State-Level Databook on

Health Care

Access and Financing

Second Edition

Colin Winterbottom
David W. Liska
Karen M. Obermaier

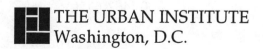

THE URBAN INSTITUTE
Washington, D.C.

THE URBAN INSTITUTE PRESS
2100 M Street, N.W.
Washington, D.C. 20037

Library of Congress Cataloging in Publication Data

State-Level Databook on Health Care Access and Financing, second edition / Colin Winterbottom, David W. Liska, Karen M. Obermaier

Earlier ed. by Pamela Loprest and Michael Gates

1. Medical economics—United States—States—Statistics. 2. Insurance, Health—United States—States—Statistics. 3. Medically uninsured persons—United States—States—Statistics. 4. Health status indicators—United States—States—Statistics. 5. United States—Statistics, Medical. I. Winterbottom, Colin. II. Liska, David. III. Obermaier, Karen. IV. Title.

RA410.53.L67	1995	94-46556
362.1'0973—dc20		CIP

ISBN 0-87766-633-4 (paper, alk. paper)

Printed in the United States of America.

Copies of this Databook *are available from:*
University Press of America

4720 Boston Way	3 Henrietta Street
Lanham, MD 20706	London WC2E 8LU
(800) 462-6420	ENGLAND

(To order data disk, see page iv)

THE URBAN INSTITUTE is a nonprofit policy research and educational organization established in Washington, D.C., in 1968. Its staff investigates the social and economic problems confronting the nation and public and private means to alleviate them. The Institute disseminates significant findings of its research through the publications program of its Press. The goals of the Institute are to sharpen thinking about societal problems and efforts to solve them, improve government decisions and performance, and increase citizen awareness of important policy choices.

Through work that ranges from broad conceptual studies to administrative and technical assistance, Institute researchers contribute to the stock of knowledge available to guide decision making in the public interest.

Conclusions or opinions expressed in Institute publications are those of the authors and do not necessarily reflect the views of staff members, officers or trustees of the Institute, advisory groups, or any organizations that provide financial support to the Institute.

To Order Data Disk

The tables are available on disk. Send check or money order for $12.50, made out to the Urban Institute, to: Publications Sales Office, P.O. Box 7273, Department C, Washington, D.C. 20044. Please request "Data disk for *State-Level Databook,* second edition." To order the *Databook* itself, see the copyright page.

☆   ☆   ☆

We also welcome written comments and questions related to this volume. Please contact us at our e-mail address via internet at *state.databook@ui.urban.org,* by fax at (202) 833-4388, or by mail, care of the Urban Institute, 2100 M Street, N.W., Washington, D.C. 20037.

Acknowledgments

The authors would like to thank Pamela Loprest and Michael Gates, the authors of the first edition of this volume, for forging the path we have followed. We are also grateful to Paul Johnson and Eric Meier for their contributions to this report, and to John Holahan, Korbin Lu, Peggy Sulvetta, Sheila Zedlewski, and Steve Zuckerman for important comments on early drafts. Funding for this project was provided by The Robert Wood Johnson Foundation under the State Initiatives in Health Care Financing Reform program.

CONTENTS

PREFACE   xiii

INTRODUCTION   1
  Data Sources   3
    Current Population Survey   4
    Medicaid Program Data   4
    Other Sources   5
  Reliability of Estimates   5
    CPS Data   5
    Health Insurance Coverage   6
    Medicaid   7
  Changes to this Edition   7

A HEALTH INSURANCE COVERAGE   11
  Types of Insurance Coverage   12
  Demographic Characteristics   13
  Family Income   14
  Work Status of Family Head and Spouse   15

B HEALTH INSURANCE COVERAGE OF WORKERS   59
  Hours of Work   60
  Employment Characteristics   61

C	CHARACTERISTICS OF THE UNINSURED	83
	Demographic Characteristics	84
	Income Characteristics	85
	Worker Characteristics	85

D	MEDICAID	109
	Eligibility and Participation, 1990–92	111
	Enrollment and Enrollment Rates, 1992	113
	Enrollment and Expenditure Growth, 1990–93	114
	Expenditures per Enrollee, 1993	114
	Acute Care Expenditures by Cash Assistance Status, 1993	115
	Expenditures by Service Type, 1993	116
	Medicaid Physician Fees Compared to Medicare Rates	119
	Data	119

E	INDICES OF HEALTH STATUS	141
	Pregnant Women and Infants	141
	Total Population	142
	Selected Populations	143

F	HEALTH CARE COSTS, ACCESS, AND UTILIZATION	153
	Hospital and Physician Costs	153
	Hospitals and Nursing Homes	154
	Physicians and HMOs	155

G	STATE DEMOGRAPHIC AND ECONOMIC PROFILES	163
	Population Characteristics	163
	Family Income Characteristics	164
	Worker Characteristics	165
	Employer Characteristics	166
	State Finances	167

APPENDICES

One: Trends in Health Insurance Coverage	211
Two: The Three-Year Merged March Current Population Survey	227
Three: Issues in Using the CPS to Measure Health Insurance Coverage	239

TABLES

Health Insurance Coverage of the Nonelderly, 1990–92
A1	All Nonelderly		18
A2	By Age		
		a. Children under 18	20
		b. Adults 18–64	22
A3	By Sex		
		a. Males	24
		b. Females	26

A4   By Race
       a. Whites   28
       b. Nonwhites   30
A5   By Family Type
       a. Married Couple with Children   32
       b. Married Couple without Children   34
       c. Single Parent   36
       d. Single Persons   38
A6   By Family Income as Percent of Poverty
       a. Below 100 Percent of Poverty   40
       b. 100–199 Percent of Poverty   42
       c. 200–399 Percent of Poverty   44
       d. 400 Percent of Poverty and Higher   46
A7   By Work Status of Family Adults
       a. Two Full-Time Workers   48
       b. One Full-Time Worker   50
       c. Some Part-Time Work   52
       d. No Work   54

Health Insurance Coverage of Workers Ages 18–64, 1990–92
B1   All Workers Ages 18–64   64
B2   By Hours of Work
       a. Full-Time   66
       b. Part-Time   68
B3   Percentage with Own-Employer Group Insurance by Firm Size   70
B4   Percentage Uninsured by Firm Size   72
B5   Percentage with Own-Employer Group Insurance by Sector   74
B6   Percentage Uninsured by Sector   76
B7   Percentage of Private-Sector Workers with Own-Employer
       Group Insurance by Industry   78
B8   Percentage of Private-Sector Workers Uninsured by Industry   80

Uninsured, 1990–92
C1   Nonelderly by Race and Sex   88
C2   Nonelderly by Age   90
C3   Nonelderly by Family Type   92
C4   Nonelderly by Work Status of Family Adults   94
C5   Nonelderly by Family Income Relative to Poverty   96
C6   Adults Ages 18–64: By Own Work Status   98
C7   Workers Ages 18–64: By Firm Size   100
C8   Workers Ages 18–64: By Sector   102
C9   Private-Sector Uninsured Workers Ages 18–64: By Industry   104

Medicaid Program
D1   Eligibility, Enrollment, and Program Participation
       of the Nonelderly, 1990–92   122
D2   Eligibility and Program Participation of Nonelderly by Age,
       1990–92   124
D3   Enrollees and Enrollment Rates, 1992   126

D4 Growth in Enrollment and Expenditures, 1990–93 127
D5 Enrollees, Expenditures, and Expenditures per Enrollee
by Enrollment Group (non-DSH), 1993 128
D6 Spending for Non-Aged Acute Care (non-DSH), 1993
   a. All Enrollees 130
   b. Cash Assistance Enrollees 131
   c. Non-Cash Assistance Enrollees 132
D7 Expenditures by Service, 1993
   a. All Expenditures 133
   b. Acute Care Expenditures (non-DSH) 134
   c. Long-Term Care Expenditures (non-DSH) 135
   d. Payments to HMOs and Medicare 136
   e. Disproportionate Share Payments, 1992–93 137
D8 Ratio of Medicaid Maximum Fees to New Medicare
Fee Schedule Levels, 1993 138

Indices of Health Status
E1 Infant Mortality by Race, 1989 144
E2 Infant Health Indicators, 1989 145
E3 Births to Unmarried Women by Race, 1989 146
E4 Total Births and Deaths, 1989 147
E5 Deaths per 100,000 Population by Cause, 1989 148
E6 AIDS Cases and Rates 149
E7 Adults Ages 18–64 with Disabilities That Prevent or
Limit Work, 1990–92 150

Health Care Costs, Access, and Utilization
F1 Relative Hospital and Physician Costs 156
F2 Hospital Utilization, 1992 157
F3 Nursing Home Facilities and Beds, 1992 158
F4 Total and Patient Care Physicians, 1992 159
F5 HMOs and HMO Membership, 1992 160

State Demographic and Economic Profiles
G1 Nonelderly Population by Age, 1990–92 170
G2 Nonelderly Population by Race and Sex, 1990–92 172
G3 Nonelderly Population by Family Type, 1990–92 174
G4 Nonelderly Family Income, 1990–92: Upper Limit of Quartiles 176
G5 Nonelderly Family Income, 1990–92: Persons in All Families 178
G6 Nonelderly Family Income, 1990–92: Persons by Age
   a. Children under Age 18 180
   b. Adults Ages 18–64 182
G7 Nonelderly Family Income, 1990–92: Persons by Family Type
   a. Married Couples with Children 184
   b. Married Couples without Children 186
   c. Single-Parent Families 188
   d. Single Persons 190
G8 Labor Force Status, 1991–93: Adults Ages 18–64 192
G9 Employment by Firm Size, 1990–92: Workers Ages 18–64 194

G10 Employment by Sector, 1990–92: Workers Ages 18–64   196

G11 Employment by Industry, 1990–92: Private-Sector Workers Ages 18–64   198

G12 Private Establishments by Size, 1991   200

G13 Employment by Establishment Size: Private-Sector Jobs, 1991   201

G14 Annualized Payroll per Private-Sector Worker by Establishment Size, 1991   202

G15 General Revenue and Revenue Sources, Fiscal Year 1990–91   203

G16 Tax Revenue and Tax Revenue Sources, Fiscal Year 1990–91   204

G17 General Expenditures, Fiscal Year 1990–91   205

Appendix One

1.1 Health Insurance Coverage of the Nonelderly, 1988–90   216

1.2 Health Insurance Coverage of the Nonelderly, by Age, 1988–90

    a. Children under Age 18   218

    b. Adults Ages 18–64   220

1.3 Change in Nonelderly Health Insurance Coverage, 1990–92 Relative to 1988–90   222

1.4 Change in Nonelderly Health Insurance Coverage, by Age, 1990–92 Relative to 1988–90

    a. Children under Age 18   223

    b. Adults Ages 18–64   224

Appendix Two

2.1 Unweighted Nonelderly Counts by Type of Health Insurance Coverage   235

Appendix Three

3.1 CPS Health Insurance Questions   241

FIGURES

Appendix Two

2.1 Nonelderly Uninsured Rate, 1990–92   236

2.2 Nonelderly Medicaid Enrollment Rate, 1990–92   237

2.3 Nonelderly Medicaid Participation Rate, 1990–92   238

Preface

The first edition of the *State-Level Data Book on Health Care Access and Financing*, published in 1993, provided state policymakers and health policy researchers with valuable information on health systems at the state level. This new edition provides more recent data related to the same issues. While seeking to maintain consistency with the prior edition, we have introduced some changes that we feel make the data more precise and more useful. These changes are described in the last subsection of the introduction. Because of these modifications, we generally discourage comparing data from the two editions to estimate trends over time. Where possible, to enable such comparisons, we have included appendix tables of previous-year data that are consistent with our new definitions. These appear in Appendix One, along with an analysis of state-level trends in health coverage.

C. *Characteristics of the Uninsured:* A profile of persons in the states who have no apparent, regular source of health insurance coverage by age, sex, race, family type, work status, income, firm size, sector, and industry.

D. *Medicaid:* The number and characteristics of persons eligible for and enrolled in Medicaid, detail on Medicaid expenditures by service, data on program trends, and how fees for various services relate to Medicare fees.

E. *Indices of Health Status:* A profile of the health status of the population including infant mortality, AIDS-related statistics, and adult disability indicators.

F. *Health Care Costs, Access, and Utilization:* Indicators of health care costs including hospital costs, physician costs, Medicare spending, and access and utilization, including number of hospital and nursing home beds, length of hospital stays, number of physicians, and enrollment in health maintenance organizations (HMOs).

G. *State Demographic and Economic Profiles:* A profile of the states' population characteristics, worker characteristics, number of establishments and worker pay by establishment size, and data on state financing and expenditure.

Each section begins with a short introduction that discusses the measures included and highlights a few results to provide a contextual basis for the data presented. We also mention important differences between data in this volume and data in the first edition. However, since this volume is intended to serve primarily as a data reference, we do not attempt to analyze all the differences in these measures across states or to draw policy conclusions.

DATA SOURCES

The two primary data sources for this volume are, first, the March Current Population Survey (CPS) of the U.S. Bureau of the Census, which provides data on a wide range of characteristics; and, second, reports from the Health Care Financing Administration on Medicaid program data.

Current Population Survey

The CPS provides data on work status and income, demographic characteristics, health insurance coverage, and other family and individual characteristics. The CPS sample is based on the civilian non-institutionalized population of the United States. In one year the survey interviews approximately 57,000 households, or 160,000 individuals, nationally. However, the sample size for a given state can be relatively small, leading to less-reliable estimates of population characteristics at the state level.

To report more-reliable statistics, we merged three consecutive March CPS files, from 1991, 1992, and 1993. As noted in more detail in Appendix Two, this procedure effectively doubles state sample sizes. Since households were interviewed in two consecutive years and we only wanted to include each household once, we included all of the observations from the 1993 survey, plus approximately half from the 1991 and 1992 surveys. Thus, each household is represented by its most recent interview. The CPS data compiled for this volume relate to the previous calendar year, so the CPS-based estimates included here represent an average value for the 1990–92 period (weighted toward the most recent year).

In a number of cases, data from the Current Population Survey have been augmented by estimates derived from the Urban Institute's microsimulation model, the Transfer Income Model (TRIM2).[2] TRIM2 has been used by various government agencies over the last 20 years to provide more information about the tax, health benefit, and income transfer systems in the United States. It includes modules that simulate the program rules for Medicaid, Aid to Families with Dependent Children (AFDC), and Supplemental Security Income (SSI). These modules correct for underreporting of benefits on the Current Population Survey (see Appendix Three) and generate estimates of the size of the population eligible for benefits.

Medicaid Program Data

The Medicaid enrollment and expenditure data used in this volume were drawn from the HCFA 2082 (*Statistical Report on Medical Care: Eligibles, Recipients, Payments, and Services*) and the HCFA 64 (*State*

Quarterly Statements of Medicaid Expenditures for the Medical Assistance Program) forms. The HCFA 2082 is essentially a statistical report filed by each state, providing detailed state-level information on Medicaid enrollment, recipiency, and expenditures for numerous types of Medicaid service categories. The HCFA 64, in contrast, is the report from which federal Medicaid reimbursement levels to states are determined, and therefore contains expenditure levels generally considered more reflective of actual spending. The HCFA 64 form, however, lacks enrollment data and reports spending only at the level of state and type of medical service. We implement a "crosswalk" to draw upon the strengths of both sources of data. In addition, a number of adjustments were made to reconcile the two data sources and are described in Section D.

Other Sources

Other data sources are also utilized in this volume, covering health costs, status, access, and utilization, as well as background data on states and summary information on state finances and spending. In all cases the most recently available data are presented. Data sources are cited for each table, and explanatory notes defining variables and concepts are included at the end of each section.

RELIABILITY OF ESTIMATES

CPS Data

To help the user evaluate the precision of the estimates, we provide standard errors on all of the estimates reported from the CPS. The CPS sample estimate and the standard error can be used to construct a confidence interval around the estimate. For example, a confidence interval defined as the estimate plus or minus 1.96 times its standard error indicates that the true estimate is within that interval with 95 percent probability. If we estimate that 10 percent of a given population are uninsured with a standard error of 1 percent, a user can say with 95 percent certainty that the true percentage of uninsured falls somewhere between 8 percent and 12 percent. The standard errors are also important for determining whether two estimates are statistically different. For example, the standard errors can be used to compare whether the percentage of uninsured is significantly different in two states, or whether it differs significantly from the percentage on Medicaid in a single state. Appendix Two describes how to use standard errors to make these comparisons. We have also added to this edition graphic illustrations of confidence intervals for several key statistics; these are shown and discussed in Appendix Two.

Even given the increased number of observations in the merged sample used here, there are some limitations to the state-level estimates. The CPS is designed to provide state and national estimates; however, the survey does not interview individuals from every county in a state. The sample is located in 729 sample areas comprising 1,973 counties and independent cities. In some states, the sample areas may not be representative of the whole state population. In addition, certain state subsamples, such as the non-white population, may still be small in the merged CPS sample, and therefore estimates based on this subsample may be unreliable. For this reason, we do not report estimates based on less than 100 unweighted sample observations.[3]

Health Insurance Coverage

Among the more significant measures we use from the CPS are the counts of health insurance coverage among the nonelderly. The estimates of the number of Americans without health insurance discussed during the recent health reform debates were frequently based on the CPS. The CPS is, in fact, the only available source of reliable estimates of the uninsured population at the state level. Like all survey data, however, the health coverage data from the CPS are not without flaws (some of these are discussed in Appendix Three). However, recent data from other sources serve to reinforce confidence in the reliability of CPS health insurance counts. Whereas the lengthy CPS survey is designed to measure many indicators of social welfare in addition to health coverage—including employment and poverty rates—recent surveys of households in 10 states conducted by the Robert Wood Johnson Foundation and RAND were designed specifically to provide the best possible measures of health coverage. For small states, these surveys also drew larger samples than the CPS. Yet, the estimates of the uninsured from these data compare well with estimates from the CPS. In fact, the differences in uninsured estimates from the CPS and these specialized surveys were statistically significant in only 3 of the 10 states surveyed.[4] The Robert Wood Johnson Foundation survey results also compare well to the estimates in this volume.

Also note that the Census Bureau has begun to publish state-specific estimates of the uninsured rate, including a three-year average. Our estimates yield similar levels across states, but the point estimates published by the Census Bureau are difficult to compare to the estimates in this volume, for several reasons. First, our TRIM2-based augmentation of the CPS to correct for underreporting of Medicaid coverage tends to reduce the uninsured counts. Second, there are differences between our method and the method used by the Census Bureau to reconcile inconsistent responses to questions. These are discussed in Appendix Three. Third, and most importantly, the percentages published by the Census Bureau include the elderly in the population denominator; we do not include the aged (65 and older). This will significantly reduce the percentage published by the Census Bureau relative to our figures.[5]

Medicaid

Historically, the quality of the HCFA form 2082 data has been somewhat inconsistent—for example, the reporting of zero expenditures (or underreporting) for certain enrollment groups or medical services, several 209(b) states categorizing most of their SSI disabled populations as noncash recipients, and patterns of expenditures that exhibit large deviations from those of the past (or future). Over the last few years, the quality of the data from the HCFA 2082 form has improved significantly. Nonetheless, we have edited some of these data to eliminate remaining inconsistencies. These procedures are discussed in Section D.

CHANGES TO THIS EDITION

This updated and revised edition of the *State-Level Data Book* incorporates a number of changes to the way data are presented. Some of these changes follow changes made by the sources from which we draw data. For example, our source for data on state revenues and expenditures changed the way government revenue sources are grouped together. We have followed the changes in these source data. We have also introduced several other changes to the original data in this volume. In each case, we believe these changes make the data better suited to the needs of states considering reform to health finance systems. However, these changes may make it difficult to compare the data in this edition to data in the prior version. We discuss these changes here.

First, we have changed the way we define family units for tables based on the Current Population Survey. We now group individuals into *health insurance units* (HIUs) rather than *families*. A health insurance unit includes the members of a nuclear family who can be covered under one health insurance policy. The standard we use follows a typical insurance industry standard: a policyholder may cover his or her spouse, all children under 18, and children between 18 and 21 who are full-time students. Thus, while a single twenty-five-year-old child living with his or her parents may be included in the parents' nuclear family, he or she would be treated as a separate, single health insurance unit. We have made this change because most health reform initiatives have adopted the health insurance unit definition. We feel this change in the definition of family units makes the data more useful. For example, the A7 table series, which shows workers and their dependents by the work status of adults in the health insurance unit, can be used by analysts to anticipate the number of people who may gain health coverage if there is an expansion of employer-sponsored health insurance. Using the nuclear family definition would overstate the number of dependents who could gain coverage through a worker in the family because older children usually cannot be covered through employer plans. This change in definition affects the following tables or table series: A5, A7, C3, C4, G3, and G7.

Second, we have changed our definition of coverage for children based on CPS reports. This change, which relates to the handling of inconsistent responses on the CPS interview, reduces the uninsured count by about 0.5 percent. As discussed in greater detail in Appendix Three, the CPS survey provides several opportunities for families to report private coverage of children under age 15. In some cases, families give inconsistent responses, reporting that children are not covered under one set of questions and that they are covered under another set. After reviewing the way we handle these inconsistent responses, we made a change which increases the number of children counted as covered. This change affects all of the health insurance coverage tables in Sections A and C, except table A2b. That table and the coverage tables in section B are not affected because they do not include any children under age 15. We have reproduced tables A1 and A2 applying this new definition to the 1989-1991 CPS data as appendix tables 1.1 and 1.2. That appendix also includes a discussion of state-level trends in health insurance coverage.

Third, we have changed the way we merge the three years of March CPS data. As discussed in greater detail in Appendix Two, households are interviewed in two consecutive years. To avoid including households in the merged file more than once, we need to eliminate those households interviewed more than once over the three-year period from one of the files. For the merged file used in the previous edition, we used all observations from the middle year, and eliminated "repeat" households in the first and third years. Thus the merged file represented an average of health coverage for the three years covered (1988-1990) *weighted toward the middle year*. For this edition, we chose to include all observations from the third-year file, eliminating repeats from the first and second years. Thus our new merged file represents average health insurance coverage for the three years covered (1990-1992) *weighted toward the last year*. We made this change so the data more closely reflect the most recent data on health coverage available. This affects all tables based on the three-year merged CPS.

Fourth, the Medicaid data presented in this edition treat Medicaid payments to Disproportionate Share Hospitals (called "DSH payments") as a separate category of spending. States make payments to hospitals which care for a significant share of Medicaid and indigent populations through the Medicaid program. Some tables may include only "non-DSH payments"; others include DSH payments as a separate spending item. We have added this separate category of spending primarily because it is fairly new. While there were some DSH programs during the period covered in the previous edition, DSH payments are a much larger share of Medicaid spending in many states than before. The text preceding Section D discusses the importance of considering these forms of spending separately from direct spending for services.

Notes, Introduction

1. John Holahan et al., 1993, "Understanding the Recent Growth in Medicaid Spending," in *Medicaid Financing Crisis: Balancing Responsibilities, Priorities, and Dollars*, edited by Diane Rowland, Judith Feder, and Alina Salganicoff (Washington, D.C.: American Association for Advancement of Sciences Press).

2. See Linda Giannarelli, 1992, *An Analyst's Guide to TRIM2* (Washington, D.C.: Urban Institute Press).

3. For further information on data reliability, see the Current Population Survey, March 1991, 1992, and 1993, and U.S. Bureau of the Census, *The Current Population Survey: Design and Methodology*, CPS Technical Paper No. 40 (Washington, D.C.: Author).

4. Specifically, the Robert Wood Johnson Foundation 10-state survey's point estimates of the percentage of people without coverage for the previous 12 months were within the 90 percent confidence interval of the CPS 1992 single-year estimate of the uninsured in 7 states: Colorado, Minnesota, New Mexico, North Dakota, Oregon, Vermont, and Washington. Differences in uninsured estimates were statistically significant in Florida, New York, and Oklahoma. The difference in Oklahoma could be explained by the failure of the CPS to count health coverage through the Indian Health Service (see Appendix Three). Policymakers in the 10 states included in the Robert Wood Johnson Foundation surveys will gain significant information from these new data; other states can be assured that the magnitude of coverage estimates from the CPS is substantially confirmed by the Robert Wood Johnson Foundation surveys.

5. Some of these same reasons account for differences in our counts and state-specific measures published by the Employee Benefits Research Institute (EBRI). Although EBRI publishes counts by age group (so the elderly could be backed out), they do not have corrections for the CPS undercount of Medicaid participation. Also note that EBRI's method for reconciling inconsistent responses is also different from our own, and that EBRI insurance counts indicate people with more than one type of coverage in each group indicated. We use a hierarchical presentation that categorizes individuals by their primary source of coverage.

Health Insurance Coverage

The tables in Section A outline health insurance coverage for various subsets of the nonelderly population. Persons are included in only one health insurance category, even though some report more than one source of coverage on the Current Population Survey. We used a hierarchy to assign each person to one category representing a primary source of coverage. First we identified persons insured through their own employer's group health plan; then those with primary coverage through another worker's employer group plan. The latter group includes dependents who do not work and dependents who work but receive coverage through their spouse's or parent's employer group plan. Then we identified those without employer coverage who are enrolled in Medicaid, and from the remainder those with coverage from other government insurance programs (CHAMPUS and Medicare). The last covered group comprised those with other private insurance plans (such as individually purchased nongroup coverage), but none of the types of coverage identified previously. The remaining people were the uninsured. We show each of these groups as a percentage of the nonelderly population.

In the Current Population Survey, respondents are not asked directly if they were uninsured. Persons are asked to report health coverage they had for any period during the prior year. The uninsured are the residual group. Therefore, coverage types other than

12-month period. Some people had spells of uninsurance interspersed with spells of employer group insurance. The fact that we defined "uninsurance" as the residual category in this hierarchy means that we have understated the number of persons who experienced a spell of uninsurance during the year. (See Appendix Three for a more complete description of these measurement issues.)

TYPES OF INSURANCE COVERAGE

About 64 percent of the nonelderly population in the United States are insured through employer group plans. Thirty-two percent have coverage through their own employers, and 32 percent have coverage as dependents on another family member's employer group policy (table A1). The extent of employer group coverage varies geographically. In general, persons in the New England, Middle Atlantic, and East North Central regions are more likely to have coverage through an employer group plan than persons living elsewhere in the country. As we show later, in Sections B and G, this probably reflects the higher concentration of large manufacturing employers in these areas, which are more likely to provide insurance. These data also show important variations in coverage across states within geographic regions. For example, within the South Atlantic region, the percentage of persons with insurance through *their own* employers' plans ranges from 27.5 percent in West Virginia to 37.5 percent in Maryland.

Medicaid coverage is more common in the East South Central and Pacific regions than elsewhere. In addition, the percentage of the population insured through Medicaid varies considerably across the states. For example, Medicaid insures 15.8 percent of Mississippi's population compared to 4.8 percent of New Hampshire's population. Higher rates of Medicaid coverage can reflect both relatively lower incomes of some states' populations as well as relatively generous eligibility standards of the states' Medicaid program. (Data in Section D further illuminate differences in Medicaid eligibility and enrollment across states.)

The uninsured rate for the nonelderly population is 15.8 percent for the period analyzed. The extent of uninsurance varies widely across states, however, and, not surprisingly, it varies inversely with the extent of employer group coverage. The New England, Middle Atlantic, and North Central regions have the lowest rates of uninsurance—from 11 percent to 13 percent, whereas

England, Middle Atlantic, and North Central regions have the lowest rates of uninsurance—from 11 percent to 13 percent, whereas the uninsured rates in other regions range from about 17 percent to 23 percent. However, there are notable exceptions to these general regional patterns. For example, although the uninsured rate in the Pacific region is above the national average, Hawaii has a low rate of uninsurance (8.3 percent). (Figure 2.1 in Appendix Two compares the uninsured rates across states, showing the statistical confidence interval around these estimates.)

DEMOGRAPHIC CHARACTERISTICS

We show insurance coverage separately for children (under age 18) and adults (18 to 64) in tables A2a and b, respectively. (Only one category is shown for employer group insurance for children, because nearly all receive coverage as dependents on a parent's health plan.) The geographic patterns in insurance coverage by age are similar to those for the general population, with the exception that more children have Medicaid coverage than do adults. In six states (California, Louisiana, Mississippi, New York, Tennessee, and West Virginia) and the District of Columbia, more than one-quarter of all children are enrolled in Medicaid, whereas the percentage of adults enrolled in Medicaid rarely exceeds 9 percent to 11 percent. Recent federal and state expansions to Medicaid eligibility have been specifically targeted to improve coverage among children. During 1990 to 1992, the period covered by these tables, states were required to continuously expand the age limit for poor children to qualify for coverage: states covered all poor children up to age six in 1990 and age eight by 1992.

The A3 and A4 table series shows insurance coverage by sex and race (white and nonwhite), respectively. We then show the insurance status of nonelderly persons by the type of family in which they live—married couples with children, married couples without children, single parents with children, and single persons without children (the A5 table series). These tables demonstrate some important differences in access to health insurance for families.[1]

A large share of persons living in married-couple families with children (table A5a) are covered by employer group insurance (74.3 percent). However, more of these are covered as dependents (50.1 percent) than as workers covered under their own employer's plan

with Dependent Children (AFDC), and low-income children as old as eight may qualify for Medicaid even though both parents are present.

Nearly half of all persons living in married-couple families with no children have coverage through their own employer's group policy, and another 24.9 percent are insured as dependents on their spouse's policy, bringing coverage under employer group insurance for this type of family to 74.2 percent. On the other hand, only 1.3 percent of persons in this group have Medicaid coverage; most likely these are persons qualifying under the program's disability provisions.

Medicaid is the largest insurer for persons living in single-parent families with children (table A5c). The program covers 44.3 percent of persons in single-parent families, ranging from less than one-third in Delaware, Nevada, and South Dakota to over one-half in California, Illinois, Louisiana, New York, and West Virginia. Broad levels of Medicaid coverage keep the rate of uninsurance for this group at 11.9 percent, below the national average for all persons.

Single adults without children (table A5d) have the highest rate of uninsurance (30.7 percent) among all family types. Nationwide, 47.5 percent have employer group insurance (45.7 percent through their own employer and 1.8 percent through another person's employer plan),[2] 7.1 percent have Medicaid, and 14.8 percent have other types of private insurance such as individually purchased, nongroup insurance policies. In many states, more than one in three single adults have no source of health insurance. These states include Florida, Georgia, Mississippi, most of the states in the West South Central Region, New Mexico, Alaska, and California.

FAMILY INCOME

The next set of tables (the A6 series) shows insurance status by income relative to the poverty line (below poverty, 100–199 percent of poverty, 200–399 percent, and 400 percent or higher).[3] These data show important differences in coverage across income levels. They also roughly indicate the population's ability to pay for additional health care coverage, as well as the potential need for government subsidization of coverage or expansion of Medicaid. Relatively few persons (11.9 percent) with incomes below the poverty threshold have employer group coverage (table A6a). Medicaid covers 49 percent of the

(11.9 percent) with incomes below the poverty threshold have employer group coverage (table A6a). Medicaid covers 49 percent of the poor, 9.9 percent have coverage from other sources, and 29.2 percent have no health insurance. Coverage for persons in families with incomes above 400 percent of poverty stands in stark contrast to that for the poor—87.3 percent have coverage through employer group plans (48.6 percent are covered as workers and 38.7 percent as dependents), and 4.3 percent have no health insurance.

Some important differences in coverage by income level emerge across states following patterns noted earlier. For example, persons in the southern states are less likely to have employer group insurance coverage across all income groups. However, more generous Medicaid coverage policies in some states fill a larger share of the insurance gap than in others. For example, the Middle Atlantic region has the lowest rate of employer coverage among its poverty population—only 11.5 percent have employer-sponsored coverage—significantly lower than the 15.8 percent coverage in the Mountain states. However, because the Middle Atlantic region has a high rate of Medicaid enrollment in the poverty population—53 percent of the poor get their primary coverage through the program—its uninsured rate of 25.1 percent is not the highest. The Mountain states, with greater employer coverage among the poor, have a higher uninsured rate (32.6 percent) than the Middle Atlantic region because Medicaid covers fewer of the poor in the region (40 percent).

WORK STATUS OF FAMILY HEAD AND SPOUSE

The last group of tables in this section (the A7 series) shows health coverage by the work status of each family's head and spouse.[4] These tables are important because most families gain health coverage through the employer of an adult in the family. The data demonstrate the importance of this link. Policymakers can also use these tables to assess the potential effects on coverage if employers are required to contribute to health benefits for their full- or part-time workers.

We categorize people by whether the family head and spouse both work full-time (35 hours or more), one works full-time, at least one works part-time (less than 35 hours), or neither works. Table A7a shows that 83.6 percent of people in families with two full-time employed adults have employer coverage (the sum of employer-

works full-time (68.2 percent), where there is no full-time but some part-time work (28.2 percent), and families without a working head or spouse (13.3 percent). Uninsured rates increase as the work of the head and spouse declines, except that families in which neither works have lower uninsured rates than families with only some part-time work. Families with two full-time workers have uninsured rates of 8.6 percent. The rate increases to 16.7 percent if only one adult works full-time, and nearly doubles to 30.2 if neither works full-time but there is part-time work. Despite the drop-off of employer-sponsored coverage for families with no workers, the uninsured rate *declines* to 20.3 percent, owing to the significance of Medicaid coverage for this group.

The pattern of coverage within these family types can vary across states. Consider the extent of employer coverage, and the uninsured rate for families with dual full-time workers. In Pennsylvania, for example, 91.2 percent of people in families with two full-time workers have employer coverage, and the uninsured rate for this group is 3.8 percent. In Texas, however, the rate of employer coverage in dual full-time worker families is 76.5 percent, and 15.2 percent of people in these families remain uninsured. Employer coverage of persons in families with a part-time worker ranges from 52.9 percent in Hawaii to 14.4 percent in Oklahoma. The uninsured rate in families where neither the head nor spouse works ranges from 11 percent in Maine to 37.2 percent in Nevada.

Note that employer group coverage among persons in families with no workers includes persons with retiree health benefits, as well as persons covered under the provisions of the Consolidated Budget Reconciliation Act of 1986 (COBRA), which requires employers to extend employer group insurance for 18 months after job termination (while allowing employers to require the terminating worker to pay the full cost of the insurance). In addition, some children may have employer group coverage from a working parent not living with the family.

Notes, Section A

1. Throughout this volume, we define families as "health insurance units." A health insurance unit includes the members of a nuclear family who can be covered under one health policy. The standard we use follows a typical insurance industry standard: a policyholder may cover his or her spouse, all children under age 18, and children between ages 18 and 21 who are full-time students. Thus, whereas a single 25-year-old child living with his or her parents may be included in the parents' nuclear family, he or she would be treated as a separate, single health unit. Because the CPS is a household-based survey, children not

included in the parents' nuclear family, he or she would be treated as a separate, single health unit. Because the CPS is a household-based survey, children not living in their parents' household may be treated as separate health units, even if they qualify for coverage as students.

In the first edition of this volume, family type was defined as consistent with a nuclear family concept. Thus, it is not straightforward to compare the A5 tables with corresponding tables from the prior edition. This is true in particular for families with children and single units, because the new definition moves non-dependent children living with their parents from units with children to single units.

2. A single person may be a dependent on another family member's health policy under several circumstances. Some health plans may cover children at ages older than is consistent with our definition of health insurance units (see note 2 following the tables). Also, some children living outside their parents' household (such as college students) may qualify for dependent coverage. However, because they are living outside their parents' household, we categorize them as single.

3. Incomes used in these tables are primarily the incomes reported on the CPS. However, we incorporated some corrections to incomes estimated by the Urban Institute's TRIM2 model. The model corrects for underreporting of income from the cash welfare programs—Aid to Families with Dependent Children (AFDC) and Supplemental Security Income (SSI)—and makes corrections to reported interest and dividend incomes. See Linda Giannarelli, 1992, *An Analyst's Guide to TRIM2* (Washington, D.C.: Urban Institute Press) for details.

4. Once again, we use the health insurance unit concept in this series, whereas the first edition used the broader nuclear family concept.

Table A1
Health Insurance Coverage of the Nonelderly, 1990-92[1]
(Persons in thousands, standard errors in parentheses)

	Number	Employer (own)	Employer (other)[2]	Medicaid[3]	Other Public[4]	Other Private[5]	Uninsured[6]
United States	**218,586**	**31.8%**	**31.9%**	**10.9%**	**2.1%**	**7.5%**	**15.8%**
		(0.10)	**(0.10)**	**(0.07)**	**(0.03)**	**(0.06)**	**(0.08)**
New England	**11,286**	**35.8%**	**35.2%**	**9.0%**	**1.6%**	**7.6%**	**10.9%**
		(0.36)	**(0.36)**	**(0.21)**	**(0.09)**	**(0.20)**	**(0.23)**
Connecticut	2,820	37.9%	38.5%	6.8%	1.1%	7.3%	8.4%
		(1.00)	(1.00)	(0.52)	(0.22)	(0.54)	(0.57)
Maine	1,102	31.3%	33.7%	11.4%	2.3%	8.8%	12.5%
		(0.85)	(0.86)	(0.58)	(0.28)	(0.52)	(0.60)
Massachusetts	5,025	35.8%	33.6%	10.3%	1.5%	7.4%	11.3%
		(0.47)	(0.47)	(0.30)	(0.12)	(0.26)	(0.31)
New Hampshire	1,016	34.3%	37.0%	4.8%	2.4%	8.0%	13.6%
		(0.95)	(0.97)	(0.43)	(0.30)	(0.54)	(0.69)
Rhode Island	806	37.4%	32.5%	10.0%	1.2%	7.8%	11.0%
		(1.01)	(0.98)	(0.62)	(0.23)	(0.56)	(0.65)
Vermont	518	33.2%	37.1%	9.4%	1.9%	7.8%	10.7%
		(0.92)	(0.95)	(0.57)	(0.27)	(0.53)	(0.61)
Middle Atlantic	**32,501**	**33.7%**	**34.0%**	**11.1%**	**1.4%**	**6.9%**	**12.9%**
		(0.23)	**(0.23)**	**(0.15)**	**(0.06)**	**(0.12)**	**(0.17)**
New Jersey	6,752	36.6%	34.6%	8.1%	1.1%	7.0%	12.7%
		(0.46)	(0.45)	(0.26)	(0.10)	(0.24)	(0.32)
New York	15,479	31.8%	31.9%	13.2%	1.5%	7.0%	14.6%
		(0.33)	(0.33)	(0.24)	(0.09)	(0.18)	(0.25)
Pennsylvania	10,270	34.9%	36.8%	9.8%	1.5%	6.6%	10.5%
		(0.45)	(0.45)	(0.28)	(0.11)	(0.23)	(0.29)
South Atlantic	**37,562**	**32.5%**	**28.8%**	**10.2%**	**2.9%**	**7.0%**	**18.5%**
		(0.25)	**(0.24)**	**(0.16)**	**(0.09)**	**(0.14)**	**(0.21)**
Delaware	623	35.4%	35.3%	6.3%	2.0%	6.5%	14.5%
		(0.92)	(0.92)	(0.47)	(0.27)	(0.47)	(0.68)
District of Columbia	477	32.5%	16.6%	19.6%	1.5%	6.8%	23.0%
		(1.03)	(0.81)	(0.87)	(0.27)	(0.55)	(0.92)
Florida	10,995	29.7%	25.1%	10.5%	3.2%	8.3%	23.1%
		(0.41)	(0.39)	(0.28)	(0.16)	(0.25)	(0.38)
Georgia	5,612	31.6%	28.7%	11.5%	2.8%	6.8%	18.7%
		(0.83)	(0.80)	(0.57)	(0.29)	(0.45)	(0.69)
Maryland	4,140	37.5%	33.2%	9.0%	2.2%	5.5%	12.7%
		(0.93)	(0.90)	(0.55)	(0.28)	(0.44)	(0.64)
North Carolina	5,640	35.5%	29.0%	10.1%	2.7%	7.3%	15.4%
		(0.45)	(0.42)	(0.28)	(0.15)	(0.24)	(0.34)
South Carolina	3,122	31.9%	29.4%	10.7%	3.6%	6.0%	18.3%
		(0.75)	(0.73)	(0.50)	(0.30)	(0.38)	(0.62)
Virginia	5,428	33.7%	31.7%	7.0%	3.4%	6.5%	17.8%
		(0.76)	(0.74)	(0.41)	(0.29)	(0.39)	(0.61)
West Virginia	1,523	27.5%	32.6%	16.0%	3.2%	5.8%	14.9%
		(0.82)	(0.86)	(0.68)	(0.32)	(0.43)	(0.66)
East South Central	**13,386**	**29.1%**	**31.3%**	**12.8%**	**3.3%**	**6.2%**	**17.3%**
		(0.41)	**(0.42)**	**(0.30)**	**(0.16)**	**(0.22)**	**(0.34)**
Alabama	3,600	29.5%	32.3%	9.5%	3.4%	5.7%	19.6%
		(0.81)	(0.83)	(0.52)	(0.32)	(0.41)	(0.71)
Kentucky	3,132	30.2%	32.8%	13.2%	3.2%	6.5%	14.1%
		(0.84)	(0.86)	(0.62)	(0.32)	(0.45)	(0.64)
Mississippi	2,351	23.7%	28.9%	15.8%	3.4%	7.0%	21.2%
		(0.71)	(0.76)	(0.61)	(0.31)	(0.43)	(0.68)
Tennessee	4,304	31.0%	30.7%	13.7%	3.1%	5.9%	15.7%
		(0.80)	(0.79)	(0.59)	(0.30)	(0.40)	(0.63)
West South Central	**23,629**	**27.3%**	**28.5%**	**11.3%**	**2.7%**	**7.5%**	**22.7%**
		(0.31)	**(0.32)**	**(0.22)**	**(0.11)**	**(0.18)**	**(0.29)**
Arkansas	2,068	26.3%	29.4%	11.8%	3.6%	9.0%	19.9%
		(0.79)	(0.81)	(0.57)	(0.33)	(0.51)	(0.71)
Louisiana	3,679	23.2%	29.2%	15.2%	2.1%	8.5%	21.8%
		(0.79)	(0.85)	(0.67)	(0.27)	(0.52)	(0.77)
Oklahoma	2,719	25.4%	30.8%	9.9%	3.8%	8.5%	21.5%
		(0.78)	(0.83)	(0.54)	(0.34)	(0.50)	(0.74)
Texas	15,163	28.8%	27.8%	10.5%	2.6%	6.8%	23.6%
		(0.41)	(0.41)	(0.28)	(0.14)	(0.23)	(0.39)

Table A1 (continued)

Health Insurance Coverage of the Nonelderly, 1990-92[1]

(Persons in thousands, standard errors in parentheses)

	Number	Employer (own)	Employer (other)[2]	Medicaid[3]	Other Public[4]	Other Private[5]	Uninsured[6]
East North Central	**37,385**	**33.7%**	**35.8%**	**10.5%**	**1.8%**	**6.8%**	**11.4%**
		(0.24)	**(0.25)**	**(0.16)**	**(0.07)**	**(0.13)**	**(0.16)**
Illinois	10,419	33.8%	32.5%	11.9%	1.7%	7.5%	12.7%
		(0.45)	(0.44)	(0.31)	(0.12)	(0.25)	(0.31)
Indiana	4,858	34.2%	35.9%	7.2%	2.8%	6.9%	13.0%
		(0.89)	(0.90)	(0.48)	(0.31)	(0.47)	(0.63)
Michigan	8,169	33.0%	36.4%	12.5%	1.4%	6.2%	10.6%
		(0.44)	(0.45)	(0.31)	(0.11)	(0.23)	(0.29)
Ohio	9,628	33.8%	37.1%	10.2%	1.8%	6.2%	10.9%
		(0.44)	(0.45)	(0.28)	(0.12)	(0.22)	(0.29)
Wisconsin	4,311	34.3%	39.7%	8.2%	1.6%	7.4%	8.8%
		(0.80)	(0.83)	(0.46)	(0.21)	(0.44)	(0.48)
West North Central	**15,577**	**31.4%**	**34.5%**	**8.2%**	**1.7%**	**11.7%**	**12.5%**
		(0.38)	**(0.39)**	**(0.22)**	**(0.11)**	**(0.26)**	**(0.27)**
Iowa	2,460	30.4%	37.1%	7.2%	1.5%	13.3%	10.5%
		(0.81)	(0.85)	(0.45)	(0.21)	(0.60)	(0.54)
Kansas	2,205	30.3%	37.7%	7.0%	1.4%	11.6%	11.9%
		(0.79)	(0.84)	(0.44)	(0.20)	(0.55)	(0.56)
Minnesota	3,844	33.4%	33.1%	8.2%	1.4%	11.7%	12.3%
		(0.87)	(0.87)	(0.51)	(0.21)	(0.59)	(0.60)
Missouri	4,568	32.8%	32.2%	9.7%	1.9%	9.0%	14.5%
		(0.87)	(0.86)	(0.55)	(0.25)	(0.53)	(0.65)
Nebraska	1,391	29.6%	37.8%	7.4%	2.4%	12.9%	9.8%
		(0.78)	(0.83)	(0.45)	(0.26)	(0.58)	(0.51)
North Dakota	524	24.8%	34.7%	7.0%	2.1%	21.7%	9.8%
		(0.75)	(0.83)	(0.44)	(0.25)	(0.72)	(0.52)
South Dakota	585	26.9%	30.7%	7.1%	3.0%	15.4%	16.8%
		(0.73)	(0.76)	(0.42)	(0.28)	(0.60)	(0.62)
Mountain	**12,011**	**29.8%**	**34.6%**	**8.1%**	**2.8%**	**8.0%**	**16.8%**
		(0.35)	**(0.37)**	**(0.21)**	**(0.13)**	**(0.21)**	**(0.29)**
Arizona	3,021	31.2%	31.1%	9.4%	2.7%	8.1%	17.5%
		(0.87)	(0.87)	(0.55)	(0.30)	(0.51)	(0.71)
Colorado	2,882	33.2%	34.9%	7.0%	3.5%	7.6%	13.7%
		(0.90)	(0.91)	(0.49)	(0.35)	(0.51)	(0.66)
Idaho	940	26.8%	35.9%	6.8%	2.3%	10.4%	17.8%
		(0.74)	(0.80)	(0.42)	(0.25)	(0.51)	(0.63)
Montana	715	26.0%	33.2%	10.1%	2.2%	12.2%	16.3%
		(0.77)	(0.82)	(0.53)	(0.26)	(0.57)	(0.65)
Nevada	1,114	34.7%	29.7%	5.6%	2.4%	6.2%	21.3%
		(0.85)	(0.82)	(0.41)	(0.27)	(0.43)	(0.74)
New Mexico	1,341	24.0%	29.9%	11.5%	3.5%	7.3%	23.8%
		(0.75)	(0.80)	(0.56)	(0.32)	(0.45)	(0.74)
Utah	1,584	26.5%	46.4%	6.1%	1.6%	7.1%	12.2%
		(0.75)	(0.85)	(0.41)	(0.21)	(0.44)	(0.56)
Wyoming	414	27.5%	39.4%	7.8%	2.7%	9.2%	13.2%
		(0.93)	(1.02)	(0.56)	(0.34)	(0.60)	(0.71)
Pacific	**35,249**	**30.7%**	**28.6%**	**13.7%**	**1.6%**	**7.7%**	**17.7%**
		(0.27)	**(0.26)**	**(0.20)**	**(0.07)**	**(0.16)**	**(0.22)**
Alaska	451	30.0%	29.7%	10.4%	3.0%	5.5%	21.5%
		(0.78)	(0.78)	(0.52)	(0.29)	(0.39)	(0.70)
California	27,030	29.2%	27.3%	15.2%	1.5%	7.5%	19.2%
		(0.31)	(0.30)	(0.24)	(0.08)	(0.18)	(0.27)
Hawaii	903	42.0%	33.1%	8.7%	2.5%	5.5%	8.3%
		(0.97)	(0.92)	(0.55)	(0.30)	(0.45)	(0.54)
Oregon	2,582	33.5%	35.3%	8.5%	1.1%	7.2%	14.3%
		(0.90)	(0.92)	(0.53)	(0.20)	(0.50)	(0.67)
Washington	4,283	35.6%	31.0%	9.0%	2.3%	9.9%	12.2%
		(0.86)	(0.83)	(0.51)	(0.27)	(0.53)	(0.58)

Source: Three-year merged March CPS: 1991, 1992, and 1993.
Note: See table notes at end of Section A.

Table A2a
Health Insurance Coverage of the Nonelderly by Age, 1990-92:
Children under 18[1]

(Persons in thousands, standard errors in parentheses)

	Number	Employer[7]	Medicaid[3]	Other Coverage[8]	Uninsured[6]
United States	**65,262**	**61.8%**	**21.1%**	**5.7%**	**11.4%**
		(0.19)	(0.16)	(0.09)	(0.19)
New England	**3,080**	**69.9%**	**17.6%**	**5.0%**	**7.5%**
		(0.65)	**(0.54)**	**(0.31)**	**(0.37)**
Connecticut	809	75.4%	13.6%	5.5%	5.5%
		(1.66)	(1.32)	(0.87)	(0.88)
Maine	323	62.6%	20.2%	8.1%	9.1%
		(1.64)	(1.36)	(0.92)	(0.97)
Massachusetts	1,318	67.2%	21.1%	3.8%	7.8%
		(0.90)	(0.79)	(0.37)	(0.52)
New Hampshire	284	73.1%	7.8%	6.5%	12.6%
		(1.68)	(1.02)	(0.94)	(1.26)
Rhode Island	197	69.5%	20.4%	4.8%	5.3%
		(1.94)	(1.70)	(0.90)	(0.95)
Vermont	150	73.1%	17.2%	4.5%	5.2%
		(1.62)	(1.38)	(0.76)	(0.81)
Middle Atlantic	**9,345**	**66.4%**	**21.9%**	**4.3%**	**7.3%**
		(0.43)	**(0.38)**	**(0.19)**	**(0.24)**
New Jersey	1,886	70.8%	16.2%	4.6%	8.4%
		(0.82)	(0.66)	(0.38)	(0.50)
New York	4,475	61.8%	26.4%	4.2%	7.6%
		(0.65)	(0.59)	(0.27)	(0.35)
Pennsylvania	2,984	70.6%	18.9%	4.3%	6.2%
		(0.79)	(0.68)	(0.35)	(0.42)
South Atlantic	**10,637**	**58.2%**	**21.0%**	**6.1%**	**14.7%**
		(0.49)	**(0.41)**	**(0.24)**	**(0.35)**
Delaware	178	70.4%	13.5%	5.2%	11.0%
		(1.64)	(1.23)	(0.79)	(1.12)
District of Columbia	129	40.7%	41.1%	1.4%	16.8%
		(2.07)	(2.07)	(0.49)	(1.58)
Florida	3,082	50.4%	23.8%	7.2%	18.7%
		(0.85)	(0.73)	(0.44)	(0.66)
Georgia	1,658	56.9%	22.3%	5.9%	15.0%
		(1.62)	(1.36)	(0.77)	(1.17)
Maryland	1,120	66.8%	19.6%	4.2%	9.3%
		(1.73)	(1.46)	(0.74)	(1.07)
North Carolina	1,563	61.4%	20.9%	6.0%	11.7%
		(0.86)	(0.72)	(0.42)	(0.57)
South Carolina	942	60.5%	18.6%	6.4%	14.5%
		(1.43)	(1.14)	(0.72)	(1.03)
Virginia	1,531	64.7%	13.5%	6.7%	15.1%
		(1.44)	(1.03)	(0.75)	(1.08)
West Virginia	434	58.3%	27.8%	3.9%	10.0%
		(1.70)	(1.55)	(0.67)	(1.04)
East South Central	**4,057**	**57.4%**	**23.4%**	**5.4%**	**13.8%**
		(0.81)	**(0.69)**	**(0.37)**	**(0.56)**
Alabama	1,100	59.3%	17.2%	5.1%	18.4%
		(1.59)	(1.22)	(0.71)	(1.25)
Kentucky	896	61.8%	22.4%	4.8%	10.9%
		(1.67)	(1.43)	(0.73)	(1.07)
Mississippi	834	50.1%	28.0%	6.7%	15.2%
		(1.40)	(1.26)	(0.70)	(1.01)
Tennessee	1,228	57.4%	26.4%	5.3%	10.9%
		(1.59)	(1.42)	(0.72)	(1.00)
West South Central	**7,461**	**53.3%**	**22.0%**	**6.2%**	**18.5%**
		(0.62)	**(0.52)**	**(0.30)**	**(0.48)**
Arkansas	671	52.4%	21.2%	7.0%	19.5%
		(1.56)	(1.28)	(0.80)	(1.24)
Louisiana	1,195	50.8%	28.1%	5.4%	15.8%
		(1.64)	(1.47)	(0.74)	(1.20)
Oklahoma	843	56.7%	19.2%	6.5%	17.6%
		(1.60)	(1.27)	(0.80)	(1.23)
Texas	4,751	53.4%	21.2%	6.1%	19.2%
		(0.81)	(0.66)	(0.39)	(0.64)

Table A2a (continued)
Health Insurance Coverage of the Nonelderly by Age, 1990-92:
Children under 18[1]
(Persons in thousands, standard errors in parentheses)

	Number	Employer[7]	Medicaid[3]	Other Coverage[8]	Uninsured[6]
East North Central	**11,387**	**67.9%**	**20.3%**	**5.0%**	**6.8%**
		(0.44)	**(0.38)**	**(0.20)**	**(0.24)**
Illinois	3,162	63.2%	23.4%	5.6%	7.7%
		(0.83)	(0.73)	(0.39)	(0.46)
Indiana	1,430	68.9%	14.4%	6.8%	9.8%
		(1.59)	(1.21)	(0.87)	(1.03)
Michigan	2,464	67.3%	22.3%	3.8%	6.6%
		(0.81)	(0.72)	(0.33)	(0.43)
Ohio	2,953	69.8%	20.6%	4.5%	5.1%
		(0.77)	(0.68)	(0.35)	(0.37)
Wisconsin	1,378	74.3%	15.1%	4.8%	5.9%
		(1.30)	(1.07)	(0.63)	(0.70)
West North Central	**4,787**	**64.9%**	**15.8%**	**9.7%**	**9.6%**
		(0.70)	**(0.54)**	**(0.43)**	**(0.43)**
Iowa	754	69.9%	13.2%	10.1%	6.8%
		(1.45)	(1.07)	(0.95)	(0.80)
Kansas	726	70.1%	12.4%	7.8%	9.7%
		(1.38)	(0.99)	(0.81)	(0.89)
Minnesota	1,119	64.1%	16.8%	10.9%	8.1%
		(1.64)	(1.28)	(1.06)	(0.93)
Missouri	1,380	60.6%	19.3%	7.4%	12.7%
		(1.65)	(1.33)	(0.88)	(1.12)
Nebraska	449	66.8%	14.9%	10.8%	7.5%
		(1.42)	(1.08)	(0.94)	(0.80)
North Dakota	167	63.0%	11.9%	18.7%	6.3%
		(1.49)	(1.00)	(1.21)	(0.75)
South Dakota	193	57.3%	13.4%	13.9%	15.4%
		(1.42)	(0.98)	(1.00)	(1.04)
Mountain	**3,901**	**65.2%**	**15.0%**	**6.7%**	**13.1%**
		(0.65)	**(0.48)**	**(0.34)**	**(0.46)**
Arizona	904	61.6%	19.9%	6.2%	12.3%
		(1.66)	(1.36)	(0.83)	(1.12)
Colorado	855	69.2%	13.6%	6.5%	10.7%
		(1.62)	(1.20)	(0.87)	(1.09)
Idaho	340	63.1%	11.5%	10.7%	14.7%
		(1.33)	(0.88)	(0.85)	(0.98)
Montana	244	59.3%	18.2%	10.1%	12.4%
		(1.47)	(1.16)	(0.91)	(0.99)
Nevada	328	64.2%	10.9%	5.1%	19.8%
		(1.59)	(1.03)	(0.73)	(1.32)
New Mexico	437	52.8%	21.6%	5.6%	20.0%
		(1.53)	(1.26)	(0.71)	(1.22)
Utah	653	76.2%	8.7%	6.0%	9.1%
		(1.13)	(0.75)	(0.63)	(0.76)
Wyoming	140	70.1%	13.2%	6.0%	10.7%
		(1.64)	(1.21)	(0.85)	(1.10)
Pacific	**10,606**	**57.1%**	**25.6%**	**5.2%**	**12.0%**
		(0.53)	**(0.46)**	**(0.24)**	**(0.35)**
Alaska	147	58.0%	19.8%	5.9%	16.3%
		(1.47)	(1.18)	(0.70)	(1.10)
California	8,203	53.9%	28.3%	5.0%	12.9%
		(0.61)	(0.55)	(0.27)	(0.41)
Hawaii	254	71.3%	17.6%	4.8%	6.2%
		(1.68)	(1.41)	(0.79)	(0.90)
Oregon	776	70.4%	16.0%	4.0%	9.7%
		(1.60)	(1.28)	(0.68)	(1.03)
Washington	1,227	67.5%	16.5%	7.9%	8.2%
		(1.56)	(1.24)	(0.90)	(0.92)

Source: Three-year merged March CPS: 1991, 1992, and 1993.
Note: See table notes at end of Section A.

Table A2b
Health Insurance Coverage of the Nonelderly by Age, 1990-92:
Adults 18-64[1]
(Persons in thousands, standard errors in parentheses)

	Number	Employer (own)	Employer (other)[2]	Medicaid[3]	Other Coverage[8]	Uninsured[6]
United States	153,323	45.3% (0.13)	19.2% (0.10)	6.6% (0.06)	11.3% (0.08)	17.7% (0.10)
New England	8,206	49.1% (0.44)	22.3% (0.36)	5.7% (0.20)	10.8% (0.27)	12.1% (0.28)
Connecticut	2,011	53.1% (1.22)	23.7% (1.04)	4.0% (0.48)	9.6% (0.72)	9.6% (0.72)
Maine	779	44.1% (1.08)	21.9% (0.90)	7.7% (0.58)	12.4% (0.72)	13.8% (0.75)
Massachusetts	3,707	48.5% (0.57)	21.7% (0.47)	6.4% (0.28)	10.8% (0.36)	12.5% (0.38)
New Hampshire	732	47.5% (1.18)	23.0% (1.00)	3.6% (0.44)	11.8% (0.76)	14.1% (0.82)
Rhode Island	609	49.5% (1.20)	20.6% (0.97)	6.7% (0.60)	10.4% (0.73)	12.8% (0.80)
Vermont	368	46.7% (1.16)	22.5% (0.97)	6.2% (0.56)	11.7% (0.75)	12.9% (0.78)
Middle Atlantic	23,156	47.3% (0.29)	21.0% (0.24)	6.7% (0.15)	9.9% (0.17)	15.1% (0.21)
New Jersey	4,866	50.7% (0.56)	20.6% (0.45)	5.0% (0.24)	9.4% (0.33)	14.4% (0.39)
New York	11,004	44.6% (0.42)	19.8% (0.34)	7.8% (0.23)	10.3% (0.26)	17.4% (0.32)
Pennsylvania	7,286	49.1% (0.55)	23.0% (0.47)	6.0% (0.26)	9.6% (0.33)	12.2% (0.36)
South Atlantic	26,924	45.4% (0.31)	17.2% (0.24)	6.0% (0.15)	11.5% (0.20)	20.0% (0.25)
Delaware	445	49.5% (1.13)	21.3% (0.93)	3.5% (0.42)	9.7% (0.67)	16.0% (0.83)
District of Columbia	348	44.6% (1.28)	7.6% (0.68)	11.6% (0.82)	11.0% (0.80)	25.3% (1.11)
Florida	7,913	41.3% (0.52)	15.3% (0.38)	5.3% (0.24)	13.2% (0.36)	24.8% (0.46)
Georgia	3,954	44.8% (1.05)	16.9% (0.79)	7.0% (0.54)	11.1% (0.66)	20.2% (0.85)
Maryland	3,020	51.4% (1.12)	20.7% (0.91)	5.0% (0.49)	8.9% (0.64)	14.0% (0.78)
North Carolina	4,077	49.1% (0.55)	16.6% (0.41)	6.0% (0.26)	11.6% (0.35)	16.8% (0.41)
South Carolina	2,180	45.7% (0.96)	16.0% (0.71)	7.3% (0.50)	11.0% (0.60)	19.9% (0.77)
Virginia	3,898	46.9% (0.94)	18.7% (0.74)	4.5% (0.39)	11.1% (0.59)	18.8% (0.74)
West Virginia	1,089	38.5% (1.06)	22.3% (0.91)	11.3% (0.69)	11.0% (0.68)	16.8% (0.82)
East South Central	9,329	41.8% (0.53)	20.0% (0.43)	8.2% (0.30)	11.2% (0.34)	18.9% (0.42)
Alabama	2,500	42.5% (1.06)	20.5% (0.86)	6.1% (0.51)	10.8% (0.67)	20.1% (0.86)
Kentucky	2,237	42.3% (1.07)	21.2% (0.89)	9.5% (0.64)	11.6% (0.70)	15.4% (0.78)
Mississippi	1,517	36.7% (1.00)	17.2% (0.79)	9.1% (0.60)	12.5% (0.69)	24.5% (0.90)
Tennessee	3,076	43.3% (1.01)	20.0% (0.82)	8.6% (0.57)	10.4% (0.62)	17.6% (0.78)
West South Central	16,168	39.8% (0.41)	17.1% (0.32)	6.3% (0.21)	12.0% (0.28)	24.7% (0.37)
Arkansas	1,396	38.8% (1.06)	18.4% (0.84)	7.2% (0.56)	15.4% (0.78)	20.1% (0.87)
Louisiana	2,484	34.3% (1.08)	18.8% (0.89)	9.0% (0.65)	13.2% (0.77)	24.7% (0.98)
Oklahoma	1,876	36.8% (1.04)	19.2% (0.85)	5.8% (0.51)	14.9% (0.77)	23.3% (0.91)
Texas	10,412	41.8% (0.54)	16.1% (0.40)	5.7% (0.25)	10.8% (0.34)	25.6% (0.48)

Table A2b (continued)
Health Insurance Coverage of the Nonelderly by Age, 1990-92:
Adults 18-64[1]
(Persons in thousands, standard errors in parentheses)

	Number	Employer (own)	Employer (other)[2]	Medicaid[3]	Other Coverage[8]	Uninsured[6]
East North Central	**25,998**	**48.4%**	**21.8%**	**6.3%**	**10.1%**	**13.4%**
		(0.31)	**(0.26)**	**(0.15)**	**(0.19)**	**(0.21)**
Illinois	7,257	48.4%	19.2%	6.8%	10.7%	14.9%
		(0.56)	(0.45)	(0.29)	(0.35)	(0.40)
Indiana	3,428	48.5%	22.1%	4.2%	10.8%	14.3%
		(1.11)	(0.92)	(0.45)	(0.69)	(0.78)
Michigan	5,706	47.2%	23.0%	8.2%	9.2%	12.4%
		(0.56)	(0.48)	(0.31)	(0.33)	(0.37)
Ohio	6,675	48.7%	22.7%	5.6%	9.6%	13.5%
		(0.56)	(0.47)	(0.26)	(0.33)	(0.38)
Wisconsin	2,933	50.4%	23.5%	4.9%	11.0%	10.2%
		(1.02)	(0.87)	(0.44)	(0.64)	(0.62)
West North Central	**10,790**	**45.4%**	**21.0%**	**4.8%**	**15.1%**	**13.7%**
		(0.49)	**(0.40)**	**(0.21)**	**(0.35)**	**(0.34)**
Iowa	1,707	43.9%	22.6%	4.5%	16.9%	12.1%
		(1.05)	(0.88)	(0.44)	(0.79)	(0.69)
Kansas	1,479	45.1%	21.8%	4.4%	15.6%	13.0%
		(1.05)	(0.87)	(0.43)	(0.77)	(0.71)
Minnesota	2,725	47.1%	20.3%	4.7%	13.9%	14.0%
		(1.09)	(0.88)	(0.46)	(0.76)	(0.76)
Missouri	3,188	47.0%	19.9%	5.6%	12.3%	15.3%
		(1.11)	(0.88)	(0.51)	(0.73)	(0.80)
Nebraska	942	43.7%	24.1%	3.8%	17.5%	10.9%
		(1.03)	(0.89)	(0.40)	(0.79)	(0.65)
North Dakota	357	36.4%	21.4%	4.7%	26.1%	11.4%
		(1.02)	(0.87)	(0.45)	(0.93)	(0.67)
South Dakota	392	40.1%	17.7%	4.0%	20.6%	17.5%
		(0.99)	(0.77)	(0.40)	(0.82)	(0.77)
Mountain	**8,110**	**44.1%**	**19.9%**	**4.7%**	**12.8%**	**18.5%**
		(0.47)	**(0.37)**	**(0.20)**	**(0.31)**	**(0.36)**
Arizona	2,117	44.5%	18.2%	4.9%	12.7%	19.7%
		(1.11)	(0.86)	(0.48)	(0.74)	(0.89)
Colorado	2,027	47.1%	20.5%	4.3%	13.1%	15.0%
		(1.14)	(0.92)	(0.46)	(0.77)	(0.82)
Idaho	600	42.0%	20.5%	4.2%	13.8%	19.5%
		(1.03)	(0.84)	(0.42)	(0.72)	(0.82)
Montana	471	39.5%	19.6%	5.9%	16.6%	18.3%
		(1.05)	(0.86)	(0.51)	(0.80)	(0.83)
Nevada	786	49.1%	15.5%	3.4%	10.1%	22.0%
		(1.07)	(0.77)	(0.39)	(0.64)	(0.88)
New Mexico	904	35.5%	18.9%	6.6%	13.3%	25.7%
		(1.02)	(0.83)	(0.53)	(0.72)	(0.93)
Utah	932	45.0%	25.7%	4.3%	10.7%	14.3%
		(1.10)	(0.97)	(0.45)	(0.69)	(0.78)
Wyoming	273	41.7%	23.7%	5.1%	15.1%	14.5%
		(1.26)	(1.09)	(0.56)	(0.92)	(0.90)
Pacific	**24,642**	**43.8%**	**16.3%**	**8.6%**	**11.1%**	**20.2%**
		(0.35)	**(0.26)**	**(0.20)**	**(0.22)**	**(0.28)**
Alaska	304	44.4%	16.1%	5.8%	9.7%	24.0%
		(1.03)	(0.76)	(0.48)	(0.61)	(0.88)
California	18,827	42.0%	15.8%	9.5%	10.8%	21.9%
		(0.40)	(0.30)	(0.24)	(0.25)	(0.34)
Hawaii	649	58.4%	18.1%	5.2%	9.2%	9.1%
		(1.14)	(0.89)	(0.52)	(0.67)	(0.67)
Oregon	1,807	47.8%	20.3%	5.3%	10.2%	16.3%
		(1.14)	(0.92)	(0.51)	(0.69)	(0.85)
Washington	3,056	49.9%	16.4%	6.0%	13.9%	13.8%
		(1.06)	(0.78)	(0.50)	(0.73)	(0.73)

Source: Three-year merged March CPS: 1991, 1992, and 1993.
Note: See table notes at end of Section A.

Table A3a
Health Insurance Coverage of the Nonelderly by Sex, 1990-92:
Males[1]

(Persons in thousands, standard errors in parentheses)

	Number	Employer (own)	Employer (other)[2]	Medicaid[3]	Other Coverage[8]	Uninsured[6]
United States	108,625	37.4% (0.15)	26.4% (0.13)	8.8% (0.09)	9.7% (0.09)	17.8% (0.12)
New England	5,632	41.9% (0.52)	29.3% (0.48)	7.0% (0.27)	9.2% (0.30)	12.6% (0.35)
Connecticut	1,387	45.8% (1.46)	32.1% (1.37)	4.4% (0.60)	7.6% (0.78)	10.1% (0.89)
Maine	556	38.3% (1.25)	28.4% (1.16)	8.9% (0.73)	10.9% (0.80)	13.5% (0.88)
Massachusetts	2,527	41.3% (0.68)	27.8% (0.62)	8.4% (0.39)	9.6% (0.41)	12.9% (0.47)
New Hampshire	513	40.3% (1.38)	29.7% (1.29)	4.3% (0.57)	10.4% (0.86)	15.3% (1.02)
Rhode Island	392	42.8% (1.48)	26.9% (1.32)	7.5% (0.79)	8.9% (0.85)	14.0% (1.03)
Vermont	255	36.9% (1.35)	32.7% (1.31)	7.2% (0.72)	9.7% (0.83)	13.4% (0.95)
Middle Atlantic	16,054	40.1% (0.34)	27.9% (0.31)	9.2% (0.20)	8.3% (0.19)	14.5% (0.25)
New Jersey	3,385	43.0% (0.66)	28.6% (0.61)	6.7% (0.33)	7.8% (0.36)	13.9% (0.46)
New York	7,571	37.2% (0.50)	26.7% (0.45)	11.0% (0.32)	8.7% (0.29)	16.3% (0.38)
Pennsylvania	5,097	42.6% (0.66)	29.1% (0.60)	8.3% (0.37)	8.0% (0.36)	12.1% (0.43)
South Atlantic	18,481	36.2% (0.36)	24.8% (0.33)	8.0% (0.21)	10.0% (0.23)	21.0% (0.31)
Delaware	318	40.4% (1.32)	30.6% (1.24)	5.0% (0.59)	8.2% (0.74)	15.8% (0.98)
District of Columbia	227	33.0% (1.50)	14.0% (1.10)	16.8% (1.19)	8.9% (0.91)	27.4% (1.42)
Florida	5,365	32.2% (0.60)	21.6% (0.53)	8.4% (0.36)	11.5% (0.41)	26.3% (0.57)
Georgia	2,724	34.0% (1.21)	26.4% (1.13)	8.9% (0.73)	9.3% (0.74)	21.4% (1.05)
Maryland	2,093	41.5% (1.33)	27.7% (1.20)	7.2% (0.69)	8.3% (0.74)	15.4% (0.97)
North Carolina	2,748	39.6% (0.65)	25.5% (0.58)	7.7% (0.36)	9.9% (0.40)	17.3% (0.50)
South Carolina	1,545	35.9% (1.10)	26.5% (1.01)	8.6% (0.64)	9.5% (0.67)	19.6% (0.91)
Virginia	2,698	39.2% (1.11)	25.8% (0.99)	4.8% (0.48)	9.9% (0.68)	20.2% (0.91)
West Virginia	764	35.1% (1.24)	24.7% (1.12)	14.3% (0.91)	10.0% (0.78)	16.0% (0.95)
East South Central	6,589	34.4% (0.61)	25.8% (0.56)	10.1% (0.39)	9.8% (0.38)	19.8% (0.51)
Alabama	1,753	36.0% (1.23)	24.9% (1.11)	7.0% (0.65)	9.5% (0.75)	22.6% (1.07)
Kentucky	1,547	35.5% (1.25)	26.3% (1.15)	10.5% (0.80)	10.6% (0.80)	17.1% (0.99)
Mississippi	1,177	28.0% (1.06)	25.5% (1.03)	12.0% (0.77)	11.0% (0.74)	23.6% (1.00)
Tennessee	2,111	36.0% (1.18)	26.2% (1.08)	11.4% (0.78)	8.9% (0.70)	17.4% (0.93)
West South Central	11,617	32.5% (0.47)	23.2% (0.42)	9.4% (0.29)	10.3% (0.30)	24.6% (0.43)
Arkansas	1,037	31.3% (1.17)	24.7% (1.09)	10.1% (0.76)	12.6% (0.83)	21.3% (1.03)
Louisiana	1,753	28.8% (1.23)	24.3% (1.16)	12.5% (0.90)	11.3% (0.86)	23.1% (1.14)
Oklahoma	1,338	32.3% (1.20)	24.7% (1.10)	7.9% (0.69)	11.9% (0.83)	23.2% (1.08)
Texas	7,489	33.6% (0.61)	22.5% (0.54)	8.8% (0.37)	9.4% (0.38)	25.7% (0.57)

Table A3a (continued)
Health Insurance Coverage of the Nonelderly by Sex, 1990-92:
Males[1]
(Persons in thousands, standard errors in parentheses)

	Number	Employer (own)	Employer (other)[2]	Medicaid[3]	Other Coverage[8]	Uninsured[6]
East North Central	**18,552**	**41.4%**	**28.7%**	**8.4%**	**8.6%**	**12.9%**
		(0.36)	**(0.33)**	**(0.20)**	**(0.21)**	**(0.25)**
Illinois	5,145	40.6%	26.4%	8.8%	9.3%	15.0%
		(0.66)	(0.59)	(0.38)	(0.39)	(0.48)
Indiana	2,371	43.0%	27.1%	6.1%	8.7%	15.0%
		(1.32)	(1.19)	(0.64)	(0.75)	(0.96)
Michigan	4,081	41.9%	28.6%	9.8%	7.7%	12.0%
		(0.66)	(0.60)	(0.40)	(0.36)	(0.43)
Ohio	4,807	40.9%	30.4%	8.6%	8.0%	12.1%
		(0.65)	(0.60)	(0.37)	(0.36)	(0.43)
Wisconsin	2,147	41.4%	32.6%	6.8%	10.0%	9.2%
		(1.18)	(1.12)	(0.60)	(0.72)	(0.69)
West North Central	**7,702**	**37.3%**	**28.5%**	**6.4%**	**13.6%**	**14.1%**
		(0.56)	**(0.52)**	**(0.28)**	**(0.40)**	**(0.40)**
Iowa	1,240	37.1%	29.8%	5.4%	15.3%	12.5%
		(1.19)	(1.13)	(0.56)	(0.89)	(0.82)
Kansas	1,118	36.2%	31.6%	6.1%	13.1%	13.1%
		(1.17)	(1.13)	(0.58)	(0.82)	(0.82)
Minnesota	1,893	39.3%	26.3%	7.0%	13.0%	14.5%
		(1.28)	(1.16)	(0.67)	(0.88)	(0.92)
Missouri	2,217	38.9%	27.2%	7.0%	10.9%	16.0%
		(1.30)	(1.18)	(0.68)	(0.83)	(0.97)
Nebraska	671	35.8%	31.7%	6.5%	15.5%	10.6%
		(1.18)	(1.15)	(0.61)	(0.89)	(0.76)
North Dakota	261	28.4%	30.0%	5.8%	23.8%	12.1%
		(1.11)	(1.13)	(0.58)	(1.05)	(0.80)
South Dakota	302	29.5%	26.8%	5.3%	19.8%	18.8%
		(1.05)	(1.02)	(0.51)	(0.91)	(0.90)
Mountain	**6,056**	**35.2%**	**29.0%**	**6.5%**	**10.9%**	**18.4%**
		(0.52)	**(0.49)**	**(0.27)**	**(0.34)**	**(0.42)**
Arizona	1,510	37.0%	26.8%	7.5%	10.0%	18.7%
		(1.28)	(1.17)	(0.70)	(0.79)	(1.03)
Colorado	1,476	38.0%	28.6%	5.3%	11.4%	16.7%
		(1.30)	(1.21)	(0.60)	(0.85)	(1.00)
Idaho	468	33.4%	30.2%	5.9%	12.7%	17.7%
		(1.11)	(1.08)	(0.56)	(0.78)	(0.90)
Montana	356	31.5%	27.8%	8.4%	15.2%	17.1%
		(1.15)	(1.11)	(0.69)	(0.89)	(0.94)
Nevada	568	39.0%	24.7%	4.8%	9.0%	22.5%
		(1.23)	(1.08)	(0.54)	(0.72)	(1.05)
New Mexico	673	28.6%	24.8%	9.1%	11.6%	25.9%
		(1.11)	(1.06)	(0.71)	(0.79)	(1.08)
Utah	802	32.0%	39.9%	5.3%	9.1%	13.8%
		(1.12)	(1.17)	(0.53)	(0.69)	(0.83)
Wyoming	203	35.0%	32.2%	5.6%	13.5%	13.7%
		(1.42)	(1.39)	(0.68)	(1.01)	(1.02)
Pacific	**17,943**	**35.4%**	**23.7%**	**11.1%**	**9.4%**	**20.3%**
		(0.39)	**(0.35)**	**(0.26)**	**(0.24)**	**(0.33)**
Alaska	230	34.4%	25.3%	7.2%	8.2%	25.0%
		(1.13)	(1.03)	(0.61)	(0.65)	(1.03)
California	13,802	33.8%	22.7%	12.4%	9.2%	22.0%
		(0.45)	(0.40)	(0.31)	(0.27)	(0.39)
Hawaii	458	48.3%	27.5%	7.2%	8.2%	8.8%
		(1.38)	(1.23)	(0.71)	(0.76)	(0.78)
Oregon	1,295	40.1%	28.8%	7.0%	8.9%	15.2%
		(1.33)	(1.22)	(0.69)	(0.77)	(0.97)
Washington	2,158	40.6%	26.2%	6.9%	11.6%	14.7%
		(1.24)	(1.11)	(0.64)	(0.81)	(0.89)

Source: Three-year merged March CPS: 1991, 1992, and 1993.
Note: See table notes at end of Section A.

Table A3b
Health Insurance Coverage of the Nonelderly by Sex, 1990-92:
Females[1]

(Persons in thousands, standard errors in parentheses)

	Number	Employer (own)	Employer (other)[2]	Medicaid[3]	Other Coverage[8]	Uninsured[6]
United States	109,961	26.3%	37.4%	13.0%	9.5%	13.8%
		(0.13)	(0.15)	(0.10)	(0.09)	(0.10)
New England	5,654	29.6%	41.2%	10.9%	9.2%	9.1%
		(0.48)	(0.52)	(0.33)	(0.30)	(0.30)
Connecticut	1,432	30.3%	44.6%	9.1%	9.2%	6.8%
		(1.33)	(1.44)	(0.83)	(0.84)	(0.73)
Maine	546	24.2%	39.1%	13.9%	11.5%	11.4%
		(1.11)	(1.27)	(0.90)	(0.83)	(0.83)
Massachusetts	2,498	30.3%	39.5%	12.1%	8.4%	9.7%
		(0.64)	(0.68)	(0.46)	(0.39)	(0.41)
New Hampshire	502	28.1%	44.4%	5.2%	10.3%	12.0%
		(1.28)	(1.42)	(0.63)	(0.87)	(0.93)
Rhode Island	413	32.3%	37.9%	12.4%	9.2%	8.2%
		(1.36)	(1.41)	(0.96)	(0.84)	(0.80)
Vermont	263	29.6%	41.4%	11.4%	9.6%	8.0%
		(1.26)	(1.36)	(0.88)	(0.81)	(0.75)
Middle Atlantic	16,447	27.5%	40.0%	12.8%	8.3%	11.4%
		(0.31)	(0.34)	(0.23)	(0.19)	(0.22)
New Jersey	3,367	30.0%	40.5%	9.6%	8.3%	11.5%
		(0.62)	(0.66)	(0.40)	(0.37)	(0.43)
New York	7,907	26.5%	36.9%	15.3%	8.4%	12.9%
		(0.44)	(0.48)	(0.36)	(0.28)	(0.34)
Pennsylvania	5,173	27.2%	44.5%	11.2%	8.1%	8.9%
		(0.59)	(0.65)	(0.42)	(0.36)	(0.38)
South Atlantic	19,081	29.0%	32.7%	12.3%	9.9%	16.1%
		(0.34)	(0.35)	(0.24)	(0.22)	(0.27)
Delaware	306	30.2%	40.3%	7.7%	8.7%	13.2%
		(1.26)	(1.34)	(0.73)	(0.77)	(0.93)
District of Columbia	251	32.1%	18.9%	22.1%	7.9%	18.9%
		(1.41)	(1.18)	(1.26)	(0.82)	(1.18)
Florida	5,630	27.4%	28.5%	12.5%	11.5%	20.0%
		(0.56)	(0.57)	(0.42)	(0.40)	(0.51)
Georgia	2,888	29.3%	30.9%	13.9%	9.8%	16.2%
		(1.13)	(1.14)	(0.86)	(0.74)	(0.91)
Maryland	2,048	33.5%	38.7%	10.8%	7.0%	10.0%
		(1.28)	(1.33)	(0.84)	(0.70)	(0.82)
North Carolina	2,892	31.6%	32.2%	12.4%	10.1%	13.6%
		(0.60)	(0.61)	(0.43)	(0.39)	(0.45)
South Carolina	1,577	28.1%	32.4%	12.7%	9.8%	17.0%
		(1.02)	(1.06)	(0.75)	(0.67)	(0.85)
Virginia	2,731	28.2%	37.4%	9.3%	9.8%	15.3%
		(1.01)	(1.09)	(0.65)	(0.67)	(0.81)
West Virginia	760	19.8%	40.6%	17.8%	8.0%	13.8%
		(1.04)	(1.28)	(1.00)	(0.71)	(0.90)
East South Central	6,798	24.0%	36.7%	15.4%	9.0%	14.9%
		(0.54)	(0.61)	(0.46)	(0.36)	(0.45)
Alabama	1,847	23.4%	39.3%	11.8%	8.7%	16.8%
		(1.05)	(1.22)	(0.80)	(0.70)	(0.93)
Kentucky	1,585	25.0%	39.2%	15.8%	8.8%	11.2%
		(1.12)	(1.26)	(0.94)	(0.73)	(0.81)
Mississippi	1,173	19.4%	32.3%	19.6%	10.0%	18.7%
		(0.94)	(1.11)	(0.94)	(0.71)	(0.92)
Tennessee	2,192	26.1%	35.0%	15.9%	9.0%	14.0%
		(1.06)	(1.15)	(0.88)	(0.69)	(0.84)
West South Central	12,013	22.2%	33.6%	13.2%	10.1%	20.9%
		(0.41)	(0.46)	(0.33)	(0.30)	(0.40)
Arkansas	1,031	21.2%	34.2%	13.4%	12.8%	18.5%
		(1.03)	(1.20)	(0.86)	(0.84)	(0.98)
Louisiana	1,926	18.1%	33.6%	17.7%	10.0%	20.6%
		(1.00)	(1.22)	(0.99)	(0.78)	(1.04)
Oklahoma	1,381	18.8%	36.7%	11.9%	12.7%	19.9%
		(0.98)	(1.21)	(0.82)	(0.84)	(1.01)
Texas	7,674	24.0%	33.0%	12.2%	9.3%	21.5%
		(0.55)	(0.60)	(0.42)	(0.37)	(0.53)

Table A3b (continued)
Health Insurance Coverage of the Nonelderly by Sex, 1990-92:
Females[1]
(Persons in thousands, standard errors in parentheses)

	Number	Employer (own)	Employer (other)[2]	Medicaid[3]	Other Coverage[8]	Uninsured[6]
East North Central	**18,833**	**26.2%**	**42.8%**	**12.7%**	**8.5%**	**9.9%**
		(0.32)	**(0.36)**	**(0.24)**	**(0.20)**	**(0.22)**
Illinois	5,274	27.1%	38.5%	14.9%	9.0%	10.5%
		(0.59)	(0.65)	(0.47)	(0.38)	(0.41)
Indiana	2,487	25.9%	44.3%	8.3%	10.5%	11.0%
		(1.14)	(1.30)	(0.72)	(0.80)	(0.82)
Michigan	4,088	24.0%	44.1%	15.1%	7.5%	9.3%
		(0.57)	(0.66)	(0.48)	(0.35)	(0.39)
Ohio	4,821	26.6%	43.8%	11.8%	8.1%	9.7%
		(0.58)	(0.65)	(0.42)	(0.36)	(0.39)
Wisconsin	2,163	27.2%	46.8%	9.5%	8.1%	8.4%
		(1.06)	(1.19)	(0.70)	(0.65)	(0.66)
West North Central	**7,875**	**25.7%**	**40.4%**	**9.9%**	**13.2%**	**10.8%**
		(0.50)	**(0.56)**	**(0.34)**	**(0.39)**	**(0.36)**
Iowa	1,220	23.7%	44.5%	9.1%	14.3%	8.4%
		(1.06)	(1.24)	(0.72)	(0.87)	(0.69)
Kansas	1,087	24.2%	44.0%	8.0%	13.0%	10.8%
		(1.05)	(1.22)	(0.67)	(0.83)	(0.76)
Minnesota	1,951	27.7%	39.7%	9.5%	13.0%	10.1%
		(1.16)	(1.27)	(0.76)	(0.87)	(0.78)
Missouri	2,350	27.0%	36.9%	12.3%	10.8%	13.0%
		(1.15)	(1.25)	(0.85)	(0.80)	(0.87)
Nebraska	720	23.9%	43.6%	8.1%	15.2%	9.1%
		(1.02)	(1.18)	(0.65)	(0.86)	(0.69)
North Dakota	263	21.2%	39.3%	8.1%	23.8%	7.6%
		(1.01)	(1.20)	(0.67)	(1.05)	(0.65)
South Dakota	282	24.2%	34.9%	9.1%	17.0%	14.8%
		(1.02)	(1.13)	(0.68)	(0.89)	(0.84)
Mountain	**5,954**	**24.4%**	**40.2%**	**9.7%**	**10.6%**	**15.1%**
		(0.47)	**(0.54)**	**(0.32)**	**(0.34)**	**(0.39)**
Arizona	1,511	25.5%	35.4%	11.3%	11.5%	16.3%
		(1.15)	(1.27)	(0.84)	(0.84)	(0.98)
Colorado	1,406	28.1%	41.6%	8.8%	10.8%	10.6%
		(1.23)	(1.35)	(0.78)	(0.85)	(0.85)
Idaho	472	20.2%	41.6%	7.7%	12.7%	17.8%
		(0.94)	(1.16)	(0.62)	(0.78)	(0.90)
Montana	359	20.7%	38.4%	11.8%	13.6%	15.5%
		(1.00)	(1.20)	(0.80)	(0.85)	(0.89)
Nevada	546	30.3%	34.9%	6.5%	8.2%	20.1%
		(1.18)	(1.22)	(0.63)	(0.70)	(1.03)
New Mexico	668	19.3%	35.1%	13.8%	10.0%	21.7%
		(0.98)	(1.18)	(0.85)	(0.74)	(1.02)
Utah	782	21.0%	53.1%	7.0%	8.4%	10.5%
		(0.99)	(1.21)	(0.62)	(0.67)	(0.74)
Wyoming	210	20.3%	46.5%	10.0%	10.5%	12.7%
		(1.18)	(1.46)	(0.88)	(0.90)	(0.97)
Pacific	**17,306**	**25.7%**	**33.6%**	**16.4%**	**9.3%**	**15.0%**
		(0.36)	**(0.39)**	**(0.31)**	**(0.24)**	**(0.30)**
Alaska	221	25.4%	34.4%	13.7%	8.7%	17.9%
		(1.05)	(1.15)	(0.83)	(0.68)	(0.93)
California	13,228	24.5%	32.2%	18.1%	8.9%	16.3%
		(0.42)	(0.45)	(0.37)	(0.28)	(0.36)
Hawaii	444	35.4%	38.8%	10.3%	7.8%	7.8%
		(1.34)	(1.37)	(0.85)	(0.75)	(0.75)
Oregon	1,288	26.8%	41.9%	10.1%	7.8%	13.5%
		(1.20)	(1.34)	(0.82)	(0.73)	(0.93)
Washington	2,126	30.5%	35.9%	11.2%	12.7%	9.6%
		(1.17)	(1.22)	(0.80)	(0.85)	(0.75)

Source: Three-year merged March CPS: 1991, 1992, and 1993.
Note: See table notes at end of Section A.

Table A4a
Health Insurance Coverage of the Nonelderly by Race, 1990-92:
Whites[1]
(Persons in thousands, standard errors in parentheses)

	Number	Employer (own)	Employer (other)[2]	Medicaid[3]	Other Coverage[8]	Uninsured[6]
United States	181,206	33.2% (0.11)	33.7% (0.11)	8.3% (0.06)	10.0% (0.07)	14.8% (0.08)
New England	10,386	36.7% (0.37)	36.0% (0.37)	7.6% (0.21)	9.2% (0.22)	10.4% (0.24)
Connecticut	2,446	39.1% (1.08)	40.2% (1.08)	4.6% (0.46)	8.7% (0.62)	7.5% (0.58)
Maine	1,076	31.6% (0.86)	33.6% (0.87)	11.3% (0.59)	11.0% (0.58)	12.5% (0.61)
Massachusetts	4,619	37.2% (0.50)	34.5% (0.49)	8.6% (0.29)	8.9% (0.29)	10.8% (0.32)
New Hampshire	975	34.6% (0.97)	37.2% (0.99)	4.8% (0.44)	10.5% (0.63)	13.0% (0.69)
Rhode Island	761	38.1% (1.04)	32.9% (1.01)	9.1% (0.62)	9.0% (0.61)	10.9% (0.67)
Vermont	508	33.4% (0.93)	37.4% (0.96)	9.1% (0.57)	9.8% (0.59)	10.3% (0.60)
Middle Atlantic	26,824	35.4% (0.26)	36.1% (0.26)	8.4% (0.15)	8.5% (0.15)	11.5% (0.17)
New Jersey	5,429	38.5% (0.52)	36.2% (0.51)	5.5% (0.24)	8.2% (0.29)	11.7% (0.34)
New York	12,197	33.5% (0.38)	34.1% (0.38)	10.6% (0.25)	8.9% (0.23)	13.0% (0.27)
Pennsylvania	9,198	36.1% (0.47)	38.9% (0.48)	7.3% (0.26)	8.2% (0.27)	9.5% (0.29)
South Atlantic	27,796	35.0% (0.29)	31.3% (0.29)	6.0% (0.15)	10.8% (0.19)	16.9% (0.23)
Delaware	485	36.9% (1.05)	38.0% (1.06)	3.2% (0.38)	8.3% (0.60)	13.6% (0.74)
District of Columbia	155	49.5% (1.92)	17.9% (1.47)	5.3% (0.86)	11.4% (1.22)	16.0% (1.41)
Florida	8,817	31.7% (0.47)	26.9% (0.45)	6.5% (0.25)	12.5% (0.33)	22.4% (0.42)
Georgia	3,676	35.7% (1.05)	32.3% (1.03)	5.0% (0.48)	10.9% (0.69)	16.1% (0.81)
Maryland	2,885	39.8% (1.12)	36.1% (1.10)	5.0% (0.50)	7.5% (0.60)	11.5% (0.73)
North Carolina	4,129	38.5% (0.53)	31.6% (0.51)	5.3% (0.24)	10.9% (0.34)	13.6% (0.37)
South Carolina	2,041	36.7% (0.96)	33.0% (0.94)	5.0% (0.43)	10.9% (0.62)	14.3% (0.70)
Virginia	4,160	35.6% (0.87)	34.4% (0.87)	4.6% (0.38)	10.2% (0.55)	15.3% (0.66)
West Virginia	1,448	27.9% (0.85)	33.0% (0.89)	15.5% (0.69)	8.6% (0.53)	15.0% (0.68)
East South Central	10,332	31.8% (0.48)	33.9% (0.49)	8.5% (0.29)	10.0% (0.31)	15.8% (0.37)
Alabama	2,526	33.2% (1.00)	36.1% (1.02)	4.2% (0.43)	9.2% (0.62)	17.3% (0.81)
Kentucky	2,949	30.4% (0.87)	33.6% (0.89)	12.5% (0.63)	10.0% (0.57)	13.4% (0.65)
Mississippi	1,432	27.7% (0.96)	34.1% (1.02)	7.0% (0.55)	12.6% (0.71)	18.7% (0.83)
Tennessee	3,425	33.7% (0.91)	32.4% (0.90)	8.9% (0.55)	9.5% (0.56)	15.6% (0.70)
West South Central	19,313	28.7% (0.35)	30.4% (0.36)	8.2% (0.21)	10.9% (0.24)	21.8% (0.32)
Arkansas	1,722	28.3% (0.88)	31.4% (0.91)	7.7% (0.52)	13.4% (0.67)	19.2% (0.77)
Louisiana	2,521	27.4% (1.01)	34.6% (1.07)	5.3% (0.51)	13.5% (0.77)	19.3% (0.89)
Oklahoma	2,252	27.3% (0.88)	32.1% (0.92)	8.0% (0.53)	12.8% (0.66)	19.8% (0.79)
Texas	12,818	29.3% (0.45)	29.2% (0.45)	8.9% (0.28)	9.7% (0.29)	23.0% (0.42)

Table A4a (continued)
Health Insurance Coverage of the Nonelderly by Race, 1990-92:
Whites[1]
(Persons in thousands, standard errors in parentheses)

	Number	Employer (own)	Employer (other)[2]	Medicaid[3]	Other Coverage[8]	Uninsured[6]
East North Central	**31,813**	**35.3%**	**38.2%**	**7.0%**	**9.0%**	**10.5%**
		(0.27)	**(0.27)**	**(0.14)**	**(0.16)**	**(0.17)**
Illinois	8,245	36.7%	35.9%	6.2%	10.0%	11.2%
		(0.51)	(0.51)	(0.26)	(0.32)	(0.33)
Indiana	4,382	35.6%	37.1%	5.7%	9.5%	12.1%
		(0.94)	(0.95)	(0.46)	(0.58)	(0.64)
Michigan	6,808	34.5%	39.3%	8.3%	7.9%	10.0%
		(0.49)	(0.51)	(0.29)	(0.28)	(0.31)
Ohio	8,412	34.5%	38.6%	8.2%	8.2%	10.5%
		(0.47)	(0.48)	(0.27)	(0.27)	(0.30)
Wisconsin	3,966	35.5%	41.2%	5.4%	9.6%	8.3%
		(0.84)	(0.87)	(0.40)	(0.52)	(0.49)
West North Central	**14,250**	**32.6%**	**35.8%**	**6.2%**	**13.8%**	**11.6%**
		(0.40)	**(0.41)**	**(0.20)**	**(0.29)**	**(0.27)**
Iowa	2,368	30.9%	38.0%	6.2%	14.7%	10.2%
		(0.83)	(0.87)	(0.43)	(0.63)	(0.54)
Kansas	1,995	31.1%	39.0%	5.8%	13.1%	11.0%
		(0.84)	(0.89)	(0.42)	(0.61)	(0.57)
Minnesota	3,589	34.8%	34.0%	5.9%	13.4%	11.9%
		(0.91)	(0.90)	(0.45)	(0.65)	(0.62)
Missouri	3,972	34.3%	33.8%	7.3%	11.4%	13.2%
		(0.94)	(0.94)	(0.52)	(0.63)	(0.67)
Nebraska	1,316	30.1%	38.7%	5.5%	15.7%	10.0%
		(0.81)	(0.86)	(0.40)	(0.64)	(0.53)
North Dakota	484	26.0%	36.2%	3.8%	25.1%	8.9%
		(0.80)	(0.87)	(0.35)	(0.79)	(0.52)
South Dakota	525	28.7%	33.7%	4.4%	19.1%	14.1%
		(0.79)	(0.82)	(0.36)	(0.69)	(0.61)
Mountain	**11,066**	**30.4%**	**35.1%**	**7.2%**	**10.9%**	**16.5%**
		(0.37)	**(0.38)**	**(0.21)**	**(0.25)**	**(0.30)**
Arizona	2,848	31.4%	31.4%	9.0%	10.6%	17.6%
		(0.89)	(0.89)	(0.55)	(0.59)	(0.73)
Colorado	2,587	34.2%	35.0%	6.1%	11.4%	13.3%
		(0.96)	(0.96)	(0.48)	(0.64)	(0.69)
Idaho	906	27.2%	35.8%	6.5%	12.9%	17.6%
		(0.75)	(0.81)	(0.42)	(0.57)	(0.64)
Montana	649	27.4%	34.5%	7.0%	15.4%	15.8%
		(0.82)	(0.87)	(0.47)	(0.66)	(0.67)
Nevada	969	35.4%	30.5%	4.6%	8.6%	21.0%
		(0.92)	(0.89)	(0.40)	(0.54)	(0.78)
New Mexico	1,165	25.3%	31.3%	9.8%	10.4%	23.2%
		(0.81)	(0.87)	(0.56)	(0.57)	(0.79)
Utah	1,537	26.5%	46.4%	6.0%	8.8%	12.2%
		(0.76)	(0.86)	(0.41)	(0.49)	(0.57)
Wyoming	405	27.9%	40.1%	7.4%	11.9%	12.8%
		(0.94)	(1.03)	(0.55)	(0.68)	(0.70)
Pacific	**29,425**	**30.9%**	**28.9%**	**13.1%**	**9.4%**	**17.7%**
		(0.29)	**(0.29)**	**(0.22)**	**(0.19)**	**(0.24)**
Alaska	337	34.2%	33.3%	7.3%	9.0%	16.2%
		(0.93)	(0.92)	(0.51)	(0.56)	(0.72)
California	22,550	29.4%	27.6%	14.8%	9.0%	19.2%
		(0.34)	(0.33)	(0.26)	(0.21)	(0.29)
Hawaii	256	45.8%	28.7%	6.0%	10.6%	8.9%
		(1.84)	(1.67)	(0.88)	(1.14)	(1.05)
Oregon	2,433	33.7%	36.0%	8.2%	8.0%	14.1%
		(0.93)	(0.95)	(0.54)	(0.53)	(0.69)
Washington	3,850	36.6%	31.8%	7.7%	12.6%	11.4%
		(0.91)	(0.88)	(0.50)	(0.62)	(0.60)

Source: Three-year merged March CPS: 1991, 1992, and 1993.
Note: See table notes at end of Section A.

Table A4b
Health Insurance Coverage of the Nonelderly by Race, 1990-92:
Nonwhites[1]
(Persons in thousands, standard errors in parentheses)

	Number	Employer (own)	Employer (other)[2]	Medicaid[3]	Other Coverage[8]	Uninsured[6]
United States	37,380	24.7%	23.0%	23.8%	7.7%	20.8%
		(0.23)	(0.23)	(0.23)	(0.14)	(0.22)
New England	900	24.8%	26.0%	24.1%	8.9%	16.2%
		(1.18)	(1.20)	(1.17)	(0.78)	(1.01)
Connecticut	374	30.1%	27.4%	21.2%	6.7%	14.6%
		(2.70)	(2.62)	(2.41)	(1.47)	(2.08)
Maine	---	---	---	---	---	---
		---	---	---	---	---
Massachusetts	405	20.0%	23.5%	29.2%	10.5%	16.7%
		(1.44)	(1.53)	(1.64)	(1.11)	(1.35)
New Hampshire	---	---	---	---	---	---
		---	---	---	---	---
Rhode Island	44	26.0%	25.7%	26.1%	9.4%	12.8%
		(4.04)	(4.03)	(4.05)	(2.69)	(3.08)
Vermont	---	---	---	---	---	---
		---	---	---	---	---
Middle Atlantic	5,676	26.0%	24.0%	23.5%	7.1%	19.3%
		(0.54)	(0.52)	(0.52)	(0.32)	(0.48)
New Jersey	1,323	28.6%	28.0%	19.1%	7.5%	16.8%
		(1.01)	(1.00)	(0.88)	(0.59)	(0.83)
New York	3,281	25.5%	24.0%	22.8%	7.1%	20.5%
		(0.71)	(0.69)	(0.68)	(0.42)	(0.66)
Pennsylvania	1,072	24.5%	19.0%	31.2%	6.6%	18.6%
		(1.29)	(1.18)	(1.39)	(0.75)	(1.17)
South Atlantic	9,766	25.3%	21.7%	22.2%	7.7%	23.1%
		(0.47)	(0.45)	(0.45)	(0.29)	(0.46)
Delaware	139	30.0%	26.0%	17.3%	8.8%	17.9%
		(1.94)	(1.86)	(1.60)	(1.20)	(1.62)
District of Columbia	322	24.3%	15.9%	26.5%	6.9%	26.3%
		(1.19)	(1.02)	(1.22)	(0.70)	(1.22)
Florida	2,177	21.6%	18.1%	26.8%	7.5%	26.1%
		(0.87)	(0.81)	(0.93)	(0.56)	(0.93)
Georgia	1,937	23.8%	21.9%	23.8%	6.9%	23.6%
		(1.34)	(1.30)	(1.34)	(0.80)	(1.34)
Maryland	1,256	32.1%	26.5%	18.0%	8.0%	15.4%
		(1.69)	(1.59)	(1.39)	(0.98)	(1.31)
North Carolina	1,511	27.2%	21.7%	23.2%	7.6%	20.4%
		(0.83)	(0.77)	(0.79)	(0.50)	(0.75)
South Carolina	1,081	22.9%	22.7%	21.4%	7.3%	25.8%
		(1.19)	(1.19)	(1.16)	(0.74)	(1.24)
Virginia	1,268	27.5%	22.8%	15.1%	8.9%	25.8%
		(1.53)	(1.44)	(1.23)	(0.98)	(1.50)
West Virginia	75	20.2%	24.9%	25.9%	15.7%	13.3%
		(3.47)	(3.74)	(3.79)	(3.14)	(2.93)
East South Central	3,054	20.1%	22.6%	27.3%	7.5%	22.5%
		(0.79)	(0.82)	(0.87)	(0.52)	(0.82)
Alabama	1,074	21.0%	23.4%	21.8%	8.7%	25.1%
		(1.38)	(1.44)	(1.40)	(0.96)	(1.47)
Kentucky	183	27.1%	19.7%	23.5%	4.4%	25.4%
		(3.51)	(3.14)	(3.35)	(1.62)	(3.44)
Mississippi	918	17.4%	20.8%	29.6%	7.1%	25.1%
		(1.06)	(1.13)	(1.27)	(0.72)	(1.21)
Tennessee	879	20.4%	24.0%	32.5%	7.0%	16.2%
		(1.60)	(1.69)	(1.86)	(1.01)	(1.46)
West South Central	4,316	20.8%	19.9%	25.2%	7.1%	27.0%
		(0.69)	(0.68)	(0.74)	(0.44)	(0.76)
Arkansas	346	16.4%	19.6%	31.8%	8.8%	23.4%
		(1.68)	(1.80)	(2.11)	(1.29)	(1.92)
Louisiana	1,159	14.1%	17.4%	36.9%	4.5%	27.1%
		(1.21)	(1.31)	(1.67)	(0.72)	(1.54)
Oklahoma	467	16.7%	24.5%	19.4%	9.7%	29.7%
		(1.68)	(1.94)	(1.78)	(1.33)	(2.06)
Texas	2,345	25.6%	20.3%	19.6%	7.6%	26.9%
		(1.05)	(0.97)	(0.95)	(0.64)	(1.07)

Health Insurance Coverage of the Nonelderly by Race, 1990-92:
Nonwhites[1]

(Persons in thousands, standard errors in parentheses)

	Number	Employer (own)	Employer (other)[2]	Medicaid[3]	Other Coverage[8]	Uninsured[6]
East North Central	**5,572**	**24.4%**	**22.4%**	**30.6%**	**6.3%**	**16.3%**
		(0.60)	**(0.58)**	**(0.64)**	**(0.34)**	**(0.51)**
Illinois	2,174	22.6%	19.4%	33.4%	6.0%	18.6%
		(0.90)	(0.85)	(1.01)	(0.51)	(0.84)
Indiana	476	21.5%	25.4%	21.0%	11.2%	21.0%
		(2.55)	(2.70)	(2.53)	(1.96)	(2.53)
Michigan	1,361	25.3%	21.7%	33.1%	6.0%	13.8%
		(1.05)	(0.99)	(1.13)	(0.57)	(0.83)
Ohio	1,216	28.8%	27.1%	23.8%	6.5%	13.9%
		(1.23)	(1.21)	(1.15)	(0.67)	(0.94)
Wisconsin	345	20.4%	23.2%	40.3%	2.0%	14.1%
		(2.50)	(2.62)	(3.04)	(0.86)	(2.16)
West North Central	**1,327**	**19.5%**	**20.3%**	**29.8%**	**9.2%**	**21.2%**
		(1.15)	**(1.17)**	**(1.33)**	**(0.84)**	**(1.19)**
Iowa	92	18.1%	13.8%	33.7%	17.2%	17.1%
		(3.63)	(3.25)	(4.45)	(3.56)	(3.55)
Kansas	210	22.4%	25.2%	18.9%	12.5%	21.1%
		(2.42)	(2.53)	(2.28)	(1.92)	(2.37)
Minnesota	255	13.8%	20.2%	40.5%	7.7%	17.8%
		(2.57)	(2.99)	(3.65)	(1.98)	(2.85)
Missouri	595	22.3%	21.2%	26.1%	7.3%	23.1%
		(2.22)	(2.18)	(2.34)	(1.38)	(2.25)
Nebraska	74	21.7%	22.7%	39.9%	8.7%	7.0%
		(3.18)	(3.23)	(3.77)	(2.17)	(1.96)
North Dakota	40	10.4%	15.6%	45.7%	7.7%	20.7%
		(2.00)	(2.38)	(3.28)	(1.75)	(2.67)
South Dakota	60	11.4%	4.5%	31.4%	12.1%	40.7%
		(1.71)	(1.12)	(2.49)	(1.75)	(2.64)
Mountain	**945**	**23.2%**	**28.2%**	**18.3%**	**10.0%**	**20.3%**
		(1.21)	**(1.29)**	**(1.11)**	**(0.86)**	**(1.15)**
Arizona	173	28.7%	25.6%	16.8%	13.0%	16.0%
		(3.67)	(3.54)	(3.04)	(2.73)	(2.98)
Colorado	294	24.4%	34.4%	15.8%	8.3%	17.2%
		(2.68)	(2.96)	(2.27)	(1.72)	(2.35)
Idaho	34	16.2%	38.4%	15.2%	8.4%	21.8%
		(3.35)	(4.42)	(3.27)	(2.52)	(3.75)
Montana	66	13.3%	20.4%	40.4%	4.4%	21.5%
		(2.03)	(2.41)	(2.93)	(1.23)	(2.46)
Nevada	145	30.2%	24.7%	12.7%	8.7%	23.7%
		(2.38)	(2.23)	(1.72)	(1.46)	(2.20)
New Mexico	176	15.0%	20.8%	22.4%	13.5%	28.2%
		(1.79)	(2.03)	(2.09)	(1.71)	(2.25)
Utah	47	26.2%	45.3%	10.9%	7.1%	10.6%
		(4.51)	(5.10)	(3.19)	(2.64)	(3.15)
Wyoming	---	---	---	---	---	---
		---	---	---	---	---
Pacific	**5,823**	**29.4%**	**26.6%**	**16.6%**	**9.3%**	**18.1%**
		(0.68)	**(0.66)**	**(0.56)**	**(0.43)**	**(0.57)**
Alaska	113	17.3%	19.0%	19.5%	6.9%	37.2%
		(1.33)	(1.38)	(1.39)	(0.89)	(1.70)
California	4,480	28.4%	25.9%	17.2%	9.5%	19.0%
		(0.78)	(0.76)	(0.65)	(0.51)	(0.68)
Hawaii	647	40.4%	34.8%	9.8%	6.9%	8.1%
		(1.19)	(1.15)	(0.72)	(0.61)	(0.66)
Oregon	149	28.9%	24.1%	14.6%	14.5%	17.9%
		(3.76)	(3.54)	(2.93)	(2.92)	(3.18)
Washington	434	26.9%	24.2%	20.5%	8.9%	19.5%
		(2.59)	(2.50)	(2.36)	(1.66)	(2.31)

Source: Three-year merged March CPS: 1991, 1992, and 1993.
Note: See table notes at end of Section A.

Table A5a
Health Insurance Coverage of the Nonelderly by Family Type, 1990-92:
Persons in Married Couple with Children Families[1,9]
(Persons in thousands, standard errors in parentheses)

	Number	Employer (own)	Employer (other)[2]	Medicaid[3]	Other Coverage[8]	Uninsured[6]
United States	**105,670**	24.2% (0.20)	50.1% (0.24)	6.6% (0.12)	7.6% (0.13)	11.5% (0.15)
New England	**5,387**	25.1% (0.72)	57.1% (0.82)	4.6% (0.35)	6.6% (0.41)	6.7% (0.42)
Connecticut	1,392	26.6% (2.01)	61.1% (2.21)	2.2% (0.66)	6.0% (1.08)	4.1% (0.91)
Maine	559	23.6% (1.69)	49.3% (1.99)	7.3% (1.04)	10.5% (1.22)	9.4% (1.16)
Massachusetts	2,291	24.9% (0.98)	56.7% (1.12)	5.4% (0.51)	5.7% (0.52)	7.3% (0.59)
New Hampshire	526	23.6% (1.83)	57.3% (2.14)	1.6% (0.54)	8.0% (1.17)	9.5% (1.26)
Rhode Island	342	24.8% (2.14)	56.5% (2.45)	7.0% (1.27)	5.9% (1.16)	5.8% (1.15)
Vermont	276	24.6% (1.79)	56.7% (2.06)	6.4% (1.02)	7.1% (1.07)	5.1% (0.92)
Middle Atlantic	**15,585**	25.3% (0.48)	54.6% (0.55)	5.9% (0.26)	6.3% (0.27)	8.0% (0.30)
New Jersey	3,287	27.8% (0.94)	55.5% (1.05)	3.2% (0.37)	6.1% (0.51)	7.4% (0.55)
New York	7,207	23.9% (0.70)	52.4% (0.81)	7.4% (0.43)	6.8% (0.41)	9.5% (0.48)
Pennsylvania	5,091	25.7% (0.90)	56.9% (1.02)	5.5% (0.47)	5.6% (0.47)	6.3% (0.50)
South Atlantic	**16,829**	25.5% (0.53)	47.0% (0.61)	5.5% (0.28)	7.8% (0.33)	14.2% (0.43)
Delaware	281	26.7% (1.96)	56.7% (2.19)	2.1% (0.63)	6.5% (1.09)	8.1% (1.20)
District of Columbia	105	18.5% (2.81)	40.7% (3.55)	16.5% (2.68)	4.1% (1.43)	20.3% (2.91)
Florida	4,563	22.6% (0.91)	42.8% (1.07)	5.8% (0.51)	9.0% (0.62)	19.8% (0.86)
Georgia	2,611	25.8% (1.77)	46.8% (2.02)	5.8% (0.94)	8.1% (1.11)	13.5% (1.38)
Maryland	1,755	27.0% (2.02)	55.6% (2.26)	3.7% (0.86)	4.5% (0.94)	9.3% (1.32)
North Carolina	2,623	29.0% (0.96)	46.2% (1.05)	6.0% (0.50)	8.1% (0.58)	10.7% (0.65)
South Carolina	1,517	28.0% (1.61)	45.8% (1.78)	4.5% (0.74)	7.4% (0.94)	14.3% (1.25)
Virginia	2,576	25.5% (1.57)	49.5% (1.80)	3.1% (0.62)	8.4% (1.00)	13.5% (1.23)
West Virginia	797	22.7% (1.66)	47.1% (1.97)	13.6% (1.35)	6.0% (0.93)	10.6% (1.22)
East South Central	**6,269**	24.2% (0.87)	48.4% (1.02)	5.8% (0.48)	7.7% (0.54)	13.9% (0.70)
Alabama	1,655	23.9% (1.74)	50.4% (2.04)	3.2% (0.72)	7.9% (1.10)	14.6% (1.44)
Kentucky	1,553	24.4% (1.74)	48.2% (2.02)	7.7% (1.07)	8.3% (1.11)	11.5% (1.29)
Mississippi	1,165	22.3% (1.53)	44.9% (1.83)	6.4% (0.90)	8.7% (1.04)	17.7% (1.41)
Tennessee	1,896	25.5% (1.75)	49.0% (2.01)	6.1% (0.96)	6.6% (0.99)	12.9% (1.35)
West South Central	**12,070**	22.2% (0.63)	43.0% (0.75)	6.6% (0.38)	8.4% (0.42)	19.8% (0.60)
Arkansas	1,090	21.5% (1.56)	43.9% (1.89)	6.2% (0.92)	10.6% (1.17)	17.8% (1.46)
Louisiana	1,740	22.3% (1.75)	48.4% (2.10)	5.7% (0.97)	8.5% (1.18)	15.1% (1.51)
Oklahoma	1,441	21.1% (1.56)	45.1% (1.90)	6.0% (0.91)	9.4% (1.11)	18.4% (1.48)
Texas	7,800	22.5% (0.82)	41.3% (0.97)	7.0% (0.50)	7.9% (0.53)	21.3% (0.81)

Health Insurance Coverage of the Nonelderly by Family Type, 1990-92:
Persons in Married Couple with Children Families[1,9]

(Persons in thousands, standard errors in parentheses)

	Number	Employer (own)	Employer (other)[2]	Medicaid[3]	Other Coverage[8]	Uninsured[6]
East North Central	**18,208**	**25.7%** (0.50)	**55.4%** (0.57)	**5.8%** (0.27)	**6.4%** (0.28)	**6.8%** (0.29)
Illinois	4,842	26.1% (0.94)	53.3% (1.07)	5.0% (0.47)	7.6% (0.57)	8.0% (0.58)
Indiana	2,262	25.9% (1.86)	54.8% (2.11)	2.1% (0.61)	8.3% (1.17)	8.9% (1.21)
Michigan	3,933	25.1% (0.91)	56.1% (1.05)	8.1% (0.57)	5.2% (0.47)	5.5% (0.48)
Ohio	4,939	25.3% (0.87)	55.6% (1.00)	7.2% (0.52)	5.7% (0.46)	6.2% (0.48)
Wisconsin	2,232	26.3% (1.60)	58.7% (1.79)	3.7% (0.69)	5.8% (0.85)	5.5% (0.83)
West North Central	**8,095**	**23.4%** (0.74)	**51.8%** (0.88)	**4.7%** (0.37)	**11.6%** (0.56)	**8.5%** (0.49)
Iowa	1,370	23.0% (1.53)	54.3% (1.82)	4.2% (0.73)	12.5% (1.20)	6.1% (0.87)
Kansas	1,204	22.8% (1.52)	54.3% (1.80)	3.6% (0.67)	11.3% (1.15)	8.0% (0.98)
Minnesota	1,855	23.6% (1.75)	51.5% (2.05)	4.4% (0.85)	12.0% (1.34)	8.5% (1.14)
Missouri	2,245	25.2% (1.78)	49.7% (2.05)	6.1% (0.98)	8.3% (1.13)	10.8% (1.27)
Nebraska	798	22.3% (1.46)	53.7% (1.75)	4.2% (0.70)	13.0% (1.18)	6.8% (0.88)
North Dakota	311	18.8% (1.37)	48.7% (1.75)	3.9% (0.68)	21.8% (1.45)	6.8% (0.88)
South Dakota	313	21.4% (1.43)	46.5% (1.74)	4.5% (0.72)	15.9% (1.28)	11.8% (1.13)
Mountain	**6,268**	**21.7%** (0.68)	**51.6%** (0.83)	**5.4%** (0.37)	**8.0%** (0.45)	**13.3%** (0.56)
Arizona	1,413	21.5% (1.74)	48.5% (2.12)	7.2% (1.09)	7.8% (1.13)	15.0% (1.51)
Colorado	1,461	23.7% (1.77)	54.4% (2.08)	3.9% (0.81)	7.6% (1.10)	10.3% (1.27)
Idaho	556	19.7% (1.33)	49.3% (1.67)	4.7% (0.71)	11.3% (1.06)	14.9% (1.19)
Montana	393	20.2% (1.47)	46.8% (1.83)	7.9% (0.99)	12.5% (1.21)	12.6% (1.22)
Nevada	493	26.2% (1.84)	47.9% (2.09)	3.9% (0.81)	5.7% (0.97)	16.3% (1.54)
New Mexico	670	18.6% (1.49)	45.5% (1.91)	6.8% (0.96)	7.6% (1.01)	21.6% (1.57)
Utah	1,042	20.7% (1.32)	59.6% (1.59)	4.1% (0.65)	6.4% (0.80)	9.2% (0.94)
Wyoming	240	22.4% (1.77)	55.2% (2.11)	5.1% (0.93)	9.5% (1.24)	7.8% (1.13)
Pacific	**16,959**	**22.5%** (0.54)	**45.2%** (0.65)	**12.0%** (0.42)	**7.6%** (0.35)	**12.7%** (0.43)
Alaska	219	23.7% (1.60)	44.8% (1.88)	7.4% (0.99)	7.2% (0.98)	16.9% (1.41)
California	12,937	21.3% (0.62)	43.7% (0.75)	13.6% (0.52)	7.4% (0.40)	14.1% (0.53)
Hawaii	405	29.2% (2.07)	55.9% (2.26)	5.4% (1.03)	4.8% (0.97)	4.6% (0.96)
Oregon	1,298	26.0% (1.84)	53.5% (2.09)	5.5% (0.95)	5.7% (0.97)	9.2% (1.21)
Washington	2,101	26.2% (1.74)	47.5% (1.97)	7.5% (1.04)	10.8% (1.23)	7.9% (1.07)

Source: Three-year merged March CPS: 1991, 1992, and 1993.
Note: See table notes at end of Section A.

Table A5b
Health Insurance Coverage of the Nonelderly by Family Type, 1990-92:
Persons in Married Couple without Children Families[1,9]

(Persons in thousands, standard errors in parentheses)

	Number	Employer (own)	Employer (other)[2]	Medicaid[3]	Other Coverage[8]	Uninsured[6]
United States	**37,122**	**49.3%**	**24.9%**	**1.3%**	**12.1%**	**12.4%**
		(0.40)	(0.35)	(0.09)	(0.26)	(0.26)
New England	**1,920**	**53.4%**	**27.1%**	**1.1%**	**10.4%**	**7.9%**
		(1.39)	**(1.24)**	**(0.29)**	**(0.85)**	**(0.75)**
Connecticut	468	55.4%	27.1%	0.9%	9.4%	7.2%
		(3.89)	(3.48)	(0.74)	(2.29)	(2.03)
Maine	192	51.4%	26.6%	2.1%	12.3%	7.7%
		(3.39)	(3.00)	(0.97)	(2.22)	(1.81)
Massachusetts	846	53.3%	27.2%	1.0%	9.4%	9.1%
		(1.86)	(1.66)	(0.38)	(1.09)	(1.07)
New Hampshire	179	50.9%	28.4%	1.4%	13.5%	5.9%
		(3.70)	(3.34)	(0.85)	(2.53)	(1.75)
Rhode Island	155	55.8%	27.2%	0.8%	9.9%	6.3%
		(3.65)	(3.27)	(0.66)	(2.19)	(1.78)
Vermont	80	49.6%	25.2%	0.9%	16.5%	8.0%
		(3.86)	(3.35)	(0.71)	(2.87)	(2.09)
Middle Atlantic	**5,386**	**52.4%**	**26.9%**	**1.3%**	**9.0%**	**10.4%**
		(0.94)	**(0.83)**	**(0.21)**	**(0.54)**	**(0.57)**
New Jersey	1,126	54.4%	24.9%	0.6%	10.2%	9.8%
		(1.79)	(1.56)	(0.28)	(1.09)	(1.07)
New York	2,415	50.3%	25.8%	1.6%	9.2%	13.2%
		(1.41)	(1.23)	(0.35)	(0.81)	(0.95)
Pennsylvania	1,845	54.1%	29.6%	1.4%	7.9%	7.0%
		(1.70)	(1.56)	(0.40)	(0.92)	(0.87)
South Atlantic	**6,897**	**48.9%**	**22.9%**	**1.2%**	**12.8%**	**14.1%**
		(0.96)	**(0.81)**	**(0.21)**	**(0.64)**	**(0.67)**
Delaware	97	53.2%	30.3%	***	9.5%	7.0%
		(3.75)	(3.45)	***	(2.20)	(1.92)
District of Columbia	55	52.8%	18.3%	1.5%	7.5%	19.8%
		(4.99)	(3.87)	(1.22)	(2.63)	(3.99)
Florida	2,177	43.9%	21.2%	0.9%	15.5%	18.5%
		(1.56)	(1.29)	(0.29)	(1.14)	(1.22)
Georgia	937	50.6%	22.0%	0.9%	12.2%	14.4%
		(3.37)	(2.79)	(0.63)	(2.21)	(2.37)
Maryland	765	54.2%	29.1%	1.2%	7.6%	7.9%
		(3.44)	(3.13)	(0.76)	(1.83)	(1.86)
North Carolina	1,066	53.0%	21.0%	1.5%	12.2%	12.4%
		(1.66)	(1.35)	(0.40)	(1.09)	(1.09)
South Carolina	530	50.9%	19.2%	2.1%	14.2%	13.7%
		(3.02)	(2.38)	(0.86)	(2.11)	(2.08)
Virginia	995	49.7%	24.6%	1.2%	12.1%	12.4%
		(2.89)	(2.49)	(0.62)	(1.89)	(1.90)
West Virginia	275	44.8%	29.8%	3.2%	12.3%	10.0%
		(3.35)	(3.08)	(1.18)	(2.21)	(2.02)
East South Central	**2,392**	**46.9%**	**25.0%**	**2.7%**	**12.4%**	**13.0%**
		(1.65)	**(1.43)**	**(0.54)**	**(1.09)**	**(1.11)**
Alabama	697	47.1%	26.3%	1.3%	11.6%	13.8%
		(3.14)	(2.77)	(0.72)	(2.01)	(2.17)
Kentucky	595	47.2%	26.1%	3.7%	12.9%	10.0%
		(3.26)	(2.87)	(1.24)	(2.19)	(1.96)
Mississippi	297	41.3%	20.5%	2.7%	16.2%	19.3%
		(3.59)	(2.94)	(1.19)	(2.69)	(2.87)
Tennessee	803	48.7%	24.6%	3.2%	11.2%	12.3%
		(3.09)	(2.66)	(1.08)	(1.95)	(2.03)
West South Central	**3,847**	**42.2%**	**21.3%**	**1.9%**	**15.1%**	**19.4%**
		(1.33)	**(1.10)**	**(0.37)**	**(0.96)**	**(1.06)**
Arkansas	368	43.0%	22.1%	3.8%	16.1%	15.0%
		(3.24)	(2.72)	(1.26)	(2.41)	(2.34)
Louisiana	562	36.9%	20.7%	3.2%	18.1%	21.2%
		(3.58)	(3.00)	(1.30)	(2.85)	(3.03)
Oklahoma	504	41.2%	22.6%	1.8%	15.6%	18.8%
		(3.18)	(2.70)	(0.87)	(2.34)	(2.53)
Texas	2,413	43.6%	21.1%	1.3%	14.1%	19.9%
		(1.75)	(1.44)	(0.41)	(1.23)	(1.41)

Table A5b (continued)

Health Insurance Coverage of the Nonelderly by Family Type, 1990-92:
Persons in Married Couple without Children Families[1,9]

(Persons in thousands, standard errors in parentheses)

	Number	Employer (own)	Employer (other)[2]	Medicaid[3]	Other Coverage[8]	Uninsured[6]
East North Central	**6,251**	**52.5%**	**28.8%**	**0.8%**	**9.8%**	**8.1%**
		(0.98)	**(0.88)**	**(0.17)**	**(0.58)**	**(0.53)**
Illinois	1,723	54.4%	24.9%	0.3%	10.9%	9.5%
		(1.79)	(1.55)	(0.20)	(1.12)	(1.05)
Indiana	883	52.2%	29.9%	0.3%	11.4%	6.3%
		(3.39)	(3.11)	(0.37)	(2.16)	(1.64)
Michigan	1,321	51.9%	32.7%	1.1%	7.4%	6.9%
		(1.82)	(1.71)	(0.38)	(0.95)	(0.92)
Ohio	1,653	52.0%	28.6%	1.2%	8.7%	9.5%
		(1.73)	(1.57)	(0.37)	(0.98)	(1.02)
Wisconsin	671	50.7%	30.1%	1.2%	12.4%	5.6%
		(3.31)	(3.04)	(0.72)	(2.18)	(1.53)
West North Central	**2,674**	**49.3%**	**25.8%**	**0.8%**	**15.8%**	**8.4%**
		(1.52)	**(1.33)**	**(0.26)**	**(1.11)**	**(0.84)**
Iowa	397	45.3%	24.3%	1.1%	20.3%	9.1%
		(3.37)	(2.90)	(0.70)	(2.72)	(1.94)
Kansas	340	50.0%	25.1%	0.9%	16.3%	7.7%
		(3.41)	(2.96)	(0.63)	(2.52)	(1.81)
Minnesota	662	52.3%	29.1%	0.2%	11.5%	6.9%
		(3.44)	(3.13)	(0.31)	(2.19)	(1.75)
Missouri	860	51.9%	25.7%	0.8%	12.6%	9.0%
		(3.30)	(2.89)	(0.60)	(2.19)	(1.89)
Nebraska	245	43.9%	24.9%	1.0%	22.1%	8.1%
		(3.14)	(2.74)	(0.62)	(2.62)	(1.73)
North Dakota	78	37.7%	22.2%	1.9%	31.3%	7.0%
		(3.39)	(2.91)	(0.95)	(3.25)	(1.78)
South Dakota	92	41.5%	18.2%	0.6%	25.9%	13.8%
		(3.18)	(2.49)	(0.50)	(2.82)	(2.22)
Mountain	**2,045**	**46.7%**	**24.4%**	**0.8%**	**14.1%**	**14.0%**
		(1.45)	**(1.24)**	**(0.25)**	**(1.01)**	**(1.01)**
Arizona	596	47.1%	25.0%	0.8%	14.0%	13.1%
		(3.26)	(2.82)	(0.60)	(2.26)	(2.20)
Colorado	501	50.4%	25.1%	1.1%	12.4%	11.0%
		(3.56)	(3.09)	(0.73)	(2.35)	(2.23)
Idaho	154	44.5%	21.8%	0.8%	17.2%	15.8%
		(3.15)	(2.62)	(0.57)	(2.39)	(2.32)
Montana	114	43.6%	25.1%	1.1%	19.1%	11.0%
		(3.37)	(2.95)	(0.71)	(2.67)	(2.13)
Nevada	196	49.3%	20.1%	***	12.1%	18.6%
		(3.32)	(2.66)	***	(2.16)	(2.58)
New Mexico	213	36.8%	25.6%	0.6%	17.0%	20.0%
		(3.28)	(2.96)	(0.54)	(2.55)	(2.72)
Utah	204	47.6%	26.0%	0.3%	12.3%	13.8%
		(3.67)	(3.22)	(0.38)	(2.41)	(2.54)
Wyoming	68	45.3%	23.6%	1.5%	15.8%	13.8%
		(3.96)	(3.38)	(0.96)	(2.90)	(2.74)
Pacific	**5,710**	**48.4%**	**22.5%**	**1.7%**	**12.4%**	**15.0%**
		(1.12)	**(0.94)**	**(0.29)**	**(0.74)**	**(0.80)**
Alaska	66	48.9%	23.8%	0.6%	10.0%	16.7%
		(3.43)	(2.92)	(0.54)	(2.06)	(2.56)
California	4,253	47.2%	22.4%	2.0%	11.7%	16.7%
		(1.32)	(1.11)	(0.37)	(0.85)	(0.99)
Hawaii	164	60.9%	20.9%	0.6%	11.6%	5.9%
		(3.48)	(2.91)	(0.55)	(2.29)	(1.69)
Oregon	474	49.9%	24.3%	0.3%	12.8%	12.7%
		(3.46)	(2.97)	(0.38)	(2.31)	(2.31)
Washington	752	51.5%	22.4%	1.3%	16.2%	8.6%
		(3.30)	(2.75)	(0.76)	(2.43)	(1.85)

Source: Three-year merged March CPS: 1991, 1992, and 1993.
Note: See table notes at end of Section A.

Table A5c
Health Insurance Coverage of the Nonelderly by Family Type, 1990-92:
Persons in Single Parent Families[1,9]
(Persons in thousands, standard errors in parentheses)

	Number	Employer (own)	Employer (other)[2]	Medicaid[3]	Other Coverage[8]	Uninsured[6]
United States	29,398	15.1% (0.32)	23.1% (0.38)	44.3% (0.45)	5.6% (0.21)	11.9% (0.29)
New England	1,344	15.8% (1.22)	24.6% (1.44)	43.5% (1.65)	7.1% (0.86)	8.9% (0.95)
Connecticut	346	19.4% (3.61)	27.5% (4.07)	36.5% (4.39)	8.6% (2.56)	8.0% (2.47)
Maine	146	13.9% (2.69)	27.0% (3.45)	42.5% (3.84)	7.7% (2.07)	9.0% (2.22)
Massachusetts	616	14.6% (1.54)	22.4% (1.82)	48.3% (2.18)	6.3% (1.06)	8.5% (1.22)
New Hampshire	93	15.0% (3.68)	22.2% (4.28)	34.6% (4.89)	8.3% (2.83)	19.8% (4.10)
Rhode Island	90	16.5% (3.57)	27.0% (4.27)	46.5% (4.80)	6.5% (2.37)	3.5% (1.76)
Vermont	53	12.7% (3.18)	25.9% (4.18)	47.4% (4.77)	4.2% (1.92)	9.7% (2.83)
Middle Atlantic	4,287	15.0% (0.75)	23.1% (0.89)	47.5% (1.05)	5.4% (0.47)	9.1% (0.61)
New Jersey	803	17.3% (1.61)	25.2% (1.85)	42.5% (2.11)	5.4% (0.96)	9.7% (1.26)
New York	2,269	13.6% (1.00)	21.7% (1.20)	50.6% (1.45)	5.4% (0.66)	8.7% (0.82)
Pennsylvania	1,215	16.1% (1.55)	24.3% (1.80)	44.9% (2.09)	5.3% (0.94)	9.4% (1.23)
South Atlantic	5,393	15.6% (0.79)	21.7% (0.89)	42.4% (1.07)	6.1% (0.52)	14.3% (0.76)
Delaware	95	19.8% (3.04)	32.0% (3.55)	30.5% (3.51)	3.1% (1.32)	14.6% (2.69)
District of Columbia	121	12.5% (2.23)	19.4% (2.67)	47.8% (3.37)	4.5% (1.40)	15.7% (2.46)
Florida	1,702	15.6% (1.29)	18.4% (1.38)	42.4% (1.76)	5.8% (0.83)	17.8% (1.36)
Georgia	835	13.7% (2.46)	19.7% (2.84)	48.9% (3.57)	5.3% (1.60)	12.4% (2.35)
Maryland	596	17.1% (2.94)	25.6% (3.41)	43.8% (3.88)	6.5% (1.92)	7.0% (1.99)
North Carolina	743	17.0% (1.49)	23.2% (1.68)	40.6% (1.95)	5.4% (0.90)	13.8% (1.37)
South Carolina	465	15.5% (2.34)	23.9% (2.75)	41.1% (3.17)	6.0% (1.53)	13.4% (2.20)
Virginia	657	16.6% (2.65)	25.5% (3.10)	33.5% (3.36)	9.4% (2.08)	14.9% (2.53)
West Virginia	180	8.9% (2.37)	18.1% (3.20)	54.0% (4.15)	4.5% (1.72)	14.5% (2.93)
East South Central	2,182	13.8% (1.19)	23.1% (1.46)	45.3% (1.72)	4.0% (0.68)	13.8% (1.19)
Alabama	545	14.5% (2.51)	23.7% (3.02)	38.5% (3.46)	2.1% (1.01)	21.2% (2.91)
Kentucky	435	14.9% (2.71)	27.0% (3.39)	45.4% (3.80)	3.4% (1.39)	9.3% (2.22)
Mississippi	468	10.4% (1.77)	18.3% (2.25)	48.5% (2.90)	7.9% (1.57)	14.9% (2.07)
Tennessee	735	14.8% (2.29)	23.3% (2.73)	48.2% (3.23)	3.4% (1.18)	10.2% (1.95)
West South Central	3,240	13.0% (0.98)	20.1% (1.17)	45.4% (1.46)	4.6% (0.61)	17.0% (1.10)
Arkansas	259	10.7% (2.42)	16.1% (2.87)	47.0% (3.90)	6.8% (1.96)	19.4% (3.09)
Louisiana	692	9.0% (1.92)	14.9% (2.38)	53.3% (3.33)	3.1% (1.16)	19.6% (2.65)
Oklahoma	309	13.4% (2.81)	20.9% (3.36)	43.3% (4.09)	4.4% (1.69)	18.0% (3.18)
Texas	1,980	14.6% (1.38)	22.2% (1.62)	42.8% (1.93)	4.8% (0.84)	15.6% (1.41)

Table A5c (continued)

Health Insurance Coverage of the Nonelderly by Family Type, 1990-92:
Persons in Single Parent Families[1,9]

(Persons in thousands, standard errors in parentheses)

	Number	Employer (own)	Employer (other)[2]	Medicaid[3]	Other Coverage[8]	Uninsured[6]
East North Central	**5,301**	**15.7%**	**25.0%**	**43.4%**	**6.4%**	**9.6%**
		(0.77)	**(0.92)**	**(1.05)**	**(0.52)**	**(0.62)**
Illinois	1,571	14.3%	21.5%	50.8%	4.8%	8.5%
		(1.32)	(1.55)	(1.88)	(0.81)	(1.05)
Indiana	793	18.5%	27.4%	32.7%	6.9%	14.5%
		(2.78)	(3.20)	(3.36)	(1.81)	(2.52)
Michigan	1,169	14.0%	24.6%	45.8%	6.0%	9.7%
		(1.34)	(1.66)	(1.93)	(0.92)	(1.14)
Ohio	1,188	15.4%	25.7%	42.9%	7.4%	8.6%
		(1.48)	(1.79)	(2.02)	(1.07)	(1.15)
Wisconsin	580	19.5%	30.0%	34.3%	8.4%	7.7%
		(2.82)	(3.27)	(3.38)	(1.98)	(1.89)
West North Central	**1,825**	**16.2%**	**23.7%**	**39.8%**	**7.9%**	**12.4%**
		(1.36)	**(1.57)**	**(1.81)**	**(1.00)**	**(1.22)**
Iowa	231	17.6%	27.3%	39.7%	5.7%	9.8%
		(3.38)	(3.95)	(4.34)	(2.06)	(2.63)
Kansas	272	18.7%	31.1%	33.6%	6.1%	10.5%
		(2.97)	(3.53)	(3.60)	(1.82)	(2.33)
Minnesota	468	15.4%	23.9%	43.6%	8.1%	8.9%
		(2.96)	(3.49)	(4.06)	(2.24)	(2.33)
Missouri	608	15.4%	18.7%	40.1%	8.6%	17.3%
		(2.84)	(3.06)	(3.85)	(2.20)	(2.97)
Nebraska	137	16.8%	23.7%	41.4%	7.6%	10.5%
		(3.17)	(3.60)	(4.17)	(2.25)	(2.59)
North Dakota	43	12.9%	26.2%	42.9%	12.4%	5.7%
		(3.16)	(4.15)	(4.68)	(3.11)	(2.19)
South Dakota	67	14.2%	23.8%	30.8%	12.9%	18.3%
		(2.63)	(3.21)	(3.48)	(2.53)	(2.92)
Mountain	**1,424**	**16.8%**	**26.9%**	**36.3%**	**6.8%**	**13.2%**
		(1.30)	**(1.54)**	**(1.67)**	**(0.87)**	**(1.18)**
Arizona	376	16.9%	25.9%	38.6%	5.6%	13.0%
		(3.08)	(3.60)	(4.00)	(1.89)	(2.76)
Colorado	338	17.8%	25.0%	37.2%	10.2%	9.9%
		(3.31)	(3.75)	(4.18)	(2.62)	(2.58)
Idaho	88	16.5%	26.9%	33.6%	9.0%	14.0%
		(3.11)	(3.72)	(3.97)	(2.41)	(2.91)
Montana	85	12.0%	27.7%	37.8%	6.6%	15.9%
		(2.56)	(3.53)	(3.82)	(1.95)	(2.88)
Nevada	156	22.2%	32.4%	23.6%	5.0%	16.8%
		(3.08)	(3.47)	(3.15)	(1.62)	(2.78)
New Mexico	194	13.5%	19.9%	44.1%	4.7%	17.8%
		(2.43)	(2.84)	(3.53)	(1.51)	(2.72)
Utah	137	16.5%	36.9%	33.2%	5.7%	7.7%
		(3.32)	(4.32)	(4.21)	(2.08)	(2.38)
Wyoming	48	15.2%	28.3%	33.2%	4.6%	18.7%
		(3.39)	(4.25)	(4.44)	(1.98)	(3.68)
Pacific	**4,402**	**14.6%**	**22.7%**	**48.2%**	**4.2%**	**10.3%**
		(0.90)	**(1.07)**	**(1.28)**	**(0.51)**	**(0.78)**
Alaska	69	16.5%	27.6%	35.0%	4.4%	16.5%
		(2.49)	(2.99)	(3.20)	(1.38)	(2.49)
California	3,439	13.3%	20.4%	51.7%	3.6%	11.1%
		(1.00)	(1.19)	(1.47)	(0.55)	(0.93)
Hawaii	108	18.3%	31.6%	37.4%	5.2%	7.4%
		(3.40)	(4.09)	(4.26)	(1.96)	(2.31)
Oregon	305	16.0%	30.6%	40.1%	4.6%	8.8%
		(3.16)	(3.98)	(4.23)	(1.81)	(2.44)
Washington	481	21.9%	31.7%	33.4%	8.0%	5.0%
		(3.41)	(3.84)	(3.89)	(2.23)	(1.81)

Source: Three-year merged March CPS: 1991, 1992, and 1993.
Note: See table notes at end of Section A.

Table A5d
Health Insurance Coverage of the Nonelderly by Family Type, 1990-92:
Single Persons[1,9]
(Persons in thousands, standard errors in parentheses)

	Number	Employer (own)	Employer (other)[2]	Medicaid[3]	Other Coverage[8]	Uninsured[6]
United States	46,395	45.7%	1.8%	7.1%	14.8%	30.7%
		(0.36)	(0.09)	(0.18)	(0.25)	(0.33)
New England	2,635	54.9%	1.7%	6.0%	14.9%	22.5%
		(1.19)	(0.31)	(0.57)	(0.85)	(0.99)
Connecticut	614	60.6%	2.0%	5.0%	13.1%	19.3%
		(3.34)	(0.96)	(1.49)	(2.31)	(2.70)
Maine	204	46.1%	2.6%	8.9%	14.7%	27.8%
		(3.28)	(1.04)	(1.87)	(2.33)	(2.95)
Massachusetts	1,272	54.2%	1.7%	6.7%	16.0%	21.4%
		(1.51)	(0.39)	(0.76)	(1.11)	(1.25)
New Hampshire	218	54.4%	1.3%	2.6%	14.3%	27.5%
		(3.34)	(0.75)	(1.07)	(2.35)	(2.99)
Rhode Island	217	52.8%	0.8%	6.1%	14.5%	25.7%
		(3.10)	(0.57)	(1.48)	(2.19)	(2.71)
Vermont	109	52.7%	2.0%	4.7%	13.6%	27.1%
		(3.30)	(0.91)	(1.40)	(2.26)	(2.94)
Middle Atlantic	7,243	49.0%	1.6%	8.0%	13.8%	27.5%
		(0.81)	(0.21)	(0.44)	(0.56)	(0.72)
New Jersey	1,536	52.3%	1.6%	6.3%	12.0%	27.8%
		(1.54)	(0.39)	(0.75)	(1.00)	(1.38)
New York	3,589	46.5%	1.4%	9.1%	13.6%	29.4%
		(1.15)	(0.27)	(0.66)	(0.79)	(1.05)
Pennsylvania	2,119	50.9%	2.0%	7.3%	15.6%	24.1%
		(1.59)	(0.45)	(0.83)	(1.16)	(1.36)
South Atlantic	8,443	43.9%	1.8%	6.5%	14.5%	33.4%
		(0.86)	(0.23)	(0.43)	(0.61)	(0.82)
Delaware	150	49.8%	0.8%	3.2%	14.7%	31.5%
		(3.03)	(0.54)	(1.07)	(2.14)	(2.81)
District of Columbia	196	46.7%	1.4%	8.9%	13.3%	29.8%
		(2.64)	(0.62)	(1.51)	(1.80)	(2.42)
Florida	2,553	39.8%	1.3%	6.0%	16.3%	36.6%
		(1.42)	(0.33)	(0.69)	(1.07)	(1.40)
Georgia	1,230	41.4%	1.5%	6.3%	13.3%	37.4%
		(2.90)	(0.72)	(1.43)	(2.00)	(2.85)
Maryland	1,024	55.0%	2.0%	3.5%	13.9%	25.5%
		(2.96)	(0.84)	(1.10)	(2.06)	(2.60)
North Carolina	1,208	45.6%	2.0%	7.8%	15.1%	29.4%
		(1.55)	(0.44)	(0.84)	(1.12)	(1.42)
South Carolina	610	37.6%	2.0%	10.3%	14.0%	36.1%
		(2.73)	(0.78)	(1.72)	(1.95)	(2.71)
Virginia	1,200	47.4%	2.6%	5.9%	11.3%	32.8%
		(2.63)	(0.83)	(1.24)	(1.67)	(2.47)
West Virginia	272	36.2%	2.6%	11.1%	17.6%	32.5%
		(3.25)	(1.07)	(2.12)	(2.58)	(3.17)
East South Central	2,543	37.6%	2.3%	11.7%	15.4%	33.0%
		(1.55)	(0.48)	(1.03)	(1.16)	(1.51)
Alabama	703	37.1%	2.5%	9.7%	14.8%	35.9%
		(3.02)	(0.99)	(1.85)	(2.22)	(3.00)
Kentucky	549	40.2%	1.2%	13.5%	15.1%	30.0%
		(3.33)	(0.75)	(2.32)	(2.43)	(3.12)
Mississippi	421	29.8%	2.3%	14.6%	14.2%	39.0%
		(2.80)	(0.92)	(2.17)	(2.14)	(2.99)
Tennessee	870	40.2%	2.7%	10.8%	16.7%	29.5%
		(2.91)	(0.96)	(1.84)	(2.21)	(2.71)
West South Central	4,473	38.5%	1.5%	7.3%	14.8%	37.8%
		(1.21)	(0.31)	(0.65)	(0.89)	(1.21)
Arkansas	351	35.2%	1.9%	11.2%	19.9%	31.9%
		(3.20)	(0.93)	(2.11)	(2.68)	(3.13)
Louisiana	685	28.5%	1.7%	10.9%	17.5%	41.4%
		(3.03)	(0.87)	(2.09)	(2.55)	(3.30)
Oklahoma	466	29.8%	1.8%	8.9%	23.0%	36.6%
		(3.08)	(0.89)	(1.91)	(2.83)	(3.24)
Texas	2,971	42.6%	1.4%	5.8%	12.3%	37.9%
		(1.58)	(0.38)	(0.74)	(1.05)	(1.55)

Health Insurance Coverage of the Nonelderly by Family Type, 1990-92:
Single Persons[1,9]

(Persons in thousands, standard errors in parentheses)

	Number	Employer (own)	Employer (other)[2]	Medicaid[3]	Other Coverage[8]	Uninsured[6]
East North Central	**7,625**	**50.0%**	**2.3%**	**7.1%**	**14.2%**	**26.4%**
		(0.88)	**(0.27)**	**(0.45)**	**(0.62)**	**(0.78)**
Illinois	2,283	47.8%	1.6%	8.4%	14.0%	28.2%
		(1.56)	(0.40)	(0.86)	(1.08)	(1.40)
Indiana	920	51.1%	2.4%	4.4%	13.9%	28.2%
		(3.32)	(1.03)	(1.36)	(2.30)	(2.99)
Michigan	1,746	49.0%	2.5%	8.6%	14.3%	25.6%
		(1.58)	(0.50)	(0.89)	(1.11)	(1.38)
Ohio	1,848	51.8%	2.5%	5.3%	14.1%	26.3%
		(1.64)	(0.51)	(0.74)	(1.14)	(1.44)
Wisconsin	828	52.9%	3.1%	7.6%	15.4%	21.0%
		(2.98)	(1.03)	(1.58)	(2.15)	(2.43)
West North Central	**2,982**	**46.6%**	**1.9%**	**5.0%**	**19.7%**	**26.8%**
		(1.44)	**(0.40)**	**(0.63)**	**(1.15)**	**(1.28)**
Iowa	463	46.3%	2.0%	5.2%	21.4%	25.1%
		(3.12)	(0.89)	(1.39)	(2.57)	(2.72)
Kansas	390	44.3%	2.1%	4.5%	20.2%	28.9%
		(3.16)	(0.92)	(1.32)	(2.55)	(2.89)
Minnesota	860	49.8%	1.5%	3.4%	19.0%	26.3%
		(3.02)	(0.73)	(1.09)	(2.37)	(2.66)
Missouri	855	45.8%	2.2%	6.7%	17.4%	27.7%
		(3.30)	(0.98)	(1.66)	(2.52)	(2.97)
Nebraska	212	48.9%	2.4%	4.7%	21.3%	22.7%
		(3.40)	(1.03)	(1.45)	(2.79)	(2.85)
North Dakota	92	39.5%	1.7%	4.9%	29.4%	24.5%
		(3.16)	(0.84)	(1.39)	(2.94)	(2.78)
South Dakota	112	38.3%	0.8%	5.7%	22.6%	32.6%
		(2.85)	(0.51)	(1.36)	(2.45)	(2.75)
Mountain	**2,273**	**45.1%**	**1.6%**	**4.4%**	**18.0%**	**30.9%**
		(1.37)	**(0.35)**	**(0.56)**	**(1.06)**	**(1.27)**
Arizona	635	46.5%	1.2%	5.0%	17.4%	29.8%
		(3.15)	(0.70)	(1.38)	(2.40)	(2.89)
Colorado	582	51.1%	0.3%	2.5%	19.3%	26.8%
		(3.30)	(0.35)	(1.03)	(2.61)	(2.93)
Idaho	141	42.0%	4.1%	4.8%	15.5%	33.5%
		(3.28)	(1.32)	(1.42)	(2.40)	(3.13)
Montana	124	38.1%	1.0%	6.3%	21.4%	33.1%
		(3.17)	(0.66)	(1.59)	(2.67)	(3.07)
Nevada	268	47.2%	1.9%	2.4%	13.4%	35.1%
		(2.83)	(0.77)	(0.86)	(1.93)	(2.70)
New Mexico	265	34.9%	1.4%	8.1%	18.5%	37.0%
		(2.90)	(0.73)	(1.66)	(2.36)	(2.94)
Utah	201	42.3%	5.1%	4.0%	19.4%	29.1%
		(3.66)	(1.63)	(1.45)	(2.93)	(3.36)
Wyoming	57	38.3%	1.1%	5.5%	24.3%	30.8%
		(4.23)	(0.91)	(1.99)	(3.73)	(4.02)
Pacific	**8,178**	**43.9%**	**1.3%**	**7.1%**	**13.7%**	**34.0%**
		(0.93)	**(0.21)**	**(0.48)**	**(0.64)**	**(0.89)**
Alaska	97	40.8%	1.4%	6.1%	13.0%	38.8%
		(2.79)	(0.65)	(1.35)	(1.91)	(2.76)
California	6,401	42.0%	1.3%	7.5%	13.7%	35.6%
		(1.07)	(0.24)	(0.57)	(0.74)	(1.03)
Hawaii	226	62.3%	1.6%	6.8%	12.4%	17.0%
		(2.95)	(0.76)	(1.53)	(2.01)	(2.29)
Oregon	506	47.6%	1.9%	5.0%	13.2%	32.4%
		(3.35)	(0.90)	(1.45)	(2.27)	(3.14)
Washington	949	50.7%	0.9%	6.1%	14.3%	28.0%
		(2.94)	(0.57)	(1.41)	(2.06)	(2.64)

Source: Three-year merged March CPS: 1991, 1992, and 1993.
Note: See table notes at end of Section A.

Table A6a

Health Insurance Coverage of the Nonelderly by Family Income, 1990-92:

Below 100 Percent of Poverty[1,9,10]

(Persons in thousands, standard errors in parentheses)

	Number	Employer (own)	Employer (other)[2]	Medicaid[3]	Other Coverage[8]	Uninsured[6]
United States	**39,487**	4.4%	7.5%	49.0%	9.9%	29.2%
		(0.23)	(0.29)	(0.55)	(0.33)	(0.50)
New England	**1,446**	**5.1%**	**8.8%**	**53.2%**	**10.5%**	**22.4%**
		(1.00)	**(1.28)**	**(2.26)**	**(1.39)**	**(1.89)**
Connecticut	260	5.8%	12.3%	55.9%	8.8%	17.2%
		(3.46)	(4.86)	(7.35)	(4.19)	(5.58)
Maine	178	4.2%	9.8%	54.8%	11.1%	20.1%
		(2.00)	(2.96)	(4.95)	(3.12)	(3.98)
Massachusetts	722	4.7%	7.2%	54.9%	10.3%	23.0%
		(1.21)	(1.46)	(2.83)	(1.72)	(2.39)
New Hampshire	108	6.3%	10.9%	36.0%	13.1%	33.7%
		(3.28)	(4.19)	(6.46)	(4.54)	(6.36)
Rhode Island	116	6.3%	6.2%	54.0%	10.5%	23.0%
		(2.90)	(2.89)	(5.97)	(3.67)	(5.04)
Vermont	63	4.2%	11.1%	47.3%	14.8%	22.6%
		(2.46)	(3.87)	(6.14)	(4.38)	(5.15)
Middle Atlantic	**5,429**	**4.2%**	**7.3%**	**53.0%**	**10.4%**	**25.1%**
		(0.53)	**(0.68)**	**(1.31)**	**(0.81)**	**(1.14)**
New Jersey	900	4.7%	6.3%	51.1%	12.0%	25.9%
		(1.21)	(1.38)	(2.84)	(1.84)	(2.48)
New York	2,971	3.6%	7.8%	53.7%	9.2%	25.8%
		(0.67)	(0.96)	(1.78)	(1.03)	(1.56)
Pennsylvania	1,558	4.9%	6.9%	52.8%	12.0%	23.4%
		(1.13)	(1.32)	(2.61)	(1.70)	(2.22)
South Atlantic	**7,128**	**4.7%**	**7.5%**	**46.0%**	**10.4%**	**31.5%**
		(0.56)	**(0.70)**	**(1.32)**	**(0.81)**	**(1.23)**
Delaware	73	6.1%	8.3%	45.1%	11.4%	29.1%
		(2.93)	(3.38)	(6.10)	(3.89)	(5.57)
District of Columbia	130	3.2%	4.8%	60.5%	5.8%	25.6%
		(1.62)	(1.96)	(4.48)	(2.15)	(4.00)
Florida	2,243	3.7%	5.5%	43.9%	11.1%	35.8%
		(0.83)	(0.99)	(2.17)	(1.37)	(2.09)
Georgia	1,182	3.9%	7.2%	47.2%	9.0%	32.8%
		(1.63)	(2.18)	(4.22)	(2.42)	(3.97)
Maryland	620	7.3%	11.6%	48.9%	10.6%	21.6%
		(2.81)	(3.45)	(5.40)	(3.33)	(4.44)
North Carolina	1,003	5.2%	8.8%	48.1%	11.3%	26.6%
		(1.07)	(1.36)	(2.41)	(1.53)	(2.13)
South Carolina	671	5.5%	8.7%	45.0%	9.8%	30.9%
		(1.73)	(2.13)	(3.77)	(2.25)	(3.50)
Virginia	841	6.3%	8.5%	39.5%	11.1%	34.7%
		(2.15)	(2.47)	(4.33)	(2.78)	(4.22)
West Virginia	366	2.8%	6.0%	55.5%	8.3%	27.3%
		(1.37)	(1.96)	(4.08)	(2.27)	(3.66)
East South Central	**3,050**	**4.6%**	**7.4%**	**49.5%**	**8.5%**	**30.1%**
		(0.86)	**(1.08)**	**(2.06)**	**(1.15)**	**(1.89)**
Alabama	789	5.7%	7.7%	39.2%	8.5%	39.0%
		(1.93)	(2.22)	(4.06)	(2.32)	(4.06)
Kentucky	680	3.4%	7.6%	55.2%	8.4%	25.4%
		(1.57)	(2.29)	(4.28)	(2.38)	(3.74)
Mississippi	659	3.4%	6.9%	50.8%	8.7%	30.2%
		(1.26)	(1.75)	(3.45)	(1.94)	(3.17)
Tennessee	921	5.4%	7.2%	53.1%	8.4%	26.0%
		(1.83)	(2.11)	(4.06)	(2.25)	(3.56)
West South Central	**5,182**	**3.9%**	**6.6%**	**44.7%**	**8.3%**	**36.4%**
		(0.63)	**(0.81)**	**(1.62)**	**(0.90)**	**(1.57)**
Arkansas	427	3.9%	5.2%	49.3%	11.7%	29.9%
		(1.67)	(1.90)	(4.29)	(2.75)	(3.93)
Louisiana	975	3.4%	6.4%	52.7%	8.0%	29.5%
		(1.43)	(1.94)	(3.96)	(2.15)	(3.62)
Oklahoma	520	2.3%	4.9%	43.7%	13.5%	35.6%
		(1.34)	(1.94)	(4.45)	(3.06)	(4.29)
Texas	3,260	4.3%	7.1%	41.9%	7.2%	39.5%
		(0.87)	(1.10)	(2.11)	(1.11)	(2.09)

Table A6a   (continued)
Health Insurance Coverage of the Nonelderly by Family Income, 1990-92:
Below 100 Percent of Poverty[1,9,10]

(Persons in thousands, standard errors in parentheses)

	Number	Employer (own)	Employer (other)[2]	Medicaid[3]	Other Coverage[8]	Uninsured[6]
East North Central	**6,322**	**4.7%**	**8.9%**	**53.3%**	**9.9%**	**23.2%**
		(0.58)	**(0.78)**	**(1.37)**	**(0.82)**	**(1.15)**
Illinois	1,953	4.1%	6.9%	56.3%	8.8%	23.9%
		(0.95)	(1.20)	(2.36)	(1.35)	(2.03)
Indiana	733	5.3%	10.1%	42.6%	12.6%	29.3%
		(2.36)	(3.16)	(5.19)	(3.49)	(4.78)
Michigan	1,588	5.0%	9.5%	55.4%	8.8%	21.2%
		(1.02)	(1.37)	(2.32)	(1.32)	(1.91)
Ohio	1,504	4.8%	8.1%	53.9%	10.8%	22.3%
		(1.10)	(1.40)	(2.55)	(1.59)	(2.13)
Wisconsin	545	5.0%	14.4%	49.2%	11.1%	20.3%
		(2.25)	(3.64)	(5.18)	(3.26)	(4.17)
West North Central	**2,307**	**4.1%**	**8.2%**	**45.8%**	**15.9%**	**26.0%**
		(0.92)	**(1.27)**	**(2.30)**	**(1.69)**	**(2.03)**
Iowa	323	4.9%	9.9%	43.0%	18.8%	23.4%
		(2.28)	(3.16)	(5.23)	(4.13)	(4.47)
Kansas	302	3.9%	11.6%	43.1%	14.9%	26.6%
		(1.96)	(3.26)	(5.04)	(3.62)	(4.50)
Minnesota	542	4.1%	6.0%	48.9%	16.7%	24.3%
		(2.12)	(2.54)	(5.35)	(3.99)	(4.60)
Missouri	784	3.5%	7.3%	48.7%	12.0%	28.5%
		(1.79)	(2.54)	(4.88)	(3.17)	(4.40)
Nebraska	171	4.8%	8.3%	45.6%	21.3%	20.0%
		(2.28)	(2.94)	(5.31)	(4.37)	(4.27)
North Dakota	82	3.6%	11.0%	32.4%	31.7%	21.3%
		(1.80)	(3.01)	(4.49)	(4.47)	(3.93)
South Dakota	102	7.2%	8.4%	34.4%	14.7%	35.3%
		(2.23)	(2.39)	(4.10)	(3.06)	(4.13)
Mountain	**1,992**	**5.5%**	**10.3%**	**40.0%**	**11.6%**	**32.6%**
		(0.94)	**(1.26)**	**(2.03)**	**(1.33)**	**(1.94)**
Arizona	534	4.8%	7.8%	45.1%	8.5%	33.9%
		(2.07)	(2.60)	(4.83)	(2.71)	(4.60)
Colorado	402	6.7%	9.7%	42.9%	12.1%	28.7%
		(2.79)	(3.31)	(5.54)	(3.65)	(5.06)
Idaho	158	7.2%	16.4%	29.8%	12.4%	34.2%
		(2.28)	(3.27)	(4.04)	(2.92)	(4.19)
Montana	134	4.1%	10.8%	40.0%	15.4%	29.6%
		(1.76)	(2.74)	(4.33)	(3.20)	(4.04)
Nevada	175	7.2%	8.3%	28.8%	13.8%	41.9%
		(2.56)	(2.72)	(4.47)	(3.41)	(4.87)
New Mexico	334	3.9%	7.4%	40.6%	9.5%	38.5%
		(1.48)	(2.00)	(3.75)	(2.24)	(3.72)
Utah	204	6.0%	19.3%	36.5%	16.4%	21.9%
		(2.45)	(4.08)	(4.99)	(3.84)	(4.28)
Wyoming	52	5.1%	10.5%	45.6%	14.7%	24.1%
		(2.82)	(3.95)	(6.41)	(4.56)	(5.50)
Pacific	**6,629**	**4.0%**	**5.9%**	**50.7%**	**7.9%**	**31.5%**
		(0.58)	**(0.69)**	**(1.47)**	**(0.79)**	**(1.36)**
Alaska	80	2.6%	6.1%	42.7%	5.3%	43.2%
		(1.41)	(2.11)	(4.36)	(1.98)	(4.36)
California	5,477	3.7%	5.0%	51.6%	7.8%	32.0%
		(0.62)	(0.72)	(1.65)	(0.88)	(1.54)
Hawaii	141	7.2%	15.3%	47.4%	8.4%	21.7%
		(2.80)	(3.91)	(5.42)	(3.01)	(4.47)
Oregon	355	5.9%	10.6%	44.8%	8.8%	29.8%
		(2.66)	(3.47)	(5.61)	(3.20)	(5.16)
Washington	577	5.6%	9.0%	48.3%	8.8%	28.3%
		(2.45)	(3.03)	(5.31)	(3.02)	(4.79)

Source: Three-year merged March CPS: 1991, 1992, and 1993.
Note: See table notes at end of Section A.

Table A6b
Health Insurance Coverage of the Nonelderly by Family Income, 1990-92:
100-199 Percent of Poverty[1,9,10]
(Persons in thousands, standard errors in parentheses)

	Number	Employer (own)	Employer (other)[2]	Medicaid[3]	Other Coverage[8]	Uninsured[6]
United States	**38,527**	**20.5%**	**27.4%**	**10.1%**	**12.3%**	**29.7%**
		(0.45)	(0.49)	(0.33)	(0.36)	(0.51)
New England	**1,517**	**20.9%**	**25.9%**	**12.8%**	**15.6%**	**24.8%**
		(1.80)	**(1.94)**	**(1.48)**	**(1.61)**	**(1.91)**
Connecticut	315	18.9%	25.0%	11.7%	19.1%	25.3%
		(5.27)	(5.83)	(4.32)	(5.29)	(5.85)
Maine	221	19.9%	31.8%	10.0%	13.1%	25.2%
		(3.56)	(4.16)	(2.68)	(3.02)	(3.88)
Massachusetts	608	21.2%	22.7%	15.9%	15.8%	24.4%
		(2.53)	(2.59)	(2.26)	(2.26)	(2.66)
New Hampshire	149	20.2%	29.8%	6.5%	13.2%	30.3%
		(4.59)	(5.23)	(2.82)	(3.88)	(5.25)
Rhode Island	134	27.0%	29.4%	9.1%	13.9%	20.7%
		(4.94)	(5.07)	(3.20)	(3.85)	(4.51)
Vermont	90	20.2%	23.4%	19.1%	15.1%	22.1%
		(4.12)	(4.34)	(4.03)	(3.67)	(4.26)
Middle Atlantic	**5,051**	**22.7%**	**30.1%**	**12.1%**	**11.6%**	**23.5%**
		(1.14)	**(1.25)**	**(0.89)**	**(0.88)**	**(1.16)**
New Jersey	842	23.5%	28.3%	8.9%	10.8%	28.5%
		(2.49)	(2.64)	(1.67)	(1.82)	(2.65)
New York	2,524	20.6%	28.3%	15.1%	11.6%	24.3%
		(1.57)	(1.75)	(1.39)	(1.24)	(1.66)
Pennsylvania	1,684	25.4%	33.7%	9.1%	12.1%	19.8%
		(2.19)	(2.38)	(1.45)	(1.64)	(2.01)
South Atlantic	**6,762**	**22.3%**	**24.5%**	**6.8%**	**11.9%**	**34.4%**
		(1.14)	**(1.17)**	**(0.69)**	**(0.88)**	**(1.29)**
Delaware	113	22.4%	31.4%	5.3%	12.5%	28.4%
		(4.09)	(4.55)	(2.20)	(3.25)	(4.42)
District of Columbia	82	19.1%	13.9%	16.4%	10.1%	40.4%
		(4.53)	(3.99)	(4.27)	(3.48)	(5.66)
Florida	2,096	19.9%	18.7%	6.4%	13.9%	41.2%
		(1.80)	(1.76)	(1.10)	(1.56)	(2.22)
Georgia	1,051	21.6%	28.7%	6.7%	10.9%	32.0%
		(3.69)	(4.06)	(2.24)	(2.80)	(4.18)
Maryland	533	26.3%	24.3%	10.7%	8.5%	30.2%
		(5.12)	(4.99)	(3.59)	(3.25)	(5.34)
North Carolina	1,056	26.1%	25.9%	7.2%	11.4%	29.3%
		(2.06)	(2.06)	(1.21)	(1.49)	(2.14)
South Carolina	635	24.5%	29.4%	4.3%	9.7%	32.0%
		(3.35)	(3.55)	(1.58)	(2.31)	(3.63)
Virginia	860	21.5%	25.5%	4.9%	12.9%	35.2%
		(3.60)	(3.82)	(1.90)	(2.93)	(4.18)
West Virginia	335	19.8%	32.8%	11.0%	12.2%	24.2%
		(3.42)	(4.03)	(2.69)	(2.81)	(3.68)
East South Central	**2,805**	**21.9%**	**29.6%**	**6.8%**	**12.4%**	**29.3%**
		(1.78)	**(1.96)**	**(1.08)**	**(1.41)**	**(1.96)**
Alabama	771	22.8%	32.3%	3.6%	11.5%	29.8%
		(3.53)	(3.94)	(1.57)	(2.68)	(3.85)
Kentucky	587	24.7%	28.4%	6.1%	15.1%	25.8%
		(3.99)	(4.17)	(2.22)	(3.31)	(4.05)
Mississippi	551	20.3%	28.6%	5.8%	11.6%	33.6%
		(3.04)	(3.41)	(1.77)	(2.42)	(3.56)
Tennessee	896	20.2%	28.7%	10.7%	11.8%	28.6%
		(3.31)	(3.73)	(2.54)	(2.66)	(3.72)
West South Central	**4,701**	**18.1%**	**24.5%**	**6.2%**	**11.4%**	**39.8%**
		(1.32)	**(1.48)**	**(0.82)**	**(1.09)**	**(1.68)**
Arkansas	471	18.3%	26.9%	5.7%	13.5%	35.5%
		(3.16)	(3.62)	(1.90)	(2.79)	(3.90)
Louisiana	665	15.8%	21.5%	5.6%	12.7%	44.5%
		(3.50)	(3.94)	(2.21)	(3.19)	(4.77)
Oklahoma	624	14.6%	28.1%	6.1%	14.2%	37.0%
		(2.89)	(3.68)	(1.95)	(2.86)	(3.95)
Texas	2,940	19.3%	24.1%	6.4%	10.1%	40.1%
		(1.78)	(1.93)	(1.10)	(1.36)	(2.21)

Table A6b (continued)
Health Insurance Coverage of the Nonelderly by Family Income, 1990-92:
100-199 Percent of Poverty[1,9,10]

(Persons in thousands, standard errors in parentheses)

	Number	Employer (own)	Employer (other)[2]	Medicaid[3]	Other Coverage[8]	Uninsured[6]
East North Central	**6,005**	**22.8%**	**33.0%**	**8.5%**	**12.7%**	**23.0%**
		(1.18)	**(1.32)**	**(0.78)**	**(0.93)**	**(1.18)**
Illinois	1,559	22.3%	29.8%	7.8%	14.7%	25.4%
		(2.22)	(2.44)	(1.43)	(1.88)	(2.32)
Indiana	947	24.1%	38.9%	3.9%	11.4%	21.8%
		(3.95)	(4.50)	(1.79)	(2.94)	(3.81)
Michigan	1,175	21.9%	31.6%	10.6%	12.0%	23.9%
		(2.25)	(2.53)	(1.67)	(1.76)	(2.32)
Ohio	1,638	23.4%	34.6%	9.4%	11.6%	21.0%
		(2.08)	(2.33)	(1.43)	(1.57)	(2.00)
Wisconsin	687	22.0%	31.1%	11.1%	13.4%	22.4%
		(3.82)	(4.27)	(2.90)	(3.14)	(3.85)
West North Central	**3,000**	**19.2%**	**27.3%**	**6.4%**	**20.4%**	**26.7%**
		(1.60)	**(1.81)**	**(0.99)**	**(1.63)**	**(1.79)**
Iowa	503	18.3%	34.5%	6.3%	20.7%	20.2%
		(3.28)	(4.03)	(2.06)	(3.43)	(3.40)
Kansas	405	20.3%	33.2%	5.6%	16.2%	24.7%
		(3.54)	(4.15)	(2.03)	(3.24)	(3.80)
Minnesota	627	17.0%	20.3%	6.7%	27.0%	29.0%
		(3.74)	(4.01)	(2.49)	(4.43)	(4.52)
Missouri	976	21.3%	24.3%	6.2%	16.3%	32.0%
		(3.58)	(3.75)	(2.10)	(3.23)	(4.08)
Nebraska	263	18.0%	31.4%	8.2%	19.6%	22.8%
		(3.30)	(3.99)	(2.36)	(3.42)	(3.61)
North Dakota	101	15.3%	25.4%	9.0%	33.6%	16.6%
		(3.12)	(3.77)	(2.48)	(4.09)	(3.22)
South Dakota	125	19.1%	31.8%	4.2%	22.8%	22.0%
		(3.07)	(3.63)	(1.56)	(3.27)	(3.23)
Mountain	**2,383**	**19.0%**	**31.9%**	**6.3%**	**13.8%**	**29.0%**
		(1.48)	**(1.76)**	**(0.92)**	**(1.31)**	**(1.72)**
Arizona	577	19.8%	29.7%	6.2%	13.3%	31.0%
		(3.72)	(4.27)	(2.26)	(3.17)	(4.32)
Colorado	476	21.0%	31.4%	6.4%	16.3%	24.8%
		(4.19)	(4.78)	(2.51)	(3.80)	(4.45)
Idaho	213	18.5%	31.1%	7.0%	15.4%	28.1%
		(2.96)	(3.53)	(1.94)	(2.75)	(3.43)
Montana	162	15.3%	28.0%	9.7%	19.6%	27.5%
		(2.89)	(3.60)	(2.37)	(3.19)	(3.58)
Nevada	205	22.7%	26.6%	5.3%	9.6%	35.7%
		(3.83)	(4.04)	(2.04)	(2.70)	(4.38)
New Mexico	291	17.4%	25.1%	5.2%	13.3%	39.0%
		(3.10)	(3.54)	(1.81)	(2.78)	(3.99)
Utah	381	17.1%	46.4%	4.9%	10.3%	21.3%
		(2.85)	(3.78)	(1.64)	(2.31)	(3.10)
Wyoming	77	15.1%	30.6%	10.2%	16.0%	28.1%
		(3.77)	(4.85)	(3.19)	(3.86)	(4.74)
Pacific	**6,304**	**16.9%**	**22.6%**	**20.4%**	**8.4%**	**31.7%**
		(1.13)	**(1.26)**	**(1.21)**	**(0.84)**	**(1.40)**
Alaska	85	18.4%	26.5%	14.1%	12.9%	28.0%
		(3.31)	(3.77)	(2.98)	(2.86)	(3.83)
California	5,039	15.8%	21.5%	22.3%	7.5%	32.8%
		(1.25)	(1.41)	(1.43)	(0.90)	(1.61)
Hawaii	153	35.5%	30.5%	7.5%	14.0%	12.6%
		(4.99)	(4.80)	(2.74)	(3.61)	(3.46)
Oregon	515	20.2%	31.6%	10.9%	9.3%	28.0%
		(3.76)	(4.35)	(2.91)	(2.72)	(4.20)
Washington	512	18.8%	21.3%	15.5%	14.3%	30.1%
		(4.41)	(4.61)	(4.08)	(3.94)	(5.17)

Source: Three-year merged March CPS: 1991, 1992, and 1993.
Note: See table notes at end of Section A.

Table A6c
Health Insurance Coverage of the Nonelderly by Family Income, 1990-92:
200-399 Percent of Poverty[1,9,10]

(Persons in thousands, standard errors in parentheses)

	Number	Employer (own)	Employer (other)[2]	Medicaid[3]	Other Coverage[8]	Uninsured[6]
United States	70,557	36.6% (0.39)	41.3% (0.40)	0.7% (0.07)	9.4% (0.24)	12.0% (0.27)
New England	3,800	38.2% (1.36)	42.3% (1.38)	1.0% (0.28)	8.6% (0.78)	9.9% (0.83)
Connecticut	929	39.0% (3.82)	43.6% (3.88)	1.0% (0.76)	7.4% (2.06)	8.9% (2.24)
Maine	402	37.7% (3.21)	41.1% (3.25)	1.2% (0.73)	10.9% (2.06)	9.1% (1.90)
Massachusetts	1,605	38.2% (1.85)	41.7% (1.88)	1.1% (0.40)	8.6% (1.07)	10.4% (1.16)
New Hampshire	366	35.2% (3.48)	42.6% (3.61)	*** ***	9.2% (2.11)	12.9% (2.45)
Rhode Island	289	41.1% (3.73)	40.8% (3.73)	2.1% (1.08)	8.2% (2.08)	7.9% (2.05)
Vermont	209	36.8% (3.25)	45.7% (3.36)	0.6% (0.53)	8.2% (1.85)	8.7% (1.90)
Middle Atlantic	10,431	37.3% (0.92)	43.2% (0.94)	0.9% (0.17)	7.7% (0.51)	11.0% (0.60)
New Jersey	1,964	37.7% (1.86)	40.6% (1.89)	0.6% (0.30)	7.8% (1.03)	13.2% (1.30)
New York	4,608	35.8% (1.38)	41.6% (1.42)	1.1% (0.30)	8.7% (0.81)	12.7% (0.96)
Pennsylvania	3,858	38.7% (1.62)	46.4% (1.66)	0.7% (0.27)	6.4% (0.81)	7.9% (0.90)
South Atlantic	11,859	38.4% (1.00)	36.7% (0.99)	0.8% (0.18)	9.6% (0.61)	14.6% (0.73)
Delaware	204	39.0% (3.57)	42.2% (3.62)	0.3% (0.41)	6.1% (1.75)	12.4% (2.42)
District of Columbia	121	41.0% (4.67)	24.2% (4.06)	0.9% (0.89)	10.0% (2.84)	24.0% (4.06)
Florida	3,605	35.5% (1.65)	33.9% (1.63)	1.0% (0.35)	10.8% (1.07)	18.7% (1.34)
Georgia	1,577	37.8% (3.55)	37.1% (3.54)	1.0% (0.74)	8.8% (2.08)	15.2% (2.63)
Maryland	1,214	42.1% (3.81)	37.4% (3.73)	0.9% (0.73)	7.8% (2.07)	11.7% (2.48)
North Carolina	1,921	41.7% (1.72)	37.0% (1.68)	0.6% (0.27)	9.4% (1.02)	11.3% (1.10)
South Carolina	995	38.0% (3.02)	38.2% (3.02)	0.4% (0.37)	11.5% (1.98)	12.0% (2.02)
Virginia	1,695	38.8% (3.04)	37.8% (3.03)	0.4% (0.41)	8.6% (1.75)	14.4% (2.19)
West Virginia	526	37.9% (3.32)	45.7% (3.41)	0.7% (0.56)	9.0% (1.96)	6.8% (1.72)
East South Central	4,459	37.2% (1.65)	42.7% (1.69)	0.3% (0.20)	8.7% (0.96)	11.1% (1.07)
Alabama	1,216	36.3% (3.22)	43.1% (3.32)	0.3% (0.35)	8.0% (1.82)	12.2% (2.20)
Kentucky	1,003	36.5% (3.41)	45.5% (3.53)	0.1% (0.24)	8.2% (1.94)	9.8% (2.10)
Mississippi	740	33.2% (3.06)	43.3% (3.22)	0.7% (0.54)	10.8% (2.02)	12.0% (2.11)
Tennessee	1,500	40.3% (3.12)	40.1% (3.12)	0.4% (0.38)	8.6% (1.79)	10.6% (1.96)
West South Central	7,193	33.9% (1.31)	38.2% (1.35)	0.6% (0.21)	10.5% (0.85)	16.8% (1.04)
Arkansas	749	34.7% (3.08)	40.3% (3.17)	0.7% (0.56)	12.0% (2.10)	12.3% (2.13)
Louisiana	1,134	30.4% (3.38)	43.4% (3.64)	0.6% (0.59)	10.8% (2.29)	14.7% (2.61)
Oklahoma	839	31.7% (3.29)	41.4% (3.48)	0.6% (0.55)	10.9% (2.20)	15.4% (2.55)
Texas	4,472	35.1% (1.75)	35.9% (1.76)	0.5% (0.26)	10.2% (1.11)	18.3% (1.42)

Table A6c (continued)
Health Insurance Coverage of the Nonelderly by Family Income, 1990-92: 200-399 Percent of Poverty[1,9,10]

(Persons in thousands, standard errors in parentheses)

	Number	Employer (own)	Employer (other)[2]	Medicaid[3]	Other Coverage[8]	Uninsured[6]
East North Central	**12,773**	**37.9%**	**45.4%**	**0.4%**	**8.1%**	**8.2%**
		(0.93)	**(0.96)**	**(0.12)**	**(0.53)**	**(0.53)**
Illinois	3,312	37.7%	43.4%	0.4%	8.2%	10.3%
		(1.77)	(1.81)	(0.22)	(1.00)	(1.11)
Indiana	1,845	40.2%	41.6%	0.1%	9.0%	9.2%
		(3.24)	(3.26)	(0.18)	(1.90)	(1.91)
Michigan	2,612	37.7%	47.4%	0.4%	7.4%	7.0%
		(1.77)	(1.82)	(0.24)	(0.96)	(0.93)
Ohio	3,431	37.3%	47.5%	0.5%	6.9%	7.8%
		(1.64)	(1.69)	(0.24)	(0.86)	(0.91)
Wisconsin	1,574	37.3%	46.5%	0.5%	10.5%	5.3%
		(2.95)	(3.04)	(0.41)	(1.86)	(1.36)
West North Central	**5,656**	**36.3%**	**43.5%**	**0.4%**	**12.0%**	**7.8%**
		(1.42)	**(1.46)**	**(0.19)**	**(0.96)**	**(0.79)**
Iowa	1,008	34.9%	45.1%	0.6%	12.9%	6.6%
		(2.85)	(2.98)	(0.47)	(2.00)	(1.49)
Kansas	820	33.0%	44.9%	0.2%	13.7%	8.2%
		(2.91)	(3.08)	(0.29)	(2.12)	(1.70)
Minnesota	1,349	37.5%	41.7%	0.7%	10.3%	9.9%
		(3.29)	(3.35)	(0.56)	(2.06)	(2.03)
Missouri	1,454	40.4%	43.3%	0.1%	9.5%	6.7%
		(3.51)	(3.55)	(0.25)	(2.10)	(1.80)
Nebraska	565	33.9%	45.7%	0.5%	14.0%	5.9%
		(2.78)	(2.92)	(0.40)	(2.04)	(1.38)
North Dakota	217	30.1%	44.1%	0.3%	19.5%	6.1%
		(2.71)	(2.94)	(0.33)	(2.34)	(1.41)
South Dakota	242	32.6%	38.2%	0.3%	17.3%	11.6%
		(2.62)	(2.72)	(0.32)	(2.12)	(1.79)
Mountain	**4,155**	**33.0%**	**44.2%**	**0.5%**	**9.9%**	**12.3%**
		(1.35)	**(1.42)**	**(0.20)**	**(0.86)**	**(0.94)**
Arizona	983	35.2%	40.2%	0.8%	9.9%	13.9%
		(3.42)	(3.51)	(0.62)	(2.14)	(2.47)
Colorado	988	34.9%	43.0%	0.1%	10.3%	11.7%
		(3.40)	(3.54)	(0.17)	(2.17)	(2.30)
Idaho	382	29.4%	45.0%	0.6%	13.1%	11.9%
		(2.59)	(2.83)	(0.43)	(1.92)	(1.84)
Montana	258	30.8%	44.2%	1.1%	13.2%	10.6%
		(2.94)	(3.16)	(0.68)	(2.15)	(1.96)
Nevada	374	39.2%	37.1%	0.2%	6.5%	17.1%
		(3.30)	(3.27)	(0.26)	(1.67)	(2.54)
New Mexico	390	29.9%	42.3%	0.7%	12.3%	14.8%
		(3.24)	(3.49)	(0.61)	(2.32)	(2.51)
Utah	613	29.5%	55.3%	0.5%	6.4%	8.3%
		(2.72)	(2.97)	(0.43)	(1.46)	(1.65)
Wyoming	167	27.9%	52.2%	0.6%	10.3%	9.0%
		(3.21)	(3.57)	(0.54)	(2.17)	(2.05)
Pacific	**10,231**	**34.7%**	**38.2%**	**1.5%**	**10.5%**	**15.1%**
		(1.12)	**(1.15)**	**(0.29)**	**(0.72)**	**(0.84)**
Alaska	140	32.0%	37.9%	0.5%	9.5%	20.1%
		(3.10)	(3.22)	(0.48)	(1.95)	(2.66)
California	7,360	33.3%	37.3%	1.6%	10.7%	17.1%
		(1.34)	(1.37)	(0.36)	(0.88)	(1.07)
Hawaii	308	49.7%	39.6%	0.1%	5.2%	5.4%
		(3.67)	(3.59)	(0.26)	(1.63)	(1.66)
Oregon	836	36.3%	46.3%	0.5%	7.0%	9.8%
		(3.53)	(3.66)	(0.54)	(1.88)	(2.19)
Washington	1,586	37.8%	38.0%	1.8%	12.5%	9.9%
		(3.11)	(3.11)	(0.85)	(2.12)	(1.91)

Source: Three-year merged March CPS: 1991, 1992, and 1993.
Note: See table notes at end of Section A.

Table A6d
Health Insurance Coverage of the Nonelderly by Family Income, 1990-92:
400 Percent of Poverty and Higher[1,9,10]
(Persons in thousands, standard errors in parentheses)

	Number	Employer (own)	Employer (other)[2]	Medicaid[3]	Other Coverage[8]	Uninsured[6]
United States	**70,014**	**48.6%**	**38.7%**	**0.1%**	**8.2%**	**4.3%**
		(0.41)	**(0.40)**	**(0.03)**	**(0.23)**	**(0.17)**
New England	**4,523**	**48.5%**	**40.8%**	**0.2%**	**7.2%**	**3.3%**
		(1.28)	**(1.26)**	**(0.10)**	**(0.66)**	**(0.46)**
Connecticut	1,316	48.0%	43.2%	***	6.5%	2.3%
		(3.29)	(3.26)	***	(1.62)	(0.98)
Maine	302	47.1%	39.4%	0.3%	10.1%	3.1%
		(3.81)	(3.73)	(0.40)	(2.30)	(1.33)
Massachusetts	2,090	49.0%	39.7%	0.3%	6.9%	4.1%
		(1.67)	(1.63)	(0.18)	(0.84)	(0.67)
New Hampshire	393	46.3%	41.6%	***	9.6%	2.5%
		(3.51)	(3.47)	***	(2.07)	(1.11)
Rhode Island	267	52.2%	36.6%	***	6.9%	4.3%
		(3.94)	(3.80)	***	(2.00)	(1.60)
Vermont	156	47.7%	43.9%	0.1%	6.3%	1.9%
		(3.90)	(3.88)	(0.28)	(1.90)	(1.08)
Middle Atlantic	**11,590**	**49.2%**	**40.0%**	**0.2%**	**6.4%**	**4.2%**
		(0.90)	**(0.88)**	**(0.07)**	**(0.44)**	**(0.36)**
New Jersey	3,046	48.8%	40.7%	0.1%	6.3%	4.1%
		(1.54)	(1.52)	(0.09)	(0.75)	(0.61)
New York	5,375	49.1%	38.7%	0.3%	6.6%	5.4%
		(1.33)	(1.29)	(0.14)	(0.66)	(0.60)
Pennsylvania	3,169	49.9%	41.6%	0.0%	6.1%	2.4%
		(1.84)	(1.81)	(0.05)	(0.88)	(0.56)
South Atlantic	**11,812**	**49.3%**	**36.2%**	**0.0%**	**9.0%**	**5.5%**
		(1.03)	**(0.99)**	**(0.04)**	**(0.59)**	**(0.47)**
Delaware	234	47.7%	39.6%	***	7.6%	5.1%
		(3.42)	(3.34)	***	(1.81)	(1.51)
District of Columbia	144	59.5%	22.3%	0.2%	8.3%	9.7%
		(4.28)	(3.62)	(0.35)	(2.41)	(2.58)
Florida	3,051	48.8%	33.7%	0.1%	11.0%	6.5%
		(1.87)	(1.77)	(0.11)	(1.17)	(0.93)
Georgia	1,802	50.1%	35.4%	***	9.7%	4.8%
		(3.43)	(3.28)	***	(2.02)	(1.46)
Maryland	1,773	48.2%	40.5%	***	6.2%	5.0%
		(3.19)	(3.13)	***	(1.54)	(1.39)
North Carolina	1,659	52.6%	33.8%	0.0%	9.0%	4.5%
		(1.87)	(1.77)	(0.07)	(1.07)	(0.77)
South Carolina	821	51.9%	35.8%	0.1%	7.2%	5.0%
		(3.42)	(3.28)	(0.22)	(1.77)	(1.49)
Virginia	2,032	45.9%	38.8%	***	9.1%	6.2%
		(2.84)	(2.78)	***	(1.64)	(1.37)
West Virginia	296	48.3%	42.0%	0.2%	6.2%	3.4%
		(4.57)	(4.51)	(0.38)	(2.21)	(1.64)
East South Central	**3,073**	**48.4%**	**40.1%**	*****	**8.7%**	**2.8%**
		(2.05)	**(2.01)**	*****	**(1.16)**	**(0.68)**
Alabama	824	48.6%	40.0%	***	9.0%	2.4%
		(4.07)	(3.99)	***	(2.33)	(1.25)
Kentucky	862	47.8%	41.0%	***	8.7%	2.4%
		(3.82)	(3.76)	***	(2.16)	(1.17)
Mississippi	401	44.0%	38.7%	***	11.2%	6.1%
		(4.39)	(4.31)	***	(2.79)	(2.12)
Tennessee	987	50.4%	40.1%	***	7.4%	2.2%
		(3.92)	(3.85)	***	(2.05)	(1.14)
West South Central	**6,554**	**45.1%**	**38.0%**	**0.3%**	**10.4%**	**6.2%**
		(1.45)	**(1.41)**	**(0.16)**	**(0.89)**	**(0.70)**
Arkansas	422	42.8%	37.4%	***	13.9%	5.9%
		(4.27)	(4.17)	***	(2.98)	(2.03)
Louisiana	905	41.0%	41.5%	0.2%	11.7%	5.5%
		(4.05)	(4.06)	(0.33)	(2.65)	(1.88)
Oklahoma	736	43.9%	39.3%	***	11.4%	5.5%
		(3.74)	(3.68)	***	(2.39)	(1.72)
Texas	4,491	46.3%	37.1%	0.4%	9.6%	6.5%
		(1.82)	(1.76)	(0.24)	(1.08)	(0.90)

Table A6d   (continued)
Health Insurance Coverage of the Nonelderly by Family Income, 1990-92:
400 Percent of Poverty and Higher[1,9,10]
(Persons in thousands, standard errors in parentheses)

	Number	Employer (own)	Employer (other)[2]	Medicaid[3]	Other Coverage[8]	Uninsured[6]
East North Central	**12,284**	**49.6%**	**41.0%**	**0.1%**	**6.3%**	**3.0%**
		(0.98)	**(0.97)**	**(0.05)**	**(0.48)**	**(0.33)**
Illinois	3,596	51.1%	37.5%	0.1%	7.8%	3.5%
		(1.75)	(1.70)	(0.12)	(0.94)	(0.64)
Indiana	1,333	49.2%	40.2%	***	7.7%	3.0%
		(3.89)	(3.82)	***	(2.07)	(1.32)
Michigan	2,795	49.1%	43.4%	0.1%	5.2%	2.3%
		(1.76)	(1.75)	(0.10)	(0.78)	(0.53)
Ohio	3,055	49.6%	41.1%	***	5.9%	3.4%
		(1.80)	(1.77)	***	(0.85)	(0.65)
Wisconsin	1,505	47.3%	45.8%	0.1%	4.8%	2.1%
		(3.11)	(3.10)	(0.18)	(1.33)	(0.89)
West North Central	**4,613**	**47.2%**	**41.3%**	**0.0%**	**9.3%**	**2.2%**
		(1.63)	**(1.61)**	**(0.04)**	**(0.95)**	**(0.48)**
Iowa	626	46.3%	40.3%	***	11.1%	2.3%
		(3.79)	(3.73)	***	(2.38)	(1.14)
Kansas	678	44.8%	43.4%	***	9.5%	2.3%
		(3.38)	(3.37)	***	(1.99)	(1.03)
Minnesota	1,326	49.0%	41.5%	***	7.7%	1.8%
		(3.42)	(3.38)	***	(1.82)	(0.91)
Missouri	1,353	49.9%	40.4%	***	7.7%	2.1%
		(3.71)	(3.64)	***	(1.98)	(1.05)
Nebraska	392	42.1%	43.8%	***	11.8%	2.3%
		(3.48)	(3.50)	***	(2.28)	(1.05)
North Dakota	123	37.4%	41.6%	***	18.0%	3.1%
		(3.80)	(3.87)	***	(3.02)	(1.36)
South Dakota	115	41.0%	33.6%	0.5%	19.2%	5.8%
		(4.00)	(3.84)	(0.56)	(3.20)	(1.90)
Mountain	**3,480**	**47.3%**	**38.8%**	**0.0%**	**9.3%**	**4.6%**
		(1.56)	**(1.53)**	**(0.07)**	**(0.91)**	**(0.65)**
Arizona	926	49.4%	35.7%	***	11.3%	3.5%
		(3.69)	(3.53)	***	(2.34)	(1.36)
Colorado	1,016	47.8%	38.7%	***	9.0%	4.5%
		(3.52)	(3.43)	***	(2.02)	(1.46)
Idaho	187	47.5%	39.3%	***	9.0%	4.1%
		(4.06)	(3.97)	***	(2.33)	(1.62)
Montana	161	47.4%	39.2%	0.1%	10.1%	3.1%
		(4.02)	(3.93)	(0.29)	(2.43)	(1.39)
Nevada	360	50.4%	34.3%	0.1%	7.6%	7.5%
		(3.45)	(3.27)	(0.26)	(1.83)	(1.82)
New Mexico	326	43.3%	42.7%	***	8.1%	5.9%
		(3.83)	(3.82)	***	(2.11)	(1.82)
Utah	387	42.0%	46.6%	0.2%	6.9%	4.2%
		(3.71)	(3.75)	(0.34)	(1.91)	(1.51)
Wyoming	118	45.0%	39.8%	***	10.6%	4.6%
		(4.24)	(4.18)	***	(2.62)	(1.79)
Pacific	**12,085**	**49.0%**	**35.9%**	**0.3%**	**9.7%**	**5.2%**
		(1.09)	**(1.04)**	**(0.11)**	**(0.64)**	**(0.48)**
Alaska	146	49.5%	36.7%	***	6.5%	7.3%
		(3.25)	(3.13)	***	(1.61)	(1.69)
California	9,154	48.7%	35.9%	0.3%	9.4%	5.7%
		(1.27)	(1.22)	(0.15)	(0.74)	(0.59)
Hawaii	301	53.7%	36.0%	***	7.6%	2.8%
		(3.71)	(3.57)	***	(1.97)	(1.22)
Oregon	875	49.7%	37.0%	0.1%	8.8%	4.3%
		(3.59)	(3.47)	(0.22)	(2.04)	(1.46)
Washington	1,608	49.5%	35.1%	***	12.4%	2.9%
		(3.18)	(3.04)	***	(2.10)	(1.07)

Source: Three-year merged March CPS: 1991, 1992, and 1993.
Note: See table notes at end of Section A.

Table A7a
Health Insurance Coverage of the Nonelderly by Work Status of Adults in Family, 1990-92:
Two Full-Time Workers[1,9,11]

(Persons in thousands, standard errors in parentheses)

	Number	Employer (own)	Employer (other)[2]	Medicaid[3]	Other Coverage[8]	Uninsured[6]
United States	62,795	39.9% (0.22)	43.7% (0.22)	1.4% (0.05)	6.4% (0.11)	8.6% (0.12)
New England	3,059	41.8% (0.79)	47.7% (0.80)	0.6% (0.13)	5.2% (0.35)	4.6% (0.34)
Connecticut	770	43.4% (2.18)	47.9% (2.20)	*** ***	4.4% (0.90)	4.3% (0.90)
Maine	349	37.5% (1.76)	45.9% (1.81)	1.2% (0.39)	8.1% (0.99)	7.2% (0.94)
Massachusetts	1,241	43.0% (1.10)	46.8% (1.11)	0.9% (0.21)	4.7% (0.47)	4.6% (0.46)
New Hampshire	316	39.6% (1.96)	51.5% (2.01)	*** ***	5.5% (0.91)	3.4% (0.73)
Rhode Island	217	43.3% (2.22)	48.0% (2.24)	0.9% (0.42)	3.9% (0.86)	4.0% (0.87)
Vermont	167	36.1% (1.85)	49.9% (1.93)	1.2% (0.43)	8.5% (1.08)	4.2% (0.77)
Middle Atlantic	8,426	42.8% (0.54)	45.2% (0.54)	1.3% (0.12)	4.7% (0.23)	6.0% (0.26)
New Jersey	1,918	45.4% (0.99)	43.0% (0.98)	1.0% (0.20)	5.6% (0.46)	5.0% (0.43)
New York	3,860	40.5% (0.79)	45.2% (0.80)	1.5% (0.19)	4.9% (0.35)	8.0% (0.44)
Pennsylvania	2,649	44.4% (1.02)	46.8% (1.03)	1.2% (0.23)	3.8% (0.39)	3.8% (0.39)
South Atlantic	11,722	41.2% (0.52)	40.5% (0.52)	1.1% (0.11)	7.1% (0.27)	10.1% (0.32)
Delaware	180	39.1% (1.94)	47.9% (1.99)	0.1% (0.14)	7.1% (1.02)	5.8% (0.93)
District of Columbia	76	43.3% (3.04)	37.5% (2.97)	1.8% (0.81)	4.9% (1.32)	12.5% (2.03)
Florida	3,216	38.5% (0.91)	38.5% (0.91)	1.1% (0.20)	7.8% (0.50)	14.0% (0.65)
Georgia	1,719	41.3% (1.77)	40.0% (1.76)	1.1% (0.37)	8.4% (0.99)	9.2% (1.04)
Maryland	1,285	41.1% (1.89)	45.9% (1.91)	1.0% (0.38)	4.6% (0.80)	7.4% (1.01)
North Carolina	1,988	44.8% (0.87)	38.4% (0.85)	1.8% (0.23)	6.6% (0.43)	8.3% (0.48)
South Carolina	1,052	43.9% (1.54)	39.9% (1.51)	0.8% (0.27)	5.6% (0.71)	9.9% (0.92)
Virginia	1,835	40.5% (1.51)	42.2% (1.52)	0.4% (0.19)	7.8% (0.82)	9.1% (0.88)
West Virginia	372	40.3% (2.04)	43.6% (2.07)	2.1% (0.60)	6.7% (1.04)	7.4% (1.09)
East South Central	4,115	38.6% (0.88)	44.3% (0.90)	1.3% (0.21)	6.5% (0.45)	9.2% (0.52)
Alabama	1,093	39.4% (1.77)	45.1% (1.80)	0.4% (0.24)	7.2% (0.93)	7.9% (0.98)
Kentucky	957	39.2% (1.81)	44.1% (1.84)	2.0% (0.52)	6.9% (0.94)	7.9% (1.00)
Mississippi	741	31.9% (1.55)	43.4% (1.65)	1.9% (0.45)	8.8% (0.94)	14.1% (1.16)
Tennessee	1,325	41.4% (1.71)	44.4% (1.72)	1.3% (0.40)	4.3% (0.71)	8.5% (0.97)
West South Central	7,281	36.1% (0.68)	40.9% (0.69)	1.3% (0.16)	7.2% (0.36)	14.6% (0.50)
Arkansas	732	33.5% (1.58)	43.8% (1.66)	1.5% (0.41)	8.7% (0.94)	12.6% (1.11)
Louisiana	932	33.9% (1.96)	47.2% (2.07)	0.4% (0.26)	7.8% (1.11)	10.6% (1.28)
Oklahoma	889	33.9% (1.66)	40.9% (1.72)	0.5% (0.26)	7.2% (0.91)	17.4% (1.33)
Texas	4,727	37.3% (0.88)	39.2% (0.89)	1.5% (0.22)	6.8% (0.46)	15.2% (0.65)

Health Insurance Coverage of the Nonelderly by Work Status of Adults in Family, 1990-92:
Two Full-Time Workers[1,9,11]

(Persons in thousands, standard errors in parentheses)

	Number	Employer (own)	Employer (other)[2]	Medicaid[3]	Other Coverage[8]	Uninsured[6]
East North Central	**10,427**	**41.3%**	**46.9%**	**1.1%**	**5.0%**	**5.8%**
		(0.54)	**(0.54)**	**(0.11)**	**(0.24)**	**(0.25)**
Illinois	2,852	43.4%	42.8%	0.9%	6.1%	6.8%
		(1.00)	(1.00)	(0.19)	(0.48)	(0.51)
Indiana	1,423	40.6%	48.4%	0.3%	4.2%	6.5%
		(1.89)	(1.93)	(0.20)	(0.77)	(0.95)
Michigan	1,947	41.9%	47.7%	1.4%	4.2%	4.8%
		(1.07)	(1.08)	(0.25)	(0.43)	(0.46)
Ohio	2,699	41.3%	47.9%	1.3%	4.3%	5.1%
		(0.96)	(0.98)	(0.22)	(0.40)	(0.43)
Wisconsin	1,506	37.1%	50.7%	1.2%	5.6%	5.5%
		(1.54)	(1.59)	(0.34)	(0.73)	(0.73)
West North Central	**5,345**	**36.7%**	**46.0%**	**0.9%**	**9.5%**	**6.9%**
		(0.75)	**(0.77)**	**(0.14)**	**(0.46)**	**(0.39)**
Iowa	842	35.3%	48.1%	1.4%	9.5%	5.7%
		(1.60)	(1.67)	(0.40)	(0.98)	(0.77)
Kansas	760	33.7%	46.6%	1.0%	10.4%	8.4%
		(1.55)	(1.64)	(0.32)	(1.00)	(0.91)
Minnesota	1,226	38.4%	44.1%	0.2%	10.9%	6.5%
		(1.77)	(1.81)	(0.14)	(1.13)	(0.90)
Missouri	1,587	40.5%	44.9%	0.6%	6.4%	7.6%
		(1.72)	(1.74)	(0.28)	(0.86)	(0.93)
Nebraska	539	32.8%	50.2%	1.5%	10.3%	5.1%
		(1.44)	(1.54)	(0.38)	(0.93)	(0.68)
North Dakota	173	28.3%	48.7%	1.9%	16.6%	4.5%
		(1.53)	(1.69)	(0.46)	(1.26)	(0.70)
South Dakota	218	30.4%	42.5%	1.7%	14.7%	10.8%
		(1.39)	(1.49)	(0.39)	(1.07)	(0.94)
Mountain	**3,459**	**36.5%**	**45.3%**	**1.5%**	**7.1%**	**9.5%**
		(0.77)	**(0.80)**	**(0.20)**	**(0.41)**	**(0.47)**
Arizona	838	38.7%	40.6%	2.6%	8.1%	10.1%
		(1.93)	(1.95)	(0.63)	(1.08)	(1.19)
Colorado	885	37.7%	47.8%	0.8%	6.4%	7.4%
		(1.87)	(1.93)	(0.33)	(0.94)	(1.01)
Idaho	288	31.4%	43.3%	1.5%	10.3%	13.5%
		(1.55)	(1.66)	(0.41)	(1.02)	(1.14)
Montana	215	34.1%	44.2%	3.5%	11.0%	7.2%
		(1.69)	(1.77)	(0.66)	(1.12)	(0.92)
Nevada	318	42.3%	40.8%	0.5%	4.8%	11.5%
		(1.85)	(1.84)	(0.27)	(0.81)	(1.20)
New Mexico	332	30.1%	45.2%	1.9%	7.9%	14.9%
		(1.80)	(1.95)	(0.54)	(1.06)	(1.40)
Utah	446	36.5%	53.5%	0.6%	3.1%	6.3%
		(1.72)	(1.78)	(0.28)	(0.62)	(0.87)
Wyoming	137	32.3%	49.1%	1.6%	10.2%	6.8%
		(1.89)	(2.02)	(0.50)	(1.22)	(1.02)
Pacific	**8,960**	**40.1%**	**41.5%**	**3.2%**	**6.2%**	**9.0%**
		(0.63)	**(0.64)**	**(0.23)**	**(0.31)**	**(0.37)**
Alaska	133	37.8%	40.3%	1.8%	7.0%	13.1%
		(1.69)	(1.71)	(0.46)	(0.89)	(1.18)
California	6,638	38.9%	41.0%	3.7%	6.6%	9.7%
		(0.75)	(0.75)	(0.29)	(0.38)	(0.45)
Hawaii	325	43.5%	46.1%	1.9%	4.1%	4.5%
		(1.81)	(1.82)	(0.49)	(0.72)	(0.76)
Oregon	739	42.4%	42.2%	2.1%	4.8%	8.5%
		(1.98)	(1.97)	(0.57)	(0.86)	(1.11)
Washington	1,125	44.9%	43.1%	1.1%	4.7%	6.3%
		(1.93)	(1.93)	(0.40)	(0.83)	(0.94)

Source: **Three-year merged March CPS: 1991, 1992, and 1993.**
Note: **See table notes at end of Section A.**

Table A7b

Health Insurance Coverage of the Nonelderly by Work Status of Adults in Family, 1990-92: One Full-Time Worker [1,9,11]

(Persons in thousands, standard errors in parentheses)

	Number	Employer (own)	Employer (other)[2]	Medicaid[3]	Other Coverage[8]	Uninsured[6]
United States	**115,801**	**34.9%**	**33.3%**	**5.9%**	**9.1%**	**16.7%**
		(0.16)	**(0.15)**	**(0.08)**	**(0.09)**	**(0.12)**
New England	**6,246**	**40.2%**	**36.6%**	**3.3%**	**8.6%**	**11.3%**
		(0.55)	**(0.54)**	**(0.20)**	**(0.31)**	**(0.35)**
Connecticut	1,636	41.0%	39.9%	2.4%	8.0%	8.6%
		(1.49)	(1.48)	(0.46)	(0.82)	(0.85)
Maine	550	34.8%	33.4%	6.4%	11.1%	14.3%
		(1.38)	(1.36)	(0.71)	(0.91)	(1.01)
Massachusetts	2,794	41.3%	36.0%	3.0%	8.3%	11.3%
		(0.73)	(0.71)	(0.25)	(0.41)	(0.47)
New Hampshire	557	37.5%	35.7%	2.1%	9.8%	15.0%
		(1.46)	(1.45)	(0.43)	(0.90)	(1.08)
Rhode Island	443	41.8%	32.9%	4.4%	8.0%	12.9%
		(1.55)	(1.47)	(0.64)	(0.85)	(1.05)
Vermont	266	37.3%	37.9%	5.7%	7.3%	11.7%
		(1.48)	(1.48)	(0.71)	(0.80)	(0.98)
Middle Atlantic	**17,723**	**37.7%**	**37.3%**	**4.2%**	**7.7%**	**13.0%**
		(0.36)	**(0.36)**	**(0.15)**	**(0.20)**	**(0.25)**
New Jersey	3,807	39.3%	37.3%	2.9%	7.2%	13.3%
		(0.69)	(0.68)	(0.24)	(0.36)	(0.48)
New York	8,138	37.2%	35.2%	4.9%	8.3%	14.5%
		(0.53)	(0.53)	(0.24)	(0.30)	(0.39)
Pennsylvania	5,778	37.3%	40.4%	4.2%	7.4%	10.6%
		(0.67)	(0.68)	(0.28)	(0.36)	(0.43)
South Atlantic	**19,037**	**35.4%**	**28.8%**	**6.1%**	**9.2%**	**20.5%**
		(0.40)	**(0.38)**	**(0.20)**	**(0.24)**	**(0.34)**
Delaware	355	38.4%	35.1%	3.7%	7.3%	15.6%
		(1.38)	(1.35)	(0.53)	(0.74)	(1.03)
District of Columbia	273	41.4%	15.9%	9.3%	7.7%	25.7%
		(1.59)	(1.18)	(0.94)	(0.86)	(1.41)
Florida	5,555	33.0%	24.6%	6.5%	10.4%	25.5%
		(0.67)	(0.61)	(0.35)	(0.43)	(0.62)
Georgia	2,892	34.1%	29.4%	7.0%	8.5%	21.1%
		(1.31)	(1.26)	(0.70)	(0.77)	(1.13)
Maryland	2,186	42.0%	32.1%	5.1%	7.6%	13.3%
		(1.45)	(1.37)	(0.65)	(0.78)	(1.00)
North Carolina	2,733	37.3%	28.3%	6.5%	9.5%	18.4%
		(0.72)	(0.67)	(0.37)	(0.44)	(0.58)
South Carolina	1,480	32.7%	30.6%	5.9%	9.9%	20.9%
		(1.22)	(1.20)	(0.61)	(0.78)	(1.06)
Virginia	2,805	36.1%	31.5%	4.2%	8.9%	19.3%
		(1.19)	(1.15)	(0.50)	(0.71)	(0.98)
West Virginia	758	30.5%	38.6%	8.9%	7.5%	14.5%
		(1.34)	(1.42)	(0.83)	(0.77)	(1.03)
East South Central	**6,495**	**32.2%**	**33.1%**	**6.3%**	**9.0%**	**19.4%**
		(0.67)	**(0.68)**	**(0.35)**	**(0.41)**	**(0.57)**
Alabama	1,794	31.7%	32.9%	4.7%	7.9%	22.8%
		(1.31)	(1.33)	(0.59)	(0.76)	(1.18)
Kentucky	1,475	34.8%	36.6%	5.3%	9.0%	14.4%
		(1.42)	(1.44)	(0.67)	(0.86)	(1.05)
Mississippi	1,129	26.4%	29.4%	11.2%	9.5%	23.4%
		(1.19)	(1.23)	(0.85)	(0.79)	(1.14)
Tennessee	2,097	33.9%	32.7%	5.9%	9.6%	17.9%
		(1.30)	(1.29)	(0.65)	(0.81)	(1.06)
West South Central	**12,176**	**29.3%**	**28.5%**	**7.5%**	**9.8%**	**25.0%**
		(0.50)	**(0.49)**	**(0.29)**	**(0.32)**	**(0.47)**
Arkansas	939	28.6%	27.9%	8.0%	13.0%	22.5%
		(1.34)	(1.33)	(0.80)	(0.99)	(1.23)
Louisiana	1,871	26.5%	30.5%	7.4%	10.2%	25.2%
		(1.29)	(1.35)	(0.77)	(0.89)	(1.27)
Oklahoma	1,357	27.0%	32.5%	7.2%	12.2%	21.3%
		(1.26)	(1.33)	(0.73)	(0.93)	(1.16)
Texas	8,010	30.4%	27.5%	7.4%	8.9%	25.8%
		(0.64)	(0.62)	(0.37)	(0.40)	(0.61)

Table A7b (continued)
Health Insurance Coverage of the Nonelderly by Work Status of Adults in Family, 1990-92: One Full-Time Worker [1,9,11]
(Persons in thousands, standard errors in parentheses)

	Number	Employer (own)	Employer (other)[2]	Medicaid[3]	Other Coverage[8]	Uninsured[6]
East North Central	**20,346**	**37.3%**	**38.2%**	**5.4%**	**7.9%**	**11.2%**
		(0.38)	**(0.38)**	**(0.18)**	**(0.21)**	**(0.25)**
Illinois	5,602	37.8%	35.8%	4.9%	8.8%	12.6%
		(0.70)	(0.69)	(0.31)	(0.41)	(0.48)
Indiana	2,668	37.7%	36.2%	4.0%	9.1%	13.1%
		(1.36)	(1.35)	(0.55)	(0.81)	(0.95)
Michigan	4,553	37.3%	40.3%	6.1%	6.6%	9.7%
		(0.68)	(0.69)	(0.34)	(0.35)	(0.42)
Ohio	5,279	36.6%	39.6%	5.9%	7.3%	10.6%
		(0.67)	(0.68)	(0.33)	(0.36)	(0.43)
Wisconsin	2,243	37.5%	39.1%	5.5%	8.5%	9.4%
		(1.26)	(1.27)	(0.60)	(0.73)	(0.76)
West North Central	**8,060**	**33.6%**	**33.5%**	**6.4%**	**13.0%**	**13.5%**
		(0.60)	**(0.60)**	**(0.31)**	**(0.43)**	**(0.43)**
Iowa	1,290	32.0%	36.4%	5.2%	14.9%	11.4%
		(1.26)	(1.30)	(0.60)	(0.96)	(0.86)
Kansas	1,182	32.4%	37.8%	5.4%	12.5%	11.8%
		(1.23)	(1.28)	(0.59)	(0.87)	(0.85)
Minnesota	2,037	36.4%	32.3%	5.1%	12.1%	14.1%
		(1.36)	(1.32)	(0.62)	(0.92)	(0.98)
Missouri	2,267	34.7%	31.3%	8.8%	9.6%	15.5%
		(1.40)	(1.36)	(0.83)	(0.86)	(1.06)
Nebraska	712	31.4%	34.2%	6.6%	16.4%	11.5%
		(1.24)	(1.27)	(0.66)	(0.99)	(0.85)
North Dakota	281	26.3%	31.6%	5.1%	26.3%	10.7%
		(1.17)	(1.24)	(0.58)	(1.17)	(0.82)
South Dakota	291	28.5%	27.8%	5.7%	19.9%	18.2%
		(1.18)	(1.17)	(0.60)	(1.04)	(1.01)
Mountain	**6,661**	**31.5%**	**35.6%**	**5.2%**	**9.8%**	**17.9%**
		(0.54)	**(0.55)**	**(0.26)**	**(0.34)**	**(0.44)**
Arizona	1,666	33.1%	32.6%	6.7%	8.8%	18.8%
		(1.32)	(1.32)	(0.70)	(0.80)	(1.10)
Colorado	1,565	36.4%	34.8%	3.6%	10.5%	14.8%
		(1.40)	(1.38)	(0.54)	(0.89)	(1.03)
Idaho	543	27.6%	36.2%	6.7%	11.8%	17.7%
		(1.09)	(1.17)	(0.61)	(0.79)	(0.93)
Montana	383	26.5%	34.1%	5.7%	15.3%	18.4%
		(1.18)	(1.27)	(0.62)	(0.96)	(1.03)
Nevada	616	37.1%	29.5%	3.5%	7.5%	22.4%
		(1.30)	(1.23)	(0.49)	(0.71)	(1.12)
New Mexico	727	27.5%	31.9%	6.1%	8.9%	25.6%
		(1.18)	(1.23)	(0.63)	(0.76)	(1.15)
Utah	933	24.9%	48.9%	4.0%	9.1%	13.1%
		(1.07)	(1.24)	(0.48)	(0.71)	(0.84)
Wyoming	228	27.8%	39.2%	7.4%	11.0%	14.6%
		(1.40)	(1.53)	(0.82)	(0.98)	(1.11)
Pacific	**19,058**	**33.9%**	**30.1%**	**7.9%**	**9.4%**	**18.7%**
		(0.42)	**(0.41)**	**(0.24)**	**(0.26)**	**(0.35)**
Alaska	243	32.0%	30.7%	5.8%	9.2%	22.2%
		(1.20)	(1.19)	(0.60)	(0.75)	(1.07)
California	14,575	32.7%	29.1%	8.7%	9.0%	20.6%
		(0.48)	(0.47)	(0.29)	(0.30)	(0.42)
Hawaii	407	50.1%	30.8%	3.1%	7.6%	8.5%
		(1.63)	(1.51)	(0.56)	(0.86)	(0.91)
Oregon	1,384	35.8%	38.5%	4.2%	7.4%	14.2%
		(1.40)	(1.42)	(0.59)	(0.76)	(1.02)
Washington	2,448	37.3%	31.3%	6.2%	13.6%	11.7%
		(1.28)	(1.22)	(0.64)	(0.90)	(0.85)

Source: Three-year merged March CPS: 1991, 1992, and 1993.
Note: See table notes at end of Section A.

Table A7c

Health Insurance Coverage of the Nonelderly by Work Status of Adults in Family, 1990-92: Some Part-Time Work[1,9,11]

(Persons in thousands, standard errors in parentheses)

	Number	Employer (own)	Employer (other)[2]	Medicaid[3]	Other Coverage[8]	Uninsured[6]
United States	**15,593**	**15.2%**	**13.0%**	**21.0%**	**19.7%**	**31.1%**
		(0.32)	**(0.30)**	**(0.36)**	**(0.35)**	**(0.41)**
New England	**848**	**19.0%**	**16.4%**	**19.9%**	**22.2%**	**22.5%**
		(1.19)	**(1.12)**	**(1.21)**	**(1.26)**	**(1.26)**
Connecticut	178	19.7%	18.4%	19.7%	22.7%	19.5%
		(3.63)	(3.54)	(3.64)	(3.83)	(3.62)
Maine	90	15.8%	18.7%	22.2%	20.4%	22.9%
		(2.61)	(2.79)	(2.98)	(2.89)	(3.01)
Massachusetts	415	18.5%	16.9%	21.5%	21.0%	22.1%
		(1.49)	(1.44)	(1.57)	(1.56)	(1.59)
New Hampshire	68	14.4%	10.7%	12.8%	27.4%	34.7%
		(3.03)	(2.67)	(2.89)	(3.85)	(4.11)
Rhode Island	57	30.9%	11.0%	15.4%	26.5%	16.3%
		(4.03)	(2.73)	(3.15)	(3.85)	(3.22)
Vermont	39	19.6%	13.6%	17.8%	21.5%	27.4%
		(3.16)	(2.73)	(3.04)	(3.27)	(3.54)
Middle Atlantic	**2,077**	**19.6%**	**17.0%**	**17.5%**	**19.3%**	**26.6%**
		(0.86)	**(0.82)**	**(0.83)**	**(0.86)**	**(0.96)**
New Jersey	371	17.1%	13.3%	16.6%	20.3%	32.8%
		(1.70)	(1.53)	(1.68)	(1.82)	(2.12)
New York	1,040	20.4%	19.2%	15.2%	18.1%	27.1%
		(1.24)	(1.22)	(1.11)	(1.19)	(1.37)
Pennsylvania	667	19.7%	15.7%	21.6%	20.8%	22.2%
		(1.63)	(1.49)	(1.69)	(1.66)	(1.70)
South Atlantic	**2,620**	**13.6%**	**10.6%**	**20.5%**	**18.9%**	**36.5%**
		(0.77)	**(0.69)**	**(0.90)**	**(0.88)**	**(1.08)**
Delaware	42	17.5%	11.8%	18.0%	12.8%	39.9%
		(3.12)	(2.66)	(3.16)	(2.74)	(4.03)
District of Columbia	36	16.6%	8.9%	19.4%	22.6%	32.5%
		(3.32)	(2.54)	(3.53)	(3.74)	(4.18)
Florida	914	9.7%	8.1%	20.4%	20.2%	41.5%
		(1.04)	(0.96)	(1.41)	(1.41)	(1.72)
Georgia	344	12.6%	9.8%	19.6%	15.6%	42.5%
		(2.65)	(2.38)	(3.18)	(2.91)	(3.96)
Maryland	256	24.9%	16.5%	16.5%	16.6%	25.6%
		(3.71)	(3.18)	(3.19)	(3.20)	(3.75)
North Carolina	353	14.8%	12.0%	20.8%	23.7%	28.6%
		(1.48)	(1.35)	(1.69)	(1.77)	(1.88)
South Carolina	213	15.3%	13.6%	21.4%	19.8%	30.0%
		(2.48)	(2.36)	(2.82)	(2.74)	(3.15)
Virginia	345	14.5%	10.2%	17.4%	16.5%	41.5%
		(2.49)	(2.14)	(2.68)	(2.62)	(3.49)
West Virginia	117	9.6%	11.0%	39.6%	15.3%	24.5%
		(2.19)	(2.32)	(3.63)	(2.68)	(3.20)
East South Central	**926**	**12.8%**	**12.1%**	**25.6%**	**16.5%**	**33.0%**
		(1.28)	**(1.25)**	**(1.67)**	**(1.42)**	**(1.80)**
Alabama	229	15.5%	18.1%	18.4%	15.8%	32.3%
		(2.86)	(3.04)	(3.06)	(2.88)	(3.70)
Kentucky	257	13.0%	13.3%	20.6%	21.1%	32.1%
		(2.40)	(2.43)	(2.89)	(2.92)	(3.34)
Mississippi	144	11.0%	8.8%	24.0%	15.8%	40.5%
		(2.36)	(2.14)	(3.22)	(2.76)	(3.71)
Tennessee	296	11.3%	8.0%	36.4%	13.4%	30.8%
		(2.32)	(1.99)	(3.53)	(2.50)	(3.38)
West South Central	**1,637**	**9.4%**	**9.3%**	**23.4%**	**19.3%**	**38.6%**
		(0.87)	**(0.86)**	**(1.26)**	**(1.17)**	**(1.45)**
Arkansas	158	9.8%	7.1%	20.2%	19.3%	43.5%
		(2.15)	(1.86)	(2.89)	(2.84)	(3.57)
Louisiana	288	8.5%	12.2%	26.0%	22.1%	31.2%
		(2.08)	(2.45)	(3.27)	(3.10)	(3.46)
Oklahoma	206	6.3%	8.1%	24.1%	21.2%	40.4%
		(1.76)	(1.99)	(3.11)	(2.97)	(3.57)
Texas	985	10.2%	9.1%	23.1%	18.0%	39.6%
		(1.21)	(1.15)	(1.68)	(1.53)	(1.95)

Table A7c (continued)

Health Insurance Coverage of the Nonelderly by Work Status of Adults in Family, 1990-92:
Some Part-Time Work[1,9,11]

(Persons in thousands, standard errors in parentheses)

	Number	Employer (own)	Employer (other)[2]	Medicaid[3]	Other Coverage[8]	Uninsured[6]
East North Central	**2,577**	**15.4%**	**15.3%**	**21.7%**	**20.1%**	**27.4%**
		(0.79)	**(0.79)**	**(0.90)**	**(0.88)**	**(0.98)**
Illinois	657	14.3%	12.9%	21.7%	19.7%	31.4%
		(1.47)	(1.40)	(1.73)	(1.67)	(1.95)
Indiana	325	12.4%	13.4%	19.6%	23.2%	31.5%
		(2.65)	(2.74)	(3.20)	(3.40)	(3.74)
Michigan	624	13.8%	17.4%	21.5%	19.0%	28.2%
		(1.32)	(1.45)	(1.57)	(1.50)	(1.72)
Ohio	659	18.7%	16.4%	22.5%	18.3%	24.0%
		(1.54)	(1.47)	(1.65)	(1.53)	(1.69)
Wisconsin	312	17.4%	15.9%	22.6%	24.0%	20.1%
		(2.65)	(2.56)	(2.93)	(2.99)	(2.80)
West North Central	**1,103**	**15.2%**	**12.5%**	**16.8%**	**29.3%**	**26.1%**
		(1.23)	**(1.13)**	**(1.28)**	**(1.56)**	**(1.50)**
Iowa	183	15.8%	11.9%	19.3%	31.5%	21.5%
		(2.62)	(2.33)	(2.84)	(3.34)	(2.95)
Kansas	137	14.5%	14.2%	16.9%	26.1%	28.4%
		(2.72)	(2.70)	(2.89)	(3.40)	(3.48)
Minnesota	308	17.9%	16.3%	15.2%	30.2%	20.3%
		(2.79)	(2.69)	(2.61)	(3.34)	(2.93)
Missouri	335	13.9%	8.6%	17.0%	27.2%	33.2%
		(2.64)	(2.14)	(2.87)	(3.40)	(3.60)
Nebraska	65	10.1%	11.9%	19.6%	35.7%	22.8%
		(2.65)	(2.85)	(3.50)	(4.23)	(3.70)
North Dakota	38	13.7%	16.9%	9.8%	35.1%	24.6%
		(2.50)	(2.73)	(2.16)	(3.47)	(3.14)
South Dakota	37	15.1%	9.1%	18.0%	25.5%	32.4%
		(2.62)	(2.11)	(2.81)	(3.19)	(3.43)
Mountain	**903**	**14.9%**	**13.2%**	**19.7%**	**22.4%**	**29.9%**
		(1.12)	**(1.06)**	**(1.25)**	**(1.31)**	**(1.44)**
Arizona	254	14.5%	12.3%	20.6%	21.6%	31.0%
		(2.54)	(2.36)	(2.91)	(2.96)	(3.33)
Colorado	205	17.0%	10.5%	17.2%	30.2%	25.1%
		(3.01)	(2.45)	(3.02)	(3.68)	(3.47)
Idaho	53	12.0%	15.5%	10.3%	24.3%	37.8%
		(2.54)	(2.83)	(2.38)	(3.35)	(3.79)
Montana	57	14.1%	12.1%	19.3%	19.6%	34.9%
		(2.40)	(2.25)	(2.72)	(2.74)	(3.29)
Nevada	74	20.9%	17.1%	13.9%	16.0%	32.1%
		(3.17)	(2.93)	(2.69)	(2.85)	(3.63)
New Mexico	121	9.6%	9.5%	28.6%	18.1%	34.2%
		(1.92)	(1.90)	(2.94)	(2.50)	(3.09)
Utah	111	15.8%	20.5%	20.5%	18.7%	24.4%
		(2.62)	(2.90)	(2.90)	(2.80)	(3.08)
Wyoming	28	12.6%	15.0%	21.2%	23.4%	27.8%
		(2.97)	(3.21)	(3.66)	(3.80)	(4.02)
Pacific	**2,903**	**16.4%**	**11.8%**	**22.6%**	**16.5%**	**32.7%**
		(0.84)	**(0.73)**	**(0.95)**	**(0.84)**	**(1.06)**
Alaska	34	12.8%	12.8%	21.3%	9.8%	43.3%
		(2.31)	(2.31)	(2.83)	(2.06)	(3.43)
California	2,202	15.0%	10.9%	23.4%	16.1%	34.7%
		(0.95)	(0.83)	(1.12)	(0.97)	(1.26)
Hawaii	70	33.5%	19.4%	14.8%	17.4%	14.9%
		(3.72)	(3.12)	(2.80)	(2.99)	(2.81)
Oregon	256	15.8%	18.0%	23.0%	13.6%	29.5%
		(2.48)	(2.61)	(2.86)	(2.33)	(3.10)
Washington	341	22.3%	11.5%	19.2%	21.7%	25.3%
		(2.94)	(2.25)	(2.78)	(2.91)	(3.07)

Source: Three-year merged March CPS: 1991, 1992, and 1993.
Note: See table notes at end of Section A.

Table A7d
Health Insurance Coverage of the Nonelderly by Work Status of Adults in Family, 1990-92:
No Work[1,9,11]
(Persons in thousands, standard errors in parentheses)

	Number	Employer (own)	Employer (other)[2]	Medicaid[3]	Other Coverage[8]	Uninsured[6]
United States	24,396	6.5%	6.8%	52.4%	14.0%	20.3%
		(0.18)	(0.18)	(0.36)	(0.25)	(0.29)
New England	1,132	7.5%	7.9%	54.5%	13.9%	16.3%
		(0.69)	(0.71)	(1.30)	(0.91)	(0.97)
Connecticut	235	11.7%	13.0%	49.6%	13.7%	12.0%
		(2.55)	(2.68)	(3.98)	(2.74)	(2.59)
Maine	114	7.5%	9.8%	58.2%	13.4%	11.0%
		(1.68)	(1.89)	(3.14)	(2.17)	(1.99)
Massachusetts	575	6.2%	5.6%	57.7%	12.8%	17.8%
		(0.78)	(0.75)	(1.61)	(1.09)	(1.25)
New Hampshire	74	5.7%	9.1%	37.6%	19.7%	27.9%
		(1.92)	(2.38)	(4.01)	(3.30)	(3.72)
Rhode Island	89	5.6%	6.7%	56.6%	15.7%	15.4%
		(1.61)	(1.75)	(3.47)	(2.54)	(2.52)
Vermont	46	10.2%	5.8%	53.1%	16.9%	14.0%
		(2.23)	(1.73)	(3.68)	(2.77)	(2.57)
Middle Atlantic	4,275	6.2%	6.5%	55.5%	12.2%	19.6%
		(0.37)	(0.37)	(0.75)	(0.50)	(0.60)
New Jersey	657	5.7%	6.0%	54.7%	13.3%	20.4%
		(0.79)	(0.81)	(1.69)	(1.15)	(1.37)
New York	2,441	4.6%	5.6%	58.7%	11.2%	19.9%
		(0.42)	(0.46)	(0.99)	(0.64)	(0.81)
Pennsylvania	1,177	9.9%	8.6%	49.4%	13.7%	18.4%
		(0.92)	(0.86)	(1.54)	(1.06)	(1.20)
South Atlantic	4,183	7.1%	7.2%	48.0%	16.2%	21.5%
		(0.46)	(0.46)	(0.89)	(0.65)	(0.73)
Delaware	46	14.1%	9.8%	40.4%	18.6%	17.1%
		(2.73)	(2.34)	(3.86)	(3.06)	(2.96)
District of Columbia	92	3.6%	4.1%	64.6%	7.7%	20.0%
		(1.04)	(1.10)	(2.66)	(1.48)	(2.22)
Florida	1,310	8.1%	6.5%	43.6%	19.2%	22.6%
		(0.80)	(0.72)	(1.45)	(1.15)	(1.22)
Georgia	657	5.0%	6.0%	54.4%	14.1%	20.6%
		(1.26)	(1.38)	(2.89)	(2.02)	(2.34)
Maryland	413	10.3%	9.9%	49.3%	12.2%	18.4%
		(2.06)	(2.02)	(3.38)	(2.21)	(2.62)
North Carolina	566	6.9%	9.5%	50.0%	16.2%	17.5%
		(0.83)	(0.96)	(1.64)	(1.21)	(1.24)
South Carolina	378	4.7%	4.9%	51.3%	14.2%	24.9%
		(1.10)	(1.11)	(2.58)	(1.80)	(2.23)
Virginia	444	4.9%	6.0%	44.5%	19.0%	25.7%
		(1.34)	(1.48)	(3.10)	(2.44)	(2.73)
West Virginia	276	9.6%	10.6%	44.4%	13.6%	21.8%
		(1.43)	(1.49)	(2.40)	(1.66)	(2.00)
East South Central	1,851	5.3%	5.9%	54.6%	14.0%	20.2%
		(0.61)	(0.63)	(1.35)	(0.94)	(1.09)
Alabama	484	5.8%	7.9%	43.5%	14.7%	28.1%
		(1.27)	(1.47)	(2.69)	(1.92)	(2.44)
Kentucky	443	5.7%	7.3%	59.4%	11.2%	16.3%
		(1.27)	(1.42)	(2.68)	(1.72)	(2.01)
Mississippi	338	1.8%	3.7%	58.4%	15.1%	20.9%
		(0.66)	(0.93)	(2.43)	(1.77)	(2.00)
Tennessee	586	6.6%	4.2%	58.0%	15.0%	16.2%
		(1.29)	(1.05)	(2.57)	(1.86)	(1.92)
West South Central	2,536	4.3%	4.9%	50.7%	14.9%	25.1%
		(0.48)	(0.52)	(1.19)	(0.85)	(1.04)
Arkansas	239	5.9%	6.1%	52.3%	19.3%	16.5%
		(1.38)	(1.40)	(2.93)	(2.31)	(2.17)
Louisiana	588	2.8%	4.4%	58.2%	10.8%	23.8%
		(0.86)	(1.07)	(2.57)	(1.62)	(2.22)
Oklahoma	268	4.5%	6.2%	44.3%	22.9%	22.1%
		(1.33)	(1.54)	(3.18)	(2.69)	(2.65)
Texas	1,441	4.6%	4.7%	48.6%	14.4%	27.7%
		(0.69)	(0.70)	(1.65)	(1.16)	(1.47)

Table A7d (continued)
Health Insurance Coverage of the Nonelderly by Work Status of Adults in Family, 1990-92: No Work[1,9,11]

(Persons in thousands, standard errors in parentheses)

	Number	Employer (own)	Employer (other)[2]	Medicaid[3]	Other Coverage[8]	Uninsured[6]
East North Central	**4,034**	**7.4%**	**8.0%**	**54.1%**	**13.8%**	**16.7%**
		(0.46)	**(0.48)**	**(0.87)**	**(0.60)**	**(0.65)**
Illinois	1,307	5.0%	5.5%	60.9%	11.8%	16.8%
		(0.65)	(0.68)	(1.45)	(0.96)	(1.11)
Indiana	442	8.7%	10.8%	40.3%	20.8%	19.4%
		(1.95)	(2.15)	(3.39)	(2.81)	(2.73)
Michigan	1,045	8.7%	9.5%	55.5%	11.6%	14.7%
		(0.83)	(0.86)	(1.46)	(0.94)	(1.04)
Ohio	991	8.1%	8.2%	49.1%	15.1%	19.5%
		(0.88)	(0.89)	(1.61)	(1.16)	(1.28)
Wisconsin	249	9.9%	9.3%	56.2%	15.5%	9.2%
		(2.34)	(2.27)	(3.89)	(2.83)	(2.26)
West North Central	**1,069**	**6.1%**	**7.3%**	**49.4%**	**19.3%**	**18.0%**
		(0.83)	**(0.90)**	**(1.74)**	**(1.37)**	**(1.33)**
Iowa	145	6.9%	10.8%	42.6%	23.3%	16.4%
		(2.05)	(2.50)	(3.99)	(3.41)	(2.98)
Kansas	126	7.3%	8.9%	48.2%	18.9%	16.7%
		(2.10)	(2.29)	(4.03)	(3.16)	(3.01)
Minnesota	273	5.8%	8.3%	60.1%	10.4%	15.5%
		(1.80)	(2.13)	(3.78)	(2.36)	(2.79)
Missouri	380	5.2%	5.0%	46.7%	22.5%	20.7%
		(1.60)	(1.56)	(3.58)	(2.99)	(2.90)
Nebraska	74	6.7%	6.1%	46.7%	24.2%	16.3%
		(2.08)	(1.98)	(4.14)	(3.56)	(3.07)
North Dakota	33	5.6%	6.7%	47.1%	27.4%	13.2%
		(1.80)	(1.96)	(3.90)	(3.48)	(2.64)
South Dakota	39	7.6%	7.3%	38.0%	21.2%	25.9%
		(1.89)	(1.86)	(3.47)	(2.92)	(3.13)
Mountain	**988**	**8.8%**	**9.3%**	**39.7%**	**19.4%**	**22.7%**
		(0.85)	**(0.87)**	**(1.47)**	**(1.19)**	**(1.26)**
Arizona	263	12.1%	9.8%	37.2%	20.8%	20.2%
		(2.31)	(2.10)	(3.42)	(2.87)	(2.84)
Colorado	226	8.3%	8.1%	46.4%	16.7%	20.6%
		(2.10)	(2.08)	(3.81)	(2.85)	(3.09)
Idaho	56	9.0%	14.4%	31.9%	23.5%	21.2%
		(2.17)	(2.66)	(3.53)	(3.21)	(3.10)
Montana	60	5.6%	7.9%	53.3%	15.6%	17.6%
		(1.55)	(1.82)	(3.36)	(2.45)	(2.57)
Nevada	106	7.8%	6.4%	27.6%	21.0%	37.2%
		(1.74)	(1.59)	(2.91)	(2.65)	(3.14)
New Mexico	162	6.2%	5.4%	42.2%	19.6%	26.6%
		(1.36)	(1.27)	(2.77)	(2.22)	(2.48)
Utah	94	7.8%	18.8%	37.1%	20.0%	16.2%
		(2.09)	(3.05)	(3.77)	(3.13)	(2.88)
Wyoming	21	12.9%	10.9%	36.0%	19.6%	20.7%
		(3.45)	(3.21)	(4.95)	(4.09)	(4.18)
Pacific	**4,328**	**6.6%**	**6.0%**	**55.3%**	**10.8%**	**21.3%**
		(0.46)	**(0.44)**	**(0.92)**	**(0.58)**	**(0.76)**
Alaska	41	6.2%	3.4%	56.4%	7.5%	26.5%
		(1.52)	(1.14)	(3.12)	(1.66)	(2.77)
California	3,614	6.3%	5.2%	57.4%	9.5%	21.6%
		(0.50)	(0.46)	(1.03)	(0.61)	(0.85)
Hawaii	100	9.9%	9.6%	49.6%	15.6%	15.3%
		(1.96)	(1.94)	(3.30)	(2.39)	(2.37)
Oregon	203	7.2%	10.9%	43.2%	21.3%	17.5%
		(1.97)	(2.37)	(3.78)	(3.12)	(2.90)
Washington	370	8.5%	10.8%	42.4%	16.9%	21.4%
		(1.90)	(2.10)	(3.35)	(2.54)	(2.78)

Source: Three-year merged March CPS: 1991, 1992, and 1993.
Note: See table notes at end of Section A.

Notes to Tables, Section A

1. Population in the merged CPS file excludes persons aged 65 and over, those living in institutions, and those in families with active military service members. Persons with more than one type of health coverage are included only in the first category shown. Percentages may not sum to 100 owing to rounding.

2. "Employer (other)" includes persons covered as dependents on the employer group insurance of another family member.

3. Medicaid coverage reflects corrections to the reports of Medicaid on the Current Population Survey made by the Urban Institute's TRIM2 model (see Appendix Three).

4. "Other Public" includes persons covered under Medicare, CHAMPUS, VA, and military health programs.

5. "Other Private" includes persons covered through privately purchased coverage that is not obtained through an employer or union (often referred to as "nongroup" coverage).

6. "Uninsured" includes persons without insurance coverage for the entire reference year. The CPS does not currently collect information on persons who are without coverage for less than 12 months (see Appendix Three).

7. "Employer" includes individuals covered by employer group insurance either from their own employer or as dependents on another family member's plan.

8. "Other Coverage" includes persons with public coverage other than Medicaid (Medicare, CHAMPUS, VA, and military health programs) and persons with privately purchased nongroup coverage.

9. We define families as health insurance units. A health insurance unit includes the members of a nuclear family who can be covered under one health policy. The standard we use follows a typical insurance industry standard: a policy-holder may cover his or her spouse, all children under age 18, and children between ages 18 and 21 who are full-time students. Thus, whereas a single 25-year-old child living with his or her parents may be included in the parents' nuclear family, he or she would be treated as a separate, single health unit.

10. Incomes used in these tables are primarily the incomes reported on the CPS. However, we incorporated some corrections to incomes estimated by the Urban Institute's TRIM2 model. The model corrects for underreporting of income from the cash welfare programs—AFDC and SSI—and makes corrections to reported interest and dividend incomes. See Linda Giannarelli, 1992, *An Analyst's Guide to TRIM2* (Washington, D.C.: Urban Institute Press) for details.

Poverty is defined using the federal poverty guidelines from the U.S. Department of Health and Human Services.

11. These categories reflect the work status of the head and spouse only. Therefore, if both parents in a family do not work but a dependent child is employed, the family is classified as nonworking. These categories are hierarchical, so each person is shown only in the first appropriate category. For

example, a person in a health unit where the head works full-time and the spouse part-time would be classified only in the one full-time worker group.

Work status is based on the *usual* number of hours per week reported for the reference year. We define full-time work as 35 hours per week or more. Non-work reflects a report of zero hours of work.

Individuals in nonworker families may have employer group insurance for several reasons. These include early retirees, children covered by an adult not living in the household, individuals buying coverage from a former employer through the provisions in the Consolidated Budget Reconciliation Act of 1986 (COBRA), and (in rare cases) coverage by individuals who are working but are not the head or spouse.

All Tables:

*** A triple asterisk in the tables indicates no observations on the merged CPS file of this type.

--- A triple dash in the tables indicates fewer than 100 observations on the merged CPS file of this type. We have not printed estimates in these cases.

Health Insurance Coverage of Workers

Section B provides more information about insurance coverage of workers. Since many policy proposals to expand health insurance focus on the workplace, it is important to understand the job characteristics of workers with and without employment-based insurance. These tables do not include workers' dependents.

After showing coverage of all workers ages 18 to 64, we show coverage for persons working full-time (more than 35 hours a week) and persons working part-time (the B2 table series). The number of hours usually worked per week is important because many employers only insure full-time workers. Many policies seeking to expand the employment-based insurance system would also exclude part-time workers. Thus, the percentage of full-time workers without health insurance from their own employer indicates the proportion of workers in a state who could be affected by a policy that expanded employment-based coverage to all full-time workers using a definition of more than 35 hours a week. We then show rates of own-employer coverage and uninsurance among workers by other employment characteristics.

Note that these data on coverage through a worker's own employer indicate how many are *enrolled* in their own employer's plan, not the number *offered* health insurance. Workers without own-employer coverage may have been offered health benefits by their employer, but turned down the offer because they already have coverage from another source (a working spouse, for instance) or because they do not value health coverage relative to the share of premiums they are asked to pay.

Nationally, 54.1 percent of all workers have employer-sponsored coverage through their own employer, and another 16.6 percent have employer coverage through a working spouse (table B1). Few workers get their primary coverage through Medicaid (2.7 percent). The primary coverage for 10 percent of workers is private coverage purchased independent of an employer group. The uninsured rate for workers is 16.7 percent. Rates of own-employer coverage among workers vary from less than 45 percent in Louisiana, Montana, New Mexico, North Dakota, and Oklahoma to greater than 60 percent in Connecticut, Hawaii, and New Jersey. Own-employer coverage is highest in Hawaii (66.7 percent), where state law requires employers to contribute to coverage of many of their workers (but not the workers' dependents). Uninsured rates for workers are less than 10 percent in Connecticut and Hawaii, but approach 25 percent in several states including Florida, New Mexico, and Texas.

Hours of work

The usual number of hours an employee works each week is important to securing employer-sponsored coverage. The data in the B2 table series make this clear. Nationally, 62.8 percent of full-time workers get health coverage through their own employer, compared to only 16.6 percent of part-time workers—a more than three-fold difference. In fact, part-time workers are more likely to gain employer coverage as a dependent on the plan of another worker: 36.6 percent of part-time workers gain employer coverage through another worker in their family relative to 11.9 percent of full-time workers. The coverage gap between full- and part-time workers is narrowed somewhat because part-time workers are more likely to enroll in Medicaid (5.9 percent have primary coverage through the program versus 1.9 percent of full-time workers) and because part-time workers are twice as likely to have "other coverage" (most often purchases of private coverage outside of employer groups)—18 percent have non-group coverage versus 8.1 percent of full-time workers. Nonetheless, part-time workers are significantly more likely to be uninsured than their full-time colleagues: the uninsured rate for part-time workers is 22.9 percent; for full-time workers the rate is 15.3 percent.

Rates of coverage and uninsurance by hours of work vary across states. Rates of own-employer coverage among full-time workers are generally highest in the New England, Middle Atlantic, and East North Central regions where own-employer coverage rates approach 70 percent. This correlates with the higher average firm payrolls and the concentration of manufacturing firms in these regions (see Section G). Hawaii has the highest rate of own-employer coverage among full-time workers—71.6 percent. Rates of own-employer coverage are lowest among full-time workers in North Dakota (50.9 percent), South Dakota (51.9 percent), and New Mexico (52 percent). Interestingly, however, an unusually high rate of "other coverage" (mostly nongroup private coverage) in North Dakota (21.3 percent) keeps the uninsured rate for full-time workers in the state (10.5 percent) below the national average (15.3 percent). The highest uninsured rates for full-time workers are found in New Mexico (23.3 percent) and the states of the West South Central region (18–23 percent); the lowest is in Hawaii (7.6 percent).

Among part-time workers, own-employer coverage rates are highest in the New England and Middle Atlantic regions and lowest in the West Central regions. The uninsured rate exceeds one in three part-time workers in Arkansas, Florida, Mississippi, Oklahoma, and Texas, but is as low as 11.3 percent in Connecticut and about 12 percent in Hawaii and Nebraska. (Nebraska has one of the lowest rates of part-time worker coverage through an own employer, at 12.5 percent. Unusually high rates of dependent coverage and Medicaid in that state help to fill the coverage gap.)

EMPLOYMENT CHARACTERISTICS

Focusing on the employment characteristics of persons who are working, we show the incidence of employer group coverage and uninsurance by firm size (tables B3 and B4), by sector of employment (tables B5 and B6), and by industry (tables B7 and B8). For each characteristic we include one table showing the prevalence of own-employer coverage and one showing the uninsured rate. These tables show important coverage differences across employers' characteristics that generally hold across all states.

Firms with fewer than 25 workers are less likely to provide health insurance, whereas those with 100 or more workers are more likely to provide insurance. Nationally, 26.8 percent of workers in firms with fewer than 25 workers have own-employer coverage versus 68.2 percent of workers in firms with 100 or more workers (table B3). This general pattern is consistent across states, although states that have lower-than-average or higher-than-average rates of own-employer group health insurance across all firm size categories stand out. For example, employer group insurance is less common in all West South Central states (Arkansas, Louisiana, Oklahoma, and Texas) than it is across the entire United States. Thus, mandates requiring all employers to provide health insurance will have a greater impact on employers in these states than in states in the New England and Middle Atlantic regions that already have higher-than-average rates of employer group insurance coverage.

Statistics presented for workers without any source of health insurance by firm size (table B4) are consistent with the employer group insurance picture. Workers in small firms (less than 25 workers) are much more likely to lack insurance than are other private-sector workers. Nationally, the uninsured rate among workers in small firms is 27.4 percent, versus 10.6 percent among workers in firms with more than 100 employees. Although this holds true across the country, workers in some states have generally higher rates of uninsurance than in others. In general, states mentioned earlier that have lower-than-average employer group coverage rates have higher rates of uninsurance (for example, workers in all firm-size categories in the West South Central region).

Table B5, which shows employer group insurance by employment sector, highlights the high enrollment rates in employer group insurance plans among workers in the public sector. Nationwide, 71.2 percent of government employees are insured through their own employer, compared to 54.4 percent of private-sector workers. Only 15.8 percent of those who are self-employed report having health insurance through their own employment-based plans. Not surprisingly, self-employed workers have the highest rate of uninsurance (25.7 percent) among the three employment sectors (table B6). There is wide variation in the incidence of uninsurance among self-employed workers across the country, however. For example, the percentage of self-employed workers without health insurance is 16.7 percent in the West North Central region compared to 33.5 percent in the West South Central region.[1]

The last two tables in this section (tables B7 and B8) show the percentage of private-sector workers with employer group insurance and without insurance by industry, respectively. Workers in manufacturing are much more likely to have insurance through their employer than are other private-sector workers. Insurance coverage among the manufacturing industry is relatively high across all states (73.9 percent), but there are important differences across the states. For example, own-employer coverage among workers in manufacturing is nearly 80 percent or higher in most of the East North Central states (Illinois, Indiana, Michigan, and Ohio), but is less than 65 percent in Florida, Montana, and New Mexico (table B7). This reflects the high concentration of large manufacturing firms in the East North Central, many of which provide generous insurance coverage established through union bargaining agreements.

The rates of uninsurance among private-sector workers (table B8) also indicate some important variations across the states. Nationwide, 17.3 percent of workers in service industries are uninsured. However, the rate exceeds 25 percent in Louisiana, Mississippi, and Texas. Workers in the wholesale and retail industry have the highest rates of uninsurance. In many of the states in the Mountain, South Atlantic, and South Central regions, for example, one-quarter of workers in this industry group lack insurance.

Note, Section B

1. We have changed the sector definitions used in tables B5 and B6 since publication of the first edition of this volume. In this edition, the self-employed group includes only the self-employed unincorporated. Incorporated self-employed workers are in the private-sector group. In the 1993 edition, the self-employed incorporated were included in the self-employed group. Researchers wishing to track changes in coverage by sector over time must therefore use caution when comparing numbers in these editions.

Table B1
Health Insurance Coverage of Workers Ages 18-64, 1990-92[1]
(Persons in thousands)

	Number	Employer (own)	Employer (other)[2]	Medicaid[3]	Other Coverage[4]	Uninsured[5]
United States	123,962	54.1%	16.6%	2.7%	10.0%	16.7%
		(0.16)	(0.12)	(0.05)	(0.09)	(0.12)
New England	6,860	56.8%	20.0%	2.1%	9.7%	11.4%
		(0.53)	(0.43)	(0.15)	(0.32)	(0.34)
Connecticut	1,702	60.5%	20.4%	1.6%	8.5%	9.0%
		(1.45)	(1.19)	(0.37)	(0.83)	(0.85)
Maine	651	50.7%	20.9%	2.9%	11.7%	13.8%
		(1.33)	(1.08)	(0.45)	(0.85)	(0.91)
Massachusetts	3,061	56.9%	19.6%	2.2%	9.8%	11.6%
		(0.70)	(0.56)	(0.21)	(0.42)	(0.45)
New Hampshire	626	54.3%	20.5%	1.4%	10.8%	13.0%
		(1.42)	(1.15)	(0.34)	(0.88)	(0.96)
Rhode Island	502	58.2%	17.9%	2.5%	8.9%	12.4%
		(1.45)	(1.13)	(0.46)	(0.84)	(0.97)
Vermont	317	52.2%	22.6%	3.0%	10.0%	12.2%
		(1.40)	(1.17)	(0.47)	(0.84)	(0.92)
Middle Atlantic	18,132	58.1%	17.7%	1.9%	8.7%	13.7%
		(0.36)	(0.28)	(0.10)	(0.21)	(0.25)
New Jersey	3,947	60.8%	16.1%	1.6%	8.3%	13.2%
		(0.68)	(0.51)	(0.17)	(0.38)	(0.47)
New York	8,389	56.2%	17.1%	1.8%	9.2%	15.7%
		(0.54)	(0.41)	(0.14)	(0.31)	(0.40)
Pennsylvania	5,797	59.0%	19.7%	2.1%	8.2%	11.0%
		(0.68)	(0.55)	(0.20)	(0.38)	(0.43)
South Atlantic	21,925	53.7%	14.7%	2.5%	9.8%	19.3%
		(0.39)	(0.27)	(0.12)	(0.23)	(0.31)
Delaware	382	55.3%	18.5%	1.7%	8.2%	16.2%
		(1.36)	(1.06)	(0.35)	(0.75)	(1.01)
District of Columbia	274	55.1%	6.8%	3.7%	10.8%	23.6%
		(1.61)	(0.81)	(0.61)	(1.00)	(1.37)
Florida	6,345	49.2%	13.2%	2.4%	10.9%	24.4%
		(0.66)	(0.45)	(0.20)	(0.41)	(0.57)
Georgia	3,191	53.7%	14.2%	3.1%	9.3%	19.7%
		(1.31)	(0.92)	(0.45)	(0.76)	(1.05)
Maryland	2,547	59.0%	17.6%	2.0%	8.1%	13.3%
		(1.34)	(1.04)	(0.38)	(0.74)	(0.92)
North Carolina	3,370	57.4%	13.6%	2.7%	9.9%	16.4%
		(0.66)	(0.46)	(0.22)	(0.40)	(0.50)
South Carolina	1,749	55.2%	14.1%	2.6%	9.4%	18.8%
		(1.19)	(0.83)	(0.38)	(0.70)	(0.94)
Virginia	3,317	54.0%	16.5%	1.9%	9.6%	18.0%
		(1.14)	(0.85)	(0.31)	(0.67)	(0.88)
West Virginia	750	51.6%	18.1%	5.2%	9.8%	15.4%
		(1.47)	(1.13)	(0.65)	(0.87)	(1.06)
East South Central	7,196	52.3%	17.3%	2.8%	9.5%	18.1%
		(0.69)	(0.52)	(0.23)	(0.40)	(0.53)
Alabama	1,915	53.4%	16.8%	2.2%	8.9%	18.7%
		(1.36)	(1.02)	(0.40)	(0.78)	(1.06)
Kentucky	1,721	53.1%	19.0%	3.0%	10.2%	14.7%
		(1.38)	(1.08)	(0.47)	(0.84)	(0.98)
Mississippi	1,161	46.9%	14.7%	3.6%	11.1%	23.8%
		(1.33)	(0.94)	(0.49)	(0.83)	(1.13)
Tennessee	2,399	53.5%	17.7%	2.8%	8.7%	17.3%
		(1.28)	(0.98)	(0.42)	(0.73)	(0.97)
West South Central	12,891	48.6%	14.3%	2.8%	10.6%	23.7%
		(0.53)	(0.37)	(0.17)	(0.33)	(0.45)
Arkansas	1,115	46.7%	15.9%	3.2%	13.2%	21.1%
		(1.35)	(0.99)	(0.47)	(0.92)	(1.11)
Louisiana	1,852	44.3%	16.3%	3.0%	12.9%	23.5%
		(1.46)	(1.09)	(0.50)	(0.98)	(1.25)
Oklahoma	1,499	44.7%	16.4%	2.7%	13.0%	23.2%
		(1.34)	(1.00)	(0.44)	(0.91)	(1.14)
Texas	8,423	50.5%	13.3%	2.7%	9.3%	24.2%
		(0.68)	(0.46)	(0.22)	(0.40)	(0.58)

Health Insurance Coverage of Workers Ages 18-64, 1990-92[1]

(Persons in thousands)

	Number	Employer (own)	Employer (other)[2]	Medicaid[3]	Other Coverage[4]	Uninsured[5]
East North Central	**21,245**	**57.2%**	**18.8%**	**2.5%**	**8.9%**	**12.6%**
		(0.38)	**(0.30)**	**(0.12)**	**(0.22)**	**(0.25)**
Illinois	5,885	58.1%	16.4%	2.3%	9.4%	13.9%
		(0.69)	(0.52)	(0.21)	(0.41)	(0.48)
Indiana	2,842	56.3%	18.8%	2.2%	8.8%	13.8%
		(1.35)	(1.06)	(0.40)	(0.77)	(0.94)
Michigan	4,520	56.8%	19.6%	3.2%	8.4%	12.0%
		(0.70)	(0.56)	(0.25)	(0.39)	(0.46)
Ohio	5,408	57.6%	19.5%	2.3%	8.4%	12.2%
		(0.68)	(0.55)	(0.21)	(0.38)	(0.45)
Wisconsin	2,589	55.8%	21.5%	2.1%	10.2%	10.4%
		(1.21)	(1.00)	(0.35)	(0.73)	(0.74)
West North Central	**9,354**	**51.2%**	**19.5%**	**2.4%**	**13.9%**	**13.0%**
		(0.59)	**(0.47)**	**(0.18)**	**(0.41)**	**(0.40)**
Iowa	1,496	49.0%	21.2%	2.4%	15.5%	11.8%
		(1.26)	(1.03)	(0.39)	(0.91)	(0.81)
Kansas	1,278	51.0%	19.7%	2.3%	14.2%	12.8%
		(1.27)	(1.01)	(0.38)	(0.88)	(0.85)
Minnesota	2,438	51.6%	19.4%	2.0%	13.5%	13.5%
		(1.29)	(1.02)	(0.36)	(0.88)	(0.88)
Missouri	2,670	54.8%	17.7%	2.9%	10.6%	14.0%
		(1.35)	(1.03)	(0.45)	(0.83)	(0.94)
Nebraska	827	48.8%	22.7%	2.2%	16.2%	10.2%
		(1.24)	(1.04)	(0.37)	(0.91)	(0.75)
North Dakota	307	41.1%	20.8%	2.3%	24.4%	11.4%
		(1.25)	(1.03)	(0.38)	(1.09)	(0.81)
South Dakota	338	45.2%	17.1%	2.1%	19.1%	16.4%
		(1.21)	(0.91)	(0.35)	(0.95)	(0.90)
Mountain	**6,754**	**51.0%**	**17.3%**	**2.5%**	**11.3%**	**17.9%**
		(0.57)	**(0.43)**	**(0.18)**	**(0.36)**	**(0.44)**
Arizona	1,717	52.2%	15.2%	2.7%	10.7%	19.3%
		(1.38)	(0.99)	(0.45)	(0.85)	(1.09)
Colorado	1,736	53.4%	18.2%	1.9%	12.4%	14.1%
		(1.37)	(1.06)	(0.37)	(0.91)	(0.96)
Idaho	507	48.3%	17.4%	2.6%	12.2%	19.6%
		(1.26)	(0.96)	(0.40)	(0.82)	(1.00)
Montana	402	44.7%	17.9%	3.2%	15.6%	18.5%
		(1.30)	(1.00)	(0.46)	(0.95)	(1.01)
Nevada	651	57.4%	12.7%	1.4%	7.7%	20.8%
		(1.30)	(0.87)	(0.31)	(0.70)	(1.06)
New Mexico	703	43.7%	16.5%	3.2%	11.8%	24.8%
		(1.34)	(1.00)	(0.47)	(0.87)	(1.16)
Utah	801	50.8%	22.8%	2.9%	9.0%	14.5%
		(1.34)	(1.12)	(0.45)	(0.76)	(0.94)
Wyoming	237	46.2%	21.5%	3.6%	14.3%	14.5%
		(1.53)	(1.26)	(0.57)	(1.08)	(1.08)
Pacific	**19,604**	**53.0%**	**13.6%**	**4.0%**	**10.2%**	**19.1%**
		(0.44)	**(0.30)**	**(0.17)**	**(0.26)**	**(0.34)**
Alaska	259	50.2%	14.1%	3.1%	9.6%	23.0%
		(1.25)	(0.87)	(0.43)	(0.74)	(1.05)
California	14,746	51.4%	13.3%	4.3%	10.2%	20.8%
		(0.51)	(0.35)	(0.21)	(0.31)	(0.42)
Hawaii	545	66.7%	15.8%	1.7%	7.6%	8.2%
		(1.33)	(1.03)	(0.37)	(0.75)	(0.78)
Oregon	1,513	55.7%	16.9%	2.8%	8.5%	16.1%
		(1.39)	(1.05)	(0.46)	(0.78)	(1.03)
Washington	2,542	58.0%	13.2%	3.2%	12.4%	13.3%
		(1.28)	(0.88)	(0.46)	(0.85)	(0.88)

Source: Three-year merged March CPS: 1991, 1992, and 1993.
Note: See table notes at end of Section B.

Table B2a

Health Insurance Coverage of Workers Ages 18-64 by Hours of Work, 1990-92: Full-Time[1,6]

(Persons in thousands)

	Number	Employer (own)	Employer (other)[2]	Medicaid[3]	Other Coverage[4]	Uninsured[5]
United States	100,639	62.8%	11.9%	1.9%	8.1%	15.3%
		(0.17)	(0.11)	(0.05)	(0.10)	(0.13)
New England	5,455	66.6%	14.5%	1.2%	7.5%	10.2%
		(0.56)	(0.42)	(0.13)	(0.31)	(0.36)
Connecticut	1,362	71.0%	13.5%	1.0%	6.1%	8.4%
		(1.50)	(1.13)	(0.32)	(0.79)	(0.92)
Maine	513	59.2%	16.0%	1.8%	9.6%	13.3%
		(1.47)	(1.10)	(0.40)	(0.88)	(1.02)
Massachusetts	2,417	66.9%	14.3%	1.1%	7.7%	10.0%
		(0.75)	(0.56)	(0.16)	(0.42)	(0.48)
New Hampshire	505	63.7%	15.9%	1.0%	8.6%	10.9%
		(1.53)	(1.16)	(0.31)	(0.89)	(0.99)
Rhode Island	408	66.1%	13.4%	1.7%	6.6%	12.2%
		(1.55)	(1.11)	(0.42)	(0.81)	(1.07)
Vermont	249	61.4%	17.4%	2.0%	7.7%	11.5%
		(1.54)	(1.20)	(0.45)	(0.84)	(1.01)
Middle Atlantic	14,750	67.0%	12.2%	1.3%	6.9%	12.6%
		(0.38)	(0.27)	(0.09)	(0.21)	(0.27)
New Jersey	3,314	68.8%	11.0%	1.1%	7.1%	12.0%
		(0.70)	(0.47)	(0.16)	(0.39)	(0.49)
New York	6,814	64.4%	12.4%	1.3%	7.2%	14.7%
		(0.58)	(0.40)	(0.14)	(0.31)	(0.43)
Pennsylvania	4,623	69.5%	12.9%	1.5%	6.3%	9.8%
		(0.72)	(0.52)	(0.19)	(0.38)	(0.46)
South Atlantic	18,289	61.3%	11.1%	1.8%	8.2%	17.6%
		(0.41)	(0.27)	(0.11)	(0.23)	(0.32)
Delaware	319	62.7%	13.9%	1.2%	7.3%	14.9%
		(1.45)	(1.04)	(0.33)	(0.78)	(1.06)
District of Columbia	237	61.1%	5.0%	3.2%	8.5%	22.2%
		(1.69)	(0.76)	(0.61)	(0.97)	(1.44)
Florida	5,265	56.6%	10.4%	1.7%	9.2%	22.1%
		(0.72)	(0.44)	(0.19)	(0.42)	(0.60)
Georgia	2,684	60.8%	10.7%	2.5%	8.4%	17.5%
		(1.40)	(0.89)	(0.45)	(0.80)	(1.09)
Maryland	2,134	65.9%	13.4%	1.4%	6.7%	12.6%
		(1.41)	(1.01)	(0.35)	(0.75)	(0.99)
North Carolina	2,850	64.8%	10.1%	2.2%	8.0%	15.0%
		(0.70)	(0.44)	(0.21)	(0.40)	(0.52)
South Carolina	1,446	63.4%	10.0%	1.9%	7.5%	17.2%
		(1.27)	(0.79)	(0.36)	(0.69)	(1.00)
Virginia	2,750	62.3%	12.3%	1.2%	8.0%	16.3%
		(1.21)	(0.82)	(0.27)	(0.68)	(0.92)
West Virginia	604	61.7%	12.3%	3.3%	8.8%	13.9%
		(1.59)	(1.07)	(0.58)	(0.93)	(1.13)
East South Central	5,921	60.4%	13.2%	2.0%	8.0%	16.5%
		(0.74)	(0.51)	(0.21)	(0.41)	(0.56)
Alabama	1,609	60.4%	13.0%	1.5%	7.4%	17.7%
		(1.46)	(1.00)	(0.36)	(0.78)	(1.14)
Kentucky	1,361	62.7%	13.7%	2.3%	8.1%	13.2%
		(1.50)	(1.07)	(0.46)	(0.85)	(1.05)
Mississippi	970	53.4%	12.1%	2.9%	9.6%	21.9%
		(1.45)	(0.95)	(0.49)	(0.86)	(1.20)
Tennessee	1,980	62.1%	13.5%	1.7%	7.6%	15.0%
		(1.37)	(0.97)	(0.36)	(0.75)	(1.01)
West South Central	10,650	56.4%	11.0%	2.0%	8.7%	21.9%
		(0.58)	(0.36)	(0.16)	(0.33)	(0.48)
Arkansas	919	53.9%	14.0%	2.6%	11.3%	18.3%
		(1.49)	(1.04)	(0.47)	(0.95)	(1.15)
Louisiana	1,473	52.9%	12.7%	1.8%	9.8%	22.7%
		(1.65)	(1.10)	(0.44)	(0.98)	(1.38)
Oklahoma	1,216	53.3%	12.9%	1.9%	11.2%	20.7%
		(1.50)	(1.01)	(0.41)	(0.95)	(1.22)
Texas	7,042	58.1%	9.9%	1.9%	7.7%	22.4%
		(0.74)	(0.45)	(0.20)	(0.40)	(0.62)

Table B2a (continued)
Health Insurance Coverage of Workers Ages 18-64 by Hours of Work, 1990-92: Full-Time[1,6]

(Persons in thousands)

	Number	Employer (own)	Employer (other)[2]	Medicaid[3]	Other Coverage[4]	Uninsured[5]
East North Central	**17,038**	**67.4%**	**12.9%**	**1.7%**	**6.9%**	**11.1%**
		(0.40)	**(0.29)**	**(0.11)**	**(0.22)**	**(0.27)**
Illinois	4,763	68.0%	10.7%	1.7%	7.3%	12.3%
		(0.73)	(0.48)	(0.20)	(0.41)	(0.51)
Indiana	2,319	66.3%	13.7%	1.3%	6.6%	12.1%
		(1.43)	(1.04)	(0.34)	(0.75)	(0.98)
Michigan	3,548	68.4%	12.9%	2.2%	6.5%	10.0%
		(0.74)	(0.54)	(0.23)	(0.40)	(0.48)
Ohio	4,328	67.5%	13.5%	1.7%	6.3%	11.0%
		(0.72)	(0.53)	(0.20)	(0.38)	(0.48)
Wisconsin	2,079	65.2%	15.8%	1.4%	8.1%	9.4%
		(1.29)	(0.99)	(0.32)	(0.74)	(0.79)
West North Central	**7,415**	**60.8%**	**14.0%**	**1.8%**	**11.3%**	**12.1%**
		(0.64)	**(0.46)**	**(0.18)**	**(0.42)**	**(0.43)**
Iowa	1,152	60.1%	14.3%	1.7%	12.3%	11.6%
		(1.40)	(1.00)	(0.37)	(0.94)	(0.92)
Kansas	1,032	59.7%	14.5%	1.8%	12.2%	11.8%
		(1.38)	(0.99)	(0.38)	(0.92)	(0.91)
Minnesota	1,877	62.2%	12.9%	1.6%	10.4%	12.8%
		(1.43)	(0.99)	(0.37)	(0.90)	(0.99)
Missouri	2,178	63.4%	13.7%	2.0%	8.4%	12.5%
		(1.44)	(1.03)	(0.42)	(0.83)	(0.99)
Nebraska	669	57.8%	16.9%	1.9%	13.8%	9.6%
		(1.36)	(1.03)	(0.38)	(0.95)	(0.81)
North Dakota	232	50.9%	15.2%	2.1%	21.3%	10.5%
		(1.46)	(1.05)	(0.42)	(1.20)	(0.90)
South Dakota	275	51.9%	13.6%	1.7%	17.6%	15.2%
		(1.34)	(0.92)	(0.34)	(1.02)	(0.97)
Mountain	**5,365**	**60.0%**	**12.4%**	**1.7%**	**9.3%**	**16.5%**
		(0.63)	**(0.43)**	**(0.17)**	**(0.37)**	**(0.48)**
Arizona	1,386	60.7%	11.0%	2.0%	9.2%	17.1%
		(1.51)	(0.96)	(0.43)	(0.89)	(1.16)
Colorado	1,375	63.0%	13.7%	1.1%	8.9%	13.3%
		(1.49)	(1.07)	(0.32)	(0.88)	(1.05)
Idaho	407	56.7%	11.6%	2.4%	10.8%	18.5%
		(1.40)	(0.90)	(0.43)	(0.87)	(1.10)
Montana	312	53.7%	12.8%	2.8%	14.4%	16.3%
		(1.48)	(0.99)	(0.49)	(1.04)	(1.09)
Nevada	548	63.4%	8.8%	1.1%	7.0%	19.6%
		(1.38)	(0.81)	(0.30)	(0.73)	(1.14)
New Mexico	554	52.0%	13.0%	1.9%	9.8%	23.3%
		(1.52)	(1.02)	(0.42)	(0.90)	(1.28)
Utah	600	62.8%	14.9%	1.5%	7.6%	13.2%
		(1.49)	(1.10)	(0.37)	(0.82)	(1.05)
Wyoming	184	55.5%	15.8%	2.8%	11.8%	14.1%
		(1.73)	(1.27)	(0.58)	(1.13)	(1.21)
Pacific	**15,757**	**61.2%**	**9.6%**	**3.1%**	**8.6%**	**17.5%**
		(0.47)	**(0.29)**	**(0.17)**	**(0.27)**	**(0.37)**
Alaska	215	56.5%	10.9%	2.2%	9.1%	21.3%
		(1.36)	(0.85)	(0.41)	(0.79)	(1.12)
California	11,886	59.5%	9.4%	3.4%	8.6%	19.1%
		(0.56)	(0.33)	(0.21)	(0.32)	(0.45)
Hawaii	460	71.6%	13.6%	1.1%	6.1%	7.6%
		(1.39)	(1.05)	(0.32)	(0.74)	(0.81)
Oregon	1,177	65.3%	11.8%	1.8%	6.6%	14.5%
		(1.51)	(1.02)	(0.42)	(0.79)	(1.11)
Washington	2,019	66.5%	8.8%	2.2%	10.6%	11.9%
		(1.37)	(0.82)	(0.42)	(0.89)	(0.94)

Source: Three-year merged March CPS: 1991, 1992, and 1993.
Note: See table notes at end of Section B.

Table B2b
Health Insurance Coverage of Workers Ages 18-64 by Hours of Work, 1990-92: Part-Time[1,6]
(Persons in thousands)

	Number	Employer (own)	Employer (other)[2]	Medicaid[3]	Other Coverage[4]	Uninsured[5]
United States	23,323	16.6%	36.6%	5.9%	18.0%	22.9%
		(0.27)	(0.35)	(0.17)	(0.28)	(0.31)
New England	1,406	18.9%	41.5%	5.5%	18.4%	15.7%
		(0.92)	(1.16)	(0.54)	(0.91)	(0.85)
Connecticut	340	18.3%	48.2%	4.0%	18.2%	11.3%
		(2.56)	(3.31)	(1.30)	(2.56)	(2.10)
Maine	138	18.9%	39.2%	6.9%	19.5%	15.5%
		(2.26)	(2.82)	(1.46)	(2.29)	(2.09)
Massachusetts	644	19.2%	39.5%	6.2%	17.8%	17.3%
		(1.21)	(1.50)	(0.74)	(1.18)	(1.16)
New Hampshire	121	15.3%	39.7%	3.3%	19.9%	21.9%
		(2.34)	(3.18)	(1.15)	(2.59)	(2.69)
Rhode Island	94	24.2%	37.1%	6.2%	19.2%	13.3%
		(2.91)	(3.29)	(1.64)	(2.68)	(2.31)
Vermont	69	18.9%	41.5%	6.4%	18.3%	15.0%
		(2.35)	(2.96)	(1.47)	(2.33)	(2.14)
Middle Atlantic	3,382	19.3%	41.5%	4.1%	16.6%	18.5%
		(0.67)	(0.84)	(0.34)	(0.63)	(0.66)
New Jersey	633	18.7%	42.7%	4.0%	15.0%	19.6%
		(1.35)	(1.71)	(0.68)	(1.23)	(1.37)
New York	1,575	20.8%	37.3%	3.8%	17.9%	20.2%
		(1.02)	(1.21)	(0.48)	(0.96)	(1.01)
Pennsylvania	1,174	17.6%	46.5%	4.5%	15.7%	15.7%
		(1.18)	(1.54)	(0.64)	(1.12)	(1.12)
South Atlantic	3,636	15.5%	32.8%	6.0%	17.6%	28.1%
		(0.69)	(0.89)	(0.45)	(0.72)	(0.85)
Delaware	62	17.5%	42.0%	4.2%	13.2%	23.1%
		(2.57)	(3.34)	(1.35)	(2.29)	(2.85)
District of Columbia	37	16.0%	18.2%	7.6%	25.2%	32.9%
		(3.24)	(3.40)	(2.34)	(3.83)	(4.15)
Florida	1,080	12.9%	26.6%	6.0%	19.2%	35.3%
		(1.08)	(1.42)	(0.76)	(1.27)	(1.54)
Georgia	507	16.5%	32.5%	5.8%	13.9%	31.3%
		(2.45)	(3.09)	(1.54)	(2.29)	(3.06)
Maryland	413	23.2%	39.5%	5.3%	15.1%	17.0%
		(2.85)	(3.31)	(1.52)	(2.42)	(2.54)
North Carolina	521	17.0%	32.5%	5.9%	20.7%	23.9%
		(1.29)	(1.60)	(0.80)	(1.38)	(1.46)
South Carolina	303	16.2%	33.5%	5.8%	18.4%	26.1%
		(2.12)	(2.72)	(1.35)	(2.24)	(2.53)
Virginia	567	13.8%	37.0%	5.4%	17.3%	26.5%
		(1.90)	(2.66)	(1.25)	(2.09)	(2.43)
West Virginia	147	9.6%	42.3%	13.0%	13.7%	21.4%
		(1.96)	(3.28)	(2.23)	(2.28)	(2.72)
East South Central	1,275	15.0%	36.1%	6.7%	16.6%	25.6%
		(1.16)	(1.57)	(0.81)	(1.21)	(1.42)
Alabama	306	16.4%	36.7%	6.1%	17.2%	23.6%
		(2.53)	(3.30)	(1.63)	(2.58)	(2.90)
Kentucky	360	16.7%	38.9%	5.8%	18.1%	20.5%
		(2.25)	(2.95)	(1.41)	(2.33)	(2.44)
Mississippi	191	14.1%	27.7%	6.6%	18.6%	33.0%
		(2.28)	(2.93)	(1.63)	(2.55)	(3.08)
Tennessee	419	12.9%	37.2%	7.9%	13.9%	28.0%
		(2.07)	(2.98)	(1.66)	(2.13)	(2.77)
West South Central	2,241	11.3%	30.0%	6.7%	19.6%	32.5%
		(0.80)	(1.16)	(0.63)	(1.01)	(1.19)
Arkansas	196	13.3%	24.6%	5.9%	22.1%	34.1%
		(2.19)	(2.78)	(1.53)	(2.68)	(3.06)
Louisiana	380	11.0%	30.2%	7.4%	24.8%	26.7%
		(2.03)	(2.98)	(1.70)	(2.80)	(2.87)
Oklahoma	284	8.2%	31.3%	6.2%	20.7%	33.7%
		(1.70)	(2.88)	(1.49)	(2.51)	(2.93)
Texas	1,381	11.7%	30.4%	6.7%	17.5%	33.7%
		(1.08)	(1.55)	(0.84)	(1.28)	(1.59)

Table B2b (continued)
Health Insurance Coverage of Workers Ages 18-64 by Hours of Work, 1990-92: Part-Time[1,6]

(Persons in thousands)

	Number	Employer (own)	Employer (other)[2]	Medicaid[3]	Other Coverage[4]	Uninsured[5]
East North Central	**4,208**	**15.9%**	**42.6%**	**5.7%**	**17.2%**	**18.7%**
		(0.63)	**(0.85)**	**(0.40)**	**(0.65)**	**(0.67)**
Illinois	1,122	15.9%	40.4%	5.1%	18.0%	20.6%
		(1.17)	(1.57)	(0.71)	(1.23)	(1.30)
Indiana	523	12.3%	41.1%	6.4%	18.7%	21.5%
		(2.09)	(3.13)	(1.56)	(2.48)	(2.61)
Michigan	972	14.6%	43.8%	7.2%	15.3%	19.2%
		(1.08)	(1.52)	(0.79)	(1.10)	(1.20)
Ohio	1,081	17.9%	43.6%	5.1%	16.5%	17.0%
		(1.18)	(1.53)	(0.68)	(1.15)	(1.16)
Wisconsin	510	17.8%	44.6%	4.7%	18.6%	14.3%
		(2.09)	(2.72)	(1.16)	(2.13)	(1.92)
West North Central	**1,940**	**14.8%**	**40.4%**	**4.6%**	**23.8%**	**16.5%**
		(0.91)	**(1.27)**	**(0.54)**	**(1.10)**	**(0.96)**
Iowa	344	11.8%	44.2%	5.1%	26.3%	12.6%
		(1.69)	(2.60)	(1.15)	(2.31)	(1.74)
Kansas	246	14.7%	41.5%	4.3%	22.8%	16.7%
		(2.04)	(2.85)	(1.17)	(2.42)	(2.16)
Minnesota	561	16.3%	41.1%	3.2%	23.6%	15.8%
		(1.99)	(2.65)	(0.95)	(2.29)	(1.97)
Missouri	492	16.8%	35.5%	6.7%	20.2%	20.7%
		(2.35)	(3.01)	(1.58)	(2.53)	(2.55)
Nebraska	158	10.7%	47.0%	3.5%	26.3%	12.5%
		(1.76)	(2.83)	(1.05)	(2.50)	(1.88)
North Dakota	76	11.1%	37.9%	3.0%	33.6%	14.3%
		(1.61)	(2.49)	(0.88)	(2.42)	(1.79)
South Dakota	63	16.1%	32.4%	4.1%	25.9%	21.5%
		(2.06)	(2.62)	(1.12)	(2.45)	(2.30)
Mountain	**1,389**	**16.2%**	**36.1%**	**5.4%**	**19.0%**	**23.2%**
		(0.93)	**(1.22)**	**(0.58)**	**(0.99)**	**(1.07)**
Arizona	330	16.5%	32.7%	5.6%	16.9%	28.3%
		(2.34)	(2.96)	(1.46)	(2.37)	(2.84)
Colorado	361	16.8%	35.0%	4.8%	26.0%	17.4%
		(2.25)	(2.88)	(1.29)	(2.65)	(2.29)
Idaho	100	14.2%	41.0%	3.2%	17.8%	23.8%
		(1.98)	(2.79)	(0.99)	(2.17)	(2.42)
Montana	91	14.1%	35.4%	4.7%	19.5%	26.3%
		(1.91)	(2.63)	(1.17)	(2.17)	(2.42)
Nevada	103	25.4%	33.5%	3.0%	11.1%	27.0%
		(2.87)	(3.11)	(1.13)	(2.07)	(2.92)
New Mexico	150	13.1%	29.5%	7.9%	19.1%	30.4%
		(1.97)	(2.66)	(1.57)	(2.29)	(2.68)
Utah	201	15.1%	46.5%	7.0%	13.3%	18.1%
		(1.91)	(2.66)	(1.36)	(1.81)	(2.06)
Wyoming	53	13.8%	41.3%	6.1%	22.9%	15.9%
		(2.24)	(3.21)	(1.56)	(2.74)	(2.38)
Pacific	**3,848**	**19.8%**	**30.1%**	**7.6%**	**16.9%**	**25.7%**
		(0.79)	**(0.90)**	**(0.52)**	**(0.74)**	**(0.86)**
Alaska	44	19.5%	29.8%	7.1%	12.0%	31.7%
		(2.40)	(2.77)	(1.55)	(1.97)	(2.82)
California	2,859	17.9%	29.5%	8.0%	16.8%	27.8%
		(0.89)	(1.06)	(0.63)	(0.87)	(1.04)
Hawaii	85	40.4%	27.5%	4.9%	15.6%	11.7%
		(3.50)	(3.19)	(1.54)	(2.59)	(2.29)
Oregon	335	22.1%	35.1%	6.2%	15.0%	21.6%
		(2.46)	(2.83)	(1.43)	(2.12)	(2.44)
Washington	524	25.2%	30.1%	7.1%	19.2%	18.4%
		(2.47)	(2.61)	(1.47)	(2.25)	(2.21)

Source: Three-year merged March CPS: 1991, 1992, and 1993.
Note: See table notes at end of Section B.

Table B3
Health Insurance Coverage of Workers Ages 18-64, 1990-92:
Percentage with Own-Employer Group Insurance by Firm Size[1,8]
(Persons in thousands)

	Total		Firm Size < 25		Firm Size 25-99		Firm Size 100+	
	Number	Percent w/ Own-EGI[7]	Number	Percent w/ Own-EGI[7]	Number	Percent w/ Own-EGI[7]	Number	Percent w/ Own-EGI[7]
United States	123,962	54.1% (0.16)	36,070	26.8% (0.26)	16,474	52.3% (0.43)	71,418	68.2% (0.19)
New England	6,860	56.8% (0.53)	1,968	30.9% (0.92)	934	56.4% (1.43)	3,958	69.8% (0.64)
Connecticut	1,702	60.5% (1.45)	465	32.5% (2.65)	216	60.1% (4.07)	1,021	73.3% (1.69)
Maine	651	50.7% (1.33)	228	28.4% (2.03)	87	51.4% (3.63)	337	65.6% (1.76)
Massachusetts	3,061	56.9% (0.70)	808	32.1% (1.28)	412	54.6% (1.91)	1,841	68.2% (0.85)
New Hampshire	626	54.3% (1.42)	194	25.0% (2.22)	92	58.5% (3.67)	340	69.9% (1.77)
Rhode Island	502	58.2% (1.45)	149	33.3% (2.54)	80	55.4% (3.67)	273	72.7% (1.78)
Vermont	317	52.2% (1.40)	124	27.6% (2.00)	47	61.8% (3.54)	147	69.9% (1.89)
Middle Atlantic	18,132	58.1% (0.36)	4,910	32.0% (0.66)	2,585	56.3% (0.97)	10,638	70.6% (0.44)
New Jersey	3,947	60.8% (0.68)	1,038	33.6% (1.28)	580	59.0% (1.78)	2,328	73.3% (0.80)
New York	8,389	56.2% (0.54)	2,317	29.8% (0.95)	1,184	53.4% (1.45)	4,888	69.4% (0.66)
Pennsylvania	5,797	59.0% (0.68)	1,555	34.3% (1.27)	821	58.5% (1.82)	3,422	70.4% (0.83)
South Atlantic	21,925	53.7% (0.39)	6,305	25.2% (0.63)	2,644	51.8% (1.11)	12,976	68.0% (0.47)
Delaware	382	55.3% (1.36)	97	30.9% (2.51)	46	49.6% (3.96)	239	66.3% (1.63)
District of Columbia	274	55.1% (1.61)	64	27.7% (2.99)	34	54.7% (4.53)	175	65.2% (1.92)
Florida	6,345	49.2% (0.66)	2,069	23.7% (0.99)	809	46.8% (1.86)	3,467	65.0% (0.86)
Georgia	3,191	53.7% (1.31)	913	24.3% (2.11)	382	56.0% (3.78)	1,896	67.5% (1.60)
Maryland	2,547	59.0% (1.34)	671	28.5% (2.39)	293	61.1% (3.91)	1,582	71.5% (1.56)
North Carolina	3,370	57.4% (0.66)	925	26.6% (1.13)	389	53.9% (1.97)	2,056	72.0% (0.77)
South Carolina	1,749	55.2% (1.19)	456	25.4% (2.04)	195	49.1% (3.59)	1,097	68.8% (1.40)
Virginia	3,317	54.0% (1.14)	897	24.8% (1.89)	399	50.5% (3.29)	2,021	67.7% (1.37)
West Virginia	750	51.6% (1.47)	212	24.7% (2.38)	97	51.7% (4.08)	441	64.4% (1.83)
East South Central	7,196	52.3% (0.69)	2,075	23.7% (1.09)	882	49.4% (1.96)	4,238	66.9% (0.84)
Alabama	1,915	53.4% (1.36)	592	27.6% (2.20)	210	51.0% (4.13)	1,113	67.6% (1.68)
Kentucky	1,721	53.1% (1.38)	513	24.1% (2.17)	227	49.2% (3.81)	981	69.1% (1.69)
Mississippi	1,161	46.9% (1.33)	346	20.4% (1.96)	153	40.1% (3.59)	662	62.4% (1.71)
Tennessee	2,399	53.5% (1.28)	624	21.5% (2.07)	293	53.2% (3.67)	1,482	67.0% (1.54)
West South Central	12,891	48.6% (0.53)	4,067	21.3% (0.77)	1,609	44.9% (1.49)	7,215	64.8% (0.68)
Arkansas	1,115	46.7% (1.35)	362	18.1% (1.83)	146	50.3% (3.74)	607	62.9% (1.78)
Louisiana	1,852	44.3% (1.46)	587	19.4% (2.07)	233	42.0% (4.10)	1,033	59.0% (1.94)
Oklahoma	1,499	44.7% (1.34)	498	16.5% (1.74)	206	44.4% (3.62)	796	62.4% (1.79)
Texas	8,423	50.5% (0.68)	2,621	23.1% (1.03)	1,024	44.9% (1.95)	4,778	66.7% (0.85)

Health Insurance Coverage of Workers Ages 18-64, 1990-92: Percentage with Own-Employer Group Insurance by Firm Size[1,8]

(Persons in thousands)

	Total		Firm Size < 25		Firm Size 25-99		Firm Size 100+	
	Number	Percent w/ Own-EGI[7]	Number	Percent w/ Own-EGI[7]	Number	Percent w/ Own-EGI[7]	Number	Percent w/ Own-EGI[7]
East North Central	21,245	57.2% (0.38)	5,533	29.5% (0.68)	2,880	55.8% (1.03)	12,833	69.5% (0.45)
Illinois	5,885	58.1% (0.69)	1,515	28.8% (1.25)	797	55.0% (1.89)	3,574	71.2% (0.81)
Indiana	2,842	56.3% (1.35)	743	27.3% (2.38)	386	59.7% (3.63)	1,713	68.2% (1.64)
Michigan	4,520	56.8% (0.70)	1,217	29.1% (1.24)	564	56.6% (1.99)	2,740	69.2% (0.84)
Ohio	5,408	57.6% (0.68)	1,349	30.0% (1.27)	729	55.9% (1.87)	3,330	69.2% (0.81)
Wisconsin	2,589	55.8% (1.21)	710	33.0% (2.18)	403	52.1% (3.08)	1,476	67.9% (1.50)
West North Central	9,354	51.2% (0.59)	2,919	26.1% (0.92)	1,306	49.1% (1.57)	5,130	66.1% (0.75)
Iowa	1,496	49.0% (1.26)	504	23.1% (1.82)	206	49.9% (3.38)	785	65.4% (1.65)
Kansas	1,278	51.0% (1.27)	401	26.3% (1.99)	166	48.9% (3.52)	711	65.5% (1.61)
Minnesota	2,438	51.6% (1.29)	745	26.8% (2.07)	364	48.6% (3.34)	1,329	66.3% (1.65)
Missouri	2,670	54.8% (1.35)	729	29.6% (2.36)	370	47.7% (3.62)	1,571	68.2% (1.64)
Nebraska	827	48.8% (1.24)	283	24.9% (1.83)	109	52.2% (3.41)	434	63.5% (1.65)
North Dakota	307	41.1% (1.25)	128	19.1% (1.55)	43	52.7% (3.41)	137	57.9% (1.88)
South Dakota	338	45.2% (1.21)	128	21.9% (1.63)	48	51.4% (3.22)	163	61.7% (1.70)
Mountain	6,754	51.0% (0.57)	2,060	24.6% (0.90)	826	47.7% (1.64)	3,868	65.8% (0.72)
Arizona	1,717	52.2% (1.38)	516	25.7% (2.21)	181	43.7% (4.23)	1,019	67.2% (1.69)
Colorado	1,736	53.4% (1.37)	480	28.3% (2.36)	227	53.7% (3.80)	1,030	65.0% (1.71)
Idaho	507	48.3% (1.26)	183	23.2% (1.77)	64	47.2% (3.55)	260	66.3% (1.67)
Montana	402	44.7% (1.30)	172	21.7% (1.64)	56	52.5% (3.48)	174	64.9% (1.89)
Nevada	651	57.4% (1.30)	172	28.0% (2.29)	80	48.9% (3.74)	399	71.8% (1.51)
New Mexico	703	43.7% (1.34)	239	19.4% (1.82)	92	39.2% (3.63)	372	60.5% (1.81)
Utah	801	50.8% (1.34)	206	19.3% (2.08)	99	46.3% (3.79)	496	64.8% (1.62)
Wyoming	237	46.2% (1.53)	92	26.2% (2.17)	26	46.2% (4.63)	119	61.7% (2.11)
Pacific	19,604	53.0% (0.44)	6,233	26.5% (0.68)	2,809	51.9% (1.15)	10,562	69.0% (0.55)
Alaska	259	50.2% (1.25)	94	24.9% (1.80)	31	45.6% (3.62)	135	68.9% (1.60)
California	14,746	51.4% (0.51)	4,684	24.7% (0.79)	2,150	49.4% (1.34)	7,912	67.9% (0.65)
Hawaii	545	66.7% (1.33)	149	47.6% (2.70)	80	71.9% (3.32)	316	74.4% (1.62)
Oregon	1,513	55.7% (1.39)	519	30.9% (2.20)	193	57.1% (3.87)	800	71.4% (1.73)
Washington	2,542	58.0% (1.28)	787	30.2% (2.13)	355	60.9% (3.38)	1,400	72.9% (1.55)

Source: Three-year merged March CPS: 1991, 1992, and 1993.
Note: See table notes at end of Section B.

Table B4
Health Insurance Coverage of Workers Ages 18-64, 1990-92:
Percentage Uninsured by Firm Size[1,8]
(Persons in thousands)

	Total		Firm Size < 25		Firm Size 25-99		Firm Size 100+	
	Number	Percent Uninsured[5]	Number	Percent Uninsured[5]	Number	Percent Uninsured[5]	Number	Percent Uninsured[5]
United States	123,962	16.7% (0.12)	36,070	27.4% (0.26)	16,474	20.0% (0.35)	71,418	10.6% (0.13)
New England	6,860	11.4% (0.34)	1,968	19.3% (0.78)	934	13.0% (0.97)	3,958	7.1% (0.36)
Connecticut	1,702	9.0% (0.85)	465	17.0% (2.13)	216	9.5% (2.44)	1,021	5.3% (0.85)
Maine	651	13.8% (0.91)	228	19.6% (1.78)	87	15.5% (2.63)	337	9.3% (1.07)
Massachusetts	3,061	11.6% (0.45)	808	19.0% (1.08)	412	14.2% (1.34)	1,841	7.7% (0.48)
New Hampshire	626	13.0% (0.96)	194	24.9% (2.22)	92	10.7% (2.30)	340	6.9% (0.98)
Rhode Island	502	12.4% (0.97)	149	19.6% (2.14)	80	17.7% (2.81)	273	7.0% (1.02)
Vermont	317	12.2% (0.92)	124	19.8% (1.78)	47	9.3% (2.11)	147	6.8% (1.04)
Middle Atlantic	18,132	13.7% (0.25)	4,910	23.4% (0.60)	2,585	16.3% (0.72)	10,638	8.5% (0.27)
New Jersey	3,947	13.2% (0.47)	1,038	24.1% (1.16)	580	15.4% (1.30)	2,328	7.8% (0.48)
New York	8,389	15.7% (0.40)	2,317	25.9% (0.91)	1,184	20.1% (1.16)	4,888	9.9% (0.43)
Pennsylvania	5,797	11.0% (0.43)	1,555	19.3% (1.06)	821	11.6% (1.18)	3,422	7.1% (0.47)
South Atlantic	21,925	19.3% (0.31)	6,305	31.6% (0.67)	2,644	23.4% (0.94)	12,976	12.5% (0.33)
Delaware	382	16.2% (1.01)	97	24.0% (2.32)	46	22.1% (3.28)	239	12.0% (1.12)
District of Columbia	274	23.6% (1.37)	64	36.2% (3.21)	34	25.3% (3.96)	175	18.6% (1.57)
Florida	6,345	24.4% (0.57)	2,069	37.5% (1.13)	809	31.5% (1.73)	3,467	14.8% (0.64)
Georgia	3,191	19.7% (1.05)	913	32.5% (2.30)	382	20.8% (3.09)	1,896	13.4% (1.16)
Maryland	2,547	13.3% (0.92)	671	22.6% (2.22)	293	12.3% (2.64)	1,582	9.5% (1.01)
North Carolina	3,370	16.4% (0.50)	925	26.9% (1.14)	389	21.4% (1.62)	2,056	10.7% (0.53)
South Carolina	1,749	18.8% (0.94)	456	30.6% (2.16)	195	24.4% (3.08)	1,097	12.9% (1.01)
Virginia	3,317	18.0% (0.88)	897	30.4% (2.02)	399	19.7% (2.62)	2,021	12.2% (0.96)
West Virginia	750	15.4% (1.06)	212	28.3% (2.49)	97	19.5% (3.24)	441	8.2% (1.05)
East South Central	7,196	18.1% (0.53)	2,075	31.6% (1.19)	882	22.7% (1.64)	4,238	10.5% (0.55)
Alabama	1,915	18.7% (1.06)	592	31.1% (2.27)	210	22.6% (3.45)	1,113	11.3% (1.13)
Kentucky	1,721	14.7% (0.98)	513	27.4% (2.26)	227	20.1% (3.05)	981	6.9% (0.93)
Mississippi	1,161	23.8% (1.13)	346	39.0% (2.37)	153	32.0% (3.42)	662	13.9% (1.22)
Tennessee	2,399	17.3% (0.97)	624	31.5% (2.35)	293	19.9% (2.94)	1,482	10.8% (1.02)
West South Central	12,891	23.7% (0.45)	4,067	36.3% (0.91)	1,609	28.2% (1.35)	7,215	15.6% (0.51)
Arkansas	1,115	21.1% (1.11)	362	32.7% (2.23)	146	22.1% (3.10)	607	13.9% (1.27)
Louisiana	1,852	23.5% (1.25)	587	34.6% (2.49)	233	29.6% (3.79)	1,033	15.9% (1.44)
Oklahoma	1,499	23.2% (1.14)	498	36.6% (2.26)	206	23.7% (3.10)	796	14.7% (1.31)
Texas	8,423	24.2% (0.58)	2,621	37.2% (1.18)	1,024	29.6% (1.79)	4,778	15.9% (0.66)

Health Insurance Coverage of Workers Ages 18-64, 1990-92:
Percentage Uninsured by Firm Size[1,8]

(Persons in thousands)

	Total		Firm Size < 25		Firm Size 25-99		Firm Size 100+	
	Number	Percent Uninsured[5]	Number	Percent Uninsured[5]	Number	Percent Uninsured[5]	Number	Percent Uninsured[5]
East North Central	**21,245**	**12.6%** **(0.25)**	**5,533**	**21.0%** **(0.61)**	**2,880**	**15.4%** **(0.75)**	**12,833**	**8.3%** **(0.27)**
Illinois	5,885	13.9% (0.48)	1,515	22.8% (1.16)	797	16.7% (1.42)	3,574	9.4% (0.53)
Indiana	2,842	13.8% (0.94)	743	22.3% (2.22)	386	15.7% (2.69)	1,713	9.7% (1.04)
Michigan	4,520	12.0% (0.46)	1,217	20.3% (1.10)	564	14.5% (1.41)	2,740	7.7% (0.49)
Ohio	5,408	12.2% (0.45)	1,349	21.8% (1.14)	729	14.4% (1.32)	3,330	7.9% (0.47)
Wisconsin	2,589	10.4% (0.74)	710	15.7% (1.69)	403	15.7% (2.24)	1,476	6.4% (0.79)
West North Central	**9,354**	**13.0%** **(0.40)**	**2,919**	**18.9%** **(0.82)**	**1,306**	**15.1%** **(1.12)**	**5,130**	**9.1%** **(0.46)**
Iowa	1,496	11.8% (0.81)	504	16.6% (1.61)	206	14.7% (2.39)	785	8.0% (0.94)
Kansas	1,278	12.8% (0.85)	401	18.2% (1.74)	166	15.9% (2.57)	711	9.0% (0.97)
Minnesota	2,438	13.5% (0.88)	745	20.6% (1.89)	364	15.5% (2.42)	1,329	9.0% (1.00)
Missouri	2,670	14.0% (0.94)	729	21.1% (2.11)	370	16.3% (2.68)	1,571	10.1% (1.06)
Nebraska	827	10.2% (0.75)	283	14.9% (1.51)	109	10.6% (2.10)	434	7.0% (0.87)
North Dakota	307	11.4% (0.81)	128	14.8% (1.40)	43	9.8% (2.03)	137	8.7% (1.07)
South Dakota	338	16.4% (0.90)	128	21.3% (1.61)	48	16.2% (2.38)	163	12.6% (1.16)
Mountain	**6,754**	**17.9%** **(0.44)**	**2,060**	**29.0%** **(0.94)**	**826**	**21.6%** **(1.35)**	**3,868**	**11.2%** **(0.48)**
Arizona	1,717	19.3% (1.09)	516	30.3% (2.32)	181	30.4% (3.92)	1,019	11.7% (1.16)
Colorado	1,736	14.1% (0.96)	480	23.3% (2.22)	227	15.9% (2.78)	1,030	9.5% (1.05)
Idaho	507	19.6% (1.00)	183	28.1% (1.89)	64	26.5% (3.13)	260	11.9% (1.14)
Montana	402	18.5% (1.01)	172	28.2% (1.79)	56	14.5% (2.45)	174	10.4% (1.21)
Nevada	651	20.8% (1.06)	172	34.9% (2.43)	80	25.9% (3.27)	399	13.7% (1.15)
New Mexico	703	24.8% (1.16)	239	37.8% (2.24)	92	27.6% (3.32)	372	15.8% (1.35)
Utah	801	14.5% (0.94)	206	29.4% (2.40)	99	11.8% (2.45)	496	8.8% (0.96)
Wyoming	237	14.5% (1.08)	92	21.1% (2.01)	26	15.8% (3.39)	119	9.1% (1.25)
Pacific	**19,604**	**19.1%** **(0.34)**	**6,233**	**30.6%** **(0.71)**	**2,809**	**23.3%** **(0.98)**	**10,562**	**11.2%** **(0.38)**
Alaska	259	23.0% (1.05)	94	36.0% (1.99)	31	24.9% (3.15)	135	13.5% (1.19)
California	14,746	20.8% (0.42)	4,684	32.9% (0.86)	2,150	25.6% (1.17)	7,912	12.3% (0.46)
Hawaii	545	8.2% (0.78)	149	15.3% (1.94)	80	7.3% (1.92)	316	5.2% (0.82)
Oregon	1,513	16.1% (1.03)	519	25.4% (2.08)	193	19.4% (3.09)	800	9.2% (1.11)
Washington	2,542	13.3% (0.88)	787	22.3% (1.93)	355	15.1% (2.48)	1,400	7.7% (0.93)

Source: Three-year merged March CPS: 1991, 1992, and 1993.
Note: See table notes at end of Section B.

Table B5
Health Insurance Coverage of Workers Ages 18-64, 1990-92:
Percentage with Own-Employer Group Insurance by Sector[1,8]
(Persons in thousands)

	Total		Private-Sector		Public-Sector		Self-Employed[9]	
	Number	Percent w/ Own-EGI[7]	Number	Percent w/ Own-EGI[7]	Number	Percent w/ Own-EGI[7]	Number	Percent w/ Own-EGI[7]
United States	123,962	54.1% (0.16)	95,569	54.4% (0.18)	19,120	71.2% (0.36)	9,273	15.8% (0.42)
New England	6,860	56.8% (0.53)	5,463	57.8% (0.59)	902	71.6% (1.32)	495	19.4% (1.57)
Connecticut	1,702	60.5% (1.45)	1,382	60.8% (1.60)	212	79.5% (3.39)	---	---
Maine	651	50.7% (1.33)	475	51.8% (1.55)	99	68.7% (3.17)	78	20.9% (3.13)
Massachusetts	3,061	56.9% (0.70)	2,455	57.8% (0.78)	418	68.3% (1.78)	188	19.6% (2.26)
New Hampshire	626	54.3% (1.42)	506	56.9% (1.57)	66	67.2% (4.14)	55	14.9% (3.43)
Rhode Island	502	58.2% (1.45)	410	57.4% (1.61)	60	80.6% (3.35)	---	---
Vermont	317	52.2% (1.40)	236	54.5% (1.62)	48	65.9% (3.42)	34	16.7% (3.20)
Middle Atlantic	18,132	58.1% (0.36)	14,270	57.7% (0.41)	2,742	75.5% (0.82)	1,121	20.3% (1.19)
New Jersey	3,947	60.8% (0.68)	3,153	60.1% (0.76)	591	79.0% (1.46)	202	17.8% (2.34)
New York	8,389	56.2% (0.54)	6,365	55.1% (0.62)	1,457	74.9% (1.13)	567	20.9% (1.70)
Pennsylvania	5,797	59.0% (0.68)	4,752	59.7% (0.75)	694	73.9% (1.76)	351	20.6% (2.28)
South Atlantic	21,925	53.7% (0.39)	16,837	52.9% (0.44)	3,616	73.6% (0.84)	1,472	13.9% (1.03)
Delaware	382	55.3% (1.36)	318	54.7% (1.49)	45	71.9% (3.58)	---	---
District of Columbia	274	55.1% (1.61)	179	52.4% (1.99)	78	68.5% (2.82)	---	---
Florida	6,345	49.2% (0.66)	4,933	47.4% (0.75)	961	76.1% (1.45)	451	11.4% (1.58)
Georgia	3,191	53.7% (1.31)	2,524	54.1% (1.48)	461	69.1% (3.20)	206	15.6% (3.76)
Maryland	2,547	59.0% (1.34)	1,797	58.6% (1.60)	566	73.4% (2.55)	185	18.3% (3.91)
North Carolina	3,370	57.4% (0.66)	2,633	58.1% (0.75)	492	75.8% (1.51)	245	13.4% (1.70)
South Carolina	1,749	55.2% (1.19)	1,377	54.1% (1.35)	271	78.3% (2.51)	102	9.5% (2.92)
Virginia	3,317	54.0% (1.14)	2,504	52.8% (1.31)	605	72.3% (2.39)	208	15.1% (3.26)
West Virginia	750	51.6% (1.47)	572	51.2% (1.68)	139	64.3% (3.26)	---	---
East South Central	7,196	52.3% (0.69)	5,529	53.1% (0.78)	1,109	69.1% (1.61)	558	11.6% (1.57)
Alabama	1,915	53.4% (1.36)	1,461	53.6% (1.56)	286	75.3% (3.05)	169	14.5% (3.24)
Kentucky	1,721	53.1% (1.38)	1,307	53.1% (1.58)	279	71.8% (3.09)	135	14.2% (3.44)
Mississippi	1,161	46.9% (1.33)	878	48.0% (1.53)	198	57.7% (3.18)	85	10.9% (3.05)
Tennessee	2,399	53.5% (1.28)	1,883	55.0% (1.45)	346	68.3% (3.15)	169	6.9% (2.45)
West South Central	12,891	48.6% (0.53)	9,764	48.0% (0.61)	2,108	68.0% (1.22)	1,019	13.7% (1.30)
Arkansas	1,115	46.7% (1.35)	827	48.1% (1.57)	178	61.8% (3.30)	111	12.6% (2.85)
Louisiana	1,852	44.3% (1.46)	1,385	43.8% (1.69)	330	58.3% (3.44)	---	---
Oklahoma	1,499	44.7% (1.34)	1,088	46.2% (1.58)	253	59.5% (3.23)	158	11.2% (2.63)
Texas	8,423	50.5% (0.68)	6,465	49.3% (0.78)	1,346	72.8% (1.52)	612	13.9% (1.75)

Table B5 (continued)

Health Insurance Coverage of Workers Ages 18-64, 1990-92:
Percentage with Own-Employer Group Insurance by Sector[1,8]

(Persons in thousands)

	Total		Private-Sector		Public-Sector		Self-Employed[9]	
	Number	Percent w/ Own-EGI[7]	Number	Percent w/ Own-EGI[7]	Number	Percent w/ Own-EGI[7]	Number	Percent w/ Own-EGI[7]
East North Central	21,245	57.2% (0.38)	16,940	58.0% (0.42)	2,975	69.7% (0.94)	1,330	18.4% (1.18)
Illinois	5,885	58.1% (0.69)	4,707	59.1% (0.77)	795	71.9% (1.71)	383	17.1% (2.07)
Indiana	2,842	56.3% (1.35)	2,259	57.3% (1.51)	374	72.6% (3.35)	209	16.6% (3.74)
Michigan	4,520	56.8% (0.70)	3,628	57.7% (0.78)	632	67.4% (1.78)	261	18.8% (2.31)
Ohio	5,408	57.6% (0.68)	4,341	58.1% (0.76)	776	69.7% (1.68)	291	18.8% (2.33)
Wisconsin	2,589	55.8% (1.21)	2,005	57.0% (1.37)	398	66.2% (2.93)	187	21.9% (3.74)
West North Central	9,354	51.2% (0.59)	7,001	53.6% (0.68)	1,414	66.0% (1.43)	939	11.5% (1.18)
Iowa	1,496	49.0% (1.26)	1,092	52.2% (1.47)	228	65.7% (3.06)	176	7.9% (1.97)
Kansas	1,278	51.0% (1.27)	942	54.6% (1.47)	197	61.5% (3.14)	138	12.1% (2.52)
Minnesota	2,438	51.6% (1.29)	1,854	54.6% (1.48)	348	63.6% (3.29)	236	10.9% (2.58)
Missouri	2,670	54.8% (1.35)	2,099	54.8% (1.52)	378	74.2% (3.14)	193	17.9% (3.85)
Nebraska	827	48.8% (1.24)	587	52.2% (1.47)	139	62.7% (2.93)	101	9.7% (2.10)
North Dakota	307	41.1% (1.25)	201	43.8% (1.56)	60	60.2% (2.81)	46	4.3% (1.33)
South Dakota	338	45.2% (1.21)	226	49.0% (1.48)	65	58.0% (2.74)	48	10.1% (1.94)
Mountain	6,754	51.0% (0.57)	4,977	51.5% (0.67)	1,184	66.9% (1.29)	592	14.8% (1.38)
Arizona	1,717	52.2% (1.38)	1,324	52.4% (1.58)	247	71.9% (3.29)	146	17.5% (3.61)
Colorado	1,736	53.4% (1.37)	1,308	55.0% (1.58)	289	64.2% (3.24)	139	15.9% (3.55)
Idaho	507	48.3% (1.26)	361	48.5% (1.49)	91	65.4% (2.84)	55	18.5% (2.97)
Montana	402	44.7% (1.30)	251	45.3% (1.64)	95	64.1% (2.58)	57	10.3% (2.10)
Nevada	651	57.4% (1.30)	519	57.5% (1.45)	87	78.5% (2.94)	45	15.6% (3.61)
New Mexico	703	43.7% (1.34)	461	42.4% (1.64)	167	62.0% (2.68)	75	11.6% (2.64)
Utah	801	50.8% (1.34)	596	50.1% (1.55)	153	67.3% (2.86)	52	9.9% (3.15)
Wyoming	237	46.2% (1.53)	158	45.2% (1.87)	56	61.9% (3.07)	23	14.6% (3.50)
Pacific	19,604	53.0% (0.44)	14,788	53.2% (0.50)	3,069	73.0% (0.98)	1,747	16.8% (1.09)
Alaska	259	50.2% (1.25)	163	49.4% (1.57)	68	66.9% (2.29)	27	14.0% (2.67)
California	14,746	51.4% (0.51)	11,292	51.4% (0.59)	2,138	73.3% (1.19)	1,315	16.1% (1.26)
Hawaii	545	66.7% (1.33)	392	69.5% (1.53)	116	69.9% (2.81)	---	---
Oregon	1,513	55.7% (1.39)	1,117	56.2% (1.61)	251	73.7% (3.02)	145	20.9% (3.67)
Washington	2,542	58.0% (1.28)	1,823	59.0% (1.50)	496	73.0% (2.60)	223	16.7% (3.26)

Source: Three-year merged March CPS: 1991, 1992, and 1993.
Note: See table notes at end of Section B.

Table B6

Health Insurance Coverage of Workers Ages 18-64, 1990-92:
Percentage Uninsured by Sector[1,8]

(Persons in thousands)

	Total Number	Total Percent Uninsured[5]	Private-Sector Number	Private-Sector Percent Uninsured[5]	Public-Sector Number	Public-Sector Percent Uninsured[5]	Self-Employed[9] Number	Self-Employed[9] Percent Uninsured[5]
United States	123,962	16.7% (0.12)	95,569	17.8% (0.14)	19,120	7.1% (0.21)	9,273	25.7% (0.51)
New England	6,860	11.4% (0.34)	5,463	11.7% (0.38)	902	5.0% (0.64)	495	19.8% (1.58)
Connecticut	1,702	9.0% (0.85)	1,382	9.5% (0.96)	212	3.2% (1.47)	---	---
Maine	651	13.8% (0.91)	475	14.4% (1.09)	99	5.3% (1.53)	78	20.3% (3.10)
Massachusetts	3,061	11.6% (0.45)	2,455	11.8% (0.51)	418	6.5% (0.94)	188	20.2% (2.28)
New Hampshire	626	13.0% (0.96)	506	12.5% (1.05)	66	4.0% (1.73)	55	28.5% (4.35)
Rhode Island	502	12.4% (0.97)	410	13.1% (1.10)	60	3.3% (1.51)	---	---
Vermont	317	12.2% (0.92)	236	12.9% (1.09)	48	2.3% (1.08)	34	21.4% (3.53)
Middle Atlantic	18,132	13.7% (0.25)	14,270	14.4% (0.29)	2,742	6.0% (0.45)	1,121	23.8% (1.26)
New Jersey	3,947	13.2% (0.47)	3,153	13.6% (0.53)	591	5.3% (0.80)	202	29.8% (2.80)
New York	8,389	15.7% (0.40)	6,365	17.0% (0.47)	1,457	6.9% (0.66)	567	24.0% (1.79)
Pennsylvania	5,797	11.0% (0.43)	4,752	11.2% (0.48)	694	4.9% (0.86)	351	20.1% (2.26)
South Atlantic	21,925	19.3% (0.31)	16,837	20.8% (0.36)	3,616	7.6% (0.51)	1,472	31.2% (1.38)
Delaware	382	16.2% (1.01)	318	16.8% (1.12)	45	8.3% (2.20)	---	---
District of Columbia	274	23.6% (1.37)	179	26.4% (1.76)	78	16.0% (2.23)	---	---
Florida	6,345	24.4% (0.57)	4,933	26.3% (0.66)	961	7.4% (0.89)	451	39.5% (2.43)
Georgia	3,191	19.7% (1.05)	2,524	20.8% (1.20)	461	9.3% (2.01)	206	30.3% (4.76)
Maryland	2,547	13.3% (0.92)	1,797	13.9% (1.12)	566	7.4% (1.52)	185	25.2% (4.39)
North Carolina	3,370	16.4% (0.50)	2,633	17.3% (0.57)	492	7.0% (0.90)	245	25.9% (2.18)
South Carolina	1,749	18.8% (0.94)	1,377	19.8% (1.08)	271	9.9% (1.82)	102	28.1% (4.47)
Virginia	3,317	18.0% (0.88)	2,504	20.2% (1.05)	605	5.9% (1.25)	208	27.7% (4.08)
West Virginia	750	15.4% (1.06)	572	16.7% (1.25)	139	5.4% (1.54)	---	---
East South Central	7,196	18.1% (0.53)	5,529	19.6% (0.62)	1,109	6.0% (0.83)	558	27.3% (2.19)
Alabama	1,915	18.7% (1.06)	1,461	20.4% (1.26)	286	3.2% (1.25)	169	29.5% (4.20)
Kentucky	1,721	14.7% (0.98)	1,307	16.3% (1.17)	279	3.7% (1.30)	135	22.4% (4.11)
Mississippi	1,161	23.8% (1.13)	878	25.5% (1.33)	198	12.3% (2.11)	85	32.5% (4.60)
Tennessee	2,399	17.3% (0.97)	1,883	18.5% (1.13)	346	6.5% (1.67)	169	26.4% (4.28)
West South Central	12,891	23.7% (0.45)	9,764	25.5% (0.53)	2,108	10.8% (0.81)	1,019	33.5% (1.78)
Arkansas	1,115	21.1% (1.11)	827	22.1% (1.31)	178	12.6% (2.26)	111	26.7% (3.81)
Louisiana	1,852	23.5% (1.25)	1,385	25.6% (1.49)	330	12.4% (2.30)	---	---
Oklahoma	1,499	23.2% (1.14)	1,088	23.5% (1.34)	253	13.4% (2.24)	158	36.9% (4.01)
Texas	8,423	24.2% (0.58)	6,465	26.2% (0.68)	1,346	9.6% (1.01)	612	34.9% (2.41)

Table B6 (continued)
Health Insurance Coverage of Workers Ages 18-64, 1990-92:
Percentage Uninsured by Sector[1,8]

(Persons in thousands)

	Total		Private-Sector		Public-Sector		Self-Employed[9]	
	Number	Percent Uninsured[5]	Private Number	Percent Uninsured[5]	Public Number	Percent Uninsured[5]	Number	Percent Uninsured[5]
East North Central	**21,245**	**12.6%** (0.25)	**16,940**	**13.2%** (0.29)	**2,975**	**6.2%** (0.49)	**1,330**	**19.0%** (1.20)
Illinois	5,885	13.9% (0.48)	4,707	14.6% (0.55)	795	6.5% (0.94)	383	20.1% (2.20)
Indiana	2,842	13.8% (0.94)	2,259	15.2% (1.10)	374	3.3% (1.34)	209	17.8% (3.84)
Michigan	4,520	12.0% (0.46)	3,628	12.2% (0.52)	632	6.7% (0.95)	261	20.8% (2.39)
Ohio	5,408	12.2% (0.45)	4,341	12.8% (0.51)	776	6.4% (0.89)	291	19.5% (2.36)
Wisconsin	2,589	10.4% (0.74)	2,005	10.7% (0.85)	398	6.8% (1.56)	187	15.1% (3.24)
West North Central	**9,354**	**13.0%** (0.40)	**7,001**	**13.9%** (0.47)	**1,414**	**6.1%** (0.73)	**939**	**16.7%** (1.38)
Iowa	1,496	11.8% (0.81)	1,092	12.5% (0.97)	228	5.5% (1.47)	176	16.1% (2.69)
Kansas	1,278	12.8% (0.85)	942	13.0% (0.99)	197	6.8% (1.62)	138	20.0% (3.09)
Minnesota	2,438	13.5% (0.88)	1,854	14.6% (1.04)	348	6.7% (1.71)	236	15.5% (3.01)
Missouri	2,670	14.0% (0.94)	2,099	15.1% (1.09)	378	5.0% (1.57)	193	19.5% (3.98)
Nebraska	827	10.2% (0.75)	587	10.9% (0.92)	139	4.2% (1.21)	101	13.9% (2.45)
North Dakota	307	11.4% (0.81)	201	12.9% (1.05)	60	8.2% (1.57)	46	9.2% (1.89)
South Dakota	338	16.4% (0.90)	226	17.6% (1.13)	65	12.1% (1.81)	48	16.3% (2.39)
Mountain	**6,754**	**17.9%** (0.44)	**4,977**	**19.3%** (0.53)	**1,184**	**7.6%** (0.73)	**592**	**27.1%** (1.73)
Arizona	1,717	19.3% (1.09)	1,324	20.9% (1.28)	247	5.4% (1.65)	146	27.5% (4.24)
Colorado	1,736	14.1% (0.96)	1,308	14.9% (1.13)	289	6.6% (1.68)	139	22.4% (4.05)
Idaho	507	19.6% (1.00)	361	22.1% (1.24)	91	9.5% (1.75)	55	19.9% (3.06)
Montana	402	18.5% (1.01)	251	21.3% (1.35)	95	9.9% (1.61)	57	20.8% (2.81)
Nevada	651	20.8% (1.06)	519	21.2% (1.20)	87	8.7% (2.02)	45	39.2% (4.86)
New Mexico	703	24.8% (1.16)	461	26.9% (1.47)	167	11.4% (1.76)	75	41.6% (4.05)
Utah	801	14.5% (0.94)	596	15.9% (1.13)	153	5.7% (1.42)	52	23.9% (4.49)
Wyoming	237	14.5% (1.08)	158	16.3% (1.39)	56	6.4% (1.55)	23	21.7% (4.09)
Pacific	**19,604**	**19.1%** (0.34)	**14,788**	**20.5%** (0.41)	**3,069**	**7.1%** (0.57)	**1,747**	**28.5%** (1.32)
Alaska	259	23.0% (1.05)	163	23.5% (1.33)	68	14.2% (1.70)	27	42.4% (3.80)
California	14,746	20.8% (0.42)	11,292	22.4% (0.49)	2,138	6.6% (0.67)	1,315	30.2% (1.58)
Hawaii	545	8.2% (0.78)	392	8.0% (0.91)	116	4.8% (1.31)	---	---
Oregon	1,513	16.1% (1.03)	1,117	17.2% (1.23)	251	6.9% (1.73)	145	23.2% (3.81)
Washington	2,542	13.3% (0.88)	1,823	13.5% (1.04)	496	8.9% (1.67)	223	21.2% (3.57)

Source: Three-year merged March CPS: 1991, 1992, and 1993.
Note: See table notes at end of Section B.

Table B7
Health Insurance Coverage of Workers Ages 18-64, 1990-92:
Private-Sector Workers with Own-Employer Group Insurance by Industry[1,8]
(Persons in thousands)

	Private Sector	Manufacturing	Services	Wholesale/ Retail	Other[10]
United States	54.4%	73.9%	47.6%	40.8%	59.1%
	(0.18)	(0.34)	(0.33)	(0.35)	(0.36)
New England	57.8%	76.3%	51.7%	41.9%	63.5%
	(0.59)	(1.04)	(1.05)	(1.22)	(1.25)
Connecticut	60.8%	82.3%	49.7%	42.8%	68.5%
	(1.60)	(2.47)	(3.04)	(3.42)	(3.22)
Maine	51.8%	72.9%	47.2%	33.7%	55.8%
	(1.55)	(2.81)	(2.82)	(2.95)	(3.40)
Massachusetts	57.8%	74.7%	53.8%	42.9%	63.7%
	(0.78)	(1.48)	(1.33)	(1.62)	(1.67)
New Hampshire	56.9%	76.3%	46.7%	43.9%	62.8%
	(1.57)	(2.61)	(2.88)	(3.20)	(3.54)
Rhode Island	57.4%	67.8%	55.1%	41.8%	62.7%
	(1.61)	(2.84)	(3.02)	(3.44)	(3.47)
Vermont	54.5%	77.6%	52.5%	39.1%	50.0%
	(1.62)	(2.87)	(2.82)	(3.32)	(3.45)
Middle Atlantic	57.7%	75.3%	51.8%	42.5%	66.3%
	(0.41)	(0.79)	(0.73)	(0.84)	(0.82)
New Jersey	60.1%	76.7%	53.2%	45.4%	68.9%
	(0.76)	(1.45)	(1.41)	(1.58)	(1.42)
New York	55.1%	71.7%	51.2%	38.6%	63.7%
	(0.62)	(1.29)	(1.05)	(1.27)	(1.26)
Pennsylvania	59.7%	78.4%	51.9%	45.4%	67.8%
	(0.75)	(1.33)	(1.37)	(1.53)	(1.55)
South Atlantic	52.9%	71.4%	46.8%	41.4%	56.3%
	(0.44)	(0.88)	(0.83)	(0.86)	(0.87)
Delaware	54.7%	77.6%	42.9%	45.8%	55.2%
	(1.49)	(2.66)	(2.81)	(3.19)	(2.82)
District of Columbia	52.4%	---	56.0%	29.7%	58.6%
	(1.99)	---	(2.64)	(4.08)	(4.82)
Florida	47.4%	62.6%	45.5%	38.9%	50.7%
	(0.75)	(2.00)	(1.36)	(1.39)	(1.41)
Georgia	54.1%	67.0%	46.5%	42.8%	61.7%
	(1.48)	(2.90)	(2.89)	(2.88)	(2.88)
Maryland	58.6%	80.5%	55.0%	49.1%	62.0%
	(1.60)	(3.63)	(2.70)	(3.25)	(3.02)
North Carolina	58.1%	74.2%	47.4%	44.4%	59.2%
	(0.75)	(1.15)	(1.57)	(1.57)	(1.67)
South Carolina	54.1%	75.8%	39.0%	36.6%	57.1%
	(1.35)	(2.05)	(2.81)	(2.63)	(2.89)
Virginia	52.8%	73.3%	46.1%	40.4%	55.0%
	(1.31)	(2.55)	(2.43)	(2.65)	(2.54)
West Virginia	51.2%	75.7%	38.4%	38.0%	60.3%
	(1.68)	(3.42)	(3.22)	(3.10)	(3.07)
East South Central	53.1%	73.8%	44.5%	36.6%	55.8%
	(0.78)	(1.32)	(1.55)	(1.50)	(1.64)
Alabama	53.6%	75.2%	46.4%	37.9%	52.8%
	(1.56)	(2.56)	(3.13)	(3.00)	(3.35)
Kentucky	53.1%	75.6%	42.3%	37.2%	61.9%
	(1.58)	(2.88)	(3.06)	(2.94)	(3.14)
Mississippi	48.0%	66.5%	39.3%	30.9%	52.6%
	(1.53)	(2.76)	(3.14)	(2.84)	(3.02)
Tennessee	55.0%	74.9%	46.8%	37.8%	55.2%
	(1.45)	(2.28)	(2.86)	(2.91)	(3.19)
West South Central	48.0%	68.0%	40.3%	36.3%	54.4%
	(0.61)	(1.33)	(1.12)	(1.13)	(1.17)
Arkansas	48.1%	70.5%	36.1%	34.8%	47.4%
	(1.57)	(2.72)	(3.19)	(2.96)	(3.22)
Louisiana	43.8%	70.5%	36.5%	27.1%	51.9%
	(1.69)	(4.15)	(3.07)	(2.99)	(3.01)
Oklahoma	46.2%	66.6%	36.8%	31.5%	57.1%
	(1.58)	(3.33)	(2.86)	(2.81)	(3.22)
Texas	49.3%	67.3%	42.1%	39.2%	55.4%
	(0.78)	(1.75)	(1.43)	(1.46)	(1.50)

Table B7 (continued)

Health Insurance Coverage of Workers Ages 18-64, 1990-92:
Private-Sector Workers with Own-Employer Group Insurance by Industry[1,8]

(Persons in thousands)

	Private Sector	Manufacturing	Services	Wholesale/ Retail	Other[10]
East North Central	**58.0%**	**79.9%**	**48.3%**	**40.7%**	**62.2%**
	(0.42)	**(0.65)**	**(0.82)**	**(0.84)**	**(0.92)**
Illinois	59.1%	80.1%	50.4%	42.9%	66.6%
	(0.77)	(1.30)	(1.46)	(1.55)	(1.55)
Indiana	57.3%	78.9%	43.3%	38.7%	62.1%
	(1.51)	(2.21)	(3.17)	(2.98)	(3.29)
Michigan	57.7%	83.0%	47.6%	39.2%	58.0%
	(0.78)	(1.10)	(1.54)	(1.52)	(1.83)
Ohio	58.1%	79.5%	49.7%	41.0%	60.6%
	(0.76)	(1.17)	(1.45)	(1.53)	(1.72)
Wisconsin	57.0%	76.3%	46.3%	39.5%	60.9%
	(1.37)	(2.12)	(2.66)	(2.86)	(3.00)
West North Central	**53.6%**	**76.2%**	**44.4%**	**39.8%**	**61.7%**
	(0.68)	**(1.29)**	**(1.23)**	**(1.28)**	**(1.37)**
Iowa	52.2%	73.9%	42.2%	41.3%	56.6%
	(1.47)	(2.74)	(2.86)	(2.65)	(3.09)
Kansas	54.6%	79.8%	46.7%	39.2%	58.3%
	(1.47)	(2.59)	(2.79)	(2.81)	(2.91)
Minnesota	54.6%	76.7%	46.6%	40.8%	62.7%
	(1.48)	(2.78)	(2.68)	(2.76)	(3.09)
Missouri	54.8%	77.6%	42.5%	39.1%	68.5%
	(1.52)	(2.83)	(2.64)	(3.02)	(2.95)
Nebraska	52.2%	71.9%	44.9%	38.8%	60.5%
	(1.47)	(3.04)	(2.73)	(2.74)	(2.89)
North Dakota	43.8%	69.5%	41.4%	35.7%	47.3%
	(1.56)	(4.63)	(2.78)	(2.63)	(3.07)
South Dakota	49.0%	69.0%	46.6%	39.8%	50.1%
	(1.48)	(3.50)	(2.65)	(2.75)	(2.93)
Mountain	**51.5%**	**68.9%**	**48.9%**	**39.0%**	**57.7%**
	(0.67)	**(1.63)**	**(1.17)**	**(1.27)**	**(1.28)**
Arizona	52.4%	67.4%	48.4%	43.7%	58.0%
	(1.58)	(3.85)	(2.72)	(3.04)	(3.10)
Colorado	55.0%	71.9%	50.3%	41.9%	62.0%
	(1.58)	(3.52)	(2.78)	(3.21)	(2.96)
Idaho	48.5%	71.8%	45.1%	34.3%	48.2%
	(1.49)	(2.93)	(2.88)	(2.71)	(3.00)
Montana	45.3%	61.3%	40.7%	38.8%	51.2%
	(1.64)	(4.87)	(3.03)	(2.82)	(3.13)
Nevada	57.5%	---	60.9%	42.3%	63.9%
	(1.45)	---	(2.16)	(3.02)	(2.74)
New Mexico	42.4%	56.6%	40.6%	27.9%	54.4%
	(1.64)	(4.98)	(2.90)	(2.73)	(3.15)
Utah	50.1%	72.9%	46.7%	35.3%	52.9%
	(1.55)	(3.13)	(2.90)	(2.81)	(3.12)
Wyoming	45.2%	---	35.4%	30.7%	57.2%
	(1.87)	---	(3.65)	(3.27)	(2.96)
Pacific	**53.2%**	**68.9%**	**48.3%**	**44.1%**	**55.5%**
	(0.50)	**(1.04)**	**(0.93)**	**(0.98)**	**(1.00)**
Alaska	49.4%	---	43.0%	41.1%	59.0%
	(1.57)	---	(2.86)	(2.90)	(2.65)
California	51.4%	67.0%	46.8%	42.1%	53.1%
	(0.59)	(1.21)	(1.09)	(1.15)	(1.17)
Hawaii	69.5%	---	67.2%	63.1%	74.5%
	(1.53)	---	(2.63)	(3.12)	(2.60)
Oregon	56.2%	74.9%	47.5%	47.6%	59.8%
	(1.61)	(3.05)	(3.07)	(3.08)	(3.34)
Washington	59.0%	77.2%	53.6%	49.3%	62.3%
	(1.50)	(2.94)	(2.81)	(2.90)	(3.02)

Source: Three-year merged March CPS: 1991, 1992, and 1993.
Note: See table notes at end of Section B.

Table B8
Health Insurance Coverage of Workers Ages 18-64, 1990-92:
Percentage of Private-Sector Workers Uninsured by Industry[1,5,8]
(Persons in thousands)

	Private Sector	Manufacturing	Services	Wholesale/ Retail	Other[10]
United States	17.8%	11.9%	17.3%	22.8%	18.3%
	(0.14)	(0.25)	(0.25)	(0.30)	(0.29)
New England	11.7%	8.7%	11.8%	16.1%	9.9%
	(0.38)	(0.69)	(0.68)	(0.91)	(0.78)
Connecticut	9.5%	7.9%	10.2%	13.4%	6.5%
	(0.96)	(1.75)	(1.84)	(2.36)	(1.71)
Maine	14.4%	11.1%	15.9%	16.4%	13.9%
	(1.09)	(1.99)	(2.06)	(2.31)	(2.37)
Massachusetts	11.8%	9.0%	11.1%	16.4%	10.4%
	(0.51)	(0.98)	(0.84)	(1.22)	(1.06)
New Hampshire	12.5%	4.2%	13.6%	20.2%	12.6%
	(1.05)	(1.23)	(1.98)	(2.59)	(2.43)
Rhode Island	13.1%	13.7%	12.0%	17.0%	10.0%
	(1.10)	(2.08)	(1.97)	(2.62)	(2.15)
Vermont	12.9%	6.1%	15.1%	16.0%	13.3%
	(1.09)	(1.65)	(2.02)	(2.50)	(2.34)
Middle Atlantic	14.4%	10.4%	13.1%	20.3%	13.4%
	(0.29)	(0.56)	(0.49)	(0.69)	(0.59)
New Jersey	13.6%	10.2%	12.8%	19.4%	12.0%
	(0.53)	(1.04)	(0.94)	(1.25)	(1.00)
New York	17.0%	13.5%	15.0%	24.0%	16.2%
	(0.47)	(0.98)	(0.75)	(1.12)	(0.96)
Pennsylvania	11.2%	7.1%	10.6%	16.3%	10.7%
	(0.48)	(0.83)	(0.84)	(1.14)	(1.02)
South Atlantic	20.8%	14.9%	20.0%	25.0%	22.2%
	(0.36)	(0.69)	(0.66)	(0.76)	(0.73)
Delaware	16.8%	10.0%	20.3%	20.0%	16.1%
	(1.12)	(1.91)	(2.28)	(2.56)	(2.08)
District of Columbia	26.4%	---	22.9%	44.8%	21.6%
	(1.76)	---	(2.24)	(4.44)	(4.03)
Florida	26.3%	21.2%	23.0%	29.2%	29.2%
	(0.66)	(1.69)	(1.15)	(1.29)	(1.28)
Georgia	20.8%	15.9%	22.6%	24.0%	20.0%
	(1.20)	(2.26)	(2.43)	(2.48)	(2.37)
Maryland	13.9%	9.7%	11.8%	18.8%	14.1%
	(1.12)	(2.72)	(1.76)	(2.54)	(2.17)
North Carolina	17.3%	12.4%	18.3%	21.4%	19.4%
	(0.57)	(0.87)	(1.22)	(1.30)	(1.34)
South Carolina	19.8%	15.3%	20.9%	24.6%	20.1%
	(1.08)	(1.72)	(2.34)	(2.35)	(2.34)
Virginia	20.2%	13.7%	19.7%	25.2%	21.2%
	(1.05)	(1.98)	(1.94)	(2.35)	(2.08)
West Virginia	16.7%	9.2%	18.5%	21.1%	15.6%
	(1.25)	(2.31)	(2.57)	(2.61)	(2.28)
East South Central	19.6%	11.8%	19.4%	25.9%	22.2%
	(0.62)	(0.97)	(1.24)	(1.37)	(1.37)
Alabama	20.4%	12.4%	21.6%	27.2%	21.3%
	(1.26)	(1.96)	(2.58)	(2.75)	(2.75)
Kentucky	16.3%	8.6%	16.3%	22.2%	16.8%
	(1.17)	(1.88)	(2.29)	(2.53)	(2.42)
Mississippi	25.5%	19.1%	26.0%	30.9%	26.8%
	(1.33)	(2.30)	(2.82)	(2.85)	(2.68)
Tennessee	18.5%	10.0%	17.2%	25.4%	24.8%
	(1.13)	(1.58)	(2.16)	(2.61)	(2.77)
West South Central	25.5%	17.7%	25.5%	30.5%	25.8%
	(0.53)	(1.09)	(1.00)	(1.08)	(1.03)
Arkansas	22.1%	14.2%	24.0%	25.8%	25.7%
	(1.31)	(2.08)	(2.83)	(2.72)	(2.82)
Louisiana	25.6%	11.2%	25.1%	32.2%	27.1%
	(1.49)	(2.87)	(2.76)	(3.14)	(2.68)
Oklahoma	23.5%	20.0%	22.4%	31.7%	18.1%
	(1.34)	(2.82)	(2.47)	(2.81)	(2.51)
Texas	26.2%	19.1%	26.2%	30.5%	26.6%
	(0.68)	(1.46)	(1.27)	(1.37)	(1.34)

Table B8 (continued)
Health Insurance Coverage of Workers Ages 18-64, 1990-92:
Percentage of Private-Sector Workers Uninsured by Industry[1,5,8]
(Persons in thousands)

	Private Sector	Manufacturing	Services	Wholesale/ Retail	Other[10]
East North Central	13.2% (0.29)	7.2% (0.42)	14.7% (0.58)	18.3% (0.66)	13.3% (0.64)
Illinois	14.6% (0.55)	8.5% (0.91)	16.1% (1.07)	20.3% (1.26)	12.4% (1.08)
Indiana	15.2% (1.10)	7.1% (1.39)	17.2% (2.42)	21.0% (2.49)	18.6% (2.64)
Michigan	12.2% (0.52)	5.8% (0.68)	14.6% (1.09)	16.1% (1.14)	13.7% (1.27)
Ohio	12.8% (0.51)	7.0% (0.74)	14.1% (1.01)	17.6% (1.18)	13.1% (1.19)
Wisconsin	10.7% (0.85)	7.9% (1.34)	10.4% (1.62)	16.4% (2.17)	9.0% (1.76)
West North Central	13.9% (0.47)	8.3% (0.84)	13.4% (0.85)	19.9% (1.04)	12.5% (0.93)
Iowa	12.5% (0.97)	9.4% (1.83)	12.0% (1.89)	14.0% (1.87)	14.0% (2.16)
Kansas	13.0% (0.99)	7.9% (1.74)	10.4% (1.70)	18.9% (2.25)	13.9% (2.04)
Minnesota	14.6% (1.04)	6.9% (1.66)	13.4% (1.83)	22.3% (2.34)	13.5% (2.18)
Missouri	15.1% (1.09)	9.3% (1.97)	16.3% (1.98)	22.8% (2.60)	10.3% (1.93)
Nebraska	10.9% (0.92)	7.6% (1.79)	10.2% (1.66)	16.6% (2.09)	8.0% (1.60)
North Dakota	12.9% (1.05)	6.4% (2.47)	8.1% (1.54)	18.0% (2.11)	14.5% (2.16)
South Dakota	17.6% (1.13)	10.1% (2.28)	14.8% (1.89)	20.3% (2.26)	22.5% (2.45)
Mountain	19.3% (0.53)	14.4% (1.23)	16.9% (0.88)	25.3% (1.13)	18.9% (1.02)
Arizona	20.9% (1.28)	17.5% (3.12)	20.4% (2.20)	24.5% (2.63)	20.0% (2.51)
Colorado	14.9% (1.13)	10.4% (2.39)	11.4% (1.76)	24.0% (2.78)	13.9% (2.11)
Idaho	22.1% (1.24)	12.8% (2.18)	22.3% (2.41)	28.0% (2.56)	23.1% (2.53)
Montana	21.3% (1.35)	12.8% (3.35)	19.0% (2.42)	25.9% (2.53)	21.4% (2.57)
Nevada	21.2% (1.20)	--- ---	18.8% (1.73)	28.2% (2.75)	19.2% (2.25)
New Mexico	26.9% (1.47)	28.3% (4.53)	22.1% (2.45)	35.6% (2.92)	22.4% (2.63)
Utah	15.9% (1.13)	10.4% (2.15)	12.1% (1.89)	17.6% (2.24)	22.7% (2.62)
Wyoming	16.3% (1.39)	--- ---	11.8% (2.46)	21.9% (2.93)	15.7% (2.18)
Pacific	20.5% (0.41)	16.4% (0.83)	19.7% (0.74)	23.9% (0.84)	21.2% (0.82)
Alaska	23.5% (1.33)	--- ---	22.7% (2.42)	28.0% (2.65)	21.6% (2.22)
California	22.4% (0.49)	18.4% (0.99)	21.6% (0.90)	25.7% (1.02)	23.2% (0.99)
Hawaii	8.0% (0.91)	--- ---	9.1% (1.61)	9.6% (1.91)	5.9% (1.40)
Oregon	17.2% (1.23)	10.6% (2.17)	17.5% (2.33)	21.4% (2.53)	17.9% (2.61)
Washington	13.5% (1.04)	8.0% (1.91)	12.0% (1.83)	17.7% (2.22)	14.8% (2.21)

Source: Three-year merged March CPS: 1991, 1992, and 1993.
Note: See table notes at end of Section B.

Notes to Tables, Section B

1. Population in the merged CPS file excludes persons aged 65 and over, those living in institutions, and those in families with active military service members. Persons with more than one type of health coverage are included only in the first category shown. Percentages may not sum to 100 owing to rounding. Workers are defined as persons 18 to 64 years old reporting a positive number of usual hours worked. Workers reporting work "without pay" are eliminated.

2. "Employer (other)" includes persons covered as dependents on the employer group insurance of another family member.

3. Medicaid coverage reflects corrections to the reports of Medicaid on the Current Population Survey made by the Urban Institute's TRIM2 model (see Appendix Three).

4. "Other Coverage" includes persons with public coverage other than Medicaid (Medicare, CHAMPUS, VA, and military health programs) and persons with privately purchased nongroup coverage.

5. "Uninsured" includes persons without insurance coverage for an entire year. The CPS does not currently collect information on persons without coverage for less than 12 months (see Appendix Three).

6. Full-time/part-time work is based on the *usual* hours of work reported for the prior year. We define full-time work as 35 hours per week or more; part-time as 1–34 hours per week; and nonwork as 0 hours per week.

7. The percentage of workers in each group with coverage through their own employer.

8. Firm size, sector, and industry are based on the job held for the longest period during the year preceding the March CPS interview.

9. "Self-Employed" includes self-employed unincorporated workers. The self-employed incorporated are classified as private-sector workers.

10. "Other" includes these industries: agriculture, forestry, fisheries, mining, construction, transportation, communication, other public utilities, finance, insurance, and real estate. Public-sector workers are not included in this table.

All Tables:

*** A triple asterisk in the tables indicates no observations on the merged CPS file of this type.

--- A triple dash in the tables indicates fewer than 100 observations on the merged CPS file of this type. We have not printed estimates in these cases.

Characteristics of the Uninsured

Section C highlights characteristics of persons without health insurance. The major goals of health care reforms currently being considered by states usually include extending coverage to the uninsured. Data in this section can help states to estimate the number of uninsured persons who could be targeted through various types of health insurance expansion strategies. Statistics presented earlier indicate the relative incidence of uninsurance for various subpopulations. Here we show the demographic, income, and work characteristics of the uninsured population alone. *Thus, the percentages shown here do not indicate the percentage of each group that is uninsured; rather, they show the percentage of uninsured that fall into each group.* For example, although we have shown in table B2a that full-time workers have the lowest rate of uninsurance, the majority of uninsured adults shown in table C6 are full-time workers. This occurs simply because most adults work full-time.

The statistics in this section are influenced by other characteristics of the state's population. For example, some states have larger percentages of low-income persons or persons working in small firms than other states. Because these characteristics are also associated with higher rates of uninsurance, those states will have large concentrations of their uninsured populations with these characteristics. The numbers in this section can be used with those presented elsewhere (Sections A and G, for example) to gain a more complete picture of the uninsured population in a state.

DEMOGRAPHIC CHARACTERISTICS

The first tables (C1–C3) show the percentage of the uninsured population by race and sex, by age, and by family type, respectively. The percentage of the uninsured population that is nonwhite varies widely across the states, in part because some states have higher concentrations of nonwhites and because nonwhites have characteristics that are associated with higher rates of uninsurance (low income, higher unemployment rates, and so on). More of the uninsured are men—44 percent women and 56 percent men (table C1). This partly reflects the higher rates of Medicaid coverage for women than men (see the A3 table series). Medicaid covers low-income pregnant women and single parents eligible for Aid to Families with Dependent Children.

Table C2 indicates that the uninsured tend to be young adults (aged 18–34). In fact, young adults comprise at least one-half of the uninsured population in some states (Delaware, Indiana, Minnesota, and Rhode Island). This category includes persons who are still in school; persons in part-time or entry-level jobs that do not provide health insurance; and, because young adults have a relatively high unemployment rate, persons without jobs.

Table C3 categorizes uninsured persons by family type.[1] It shows, for example, that 35 percent of uninsured persons live in two-parent families with children. In some states (for example, Arkansas, Idaho, New Mexico, Texas, and Utah) almost half of uninsured persons are in this family status category. A large share of the uninsured are single—41 percent nationally. As noted earlier, single adults have low rates of employer group insurance coverage and high rates of uninsurance. In addition, public health plan coverage is not typically available to single persons unless they have severe disabilities.

Table C4, which shows uninsured persons by the work status of the family's head and spouse, reveals some surprising statistics. Despite the fact that persons in families with a full-time worker have relatively low rates of uninsurance (8.6 percent with two full-time workers and 16.7 percent with one, as shown in the A7 table series), they comprise a large share of the uninsured population because *most* families have a full-time worker. Thus, 72 percent of the uninsured population are in families in which either the head or the spouse works 35 hours a week or more (16 percent are in families where both head and spouse work full-time, and 56 percent are in families with one adult full-time worker). This statistic has led many to conclude that expanding the employer-group health insurance system could go far toward reducing the number of uninsured Americans, even if a mandate only covered full-time workers.

Income characteristics

Table C5 provides some indication of whether the uninsured would be able to pay for a share of their insurance coverage or would need special subsidies or program expansions to gain coverage. Thirty-four percent of the uninsured live in families with incomes more than twice the poverty line (25 percent in families with incomes between 200 and 399 percent of poverty, plus 9 percent in families with incomes at 400 percent of poverty or greater). There is wide variation in this statistic across states and regions, however, reflecting widely different economic circumstances across the states. Policymakers need to assess the ability to pay for insurance within their own state environment. In the New England region, for example, 43 percent of the uninsured live in families with incomes above 200 percent of poverty, compared to 25 percent in the East South Central region. However, some families in states with high insurance costs like New York, for example, may find it difficult to afford insurance even when their incomes exceed two times the federal poverty level. On the other hand, families with incomes between 150 percent and 200 percent of the poverty line living in lower-cost areas may be able to pay a reasonable share of their health insurance costs.

Worker characteristics

The distribution of uninsured adults (table C6) by own-work status indicates that the majority of uninsured adults work full-time (57 percent), 20 percent are part-time workers, and approximately one-quarter are not working. (Unlike earlier tables in this section, this table includes only uninsured adults ages 18 to 64.) The distribution of uninsured adults across work status groups is similar across states, with notable exceptions in Alabama, Louisiana, New York, Pennsylvania, and West Virginia, where almost 30 percent or more of the uninsured adults are from the not-working group, and in Delaware, Maryland, Kansas, and Wisconsin (among others), where about 60 percent of the uninsured adults are full-time workers.

Table C7 shows that nearly one-half of all uninsured workers are in firms with fewer than 25 workers. (The remaining tables in the section include only uninsured workers.) Variations across the states in the distribution of uninsured workers by firm size indicate variations in employment patterns across the states more than they indicate different propensities for firms of a given size to provide health insurance. For example, 58 percent or more of uninsured workers are in small firms in New Hampshire, Montana, and Vermont. These states have higher-than-average concentrations of their employment base in small firms (table G9). There are important exceptions to this generalization, however, and each state's employment base must be reviewed separately.

Data for uninsured workers by sector of employment (table C8) show that a great majority of such individuals work in the private sector (82 percent). The high rate of employment-based coverage in the government sector discussed earlier means that relatively few uninsured workers are in the government sector. Nationwide, 7 percent of the uninsured work in the government sector, despite the fact that government workers comprise 15.4 percent of adult employment (shown later in table G10). In contrast, 12 percent of the uninsured are in the self-employed sector, which comprises about 8 percent of all workers (table G10).

The last table in this section (table C9) shows the distribution of the uninsured by industry. Not surprisingly, the uninsured are more likely to work in the service or wholesale and retail industries than in manufacturing. This holds true across the country, although the differences across industry groups are not as sharp in some states as they are in others. For example, among uninsured workers in North Carolina, 24 percent are employed in manufacturing, 25 percent are in the service industry, and 29 percent are in the wholesale and retail group. And in Ohio, 15 percent of the uninsured work in manufacturing, 31 percent work in services, and 34 percent work in wholesale and retail industries. As noted earlier, the extent of employment-based coverage in the manufacturing industry differs across the states. States with very large manufacturing firms and long-established benefit plans have above-average rates of employer-group coverage, and states with small manufacturers have lower-than-average rates of employer-group coverage. In addition, the concentration of workers by industry affects these results (see table G11 and others in that section to review differences in employers' characteristics across states).

Note, Section C

1. As discussed in the Introduction, our family unit definition has been changed from a nuclear family concept to the health insurance unit. Note 2, following the tables, explains this distinction.

88

Table C1
Nonelderly Uninsured, 1990-92:
By Race and Sex[1]

(Persons in thousands, standard errors in parentheses)

		Race		Sex	
	Number	White	Nonwhite	Male	Female
United States	34,515	77% (0.22)	23% (0.23)	56% (0.27)	44% (0.27)
New England	1,225	88% (0.73)	12% (0.76)	58% (1.11)	42% (1.11)
Connecticut	238	77% (2.98)	23% (3.10)	59% (3.49)	41% (3.49)
Maine	137	98% (0.74)	2% (0.77)	55% (2.58)	45% (2.58)
Massachusetts	568	88% (0.95)	12% (0.99)	57% (1.45)	43% (1.45)
New Hampshire	139	91% (1.52)	9% (1.58)	57% (2.69)	43% (2.69)
Rhode Island	89	94% (1.54)	6% (1.60)	62% (3.05)	38% (3.05)
Vermont	55	94% (1.39)	6% (1.45)	62% (2.91)	38% (2.91)
Middle Atlantic	4,191	74% (0.60)	26% (0.63)	55% (0.68)	45% (0.68)
New Jersey	858	74% (1.17)	26% (1.21)	55% (1.33)	45% (1.33)
New York	2,256	70% (0.86)	30% (0.90)	55% (0.94)	45% (0.94)
Pennsylvania	1,078	82% (1.12)	18% (1.17)	57% (1.43)	43% (1.43)
South Atlantic	6,948	68% (0.58)	32% (0.60)	56% (0.61)	44% (0.61)
Delaware	91	73% (2.24)	27% (2.33)	56% (2.50)	44% (2.50)
District of Columbia	110	23% (1.91)	77% (1.99)	57% (2.27)	43% (2.27)
Florida	2,541	78% (0.78)	22% (0.81)	56% (0.93)	44% (0.93)
Georgia	1,049	56% (2.04)	44% (2.12)	56% (2.04)	44% (2.04)
Maryland	527	63% (2.59)	37% (2.69)	61% (2.62)	39% (2.62)
North Carolina	869	65% (1.13)	35% (1.18)	55% (1.18)	45% (1.18)
South Carolina	572	51% (1.88)	49% (1.95)	53% (1.88)	47% (1.88)
Virginia	964	66% (1.80)	34% (1.87)	57% (1.88)	43% (1.88)
West Virginia	227	96% (0.98)	4% (1.02)	54% (2.38)	46% (2.38)
East South Central	2,321	70% (0.99)	30% (1.03)	56% (1.07)	44% (1.07)
Alabama	706	62% (1.96)	38% (2.04)	56% (2.00)	44% (2.00)
Kentucky	443	90% (1.50)	10% (1.56)	60% (2.39)	40% (2.39)
Mississippi	497	54% (1.81)	46% (1.89)	56% (1.81)	44% (1.81)
Tennessee	675	79% (1.77)	21% (1.84)	55% (2.17)	45% (2.17)
West South Central	5,373	78% (0.61)	22% (0.63)	53% (0.73)	47% (0.73)
Arkansas	412	80% (1.59)	20% (1.65)	54% (1.99)	46% (1.99)
Louisiana	801	61% (1.96)	39% (2.04)	50% (2.00)	50% (2.00)
Oklahoma	586	76% (1.65)	24% (1.71)	53% (1.93)	47% (1.93)
Texas	3,575	82% (0.71)	18% (0.74)	54% (0.93)	46% (0.93)

Nonelderly Uninsured, 1990-92:
By Race and Sex[1]
(Persons in thousands, standard errors in parentheses)

	Number	Race White	Race Nonwhite	Sex Male	Sex Female
East North Central	**4,254**	**79%**	**21%**	**56%**	**44%**
		(0.63)	**(0.65)**	**(0.76)**	**(0.76)**
Illinois	1,327	69%	31%	58%	42%
		(1.22)	(1.27)	(1.30)	(1.30)
Indiana	630	84%	16%	57%	43%
		(1.89)	(1.97)	(2.57)	(2.57)
Michigan	867	78%	22%	56%	44%
		(1.19)	(1.24)	(1.44)	(1.44)
Ohio	1,050	84%	16%	55%	45%
		(1.03)	(1.07)	(1.39)	(1.39)
Wisconsin	379	87%	13%	52%	48%
		(1.90)	(1.98)	(2.84)	(2.84)
West North Central	**1,941**	**86%**	**14%**	**56%**	**44%**
		(0.81)	**(0.85)**	**(1.15)**	**(1.15)**
Iowa	258	94%	6%	60%	40%
		(1.30)	(1.35)	(2.65)	(2.65)
Kansas	263	83%	17%	56%	44%
		(1.87)	(1.95)	(2.48)	(2.48)
Minnesota	471	90%	10%	58%	42%
		(1.55)	(1.61)	(2.60)	(2.60)
Missouri	661	79%	21%	54%	46%
		(1.97)	(2.05)	(2.43)	(2.43)
Nebraska	137	96%	4%	52%	48%
		(1.05)	(1.09)	(2.73)	(2.73)
North Dakota	51	84%	16%	61%	39%
		(2.05)	(2.13)	(2.71)	(2.71)
South Dakota	98	75%	25%	58%	42%
		(1.74)	(1.81)	(1.99)	(1.99)
Mountain	**2,012**	**90%**	**10%**	**55%**	**45%**
		(0.55)	**(0.58)**	**(0.94)**	**(0.94)**
Arizona	529	95%	5%	53%	47%
		(1.00)	(1.04)	(2.23)	(2.23)
Colorado	395	87%	13%	62%	38%
		(1.73)	(1.80)	(2.51)	(2.51)
Idaho	167	96%	4%	50%	50%
		(0.81)	(0.84)	(1.97)	(1.97)
Montana	117	88%	12%	52%	48%
		(1.42)	(1.48)	(2.17)	(2.17)
Nevada	238	86%	14%	54%	46%
		(1.37)	(1.42)	(1.94)	(1.94)
New Mexico	319	84%	16%	55%	45%
		(1.30)	(1.35)	(1.78)	(1.78)
Utah	193	97%	3%	58%	42%
		(0.77)	(0.81)	(2.41)	(2.41)
Wyoming	55	95%	5%	51%	49%
		(1.23)	(1.28)	(2.86)	(2.86)
Pacific	**6,250**	**83%**	**17%**	**58%**	**42%**
		(0.52)	**(0.54)**	**(0.68)**	**(0.68)**
Alaska	97	56%	44%	59%	41%
		(1.81)	(1.89)	(1.80)	(1.80)
California	5,187	84%	16%	59%	41%
		(0.57)	(0.60)	(0.76)	(0.76)
Hawaii	75	30%	70%	54%	46%
		(3.14)	(3.26)	(3.40)	(3.40)
Oregon	370	93%	7%	53%	47%
		(1.31)	(1.36)	(2.52)	(2.52)
Washington	522	84%	16%	61%	39%
		(1.88)	(1.96)	(2.50)	(2.50)

Source: Three-year merged March CPS: 1991, 1992, and 1993.
Note: See table notes at end of Section C.

Table C2
Nonelderly Uninsured, 1990-92:
By Age[1]
(Persons in thousands, standard errors in parentheses)

	Number	Age <18	Age 18-34	Age 35-53	Age 54-64
United States	34,515	22% (0.34)	43% (0.41)	26% (0.37)	9% (0.24)
New England	1,225	19% (1.37)	46% (1.74)	27% (1.55)	8% (0.95)
Connecticut	238	19% (4.29)	46% (5.48)	27% (4.88)	8% (2.95)
Maine	137	21% (3.29)	42% (3.97)	29% (3.63)	7% (2.10)
Massachusetts	568	18% (1.75)	46% (2.27)	27% (2.02)	8% (1.25)
New Hampshire	139	26% (3.68)	43% (4.17)	24% (3.57)	7% (2.21)
Rhode Island	89	12% (3.14)	56% (4.83)	25% (4.20)	8% (2.58)
Vermont	55	14% (3.23)	45% (4.63)	30% (4.27)	10% (2.84)
Middle Atlantic	4,191	16% (0.79)	47% (1.06)	27% (0.94)	10% (0.65)
New Jersey	858	19% (1.60)	44% (2.05)	28% (1.85)	10% (1.22)
New York	2,256	15% (1.04)	47% (1.45)	27% (1.30)	10% (0.87)
Pennsylvania	1,078	17% (1.69)	47% (2.23)	25% (1.93)	11% (1.41)
South Atlantic	6,948	23% (0.80)	41% (0.94)	26% (0.84)	10% (0.58)
Delaware	91	22% (3.20)	50% (3.90)	20% (3.14)	8% (2.07)
District of Columbia	110	20% (2.82)	39% (3.46)	30% (3.24)	11% (2.23)
Florida	2,541	23% (1.22)	41% (1.43)	26% (1.28)	10% (0.88)
Georgia	1,049	24% (2.71)	38% (3.10)	29% (2.88)	9% (1.87)
Maryland	527	20% (3.31)	44% (4.12)	24% (3.57)	12% (2.68)
North Carolina	869	21% (1.50)	41% (1.80)	27% (1.64)	11% (1.13)
South Carolina	572	24% (2.49)	39% (2.84)	28% (2.62)	9% (1.66)
Virginia	964	24% (2.51)	41% (2.89)	25% (2.53)	10% (1.77)
West Virginia	227	19% (2.92)	44% (3.68)	27% (3.30)	9% (2.13)
East South Central	2,321	24% (1.43)	42% (1.65)	25% (1.46)	9% (0.94)
Alabama	706	29% (2.82)	41% (3.07)	22% (2.58)	8% (1.73)
Kentucky	443	22% (3.14)	44% (3.76)	25% (3.28)	8% (2.11)
Mississippi	497	25% (2.45)	40% (2.76)	27% (2.49)	8% (1.54)
Tennessee	675	20% (2.68)	43% (3.33)	28% (3.02)	10% (1.98)
West South Central	5,373	26% (0.99)	40% (1.11)	27% (1.01)	8% (0.62)
Arkansas	412	32% (2.88)	37% (3.00)	23% (2.59)	8% (1.70)
Louisiana	801	24% (2.63)	37% (3.00)	28% (2.79)	11% (1.96)
Oklahoma	586	25% (2.61)	41% (2.95)	25% (2.59)	8% (1.66)
Texas	3,575	26% (1.27)	40% (1.42)	27% (1.29)	7% (0.76)

Table C2 (continued)
Nonelderly Uninsured, 1990-92:
By Age[1]
(Persons in thousands, standard errors in parentheses)

		Age			
	Number	**<18**	**18-34**	**35-53**	**54-64**
East North Central	**4,254**	**18%**	**48%**	**25%**	**9%**
		(0.92)	**(1.18)**	**(1.02)**	**(0.68)**
Illinois	1,327	18%	48%	26%	8%
		(1.59)	(2.05)	(1.79)	(1.13)
Indiana	630	22%	50%	21%	6%
		(3.34)	(4.02)	(3.30)	(1.95)
Michigan	867	19%	47%	24%	10%
		(1.75)	(2.24)	(1.92)	(1.33)
Ohio	1,050	14%	46%	27%	12%
		(1.52)	(2.17)	(1.94)	(1.40)
Wisconsin	379	21%	49%	23%	6%
		(3.61)	(4.40)	(3.70)	(2.13)
West North Central	**1,941**	**24%**	**44%**	**24%**	**8%**
		(1.52)	**(1.78)**	**(1.53)**	**(0.96)**
Iowa	258	20%	43%	28%	9%
		(3.34)	(4.16)	(3.76)	(2.40)
Kansas	263	27%	43%	24%	6%
		(3.43)	(3.83)	(3.33)	(1.86)
Minnesota	471	19%	52%	22%	7%
		(3.22)	(4.07)	(3.37)	(2.10)
Missouri	661	26%	43%	23%	7%
		(3.32)	(3.73)	(3.18)	(1.96)
Nebraska	137	25%	37%	28%	11%
		(3.65)	(4.08)	(3.80)	(2.63)
North Dakota	51	21%	46%	25%	8%
		(3.49)	(4.30)	(3.75)	(2.29)
South Dakota	98	30%	32%	27%	11%
		(2.86)	(2.91)	(2.76)	(1.96)
Mountain	**2,012**	**25%**	**39%**	**27%**	**9%**
		(1.27)	**(1.42)**	**(1.30)**	**(0.82)**
Arizona	529	21%	40%	28%	10%
		(2.82)	(3.40)	(3.12)	(2.11)
Colorado	395	23%	42%	28%	7%
		(3.38)	(3.95)	(3.60)	(2.07)
Idaho	167	30%	36%	26%	8%
		(2.79)	(2.93)	(2.67)	(1.68)
Montana	117	26%	40%	27%	7%
		(2.94)	(3.29)	(3.00)	(1.67)
Nevada	238	27%	36%	29%	8%
		(2.68)	(2.88)	(2.74)	(1.62)
New Mexico	319	27%	36%	27%	9%
		(2.47)	(2.66)	(2.46)	(1.60)
Utah	193	31%	40%	22%	7%
		(3.49)	(3.70)	(3.12)	(1.96)
Wyoming	55	27%	34%	27%	11%
		(3.96)	(4.21)	(3.95)	(2.80)
Pacific	**6,250**	**20%**	**45%**	**26%**	**8%**
		(0.86)	**(1.07)**	**(0.94)**	**(0.59)**
Alaska	97	25%	36%	31%	8%
		(2.44)	(2.72)	(2.62)	(1.56)
California	5,187	20%	46%	25%	8%
		(0.97)	(1.20)	(1.05)	(0.66)
Hawaii	75	21%	40%	31%	7%
		(4.32)	(5.18)	(4.91)	(2.78)
Oregon	370	20%	39%	31%	10%
		(3.15)	(3.81)	(3.62)	(2.39)
Washington	522	19%	45%	30%	5%
		(3.13)	(3.94)	(3.65)	(1.80)

Source: Three-year merged March CPS: 1991, 1992, and 1993.
Note: See table notes at end of Section C.

Table C3
Nonelderly Uninsured, 1990-92:
By Type of Family[1,2]

(Persons in thousands, standard errors in parentheses)

	Number	Married with Children	Married without Children	Single-Parent Family	Singles
United States	**34,515**	35%	13%	10%	41%
		(0.40)	(0.28)	(0.25)	(0.41)
New England	**1,225**	29%	12%	10%	48%
		(1.59)	(1.15)	(1.04)	(1.75)
Connecticut	238	24%	14%	12%	50%
		(4.71)	(3.84)	(3.52)	(5.50)
Maine	137	38%	11%	10%	41%
		(3.90)	(2.49)	(2.37)	(3.96)
Massachusetts	568	29%	14%	9%	48%
		(2.07)	(1.56)	(1.31)	(2.27)
New Hampshire	139	36%	8%	13%	43%
		(4.04)	(2.24)	(2.85)	(4.17)
Rhode Island	89	22%	11%	4%	63%
		(4.05)	(3.04)	(1.80)	(4.69)
Vermont	55	26%	12%	9%	54%
		(4.06)	(2.97)	(2.69)	(4.64)
Middle Atlantic	**4,191**	30%	13%	9%	48%
		(0.97)	(0.72)	(0.62)	(1.06)
New Jersey	858	28%	13%	9%	50%
		(1.86)	(1.38)	(1.18)	(2.06)
New York	2,256	30%	14%	9%	47%
		(1.34)	(1.01)	(0.82)	(1.45)
Pennsylvania	1,078	30%	12%	11%	47%
		(2.05)	(1.45)	(1.38)	(2.23)
South Atlantic	**6,948**	34%	14%	11%	41%
		(0.91)	(0.66)	(0.60)	(0.94)
Delaware	91	25%	8%	15%	52%
		(3.37)	(2.06)	(2.81)	(3.89)
District of Columbia	110	19%	10%	17%	53%
		(2.80)	(2.12)	(2.68)	(3.53)
Florida	2,541	35%	16%	12%	37%
		(1.39)	(1.06)	(0.94)	(1.40)
Georgia	1,049	33%	13%	10%	44%
		(3.01)	(2.13)	(1.90)	(3.16)
Maryland	527	31%	11%	8%	50%
		(3.84)	(2.65)	(2.24)	(4.15)
North Carolina	869	32%	15%	12%	41%
		(1.72)	(1.32)	(1.18)	(1.81)
South Carolina	572	38%	13%	11%	39%
		(2.82)	(1.94)	(1.82)	(2.83)
Virginia	964	36%	13%	10%	41%
		(2.82)	(1.96)	(1.77)	(2.89)
West Virginia	227	37%	12%	12%	39%
		(3.59)	(2.42)	(2.36)	(3.61)
East South Central	**2,321**	37%	13%	13%	36%
		(1.62)	(1.14)	(1.13)	(1.61)
Alabama	706	34%	14%	16%	36%
		(2.96)	(2.14)	(2.31)	(2.99)
Kentucky	443	40%	13%	9%	37%
		(3.71)	(2.58)	(2.19)	(3.66)
Mississippi	497	41%	12%	14%	33%
		(2.78)	(1.80)	(1.96)	(2.65)
Tennessee	675	36%	15%	11%	38%
		(3.24)	(2.38)	(2.12)	(3.27)
West South Central	**5,373**	44%	14%	10%	31%
		(1.13)	(0.79)	(0.69)	(1.06)
Arkansas	412	47%	13%	12%	27%
		(3.09)	(2.11)	(2.03)	(2.75)
Louisiana	801	33%	15%	17%	35%
		(2.91)	(2.21)	(2.33)	(2.97)
Oklahoma	586	45%	16%	9%	29%
		(2.98)	(2.21)	(1.76)	(2.72)
Texas	3,575	47%	13%	9%	31%
		(1.45)	(0.99)	(0.81)	(1.35)

Table C3 (continued)
Nonelderly Uninsured, 1990-92:
By Type of Family[1,2]
(Persons in thousands, standard errors in parentheses)

	Number	Married with Children	Married without Children	Single-Parent Family	Singles
East North Central	**4,254**	**29%** (1.07)	**12%** (0.77)	**12%** (0.77)	**47%** (1.18)
Illinois	1,327	29% (1.86)	12% (1.35)	10% (1.23)	49% (2.05)
Indiana	630	32% (3.74)	9% (2.27)	18% (3.10)	41% (3.95)
Michigan	867	25% (1.94)	10% (1.38)	13% (1.51)	52% (2.24)
Ohio	1,050	29% (1.97)	15% (1.55)	10% (1.29)	46% (2.17)
Wisconsin	379	32% (4.12)	10% (2.64)	12% (2.83)	46% (4.39)
West North Central	**1,941**	**36%** (1.71)	**12%** (1.14)	**12%** (1.15)	**41%** (1.76)
Iowa	258	32% (3.92)	14% (2.91)	9% (2.37)	45% (4.18)
Kansas	263	36% (3.73)	10% (2.31)	11% (2.41)	43% (3.83)
Minnesota	471	33% (3.84)	10% (2.42)	9% (2.32)	48% (4.07)
Missouri	661	37% (3.63)	12% (2.42)	16% (2.76)	36% (3.61)
Nebraska	137	40% (4.15)	15% (2.99)	10% (2.60)	35% (4.05)
North Dakota	51	41% (4.24)	11% (2.66)	5% (1.84)	44% (4.28)
South Dakota	98	38% (3.02)	13% (2.09)	13% (2.07)	37% (3.01)
Mountain	**2,012**	**41%** (1.44)	**14%** (1.02)	**9%** (0.85)	**35%** (1.39)
Arizona	529	40% (3.39)	15% (2.46)	9% (2.01)	36% (3.32)
Colorado	395	38% (3.89)	14% (2.78)	8% (2.23)	39% (3.91)
Idaho	167	50% (3.05)	15% (2.15)	7% (1.60)	28% (2.75)
Montana	117	43% (3.32)	11% (2.08)	12% (2.15)	35% (3.21)
Nevada	238	34% (2.85)	15% (2.17)	11% (1.89)	40% (2.95)
New Mexico	319	45% (2.76)	13% (1.88)	11% (1.72)	31% (2.56)
Utah	193	50% (3.78)	15% (2.67)	5% (1.72)	30% (3.47)
Wyoming	55	34% (4.21)	17% (3.35)	17% (3.30)	32% (4.14)
Pacific	**6,250**	**35%** (1.02)	**14%** (0.74)	**7%** (0.56)	**45%** (1.07)
Alaska	97	38% (2.75)	11% (1.80)	12% (1.83)	39% (2.76)
California	5,187	35% (1.15)	14% (0.83)	7% (0.63)	44% (1.19)
Hawaii	75	25% (4.58)	13% (3.56)	11% (3.27)	51% (5.29)
Oregon	370	32% (3.66)	16% (2.89)	7% (2.03)	44% (3.89)
Washington	522	32% (3.70)	12% (2.61)	5% (1.67)	51% (3.96)

Source: Three-year merged March CPS: 1991, 1992, and 1993.
Note: See table notes at end of Section C.

Table C4
Nonelderly Uninsured, 1990-92:
By Work Status of Adults in Families[1,2,3]

(Persons in thousands, standard errors in parentheses)

	Number	Both Full-time	One Full-time	Part-time	Not Working
United States	**34,515**	**16%** (0.22)	**56%** (0.30)	**14%** (0.21)	**14%** (0.21)
New England	**1,225**	**12%** (0.81)	**58%** (1.24)	**16%** (0.91)	**15%** (0.90)
Connecticut	238	14% (2.75)	59% (3.89)	15% (2.80)	12% (2.57)
Maine	137	18% (2.24)	58% (2.86)	15% (2.06)	9% (1.67)
Massachusetts	568	10% (0.98)	56% (1.63)	16% (1.20)	18% (1.26)
New Hampshire	139	8% (1.63)	60% (2.97)	17% (2.28)	15% (2.16)
Rhode Island	89	10% (2.07)	64% (3.36)	10% (2.15)	15% (2.53)
Vermont	55	13% (2.22)	56% (3.32)	19% (2.65)	12% (2.14)
Middle Atlantic	**4,191**	**12%** (0.50)	**55%** (0.76)	**13%** (0.52)	**20%** (0.61)
New Jersey	858	11% (0.94)	59% (1.46)	14% (1.04)	16% (1.08)
New York	2,256	14% (0.72)	52% (1.05)	13% (0.69)	22% (0.86)
Pennsylvania	1,078	9% (0.94)	57% (1.60)	14% (1.11)	20% (1.29)
South Atlantic	**6,948**	**17%** (0.52)	**56%** (0.68)	**14%** (0.47)	**13%** (0.46)
Delaware	91	12% (1.80)	61% (2.74)	19% (2.19)	9% (1.59)
District of Columbia	110	9% (1.44)	64% (2.45)	11% (1.57)	17% (1.91)
Florida	2,541	18% (0.80)	56% (1.04)	15% (0.75)	12% (0.67)
Georgia	1,049	15% (1.64)	58% (2.27)	14% (1.59)	13% (1.54)
Maryland	527	18% (2.31)	55% (2.98)	12% (1.98)	14% (2.10)
North Carolina	869	19% (1.04)	58% (1.31)	12% (0.85)	11% (0.84)
South Carolina	572	18% (1.62)	54% (2.09)	11% (1.32)	16% (1.56)
Virginia	964	17% (1.60)	56% (2.10)	15% (1.51)	12% (1.37)
West Virginia	227	12% (1.74)	49% (2.67)	13% (1.77)	27% (2.36)
East South Central	**2,321**	**16%** (0.89)	**54%** (1.20)	**13%** (0.82)	**16%** (0.89)
Alabama	706	12% (1.48)	58% (2.22)	10% (1.38)	19% (1.78)
Kentucky	443	17% (2.05)	48% (2.73)	19% (2.12)	16% (2.02)
Mississippi	497	21% (1.65)	53% (2.03)	12% (1.30)	14% (1.42)
Tennessee	675	17% (1.81)	56% (2.41)	14% (1.66)	14% (1.69)
West South Central	**5,373**	**20%** (0.65)	**57%** (0.81)	**12%** (0.53)	**12%** (0.53)
Arkansas	412	22% (1.86)	51% (2.23)	17% (1.66)	10% (1.31)
Louisiana	801	12% (1.47)	59% (2.20)	11% (1.41)	17% (1.70)
Oklahoma	586	26% (1.91)	49% (2.16)	14% (1.51)	10% (1.30)
Texas	3,575	20% (0.84)	58% (1.03)	11% (0.65)	11% (0.66)

Table C4 (continued)
Nonelderly Uninsured, 1990-92:
By Work Status of Adults in Families[1,2,3]
(Persons in thousands, standard errors in parentheses)

	Number	Both Full-time	One Full-time	Part-time	Not Working
East North Central	**4,254**	**14%**	**53%**	**17%**	**16%**
		(0.59)	**(0.85)**	**(0.63)**	**(0.62)**
Illinois	1,327	15%	53%	16%	17%
		(1.04)	(1.47)	(1.07)	(1.10)
Indiana	630	15%	55%	16%	14%
		(2.05)	(2.88)	(2.14)	(1.98)
Michigan	867	11%	51%	20%	18%
		(1.00)	(1.62)	(1.30)	(1.23)
Ohio	1,050	13%	53%	15%	18%
		(1.06)	(1.56)	(1.12)	(1.21)
Wisconsin	379	22%	56%	17%	6%
		(2.62)	(3.15)	(2.36)	(1.51)
West North Central	**1,941**	**19%**	**56%**	**15%**	**10%**
		(1.01)	**(1.28)**	**(0.92)**	**(0.77)**
Iowa	258	19%	57%	15%	9%
		(2.35)	(2.99)	(2.17)	(1.75)
Kansas	263	24%	53%	15%	8%
		(2.39)	(2.78)	(1.98)	(1.51)
Minnesota	471	17%	61%	13%	9%
		(2.20)	(2.87)	(1.99)	(1.68)
Missouri	661	18%	53%	17%	12%
		(2.09)	(2.71)	(2.03)	(1.76)
Nebraska	137	20%	60%	11%	9%
		(2.46)	(2.99)	(1.91)	(1.73)
North Dakota	51	15%	59%	18%	8%
		(2.23)	(3.06)	(2.39)	(1.72)
South Dakota	98	24%	54%	12%	10%
		(1.92)	(2.24)	(1.47)	(1.36)
Mountain	**2,012**	**16%**	**59%**	**13%**	**11%**
		(0.78)	**(1.03)**	**(0.72)**	**(0.66)**
Arizona	529	16%	59%	15%	10%
		(1.83)	(2.45)	(1.78)	(1.50)
Colorado	395	17%	59%	13%	12%
		(2.15)	(2.84)	(1.94)	(1.86)
Idaho	167	23%	58%	12%	7%
		(1.86)	(2.17)	(1.43)	(1.13)
Montana	117	13%	60%	17%	9%
		(1.64)	(2.37)	(1.83)	(1.39)
Nevada	238	15%	58%	10%	17%
		(1.57)	(2.14)	(1.30)	(1.61)
New Mexico	319	15%	58%	13%	13%
		(1.44)	(1.97)	(1.34)	(1.36)
Utah	193	15%	63%	14%	8%
		(1.92)	(2.62)	(1.89)	(1.47)
Wyoming	55	17%	61%	14%	8%
		(2.40)	(3.12)	(2.23)	(1.73)
Pacific	**6,250**	**13%**	**57%**	**15%**	**15%**
		(0.52)	**(0.77)**	**(0.55)**	**(0.55)**
Alaska	97	18%	56%	15%	11%
		(1.57)	(2.03)	(1.46)	(1.29)
California	5,187	12%	58%	15%	15%
		(0.57)	(0.85)	(0.61)	(0.62)
Hawaii	75	20%	46%	14%	20%
		(3.03)	(3.80)	(2.64)	(3.07)
Oregon	370	17%	53%	20%	10%
		(2.12)	(2.82)	(2.28)	(1.67)
Washington	522	14%	55%	17%	15%
		(1.95)	(2.84)	(2.12)	(2.05)

Source: Three-year merged March CPS: 1991, 1992, and 1993.
Note: See table notes at end of Section C.

Table C5
Nonelderly Uninsured, 1990-92:
By Family Income Relative to Poverty[1,2,4]
(Persons in thousands, standard errors in parentheses)

	Number	<100%	100-199%	200-399%	400% +
United States	34,515	33% (0.55)	33% (0.55)	25% (0.50)	9% (0.33)
New England	1,225	26% (2.17)	31% (2.27)	31% (2.27)	12% (1.62)
Connecticut	238	19% (6.06)	34% (7.31)	35% (7.39)	13% (5.14)
Maine	137	26% (4.97)	41% (5.56)	27% (4.99)	7% (2.86)
Massachusetts	568	29% (2.91)	26% (2.81)	29% (2.92)	15% (2.30)
New Hampshire	139	26% (5.21)	33% (5.55)	34% (5.62)	7% (3.06)
Rhode Island	89	30% (6.29)	31% (6.35)	26% (5.99)	13% (4.59)
Vermont	55	26% (5.72)	36% (6.29)	33% (6.15)	5% (2.97)
Middle Atlantic	4,191	33% (1.40)	28% (1.35)	27% (1.34)	12% (0.96)
New Jersey	858	27% (2.58)	28% (2.61)	30% (2.67)	15% (2.05)
New York	2,256	34% (1.94)	27% (1.83)	26% (1.80)	13% (1.37)
Pennsylvania	1,078	34% (2.98)	31% (2.91)	28% (2.83)	7% (1.60)
South Atlantic	6,948	32% (1.26)	33% (1.27)	25% (1.16)	9% (0.78)
Delaware	91	23% (4.65)	36% (5.26)	28% (4.93)	13% (3.72)
District of Columbia	110	30% (4.59)	30% (4.59)	27% (4.41)	13% (3.33)
Florida	2,541	32% (1.91)	34% (1.94)	27% (1.81)	8% (1.10)
Georgia	1,049	37% (4.33)	32% (4.19)	23% (3.77)	8% (2.46)
Maryland	527	25% (5.10)	31% (5.40)	27% (5.20)	17% (4.39)
North Carolina	869	31% (2.39)	36% (2.48)	25% (2.24)	8% (1.44)
South Carolina	572	36% (3.95)	36% (3.93)	21% (3.34)	7% (2.12)
Virginia	964	30% (3.80)	31% (3.84)	25% (3.60)	13% (2.79)
West Virginia	227	44% (5.18)	36% (5.00)	16% (3.80)	4% (2.13)
East South Central	2,321	40% (2.31)	35% (2.26)	21% (1.93)	4% (0.89)
Alabama	706	44% (4.36)	33% (4.12)	21% (3.59)	3% (1.45)
Kentucky	443	39% (5.20)	34% (5.06)	22% (4.43)	5% (2.26)
Mississippi	497	40% (3.89)	37% (3.84)	18% (3.04)	5% (1.71)
Tennessee	675	35% (4.54)	38% (4.60)	24% (4.03)	3% (1.66)
West South Central	5,373	35% (1.53)	35% (1.53)	22% (1.34)	8% (0.85)
Arkansas	412	31% (4.04)	41% (4.29)	22% (3.64)	6% (2.08)
Louisiana	801	36% (4.20)	37% (4.22)	21% (3.55)	6% (2.11)
Oklahoma	586	32% (3.93)	39% (4.13)	22% (3.50)	7% (2.15)
Texas	3,575	36% (1.96)	33% (1.92)	23% (1.72)	8% (1.12)

Nonelderly Uninsured, 1990-92:
By Family Income Relative to Poverty[1,2,4]
(Persons in thousands, standard errors in parentheses)

	Number	<100%	100-199%	200-399%	400% +
East North Central	4,254	34% (1.59)	32% (1.56)	25% (1.43)	9% (0.93)
Illinois	1,327	35% (2.75)	30% (2.64)	26% (2.52)	9% (1.69)
Indiana	630	34% (5.37)	33% (5.31)	27% (5.02)	6% (2.75)
Michigan	867	39% (3.08)	32% (2.96)	21% (2.59)	7% (1.66)
Ohio	1,050	32% (2.86)	33% (2.88)	25% (2.67)	10% (1.83)
Wisconsin	379	29% (5.64)	41% (6.09)	22% (5.14)	8% (3.43)
West North Central	1,941	31% (2.33)	41% (2.48)	23% (2.11)	5% (1.12)
Iowa	258	29% (5.38)	39% (5.78)	26% (5.17)	6% (2.73)
Kansas	263	30% (5.02)	38% (5.30)	26% (4.76)	6% (2.59)
Minnesota	471	28% (5.16)	39% (5.59)	28% (5.18)	5% (2.52)
Missouri	661	34% (5.02)	47% (5.30)	15% (3.78)	4% (2.13)
Nebraska	137	25% (5.18)	44% (5.93)	24% (5.13)	7% (2.95)
North Dakota	51	34% (5.77)	33% (5.71)	26% (5.31)	7% (3.18)
South Dakota	98	37% (4.23)	28% (3.95)	29% (3.97)	7% (2.21)
Mountain	2,012	32% (1.92)	34% (1.96)	25% (1.79)	8% (1.11)
Arizona	529	34% (4.63)	34% (4.62)	26% (4.27)	6% (2.34)
Colorado	395	29% (5.13)	30% (5.17)	29% (5.14)	12% (3.62)
Idaho	167	32% (4.02)	36% (4.12)	27% (3.83)	5% (1.80)
Montana	117	34% (4.48)	38% (4.60)	24% (4.02)	4% (1.91)
Nevada	238	31% (3.92)	31% (3.92)	27% (3.76)	11% (2.70)
New Mexico	319	40% (3.83)	36% (3.74)	18% (3.01)	6% (1.86)
Utah	193	23% (4.49)	42% (5.26)	26% (4.69)	8% (2.97)
Wyoming	55	23% (5.24)	40% (6.12)	28% (5.59)	10% (3.75)
Pacific	6,250	33% (1.43)	32% (1.41)	25% (1.30)	10% (0.91)
Alaska	97	36% (3.82)	24% (3.43)	29% (3.63)	11% (2.49)
California	5,187	34% (1.60)	32% (1.58)	24% (1.45)	10% (1.02)
Hawaii	75	41% (7.33)	26% (6.51)	22% (6.19)	11% (4.70)
Oregon	370	29% (4.99)	39% (5.38)	22% (4.59)	10% (3.35)
Washington	522	31% (5.18)	30% (5.10)	30% (5.12)	9% (3.20)

Source: Three-year merged March CPS: 1991, 1992, and 1993.
Note: See table notes at end of Section C.

Table C6
Uninsured Adults Ages 18-64, 1990-92:
By Own Work Status[1,5]

(Persons in thousands, standard errors in parentheses)

	Number	Full-time	Part-time	Not Working
United States	**27,068**	**57%** (0.34)	**20%** (0.27)	**23%** (0.29)
New England	**994**	**56%** (1.39)	**22%** (1.16)	**21%** (1.15)
Connecticut	193	60% (4.31)	20% (3.51)	21% (3.55)
Maine	108	63% (3.15)	20% (2.60)	17% (2.45)
Massachusetts	465	52% (1.81)	24% (1.54)	24% (1.54)
New Hampshire	103	54% (3.51)	26% (3.08)	21% (2.85)
Rhode Island	78	64% (3.58)	16% (2.74)	20% (2.99)
Vermont	48	60% (3.54)	22% (2.97)	18% (2.80)
Middle Atlantic	**3,504**	**53%** (0.84)	**18%** (0.64)	**29%** (0.76)
New Jersey	698	57% (1.63)	18% (1.26)	25% (1.43)
New York	1,914	52% (1.14)	17% (0.85)	31% (1.05)
Pennsylvania	892	51% (1.77)	21% (1.44)	28% (1.59)
South Atlantic	**5,383**	**60%** (0.77)	**19%** (0.61)	**21%** (0.64)
Delaware	71	67% (2.99)	20% (2.55)	13% (2.13)
District of Columbia	88	60% (2.80)	14% (1.96)	27% (2.52)
Florida	1,966	59% (1.17)	19% (0.94)	21% (0.98)
Georgia	801	59% (2.59)	20% (2.10)	21% (2.15)
Maryland	422	64% (3.21)	17% (2.49)	19% (2.65)
North Carolina	685	62% (1.44)	18% (1.15)	19% (1.18)
South Carolina	435	58% (2.38)	18% (1.86)	24% (2.06)
Virginia	732	61% (2.37)	21% (1.96)	18% (1.87)
West Virginia	183	46% (2.96)	17% (2.25)	37% (2.86)
East South Central	**1,760**	**56%** (1.38)	**19%** (1.08)	**26%** (1.21)
Alabama	503	57% (2.64)	14% (1.87)	29% (2.41)
Kentucky	345	53% (3.09)	22% (2.55)	26% (2.70)
Mississippi	371	58% (2.32)	17% (1.78)	25% (2.04)
Tennessee	541	55% (2.70)	22% (2.24)	23% (2.28)
West South Central	**3,991**	**59%** (0.94)	**18%** (0.74)	**23%** (0.80)
Arkansas	281	60% (2.65)	24% (2.31)	16% (1.98)
Louisiana	612	55% (2.54)	17% (1.90)	28% (2.31)
Oklahoma	437	58% (2.46)	22% (2.07)	20% (1.99)
Texas	2,661	59% (1.19)	18% (0.92)	23% (1.02)

Table C6 (continued)
Uninsured Adults Ages 18-64, 1990-92:
By Own Work Status[1,5]
(Persons in thousands, standard errors in parentheses)

	Number	Full-time	Part-time	Not Working
East North Central	**3,475**	**55%**	**23%**	**23%**
		(0.94)	**(0.79)**	**(0.79)**
Illinois	1,083	54%	21%	25%
		(1.63)	(1.34)	(1.41)
Indiana	490	58%	23%	19%
		(3.25)	(2.76)	(2.60)
Michigan	705	51%	27%	23%
		(1.79)	(1.58)	(1.51)
Ohio	900	53%	20%	26%
		(1.69)	(1.37)	(1.49)
Wisconsin	298	66%	25%	10%
		(3.40)	(3.08)	(2.13)
West North Central	**1,480**	**61%**	**22%**	**17%**
		(1.44)	**(1.22)**	**(1.11)**
Iowa	207	65%	21%	14%
		(3.23)	(2.76)	(2.35)
Kansas	193	65%	22%	14%
		(3.12)	(2.68)	(2.24)
Minnesota	380	64%	24%	13%
		(3.14)	(2.78)	(2.17)
Missouri	487	56%	21%	23%
		(3.14)	(2.58)	(2.68)
Nebraska	103	62%	19%	18%
		(3.41)	(2.77)	(2.73)
North Dakota	41	61%	27%	13%
		(3.41)	(3.08)	(2.33)
South Dakota	69	62%	21%	17%
		(2.61)	(2.19)	(2.00)
Mountain	**1,502**	**59%**	**22%**	**19%**
		(1.20)	**(1.00)**	**(0.96)**
Arizona	418	57%	22%	20%
		(2.78)	(2.34)	(2.27)
Colorado	304	60%	21%	19%
		(3.22)	(2.67)	(2.59)
Idaho	117	65%	21%	15%
		(2.51)	(2.12)	(1.86)
Montana	86	60%	28%	13%
		(2.76)	(2.52)	(1.87)
Nevada	173	62%	16%	21%
		(2.47)	(1.87)	(2.09)
New Mexico	232	56%	20%	25%
		(2.33)	(1.86)	(2.02)
Utah	133	60%	28%	12%
		(3.21)	(2.93)	(2.15)
Wyoming	40	65%	22%	13%
		(3.58)	(3.12)	(2.49)
Pacific	**4,977**	**55%**	**20%**	**24%**
		(0.86)	**(0.69)**	**(0.74)**
Alaska	73	63%	19%	18%
		(2.28)	(1.85)	(1.82)
California	4,129	55%	19%	26%
		(0.96)	(0.77)	(0.85)
Hawaii	59	59%	17%	24%
		(4.22)	(3.21)	(3.67)
Oregon	295	58%	25%	17%
		(3.12)	(2.73)	(2.38)
Washington	421	57%	23%	20%
		(3.15)	(2.67)	(2.54)

Source: Three-year merged March CPS: 1991, 1992, and 1993.
Note: See table notes at end of Section C.

Table C7
Uninsured Workers, Ages 18-64, 1990-92:
By Firm Size[1,6,7]

(Persons in thousands, standard errors in parentheses)

	Number	Number of Workers in Firm		
		Under 25	25-99	100+
United States	**20,706**	48%	16%	36%
		(0.39)	(0.28)	(0.37)
New England	**779**	49%	16%	36%
		(1.58)	(1.14)	(1.51)
Connecticut	153	52%	13%	35%
		(4.93)	(3.36)	(4.70)
Maine	90	50%	15%	35%
		(3.58)	(2.56)	(3.42)
Massachusetts	354	43%	17%	40%
		(2.06)	(1.54)	(2.03)
New Hampshire	82	59%	12%	29%
		(3.88)	(2.58)	(3.57)
Rhode Island	62	47%	23%	31%
		(4.17)	(3.49)	(3.85)
Vermont	39	63%	11%	26%
		(3.86)	(2.53)	(3.50)
Middle Atlantic	**2,480**	46%	17%	37%
		(0.99)	(0.75)	(0.96)
New Jersey	521	48%	17%	35%
		(1.90)	(1.44)	(1.82)
New York	1,320	45%	18%	37%
		(1.37)	(1.05)	(1.32)
Pennsylvania	638	47%	15%	38%
		(2.09)	(1.49)	(2.03)
South Atlantic	**4,233**	47%	15%	38%
		(0.88)	(0.62)	(0.86)
Delaware	62	38%	16%	46%
		(3.29)	(2.51)	(3.39)
District of Columbia	65	36%	14%	50%
		(3.19)	(2.27)	(3.33)
Florida	1,545	50%	16%	33%
		(1.35)	(1.00)	(1.27)
Georgia	629	47%	13%	40%
		(2.96)	(1.97)	(2.91)
Maryland	338	45%	11%	44%
		(3.72)	(2.31)	(3.71)
North Carolina	552	45%	15%	40%
		(1.65)	(1.19)	(1.63)
South Carolina	328	42%	15%	43%
		(2.74)	(1.95)	(2.74)
Virginia	598	46%	13%	41%
		(2.68)	(1.81)	(2.65)
West Virginia	115	52%	16%	32%
		(3.74)	(2.77)	(3.48)
East South Central	**1,302**	50%	15%	34%
		(1.61)	(1.16)	(1.53)
Alabama	357	52%	13%	35%
		(3.16)	(2.15)	(3.02)
Kentucky	254	55%	18%	27%
		(3.58)	(2.77)	(3.19)
Mississippi	276	49%	18%	33%
		(2.73)	(2.08)	(2.57)
Tennessee	415	47%	14%	39%
		(3.09)	(2.15)	(3.01)
West South Central	**3,058**	48%	15%	37%
		(1.09)	(0.77)	(1.05)
Arkansas	235	50%	14%	36%
		(2.95)	(2.04)	(2.84)
Louisiana	436	46%	16%	38%
		(3.02)	(2.21)	(2.94)
Oklahoma	348	52%	14%	34%
		(2.80)	(1.95)	(2.65)
Texas	2,040	48%	15%	37%
		(1.38)	(0.99)	(1.34)

Table C7 (continued)
Uninsured Workers, Ages 18-64, 1990-92:
By Firm Size[1,6,7]
(Persons in thousands, standard errors in parentheses)

	Number	Number of Workers in Firm		
		Under 25	25-99	100+
East North Central	**2,679**	**43%**	**17%**	**40%**
		(1.07)	**(0.80)**	**(1.05)**
Illinois	815	42%	16%	41%
		(1.86)	(1.39)	(1.85)
Indiana	393	42%	15%	42%
		(3.62)	(2.65)	(3.62)
Michigan	541	46%	15%	39%
		(2.04)	(1.47)	(2.00)
Ohio	661	44%	16%	40%
		(1.96)	(1.44)	(1.93)
Wisconsin	269	41%	24%	35%
		(3.71)	(3.20)	(3.59)
West North Central	**1,218**	**45%**	**16%**	**38%**
		(1.62)	**(1.20)**	**(1.58)**
Iowa	177	47%	17%	36%
		(3.64)	(2.75)	(3.50)
Kansas	163	45%	16%	39%
		(3.52)	(2.61)	(3.46)
Minnesota	330	47%	17%	36%
		(3.50)	(2.64)	(3.38)
Missouri	373	41%	16%	43%
		(3.56)	(2.66)	(3.57)
Nebraska	84	50%	14%	36%
		(3.89)	(2.68)	(3.74)
North Dakota	35	54%	12%	34%
		(3.75)	(2.44)	(3.57)
South Dakota	55	49%	14%	37%
		(3.00)	(2.08)	(2.89)
Mountain	**1,210**	**49%**	**15%**	**36%**
		(1.36)	**(0.96)**	**(1.30)**
Arizona	331	47%	17%	36%
		(3.15)	(2.35)	(3.03)
Colorado	245	46%	15%	40%
		(3.65)	(2.59)	(3.58)
Idaho	99	52%	17%	31%
		(2.85)	(2.15)	(2.64)
Montana	75	65%	11%	24%
		(2.89)	(1.89)	(2.59)
Nevada	135	44%	15%	40%
		(2.85)	(2.07)	(2.82)
New Mexico	174	52%	15%	34%
		(2.70)	(1.91)	(2.55)
Utah	116	52%	10%	38%
		(3.51)	(2.11)	(3.40)
Wyoming	34	56%	12%	32%
		(4.01)	(2.62)	(3.76)
Pacific	**3,747**	**51%**	**17%**	**32%**
		(1.00)	**(0.76)**	**(0.93)**
Alaska	60	57%	13%	31%
		(2.58)	(1.74)	(2.40)
California	3,062	50%	18%	32%
		(1.13)	(0.86)	(1.05)
Hawaii	45	51%	13%	36%
		(4.92)	(3.30)	(4.74)
Oregon	243	54%	15%	30%
		(3.47)	(2.52)	(3.20)
Washington	337	52%	16%	32%
		(3.55)	(2.60)	(3.32)

Source: Three-year merged March CPS: 1991, 1992, and 1993.
Note: See table notes at end of Section C.

Table C8
Uninsured Workers, Ages 18-64, 1990-92:
By Sector[1,6,7]

(Persons in thousands, standard errors in parentheses)

	Number	Private	Public	Self-Employed[8]
United States	20,706	82% (0.30)	7% (0.19)	12% (0.25)
New England	779	82% (1.22)	6% (0.73)	13% (1.05)
Connecticut	153	86% (3.44)	4% (2.02)	10% (2.93)
Maine	90	77% (3.04)	6% (1.68)	18% (2.73)
Massachusetts	354	82% (1.61)	8% (1.10)	11% (1.28)
New Hampshire	82	78% (3.29)	3% (1.40)	19% (3.11)
Rhode Island	62	86% (2.87)	3% (1.46)	10% (2.56)
Vermont	39	79% (3.28)	3% (1.32)	18% (3.11)
Middle Atlantic	2,480	83% (0.76)	7% (0.50)	11% (0.62)
New Jersey	521	82% (1.45)	6% (0.91)	12% (1.22)
New York	1,320	82% (1.05)	8% (0.73)	10% (0.83)
Pennsylvania	638	84% (1.55)	5% (0.94)	11% (1.31)
South Atlantic	4,233	83% (0.67)	7% (0.44)	11% (0.55)
Delaware	62	86% (2.35)	6% (1.62)	8% (1.83)
District of Columbia	65	73% (2.94)	19% (2.63)	7% (1.72)
Florida	1,545	84% (0.99)	5% (0.56)	12% (0.86)
Georgia	629	83% (2.21)	7% (1.49)	10% (1.77)
Maryland	338	74% (3.28)	12% (2.46)	14% (2.57)
North Carolina	552	82% (1.27)	6% (0.80)	11% (1.06)
South Carolina	328	83% (2.07)	8% (1.52)	9% (1.56)
Virginia	598	84% (1.95)	6% (1.27)	10% (1.59)
West Virginia	115	83% (2.82)	7% (1.85)	11% (2.30)
East South Central	1,302	83% (1.21)	5% (0.71)	12% (1.04)
Alabama	357	83% (2.35)	3% (1.00)	14% (2.19)
Kentucky	254	84% (2.64)	4% (1.42)	12% (2.34)
Mississippi	276	81% (2.13)	9% (1.54)	10% (1.64)
Tennessee	415	84% (2.28)	5% (1.40)	11% (1.92)
West South Central	3,058	81% (0.85)	7% (0.57)	11% (0.68)
Arkansas	235	78% (2.45)	10% (1.74)	13% (1.96)
Louisiana	436	81% (2.36)	9% (1.77)	9% (1.75)
Oklahoma	348	73% (2.48)	10% (1.66)	17% (2.09)
Texas	2,040	83% (1.04)	6% (0.68)	10% (0.85)

Table C8 (continued)
Uninsured Workers, Ages 18-64, 1990-92:
By Sector[1,6,7]
(Persons in thousands, standard errors in parentheses)

	Number	Private	Public	Self-Employed[8]
East North Central	**2,679**	**84%**	**7%**	**9%**
		(0.79)	**(0.54)**	**(0.63)**
Illinois	815	84%	6%	9%
		(1.37)	(0.92)	(1.10)
Indiana	393	87%	3%	9%
		(2.43)	(1.28)	(2.15)
Michigan	541	82%	8%	10%
		(1.57)	(1.10)	(1.23)
Ohio	661	84%	8%	9%
		(1.45)	(1.04)	(1.11)
Wisconsin	269	80%	10%	10%
		(3.04)	(2.26)	(2.31)
West North Central	**1,218**	**80%**	**7%**	**13%**
		(1.30)	**(0.84)**	**(1.09)**
Iowa	177	77%	7%	16%
		(3.08)	(1.87)	(2.68)
Kansas	163	75%	8%	17%
		(3.07)	(1.95)	(2.66)
Minnesota	330	82%	7%	11%
		(2.71)	(1.80)	(2.21)
Missouri	373	85%	5%	10%
		(2.59)	(1.59)	(2.18)
Nebraska	84	76%	7%	17%
		(3.31)	(1.98)	(2.90)
North Dakota	35	74%	14%	12%
		(3.32)	(2.63)	(2.46)
South Dakota	55	72%	14%	14%
		(2.70)	(2.09)	(2.08)
Mountain	**1,210**	**79%**	**7%**	**13%**
		(1.10)	**(0.71)**	**(0.92)**
Arizona	331	84%	4%	12%
		(2.32)	(1.24)	(2.06)
Colorado	245	80%	8%	13%
		(2.96)	(1.96)	(2.44)
Idaho	99	80%	9%	11%
		(2.27)	(1.61)	(1.79)
Montana	75	72%	13%	16%
		(2.73)	(2.01)	(2.21)
Nevada	135	81%	6%	13%
		(2.24)	(1.33)	(1.94)
New Mexico	174	71%	11%	18%
		(2.45)	(1.69)	(2.08)
Utah	116	82%	8%	11%
		(2.71)	(1.86)	(2.17)
Wyoming	34	75%	11%	14%
		(3.50)	(2.48)	(2.85)
Pacific	**3,747**	**81%**	**6%**	**13%**
		(0.78)	**(0.47)**	**(0.68)**
Alaska	60	64%	16%	19%
		(2.49)	(1.92)	(2.06)
California	3,062	82%	5%	13%
		(0.86)	(0.47)	(0.76)
Hawaii	45	70%	12%	17%
		(4.50)	(3.25)	(3.73)
Oregon	243	79%	7%	14%
		(2.83)	(1.79)	(2.41)
Washington	337	73%	13%	14%
		(3.16)	(2.40)	(2.47)

Source: Three-year merged March CPS: 1991, 1992, and 1993.
Note: See table notes at end of Section C.

Table C9
Private-Sector Uninsured Workers Ages 18-64, 1990-92:
By Industry[1,6,7]
(Persons in thousands, standard errors in parentheses)

	Number	Manufacturing	Services	Wholesale/ Retail	Other[9]
United States	**16,964**	**15%** (0.30)	**28%** (0.39)	**32%** (0.40)	**24%** (0.37)
New England	**637**	**18%** (1.34)	**32%** (1.64)	**32%** (1.63)	**18%** (1.34)
Connecticut	132	22% (4.38)	31% (4.93)	32% (4.96)	15% (3.84)
Maine	69	19% (3.18)	33% (3.86)	28% (3.68)	20% (3.27)
Massachusetts	289	16% (1.70)	33% (2.16)	32% (2.15)	18% (1.77)
New Hampshire	63	9% (2.56)	33% (4.22)	39% (4.38)	19% (3.51)
Rhode Island	54	30% (4.11)	26% (3.96)	28% (4.04)	16% (3.26)
Vermont	31	10% (2.76)	39% (4.39)	28% (4.06)	23% (3.78)
Middle Atlantic	**2,048**	**15%** (0.78)	**30%** (1.01)	**34%** (1.04)	**21%** (0.90)
New Jersey	430	15% (1.51)	28% (1.89)	34% (1.99)	22% (1.75)
New York	1,084	15% (1.09)	31% (1.40)	32% (1.42)	22% (1.25)
Pennsylvania	534	14% (1.60)	29% (2.08)	36% (2.20)	21% (1.85)
South Atlantic	**3,499**	**15%** (0.69)	**27%** (0.86)	**31%** (0.89)	**27%** (0.86)
Delaware	53	13% (2.48)	34% (3.46)	26% (3.22)	27% (3.25)
District of Columbia	47	4% (1.49)	49% (3.88)	34% (3.67)	14% (2.66)
Florida	1,296	11% (0.91)	27% (1.30)	31% (1.36)	32% (1.36)
Georgia	524	18% (2.47)	28% (2.93)	30% (2.97)	24% (2.78)
Maryland	250	9% (2.46)	30% (4.00)	34% (4.10)	27% (3.88)
North Carolina	455	24% (1.56)	25% (1.58)	29% (1.65)	23% (1.53)
South Carolina	273	25% (2.62)	23% (2.56)	30% (2.80)	22% (2.50)
Virginia	505	14% (2.04)	28% (2.64)	29% (2.67)	28% (2.63)
West Virginia	96	10% (2.44)	29% (3.71)	35% (3.92)	27% (3.64)
East South Central	**1,083**	**16%** (1.31)	**25%** (1.53)	**33%** (1.67)	**26%** (1.54)
Alabama	298	17% (2.59)	26% (3.05)	34% (3.28)	23% (2.90)
Kentucky	213	12% (2.54)	26% (3.46)	37% (3.80)	25% (3.40)
Mississippi	224	20% (2.44)	23% (2.55)	30% (2.77)	27% (2.68)
Tennessee	348	16% (2.51)	24% (2.88)	32% (3.16)	28% (3.02)
West South Central	**2,489**	**13%** (0.80)	**28%** (1.08)	**32%** (1.13)	**27%** (1.07)
Arkansas	183	18% (2.57)	24% (2.88)	30% (3.07)	28% (2.99)
Louisiana	355	6% (1.61)	28% (3.02)	32% (3.14)	34% (3.18)
Oklahoma	255	17% (2.47)	27% (2.91)	37% (3.16)	18% (2.53)
Texas	1,696	13% (1.01)	29% (1.38)	32% (1.41)	27% (1.35)

Table C9 (continued)
Private-Sector Uninsured Workers Ages 18-64, 1990-92:
By Industry[1,6,7]
(Persons in thousands, standard errors in parentheses)

	Number	Manufacturing	Services	Wholesale/ Retail	Other[9]
East North Central	**2,242**	**15%**	**30%**	**34%**	**20%**
		(0.84)	**(1.08)**	**(1.12)**	**(0.95)**
Illinois	686	14%	32%	35%	19%
		(1.40)	(1.91)	(1.96)	(1.62)
Indiana	343	15%	26%	34%	25%
		(2.80)	(3.43)	(3.73)	(3.39)
Michigan	444	14%	31%	34%	21%
		(1.57)	(2.10)	(2.14)	(1.82)
Ohio	555	15%	31%	34%	20%
		(1.56)	(2.00)	(2.04)	(1.71)
Wisconsin	214	23%	26%	34%	17%
		(3.54)	(3.71)	(4.01)	(3.18)
West North Central	**975**	**12%**	**29%**	**38%**	**21%**
		(1.18)	**(1.65)**	**(1.77)**	**(1.48)**
Iowa	136	17%	25%	33%	25%
		(3.11)	(3.59)	(3.93)	(3.60)
Kansas	122	13%	22%	38%	27%
		(2.73)	(3.41)	(3.98)	(3.62)
Minnesota	270	10%	28%	42%	20%
		(2.29)	(3.49)	(3.84)	(3.11)
Missouri	317	12%	35%	37%	16%
		(2.59)	(3.75)	(3.78)	(2.86)
Nebraska	64	13%	27%	42%	18%
		(3.02)	(3.95)	(4.40)	(3.43)
North Dakota	26	5%	20%	46%	30%
		(1.89)	(3.48)	(4.37)	(4.00)
South Dakota	40	9%	26%	32%	33%
		(2.00)	(3.11)	(3.30)	(3.32)
Mountain	**960**	**11%**	**29%**	**35%**	**26%**
		(0.95)	**(1.38)**	**(1.45)**	**(1.34)**
Arizona	277	12%	33%	31%	24%
		(2.26)	(3.23)	(3.19)	(2.95)
Colorado	195	11%	25%	38%	25%
		(2.62)	(3.55)	(3.99)	(3.57)
Idaho	80	12%	27%	35%	26%
		(2.09)	(2.82)	(3.04)	(2.79)
Montana	53	7%	26%	40%	28%
		(1.77)	(3.12)	(3.50)	(3.22)
Nevada	110	6%	39%	31%	24%
		(1.54)	(3.11)	(2.94)	(2.72)
New Mexico	124	11%	26%	39%	23%
		(2.04)	(2.81)	(3.13)	(2.70)
Utah	95	13%	22%	31%	35%
		(2.58)	(3.20)	(3.59)	(3.71)
Wyoming	26	6%	18%	38%	38%
		(2.24)	(3.56)	(4.53)	(4.54)
Pacific	**3,032**	**16%**	**28%**	**30%**	**26%**
		(0.82)	**(0.99)**	**(1.02)**	**(0.97)**
Alaska	38	6%	29%	34%	31%
		(1.55)	(2.93)	(3.07)	(3.01)
California	2,524	17%	28%	29%	26%
		(0.93)	(1.11)	(1.13)	(1.09)
Hawaii	---	---	---	---	---
		---	---	---	---
Oregon	192	13%	28%	35%	24%
		(2.66)	(3.54)	(3.73)	(3.34)
Washington	246	11%	26%	36%	26%
		(2.63)	(3.66)	(4.00)	(3.66)

Source: Three-year merged March CPS: 1991, 1992, and 1993.
Note: See table notes at end of Section C.

Notes to Tables, Section C

1. Population in the merged CPS file excludes persons aged 65 and over, those living in institutions, and those in families with active military service members. The tables in this section include only persons without insurance coverage for an entire year. The CPS does not currently collect information on persons who are without coverage for less than 12 months (see Appendix Three). Percentages may not sum to 100 owing to rounding.

2. We define families as health insurance units. A health insurance unit includes the members of a nuclear family who can be covered under one health policy. The standard we use follows a typical insurance industry standard: a policy-holder may cover his or her spouse, all children under age 18, and children between ages 18 and 21 who are full-time students. Thus, whereas a single 25-year-old child living with his or her parents may be included in the parents' nuclear family, he or she would be treated as a separate, single health unit.

3. These categories reflect the work status of the head and spouse only. There-fore, if both parents in a family do not work but a dependent child is employed, the family is classified as nonworking. Work status is based on the *usual* number of hours per week reported for the reference year. We define full-time work as 35 hours per week or more. Nonwork reflects a report of zero hours of work.

These categories are hierarchical, so each person is shown only in the first appropriate category. For example, a person in a health unit where the head works full-time and the spouse part-time would be classified only in the one full-time worker group.

4. Incomes used in these tables are primarily the incomes reported on the CPS. However, we incorporated some corrections to incomes estimated by the Urban Institute's TRIM2 model. The model corrects for underreporting of income from the cash welfare programs—AFDC and SSI—and makes corrections to reported interest and dividend incomes. See Linda Giannarelli, 1992, *An Analyst's Guide to TRIM2* (Washington, D.C.: Urban Institute Press) for details.

Poverty is defined using the federal poverty guidelines from the U.S. Depart-ment of Health and Human Services.

5. Own-work status is based on the report of *usual* hours worked per week during the reference year. We define full-time work as 35 hours per week or more; part-time work as 1–34 hours per week; and nonwork as 0 hours per week.

6. Workers are defined as persons 18 to 64 years old reporting a positive number of usual hours worked. Workers reporting work "without pay" are treated as nonworkers.

7. Firm size, sector, and industry are based on the job held for the longest period during the year preceding the March CPS interview.

8. "Self-Employed" includes self-employed unincorporated workers. The self-employed incorporated are classified as private-sector workers.

9. "Other" includes these industries: agriculture, forestry, fisheries, mining, construction, transportation, communication, public utilities, finance, insurance, and real estate. Public-sector workers are not included in this table.

All Tables:

*** A triple asterisk in the tables indicates no observations on the merged CPS file of this type.

--- A triple dash in the tables indicates fewer than 100 observations on the merged CPS file of this type. We have not printed estimates in these cases.

Medicaid

In the absence of health care reform, Medicaid remains the primary means for providing medical care—from physician services to long-term nursing home care—to the nation's indigent and disabled populations. Approximately 13 percent of the population received some form of medical coverage through Medicaid in 1992. Furthermore, the program's costs have been rising dramatically—reaching over $126 billion in 1993—affecting both state and federal governments responsible for financing this important source of access to medical care.

The focus on Medicaid has increased in the last few years. State governments have become alarmed by the growing share of their budgets that Medicaid consumes. The federal government, which pays for approximately 57 percent of national Medicaid expenditures, is similarly concerned by the program's recent surge in overall costs. The growing emphasis on the uninsured—including the poor who do not qualify for Medicaid—has pressured state governments to find ways to increase Medicaid enrollments while at the same time attempting to control the program's rapidly escalating costs.

Under relatively broad federal guidelines, the responsibilities of determining eligibility, paying providers, and general program administration fall to the state governments. Although the federal government mandates coverage for certain categorical groups and services, a number of groups and services are left to state discretion. Arising from this individual state control is a disparate group of 51 (including the District of Columbia) separate Medicaid programs, each with different eligibility rules and covered services.

Section D provides data on the different facets of each state's Medicaid program: eligibility, enrollment, participation, and expenditures by eligibility group and type of service. In all cases, data for the most recent year available were used. For state demographic characteristics the most recent year available was the 1990–92 period (based on the three-year merged March Current Population Surveys for 1991, 1992, and 1993—see Appendix Two), whereas the most recent year for Medicaid expenditures was 1993. Tables clearly indicate the year for which the data apply.

The issues of Medicaid eligibility, enrollment, and participation are addressed by tables D1 and D2 using data from the merged Current Population Survey file. Other tables in this section are based primarily on program administration data. Table D3 shows Medicaid enrollment rates separately for children, adults, the elderly, and the blind and disabled. The recent surge in Medicaid expenditures between 1990 and 1993 is detailed in table D4. Table D5 shows Medicaid enrollees, expenditures, and expenditures per enrollee for 1993 by major eligibility group. New to this edition is the D6 table series, which was added to provide data on acute care expenditures by cash assistance (AFDC and SSI) status of enrollees. These tables may facilitate discussions of state maintenance of effort under potential health care reform proposals. Also new is the D7 table series, which shows expenditures by service category by state. Finally, table D8 provides useful information on the payment rates for some Medicaid services relative to similar services provided by Medicare.

Another important change in this edition is the explicit exclusion of disproportionate share payments (DSH) to inpatient hospitals or mental health institutions from most of the reported Medicaid expenditures. The use of DSH payments was designed, in theory, to enable states to compensate particular institutions that served disproportionately large numbers of Medicaid patients (who are generally reimbursed at lower rates than private patients) and individuals who are under- or uninsured. These expenditures were excluded since the payments were not made on behalf of specific individuals, and thus should not be included in per enrollee numbers. Since the level of DSH payments is large (13.5 percent of total expenditures in 1993), the reader should be cautious in making time-trend comparisons with Medicaid expenditures reported in the first edition of this volume. Table D7e shows DSH payments for 1992 and 1993.

With the exception of tables D1 and D2, data for the state of Arizona are not included. Arizona currently offers medical care for its indigent populations under a 1115(a) waiver, which makes its Medicaid program less comparable to other states' programs. The U.S. Territories were excluded from all tables due to their unique financing arrangements and small cell sizes.

ELIGIBILITY AND PARTICIPATION, 1990–92

The rules and demographics governing Medicaid eligibility and enrollment vary considerably from state to state. Historically, Medicaid eligibility has been tied to the receipt of cash assistance such as Aid to Families with Dependent Children (AFDC) or Supplemental Security Income (SSI). Within federal guidelines, states have control over the income, asset, and family structure criteria determining AFDC eligibility; Medicaid eligibility levels for similar populations at different income thresholds can therefore vary from state to state. Not all states are required to grant Medicaid eligibility to individuals receiving SSI, and instead use an alternative set of criteria for determining eligibility for disabled persons. Also, differences in eligibility arise from the lack of medically needy programs in some states. Finally, states have had the option of expanding coverage (with corresponding federal financial participation) to certain poverty-related groups such as pregnant women and children; although certain guidelines for these groups are becoming standardized by the federal government, states continue to vary in their willingness and fiscal ability to extend such coverage.

The estimates of persons eligible for Medicaid presented here were developed using a microsimulation model that takes each state's different Medicaid program rules into account. The model examines the characteristics of each person on the Current Population Survey (CPS) to determine whether that person falls into at least one of the state's categorical eligibility groups, whether the person's assets fall below the limits defined for that eligibility group, and whether the person's income falls below the state's maximum threshold. Persons who actually enroll in Medicaid were chosen from the eligible population using various criteria to match states' administrative records on enrollees (see Appendix Three).

Table D1 provides data on the percentage of the population eligible for Medicaid, the percentage of the population that enrolls, and the participation rate—defined as the percentage of eligibles who enroll. The percentage of the population eligible for Medicaid is relatively low for Delaware and South Dakota, yet is high for such different areas as California, the District of Columbia, Louisiana, and Mississippi. The percentage eligible reflects both the number of low-income people in the state and the generosity of state Medicaid programs' eligibility rules. For example, New York, California, Mississippi, and Louisiana all have relatively high rates of eligibility for Medicaid (20–25 percent). However, the poverty rates in New York and California are substantially less than the poverty rates in Mississippi and Louisiana. The relatively high Medicaid eligibility rates in New York and California are associated with their liberal eligibility rules. Mississippi and Louisiana have less-generous eligibility standards, however; high eligibility in these states is associated with their high poverty rates.

The percentage of Medicaid eligibles who enroll in Medicaid (participation rate), also shown in table D1, depends on many factors, including attitudes toward welfare and Medicaid, as well as eligibility processing systems and outreach efforts by the states. Participation may also be lower among groups targeted for recent program expansions, because these generally higher-income groups may not be aware of their eligibility or may be more likely to have health coverage from some other source. The estimated participation rate varies from 49 percent in New Hampshire to 92.8 percent in West Virginia. The differences between states' Medicaid-eligible and enrollee populations give policymakers some indication of the number of additional persons who could potentially enroll in Medicaid under eligibility rules in effect during 1990–92. In areas where participation rates are low (such as the West South Central region), full program participation could increase the Medicaid rolls dramatically and significantly reduce the number of uninsured in these areas. Note that some of the estimates have large standard errors; since this concept is extremely important for reasons of interpretation, a discussion of confidence intervals around these estimates is included in Appendix Two.

Table D2 shows Medicaid program participation as a percentage of those eligible by age groups 0 to 17 and 18 to 64. Unfortunately, small cell sizes for some states lead to potentially unreliable estimates, and data for those states are therefore not shown. Participation by age is important because some Medicaid expansion policies focus on certain age groups, particularly children. In general, adults have lower participation rates than children, but adults in the East North Central and Pacific regions are more likely to enroll than adults living elsewhere. Children in the Middle Atlantic, East North Central, and Pacific regions have higher participation rates than children living elsewhere in the country. As mentioned in the discussion for table D1, the standard errors should be taken into account when interpreting any of the state-level figures.

Enrollment and Enrollment Rates, 1992

Table D3 shows 1992 Medicaid enrollments, in total and per 1,000 population by major eligibility group. The total enrollee figures in this table differ from those reported in table D1, since they are based on HCFA administrative records for 1992 (versus CPS data for 1990–92) and include the elderly and the institutionalized. The number of enrollees per 1,000 population varies considerably from a low of 70 per 1,000 population in New Hampshire to highs of over 230 enrollees per 1,000 in the District of Columbia and Rhode Island. As shown in previous tables, the different enrollment levels found in states are due not only to different underlying socioeconomic factors but to different eligibility rules.

Enrollment rates are highest for children in all states, which in part reflects the focus this group has received in recent eligibility expansion efforts. Table D3 also shows the important role that Medicaid plays in medical coverage for children in the United States; more than one out of four children receive their medical care through the Medicaid program. This ratio is especially high in the District of Columbia, which provides Medicaid services to over half of the children who reside there. The elderly have the next highest enrollment rates, which is most likely due to use of long-term care services (not offered through Medicare) that can quickly impoverish individuals into becoming eligible for Medicaid. Adults have generally lower enrollment rates and, as shown in table A2b, are those most likely to fall through the cracks of health care insurance coverage. This is owing to the categorical requirements of Medicaid eligibility, which make coverage unlikely for many nondisabled adults, regardless of income (single individuals and childless couples, for example).

ENROLLMENT AND EXPENDITURE GROWTH, 1990–93

Table D4 shows Medicaid enrollment and expenditure growth for 1990–92 and 1992–93. Figures for growth in expenditures are shown with and without disproportionate share payments (DSH) included. Including DSH, Medicaid spending grew significantly for most states, with a high of 83.4 percent per year for New Hampshire between 1990 and 1992 (27.7 percent, not including DSH payments). Nationally, Medicaid spending between 1990 and 1992 grew at an average of 28 percent per year—from $69.0 billion in 1990 to $113.1 billion in 1992.

Note that, not including DSH payments, expenditures per enrollee growth for this same period (1990–92) were relatively low; some states, like Alaska, California, Colorado, New Hampshire, Rhode Island, and Virginia, actually reported negative growth. The pattern of growth between states and regions is uneven. Regional growth rates ranged from a low of 1.3 percent for the Pacific states to a high of 13.2 percent for the East South Central states (table D4).

Enrollment, expenditure, and expenditure per enrollee growth all slowed in 1993. Most notable is the decline in overall expenditures, including DSH. This is likely due to the changes in the 1991 Medicaid Voluntary Contribution and Provider-Specific Tax Amendments, which restricted states' ability to utilize provider tax and donation mechanisms and placed a national cap on DSH expenditures. For many states, this had a marked effect on overall expenditure growth. At the national level, expenditure growth including DSH payments fell to 10.7 percent for 1992–93. For expenditures per Medicaid enrollee (excluding DSH), a few states actually reported negative growth during 1992–93, while most states reported (non-DSH) growth rates of 10 percent or more (table D4).

EXPENDITURES PER ENROLLEE, 1993

Medicaid expenditures for nondisabled children averaged $955 annually per child enrollee in 1993, as shown in table D5. Most regions were within a few hundred dollars of this average, except for the

Pacific region, which averaged $664 per enrollee. The figures for the Pacific region are heavily weighted by the large population of California, which reported a national low of $605 per child enrollee. Children—while making up the largest single group of Medicaid enrollees—cost less to cover than any other subgroup covered by Medicaid.

The pattern for expenditures and enrollees for nondisabled adults is similar to the distribution found for children. The Middle Atlantic states—New Jersey and New York, in particular—reported relative high levels of expenditures per adult enrollee. The Pacific states, again heavily influenced by California, reported an average of around $1,494. The lowest relative expenditures, although close in magnitude to the Pacific states, were reported in the West North Central region at $1,507 per adult enrollee (table D5).

Elderly Medicaid enrollees are considerably more expensive than adults or children, and averaged $8,704 per enrollee in 1993 (table D5). The higher costs associated with the elderly reflect heavy use of nursing home and home health services. SNF/ICF (skilled nursing facility/intermediate care facility-other) services are frequently picked up under the medically needy provisions in state law, according to which individuals only become eligible for Medicaid after "spending down" their income and assets to state predetermined levels. Expenditures in 1993 were particularly high in New York, at $17,464 per elderly enrollee, reflecting New York's large long-term care program. Connecticut reported a national high at $21,494.

Accurate figures for blind persons and those with disabilities were not available by age; therefore, the figures presented include children, adults, and elderly individuals. Like the aged, blind persons and those with disabilities are relatively expensive, averaging $7,216 per enrollee in 1993 (table D5).

ACUTE CARE EXPENDITURES BY CASH ASSISTANCE STATUS, 1993

With the recent focus on health care reform, the issue of state "maintenance of effort" for state expenditures on Medicaid-covered populations has been actively debated. Since many national reform plans have attempted to shift current Medicaid enrollees into "mainstream" plans, the federal government would have to assume the full cost of these individuals (compared to paying only a portion of the cost as it does now). To lessen the financial impact on the federal government, states would be required to maintain a certain level of financial "effort" in relation to current Medicaid expenditures. Maintenance of effort, as defined by several reform plans, has included per capita payments for cash assistance populations (AFDC and SSI) and absolute dollar contributions for the noncash assistance populations (medically needy, pregnant women, and poor children). Proposals required that both components of the maintenance of effort be calculated for *acute care* expenditures only, set to some base year (most likely 1993), and then be allowed to grow at a predetermined rate (growth in GDP per capita, for example). For some plans, DSH payments were to be included in the noncash portion. Medicaid benefits for the elderly were generally not affected.

Tables D6a–D6c show acute care expenditures by cash assistance status for all non-aged Medicaid enrollees in 1993. Note that the expenditures per enrollee figures are much more uniform between states than the total expenditures per enrollee shown in table D3. Although more uniform than long-term care expenditures (not shown), acute care expenditures still exhibit considerable variation between states. Variations can be attributed to more liberal payment policies and optional benefits (dental and vision services, for example) or unusual types of costs.

EXPENDITURES BY SERVICE TYPE, 1993

Medicaid expenditures for 1993 by type of service are shown in table D7a. Medical services are broken down into acute care, long-term care, payments to HMOs and Medicare, and disproportionate share payments. This table gives a broad look at each state's individual Medicaid program and where its Medicaid dollars are focused. The distribution of expenditures reflects coverage for optional services and varying generosity for medically needy programs; it also indirectly reflects the different demographic compositions, since each type of eligibility group tends to use certain services more than others. Direct comparisons across states can be misleading owing to the effect of DSH payments on the percentages.

Acute care, defined as inpatient care, physician services, laboratory/X-ray, outpatient services, drugs, and other supplemental acute care (dental, vision, EPSDT [early and periodic screening, diagnostic treatment], etc.), comprises approximately 46 percent of total Medicaid expenditures at the national level. In subsequent tables (D7b and D7c), we show acute and long-term care as a percentage of payments for direct services only (i.e., excluding payments to HMOs and Medicare and DSH payments). Most states make more than half of their payments for direct services on acute care. Notable exceptions are Connecticut, Minnesota, and New Hampshire, which spend only around 32–37 percent of direct service expenditures on acute care, as shown later in table D7b.

Table D7b looks at acute care by detailed service category. Services are separated into "basic" and "supplemental" acute care: basic acute care is defined as services most likely to be included in a basic benefit package; supplemental acute care services include EPSDT, dental, vision, family planning, hospice, and other practitioner's services. Spending on inpatient services is the largest acute care component for all states—more than half of basic acute care spending. This percentage would be even larger if DSH payments to inpatient hospitals were included. An interesting note is that although prescription drugs are an optional benefit, all states provide this service to at least some of their Medicaid enrollees.

Long-term care, which includes skilled nursing facilities/intermediate care facilities-other (SNF/ICF-other), intermediate care facilities for the mentally retarded (ICF/MR), mental health, and home health, amounted to 35.3 percent of total Medicaid expenditures for 1993 (table D7a). Long-term care used to be the largest component of total Medicaid spending—a trend that has declined generally, owing in part to the recent surge of inpatient care. Focusing on expenditures for direct services only (see table D7c), long-term care amounted to 43.6 percent of Medicaid direct care expenditures for 1993 (excluding DSH and payments to Medicare and HMOs); California has the smallest relative long-term care program, which includes only 23.1 percent of total direct care services.

Long-term care expenditures, with home and community-based care services listed separately, are detailed in table D7c. Spending on skilled nursing facilities and other intermediate care facilities included more than half (59 percent) of total spending on long-term care. Home and community-based services amounted to 15.2 percent of total long-term care spending.

The level of acute care expenditures presented is masked by the increasing role of group health plans and HMOs (shown in table D7d) in the delivery of care to the Medicaid population. Payments to HMOs increased by 34 percent from 1991 to 1992 and by another 54 percent in 1992–93 (1992 figures not shown)—which is most likely resulting in decreased expenditures for some states, or at least slowed growth in expenditures for these services. Indiana reported the largest relative expenditures on HMOs (not including Arizona, which operates its Medicaid program under a 1115[a] waiver), with 15.6 percent of total Medicaid expenditures. Since the HMO payments shown in table D7d do not include primary care case management arrangements (which classify as managed care, but are paid for on a fee-for-service basis), the actual penetration of managed care into the Medicaid program is understated here.

Payments to Medicare—on behalf of individuals who may or may not have dual Medicaid coverage—have also been growing over the last few years and are delineated in table D7d. Medicaid pays the Medicare premiums for low-income elderly, as well as for elderly individuals otherwise eligible for Medicaid for services not included in the Medicare benefit package (nursing home services and prescription drugs, for example). Some disabled individuals qualify for dual Medicaid-Medicare coverage, as well; in either case, Medicaid acts as the secondary payer. Iowa, at 8.2 percent of total program expenditures, spends the largest relative amount on these individuals.

The dramatic growth in use of DSH payments (see table D7e) became extremely controversial in the early 1990s, resulting in increased tensions between the federal and state governments. To stem this growth, the federal government capped state DSH expenditures to 12 percent of total expenditures. States with expenditures above 12 percent were capped at 1992 levels; states below 12 percent were also capped at 12 percent but were allowed to let DSH expenditures grow at an estimated rate based on overall program costs. New Hampshire has by far the largest relative DSH program in the country—DSH expenditures, at $383 million for 1993, account for over half of total program expenditures. Several states—North and South Dakota, for example—reported zero or almost no DSH expenditures.

Medicaid physician fees compared to medicare rates

Table D8 provides data on Medicaid fees relative to fees under the Medicare Fee Schedule established by the Health Care Financing Administration in 1993. The ratios of actual 1993 Medicaid fees to the Medicare fee schedule are shown for each of six services to indicate differences in Medicaid payment policies across states and service categories. The results reveal that some states pay providers fees that are very close to those required under the new Medicare fee schedule. Other states pay substantially below the Medicare fee schedule. It is important to note, however, that Medicaid obstetrical fees exceed the Medicare fee schedule in about half of the states. On the other hand, most states pay less for primary care services and hospital visits under Medicaid than they would pay under the Medicare fee schedule. This is not surprising, given that the recent changes in the Medicare fee schedule increased fees substantially for these services relative to other services.

Data

The two primary data sources used for this section (except in tables D1, D2, and D8) are the HCFA 2082 (*Statistical Report on Medical Care: Eligibles, Recipients, Payments, and Services*) and the HCFA 64 (*State Quarterly Statements of Medicaid Expenditures for the Medical Assistance Program*) forms. As described earlier in this volume, the 2082 form contains state-level data on Medicaid enrollees, reason for enrollment, type of medical services provided, and expenditure amounts. The HCFA 64, in contrast, is the report from which federal Medicaid reimbursement levels to states are determined, and therefore contains expenditure levels generally considered more reflective of actual spending. The HCFA 64 form, however, lacks enrollment data and reports spending only at the level of state and type of medical service. A "crosswalk" was implemented to draw upon the strengths of both sources of data. The 2082 expenditure data were used to determine relative expenditures by age, disability, and eligibility group; and total expenditures by state and service were adjusted to agree with the figures reported on the 64 form. Enrollment levels were generally not adjusted.

Historically, the HCFA 2082 has been a problematic data source at best, although the quality of the data has increased dramatically over the last few years. Frequent errors have been reported in the state-level data, including missing, zero, or negative expenditures for some services or eligibility groups, rapidly shifting expenditure or enrollment patterns across years, and inconsistencies between enrollment and expenditure levels. To correct for these errors, a number of edits were made to the data. Some edits were made to correct for obviously bad data, whereas others corrected for classification differences between states. It is important to note that the total level of a state's reported expenditures was not affected by these edits; only the pattern of expenditures (how much was spent for a given service on adults relative to the amount spent on children, for example) was adjusted to more accurately simulate how the dollars were actually spent.

Several states reported zero expenditures for a given service on the HCFA 2082 form, while reporting sizable expenditures for that same service on the HCFA 64 form. In these cases, the distribution of expenditures for that service (i.e., what the relative expenditures were for each type of enrollment group) for an adjacent year was used. When no adjacent pattern of expenditures was available, the national distribution was used as a proxy. This same method was utilized when the pattern of expenditures resulted in a shift that was significantly inconsistent with past (or future, in the case of 1992 figures) distributions.

Not all states are required to grant Medicaid eligibility to individuals receiving Supplemental Security Income; instead, they use an alternative set of criteria for determining eligibility for individuals with disabilities (these states are referred to as 209[b] states, named after the corresponding section in the Medicaid law). A few of these states (Connecticut and New Hampshire, for example) did not report any Medicaid eligibles as receiving SSI; these individuals were likely categorized as "noncash," since their reason for eligibility was physical disability and not the receipt of SSI. The aged and blind and disabled enrollment and expenditure patterns for 209(b) states with more consistent distributions were used as estimates.

It is also important to note that the Medicaid expenditure data from the HCFA 64 are based on dates of provider reimbursement and not dates for which the medical services were actually delivered. This lag in expenditure reporting, which usually averages out for most years, is especially problematic in light of the states' growing use of disproportionate share payments; DSH payments are usually made in lump sums and tend to be quite large. For a few select states the timing of these DSH payments (in addition to differences between state and federal fiscal years) resulted in large fluctuations in reported expenditures by year. When possible, the data for DSH expenditures were adjusted to better reflect payments by calendar year.

Table D1
Medicaid Eligibility, Enrollment, and Program Participation
of the Nonelderly, 1990-92

(Enrollees and eligibles in thousands, standard errors in parentheses)

	Number	Eligibles[1]	Eligibility Rate[2]	Enrollees[3]	Enrollment Rate[4]	Participation Rate[5]
United States	218,586	38,612	17.7%	28,478	13.0%	73.8%
			(0.17)		(0.15)	(0.48)
New England	11,286	1,757	15.6%	1,274	11.3%	72.5%
			(0.57)		(0.50)	(1.79)
Connecticut	2,820	357	12.6%	229	8.1%	64.3%
			(1.46)		(1.20)	(5.91)
Maine	1,102	209	19.0%	157	14.2%	74.9%
			(1.53)		(1.36)	(3.88)
Massachusetts	5,025	842	16.8%	635	12.6%	75.5%
			(0.78)		(0.70)	(2.21)
New Hampshire	1,016	127	12.5%	62	6.1%	49.0%
			(1.41)		(1.02)	(6.05)
Rhode Island	806	136	16.9%	123	15.2%	90.1%
			(1.66)		(1.59)	(3.22)
Vermont	518	87	16.7%	68	13.1%	78.1%
			(1.56)		(1.41)	(4.23)
Middle Atlantic	32,501	5,716	17.6%	4,359	13.4%	76.3%
			(0.40)		(0.36)	(1.07)
New Jersey	6,752	897	13.3%	648	9.6%	72.2%
			(0.69)		(0.60)	(2.49)
New York	15,479	3,237	20.9%	2,422	15.6%	74.8%
			(0.62)		(0.56)	(1.45)
Pennsylvania	10,270	1,582	15.4%	1,290	12.6%	81.5%
			(0.72)		(0.66)	(1.97)
South Atlantic	37,562	6,583	17.5%	4,463	11.9%	67.8%
			(0.43)		(0.37)	(1.27)
Delaware	623	67	10.7%	53	8.5%	79.8%
			(1.26)		(1.14)	(5.01)
District of Columbia	477	126	26.4%	104	21.8%	82.6%
			(2.06)		(1.93)	(3.45)
Florida	10,995	2,026	18.4%	1,300	11.8%	64.2%
			(0.75)		(0.62)	(2.15)
Georgia	5,612	1,076	19.2%	737	13.1%	68.5%
			(1.49)		(1.28)	(4.02)
Maryland	4,140	653	15.8%	463	11.2%	70.9%
			(1.49)		(1.28)	(4.66)
North Carolina	5,640	997	17.7%	658	11.7%	66.0%
			(0.76)		(0.64)	(2.23)
South Carolina	3,122	628	20.1%	388	12.4%	61.8%
			(1.37)		(1.13)	(3.71)
Virginia	5,428	690	12.7%	463	8.5%	67.1%
			(1.13)		(0.95)	(4.49)
West Virginia	1,523	320	21.0%	297	19.5%	92.8%
			(1.60)		(1.56)	(2.21)
East South Central	13,386	2,668	19.9%	1,975	14.8%	74.0%
			(0.77)		(0.68)	(1.88)
Alabama	3,600	556	15.4%	376	10.4%	67.6%
			(1.37)		(1.16)	(4.53)
Kentucky	3,132	641	20.5%	484	15.4%	75.4%
			(1.58)		(1.41)	(3.72)
Mississippi	2,351	545	23.2%	427	18.2%	78.3%
			(1.50)		(1.37)	(3.05)
Tennessee	4,304	926	21.5%	688	16.0%	74.3%
			(1.51)		(1.34)	(3.46)
West South Central	23,629	4,530	19.2%	3,033	12.8%	67.0%
			(0.59)		(0.50)	(1.61)
Arkansas	2,068	429	20.7%	259	12.5%	60.4%
			(1.54)		(1.26)	(4.08)
Louisiana	3,679	903	24.6%	625	17.0%	69.2%
			(1.71)		(1.50)	(3.71)
Oklahoma	2,719	524	19.3%	310	11.4%	59.3%
			(1.51)		(1.22)	(4.28)
Texas	15,163	2,674	17.6%	1,838	12.1%	68.7%
			(0.74)		(0.63)	(2.14)

Table D1 (continued)
Medicaid Eligibility, Enrollment, and Program Participation
of the Nonelderly, 1990-92
(Enrollees and eligibles in thousands, standard errors in parentheses)

	Number	Eligibles[1]	Eligibility Rate[2]	Enrollees[3]	Enrollment Rate[4]	Participation Rate[5]
East North Central	**37,385**	**6,113**	**16.4%**	**4,800**	**12.8%**	**78.5%**
			(0.41)		**(0.37)**	**(1.11)**
Illinois	10,419	1,790	17.2%	1,395	13.4%	77.9%
			(0.76)		(0.68)	(2.01)
Indiana	4,858	682	14.0%	394	8.1%	57.8%
			(1.38)		(1.09)	(5.25)
Michigan	8,169	1,554	19.0%	1,248	15.3%	80.3%
			(0.79)		(0.72)	(1.83)
Ohio	9,628	1,428	14.8%	1,279	13.3%	89.6%
			(0.70)		(0.67)	(1.57)
Wisconsin	4,311	660	15.3%	484	11.2%	73.4%
			(1.29)		(1.13)	(4.06)
West North Central	**15,577**	**2,205**	**14.2%**	**1,582**	**10.2%**	**71.7%**
			(0.61)		**(0.53)**	**(2.09)**
Iowa	2,460	332	13.5%	241	9.8%	72.4%
			(1.28)		(1.11)	(4.55)
Kansas	2,205	310	14.1%	211	9.6%	67.9%
			(1.28)		(1.08)	(4.58)
Minnesota	3,844	625	16.3%	379	9.9%	60.7%
			(1.45)		(1.17)	(4.76)
Missouri	4,568	634	13.9%	520	11.4%	82.1%
			(1.36)		(1.25)	(4.06)
Nebraska	1,391	171	12.3%	130	9.4%	76.1%
			(1.20)		(1.06)	(4.44)
North Dakota	524	67	12.7%	48	9.1%	71.6%
			(1.24)		(1.07)	(4.71)
South Dakota	585	67	11.4%	53	9.1%	79.6%
			(1.12)		(1.01)	(4.20)
Mountain	**12,011**	**1,760**	**14.7%**	**1,196**	**10.0%**	**67.9%**
			(0.57)		**(0.49)**	**(1.98)**
Arizona	3,021	477	15.8%	346	11.4%	72.4%
			(1.45)		(1.27)	(4.48)
Colorado	2,882	353	12.2%	249	8.6%	70.4%
			(1.34)		(1.15)	(5.32)
Idaho	940	135	14.4%	81	8.6%	59.9%
			(1.24)		(0.99)	(4.57)
Montana	715	141	19.7%	86	12.1%	61.2%
			(1.48)		(1.21)	(4.10)
Nevada	1,114	133	12.0%	78	7.0%	58.5%
			(1.24)		(0.98)	(5.45)
New Mexico	1,341	235	17.5%	179	13.3%	76.2%
			(1.41)		(1.26)	(3.79)
Utah	1,584	237	15.0%	138	8.7%	58.2%
			(1.29)		(1.02)	(4.62)
Wyoming	414	49	11.8%	40	9.6%	81.4%
			(1.43)		(1.31)	(5.02)
Pacific	**35,249**	**7,278**	**20.6%**	**5,797**	**16.4%**	**79.7%**
			(0.50)		**(0.46)**	**(1.10)**
Alaska	451	74	16.5%	57	12.6%	76.7%
			(1.34)		(1.20)	(3.76)
California	27,030	6,042	22.4%	4,825	17.9%	79.9%
			(0.60)		(0.55)	(1.23)
Hawaii	903	146	16.2%	96	10.7%	65.9%
			(1.54)		(1.29)	(4.93)
Oregon	2,582	408	15.8%	297	11.5%	72.8%
			(1.49)		(1.30)	(4.57)
Washington	4,283	608	14.2%	521	12.2%	85.8%
			(1.33)		(1.24)	(3.53)

Source: Three-year merged March CPS: 1991, 1992, and 1993.
Note: See table notes for Section D.

Table D2
Medicaid Eligibility and Program Participation
of the Nonelderly by Age, 1990-92[6]

(Enrollees and eligibles in thousands, standard errors in parentheses)

	Ages 0-17		Ages 18-64	
	Eligibles[1]	Participation Rate[5]	Eligibles[1]	Participation Rate[5]
United States	22,599	75.4% (0.61)	16,012	71.5% (0.76)
New England	959	74.4% (2.37)	798	70.2% (2.72)
Connecticut	211	62.6% (7.77)	---	---
Maine	112	79.6% (4.93)	97	69.5% (6.04)
Massachusetts	456	78.7% (2.85)	386	71.6% (3.42)
New Hampshire	---	--- ---	---	--- ---
Rhode Island	68	98.7% (1.71)	68	81.5% (5.92)
Vermont	46	81.2% (5.49)	41	74.7% (6.50)
Middle Atlantic	3,131	83.8% (1.25)	2,586	67.1% (1.75)
New Jersey	499	72.9% (3.31)	398	71.3% (3.77)
New York	1,764	83.9% (1.66)	1,473	63.9% (2.38)
Pennsylvania	867	89.9% (2.07)	715	71.5% (3.41)
South Atlantic	3,875	68.5% (1.64)	2,708	66.8% (1.99)
Delaware	42	80.7% (6.19)	---	--- ---
District of Columbia	74	82.7% (4.49)	53	82.3% (5.37)
Florida	1,266	65.9% (2.69)	760	61.2% (3.57)
Georgia	636	68.8% (5.21)	440	68.0% (6.32)
Maryland	387	73.4% (5.89)	266	67.3% (7.54)
North Carolina	554	68.7% (2.93)	443	62.5% (3.42)
South Carolina	355	58.4% (5.01)	272	66.3% (5.48)
Virginia	395	66.4% (5.96)	296	67.9% (6.81)
West Virginia	167	92.5% (3.13)	153	93.2% (3.12)
East South Central	1,540	74.5% (2.46)	1,129	73.2% (2.92)
Alabama	345	62.2% (5.96)	211	76.4% (6.67)
Kentucky	334	76.8% (5.06)	307	73.9% (5.49)
Mississippi	347	80.0% (3.71)	198	75.5% (5.28)
Tennessee	513	77.7% (4.42)	412	70.1% (5.43)
West South Central	2,801	67.9% (2.03)	1,729	65.4% (2.63)
Arkansas	274	54.8% (5.19)	154	70.3% (6.36)
Louisiana	530	71.1% (4.76)	373	66.5% (5.90)
Oklahoma	303	62.8% (5.54)	221	54.4% (6.69)
Texas	1,694	70.0% (2.66)	981	66.6% (3.60)

Table D2 (continued)
Medicaid Eligibility and Program Participation
of the Nonelderly by Age, 1990-92[6]
(Enrollees and eligibles in thousands, standard errors in parentheses)

	Ages 0-17		Ages 18-64	
	Eligibles[1]	Participation Rate[5]	Eligibles[1]	Participation Rate[5]
East North Central	**3,660**	**80.9%** **(1.38)**	**2,453**	**75.0%** **(1.86)**
Illinois	1,069	81.3% (2.45)	721	73.0% (3.39)
Indiana	211	55.1% (9.51)	---	--- ---
Michigan	869	81.2% (2.41)	685	79.1% (2.82)
Ohio	913	92.9% (1.65)	515	83.6% (3.16)
Wisconsin	383	79.2% (4.89)	277	65.3% (6.75)
West North Central	**1,354**	**72.3%** **(2.65)**	**852**	**70.8%** **(3.39)**
Iowa	191	75.2% (5.79)	141	68.7% (7.25)
Kansas	3,131	65.8% (1.47)	115	71.5% (7.29)
Minnesota	372	63.8% (6.07)	253	56.0% (7.60)
Missouri	1,764	79.2% (2.57)	231	87.2% (5.86)
Nebraska	109	79.9% (5.22)	62	69.3% (7.98)
North Dakota	3,875	71.3% (0.62)	26	72.0% (7.48)
South Dakota	42	78.2% (5.40)	24	82.1% (6.71)
Mountain	**1,149**	**64.8%** **(2.51)**	**611**	**73.8%** **(3.17)**
Arizona	335	67.8% (5.59)	143	83.0% (6.89)
Colorado	636	66.3% (4.11)	137	77.0% (7.87)
Idaho	92	55.6% (5.63)	43	69.1% (7.61)
Montana	85	65.6% (5.15)	56	54.5% (6.64)
Nevada	355	54.8% (3.37)	---	--- ---
New Mexico	147	76.9% (4.74)	88	74.9% (6.30)
Utah	161	52.5% (5.69)	76	70.2% (7.55)
Wyoming	1,540	82.5% (0.87)	---	--- ---
Pacific	**4,129**	**80.0%** **(1.45)**	**3,148**	**79.1%** **(1.69)**
Alaska	49	73.8% (4.81)	25	82.4% (5.85)
California	3,434	79.8% (1.63)	2,607	80.0% (1.86)
Hawaii	513	65.5% (2.64)	59	66.3% (7.76)
Oregon	2,801	73.4% (1.73)	177	72.0% (7.00)
Washington	328	92.0% (3.73)	280	78.5% (0.00)

Source: Three-year merged March CPS: 1991, 1992, and 1993.
Note: See table notes for Section D.

Table D3
Medicaid Enrollees and Enrollment Rates, 1992
(Enrollees in thousands)

	Total		Children		Adults		Elderly		Blind and Disabled	
	Enrollees[7]	Per 1,000 Population	Enrollees	Per 1,000 Children	Enrollees	Per 1,000 Adults	Enrollees	Per 1,000 Elderly	Enrollees	Per 1,000 Population
United States	35,313	144	18,376	286	8,271	55	3,778	126	4,887	20
New England	1,674	129	801	260	386	47	218	130	269	21
Connecticut	332	102	177	219	78	39	34	79	43	13
Maine	189	151	93	288	43	55	23	158	30	24
Massachusetts	765	132	358	272	177	48	99	126	131	23
New Hampshire	79	70	42	148	19	25	8	70	10	9
Rhode Island	223	235	91	462	44	73	44	301	44	46
Vermont	86	146	40	268	24	65	11	153	11	19
Middle Atlantic	5,261	140	2,770	296	1,089	47	608	118	794	21
New Jersey	790	102	387	205	198	41	84	85	121	16
New York	2,928	165	1,570	351	562	51	363	157	434	24
Pennsylvania	1,543	127	813	273	330	45	161	86	239	20
South Atlantic	5,851	135	3,069	288	1,306	48	676	118	800	18
Delaware	69	98	37	208	16	36	6	77	10	14
District of Columbia	126	233	66	509	28	81	11	186	20	38
Florida	1,803	136	1,027	333	349	44	196	85	232	17
Georgia	968	153	493	297	219	55	102	140	153	24
Maryland	534	114	296	264	115	38	48	91	75	16
North Carolina	882	136	440	282	222	54	124	148	95	15
South Carolina	475	136	235	250	94	43	73	201	73	21
Virginia	608	102	309	202	131	34	82	149	86	14
West Virginia	386	216	166	382	131	120	35	130	55	31
East South Central	2,605	171	1,252	309	516	55	319	169	518	34
Alabama	546	134	251	228	101	40	78	161	116	28
Kentucky	637	177	293	327	152	68	64	137	127	35
Mississippi	537	202	274	329	95	63	73	238	95	36
Tennessee	885	180	433	353	168	55	103	166	181	37
West South Central	3,817	144	2,070	277	817	51	479	166	451	17
Arkansas	360	150	153	228	75	54	55	168	76	32
Louisiana	735	178	375	314	152	61	95	207	113	27
Oklahoma	414	132	219	260	93	49	55	137	46	15
Texas	2,309	137	1,322	278	498	48	273	161	216	13
East North Central	5,767	136	3,110	273	1,374	53	487	94	796	19
Illinois	1,637	138	909	287	377	52	114	81	236	20
Indiana	535	97	282	197	130	38	50	76	72	13
Michigan	1,361	147	720	292	367	64	91	85	183	20
Ohio	1,619	147	864	293	382	57	165	120	208	19
Wisconsin	616	124	335	243	119	40	67	102	96	19
West North Central	2,002	113	1,041	218	474	44	240	112	247	14
Iowa	305	107	151	200	74	43	38	101	42	15
Kansas	246	98	129	178	58	39	29	95	30	12
Minnesota	501	115	274	245	121	45	54	106	51	12
Missouri	647	126	324	235	159	50	77	132	87	17
Nebraska	163	103	92	205	33	35	20	102	18	12
North Dakota	66	109	32	194	14	39	11	146	8	13
South Dakota	75	109	39	200	15	38	10	102	11	17
Mountain	1,087	108	575	192	267	45	100	93	144	14
Arizona	n/a	n/a	n/a	n/a	n/a	n/a	n/a	n/a	n/a	n/a
Colorado	330	101	174	204	76	38	35	94	45	14
Idaho	100	95	54	159	23	39	10	82	13	13
Montana	92	113	40	163	31	66	8	82	13	16
Nevada	99	79	54	164	24	30	10	71	12	9
New Mexico	241	160	123	281	52	58	25	153	40	27
Utah	175	101	102	157	47	51	9	65	16	9
Wyoming	49	107	29	205	12	45	3	73	5	11
Pacific	7,249	183	3,688	348	2,042	83	651	150	868	22
Alaska	72	151	42	287	21	68	4	149	5	11
California	6,060	200	3,065	374	1,724	92	551	171	720	24
Hawaii	111	107	59	232	26	40	11	88	14	14
Oregon	335	113	175	225	89	49	32	81	40	13
Washington	671	139	348	283	182	60	52	94	89	18

Sources: Population data from Three-year merged March CPS: 1991, 1992, 1993; Enrollee data from HCFA Form 2082.
Note: See table notes for Section D.

Table D4
Growth in Medicaid Enrollment and Expenditures: 1990-93

	1990-1992 Average Annual Growth in				1992-1993 Average Annual Growth in			
		Expenditures		Expenditures per Enrollee[8]		Expenditures		Expenditures per Enrollee[8]
	Enrollees	without DSH	with DSH		Enrollees	without DSH	with DSH	
United States	11.5%	18.9%	28.0%	6.7%	8.6%	13.2%	10.7%	4.3%
New England	9.3%	14.6%	25.5%	4.9%	1.9%	0.4%	1.2%	-1.5%
Connecticut	3.2	17.8	30.6	14.2	6.6	8.3	7.8	1.7
Maine	9.8	18.2	30.7	7.6	3.8	12.8	13.7	8.7
Massachusetts	5.3	9.9	16.2	4.3	2.0	-6.6	-5.3	-8.5
New Hampshire	23.3	27.7	83.4	3.6	8.9	3.1	.3	-5.3
Rhode Island	34.8	25.4	32.4	-7.0	-10.4	4.5	6.0	16.6
Vermont	11.9	20.2	26.3	7.4	4.5	6.7	4.2	2.1
Middle Atlantic	7.4%	16.0%	26.7%	8.0%	6.6%	10.6%	6.1%	3.8%
New Jersey	10.9	14.8	32.7	3.5	8.1	17.3	12.6	8.5
New York	5.8	12.6	21.7	6.4	6.0	14.3	8.7	7.8
Pennsylvania	8.8	28.9	40.6	18.5	6.8	-4.6	-6.4	-10.6
South Atlantic	17.2%	22.8%	28.5%	4.8%	13.8%	16.0%	14.7%	1.9%
Delaware	10.1	30.9	30.9	18.9	12.5	14.9	17.3	2.2
District of Columbia	7.7	18.2	21.6	9.8	13.8	12.9	14.4	-0.8
Florida	23.3	26.1	27.9	2.2	23.0	19.0	19.3	-3.3
Georgia	16.3	18.2	26.0	1.7	9.7	13.9	12.6	3.8
Maryland	10.1	22.6	26.5	11.4	6.5	5.9	3.7	-0.6
North Carolina	17.8	22.4	28.7	3.9	12.5	18.7	16.7	5.5
South Carolina	15.8	18.2	34.5	2.1	7.3	11.8	8.5	4.2
Virginia	17.5	16.8	22.4	-0.6	8.6	18.2	15.4	8.8
West Virginia	10.1	45.7	52.6	32.3	10.8	25.9	25.8	13.6
East South Central	10.2%	24.8%	32.9%	13.2%	12.8%	11.5%	7.5%	-1.1%
Alabama	12.5	33.3	36.6	18.5	20.2	12.5	9.1	-6.4
Kentucky	10.3	24.4	34.4	12.8	4.6	10.3	1.8	5.4
Mississippi	4.1	22.4	31.8	17.6	6.0	12.2	10.4	5.8
Tennessee	13.0	22.2	30.2	8.2	18.2	11.6	9.6	-5.5
West South Central	12.3%	24.2%	40.8%	10.7%	11.4%	16.1%	12.3%	4.2%
Arkansas	11.4	22.7	22.7	10.2	3.6	10.7	10.7	6.9
Louisiana	6.4	27.9	53.8	20.2	5.4	19.7	12.5	13.6
Oklahoma	11.8	19.2	20.2	6.6	5.9	4.3	4.3	-1.5
Texas	14.6	24.2	42.5	8.4	15.5	18.0	13.7	2.2
East North Central	9.1%	19.3%	23.9%	9.4%	4.8%	14.6%	11.8%	9.3%
Illinois	8.4	28.3	31.5	18.4	6.4	19.3	16.2	12.1
Indiana	18.8	24.1	29.5	4.5	13.0	21.8	12.8	7.8
Michigan	7.7	12.5	20.3	4.4	5.2	17.7	15.2	11.9
Ohio	10.0	16.7	21.5	6.1	0.6	8.4	7.5	7.7
Wisconsin	4.7	16.3	16.5	11.1	3.5	5.3	5.2	1.7
West North Central	9.0%	20.0%	28.0%	10.1%	7.6%	8.0%	6.3%	0.4%
Iowa	5.8	18.4	18.6	12.0	3.1	9.4	9.3	6.1
Kansas	2.9	15.4	27.4	12.2	10.4	15.6	11.4	4.7
Minnesota	11.6	13.9	14.8	2.1	7.8	12.4	11.6	4.3
Missouri	10.4	33.5	57.3	20.8	9.2	-4.0	-4.0	-12.1
Nebraska	11.2	22.4	22.7	10.1	6.7	17.5	17.5	10.1
North Dakota	8.9	11.9	11.9	2.8	6.2	8.0	8.0	1.6
South Dakota	11.7	18.3	18.3	5.9	5.5	11.6	11.5	5.7
Mountain	18.2%	28.0%	32.6%	8.3%	9.2%	12.8%	12.3%	3.3%
Arizona	n/a	n/a	n/a	n/a	n/a	n/a	n/a	n/a
Colorado	17.3	27.5	35.5	8.7	7.2	10.2	10.0	2.9
Idaho	23.6	30.4	30.7	5.5	13.9	9.8	9.6	-3.5
Montana	11.8	18.3	18.2	5.8	7.1	19.5	19.7	11.6
Nevada	25.3	41.1	57.5	12.6	12.8	15.1	13.9	2.1
New Mexico	23.2	30.0	31.3	5.5	9.6	13.4	12.5	3.5
Utah	11.8	23.2	23.6	10.2	9.3	13.5	13.3	3.8
Wyoming	16.7	33.8	33.8	14.6	8.2	11.8	11.8	3.3
Pacific	12.5%	14.0%	25.0%	1.3%	7.4%	22.8%	21.8%	14.3%
Alaska	20.1	14.8	14.8	-4.4	14.1	16.7	33.2	2.2
California	12.5	11.8	24.9	-0.6	6.9	24.9	23.2	16.9
Hawaii	8.8	15.2	23.4	5.8	13.5	22.9	21.1	8.3
Oregon	13.0	21.6	22.5	7.6	9.2	18.7	18.7	8.7
Washington	12.3	22.3	28.4	8.8	9.7	14.9	14.5	4.7

Sources: Health Care Financing Administration Form 64 and Form 2082.
Note: See table notes for Section D.

Table D5

Medicaid Enrollees, Expenditures, and Expenditures per Enrollee by Enrollment Group (non-DSH), 1993

(Expenditures in millions and enrollees in thousands, except where noted by [$])

	Total			Children[9,10]			Adults[9,11]		
	Enrollees	Expend.	Expend. per Enrollee ($)	Enrollees	Expend.	Expend. per Enrollee ($)	Enrollees	Expend.	Expend. per Enrollee ($)
United States	38,336	$108,209.1	$2,823	20,000	$19,104.1	$955	8,922	$15,318.3	$1,717
New England	1,706	$7,455.9	$4,371	809	$1,014.5	$1,255	395	$787.8	$1,993
Connecticut	354	1,860.5	5,255	189	230.1	1,219	83	149.5	1,808
Maine	196	687.0	3,511	90	87.1	968	49	69.5	1,407
Massachusetts	780	3,559.6	4,561	361	558.1	1,548	179	444.0	2,479
New Hampshire	86	380.0	4,439	46	55.6	1,217	20	39.8	1,990
Rhode Island	200	731.9	3,663	81	57.5	707	40	54.5	1,368
Vermont	90	236.9	2,631	42	26.1	619	24	30.6	1,261
Middle Atlantic	5,606	$25,488.7	$4,546	2,925	$3,656.4	$1,250	1,156	$2,494.0	$2,158
New Jersey	854	3,617.8	4,235	423	429.7	1,017	206	539.5	2,624
New York	3,104	17,069.3	5,498	1,652	2,340.2	1,416	599	1,437.9	2,401
Pennsylvania	1,648	4,801.6	2,914	850	886.4	1,043	351	516.7	1,471
South Atlantic	6,659	$16,518.1	$2,480	3,541	$3,526.3	$996	1,477	$2,365.1	$1,601
Delaware	77	247.8	3,205	43	40.8	945	17	26.3	1,502
District of Columbia	143	640.6	4,484	77	120.1	1,561	31	66.2	2,168
Florida	2,218	4,709.3	2,123	1,270	1,355.5	1,067	454	473.8	1,044
Georgia	1,062	2,489.2	2,345	545	426.4	782	240	528.2	2,205
Maryland	569	1,882.6	3,309	313	402.5	1,288	118	266.2	2,250
North Carolina	992	2,550.8	2,571	503	498.3	991	247	412.6	1,672
South Carolina	510	1,241.7	2,437	255	228.8	896	97	168.9	1,746
Virginia	661	1,661.0	2,513	347	262.6	757	134	211.3	1,572
West Virginia	428	1,095.1	2,560	187	191.3	1,022	140	211.7	1,516
East South Central	2,938	$6,234.1	$2,122	1,420	$1,167.4	$822	575	$916.8	$1,594
Alabama	656	1,218.1	1,856	309	182.4	591	125	160.8	1,290
Kentucky	666	1,726.7	2,593	308	297.3	964	150	285.3	1,906
Mississippi	570	1,044.1	1,832	291	175.8	604	101	155.9	1,551
Tennessee	1,046	2,245.1	2,146	512	512.0	1,001	200	314.7	1,571
West South Central	4,252	$10,213.1	$2,402	2,334	$2,136.0	$915	899	$1,582.0	$1,759
Arkansas	372	1,028.6	2,762	165	187.0	1,135	68	83.2	1,217
Louisiana	775	2,512.7	3,242	391	419.4	1,072	154	318.1	2,072
Oklahoma	438	1,066.3	2,435	236	253.3	1,075	96	139.7	1,448
Texas	2,666	5,605.5	2,103	1,542	1,276.3	828	581	1,041.1	1,792
East North Central	6,044	$18,178.5	$3,008	3,244	$3,408.4	$1,051	1,426	$2,600.8	$1,823
Illinois	1,741	4,741.4	2,723	955	908.4	951	398	586.5	1,473
Indiana	604	2,781.8	4,603	332	641.6	1,931	142	543.8	3,823
Michigan	1,432	3,817.9	2,666	739	655.6	887	390	670.2	1,719
Ohio	1,629	4,730.1	2,904	868	894.8	1,031	380	634.1	1,668
Wisconsin	637	2,107.4	3,306	349	308.0	883	116	166.2	1,435
West North Central	2,155	$6,468.5	$3,002	1,122	$1,025.5	$914	501	$755.5	$1,507
Iowa	314	983.2	3,131	155	165.2	1,069	75	137.5	1,834
Kansas	272	705.2	2,592	142	117.3	826	64	103.2	1,616
Minnesota	540	2,134.8	3,957	293	330.4	1,126	130	259.5	2,002
Missouri	706	1,548.5	2,192	355	224.5	633	172	157.6	918
Nebraska	174	560.8	3,219	101	118.6	1,176	32	46.3	1,440
North Dakota	70	269.7	3,867	35	32.3	923	14	28.7	1,990
South Dakota	79	266.3	3,369	42	37.1	888	15	22.7	1,528
Mountain	1,187	$3,090.1	$2,603	632	$610.2	$966	288	$523.2	$1,816
Arizona	n/a	n/a	n/a	n/a	n/a	n/a	n/a	n/a	n/a
Colorado	354	961.2	2,718	186	174.4	940	82	137.8	1,673
Idaho	114	292.7	2,558	63	44.5	705	26	40.9	1,574
Montana	99	322.7	3,267	42	71.2	1,695	34	41.8	1,234
Nevada	112	343.2	3,066	61	71.4	1,168	26	59.7	2,260
New Mexico	264	562.4	2,133	135	115.9	861	58	101.6	1,766
Utah	191	473.2	2,474	114	102.6	902	50	117.9	2,376
Wyoming	53	134.7	2,529	32	30.1	948	12	23.6	1,914
Pacific	7,789	$14,562.1	$1,870	3,973	$2,559.5	$644	2,204	$3,293.1	$1,494
Alaska	82	235.4	2,868	48	69.0	1,447	24	62.1	2,632
California	6,479	10,995.5	1,697	3,278	1,971.1	601	1,862	2,648.7	1,422
Hawaii	126	336.7	2,682	67	66.7	996	29	51.4	1,755
Oregon	366	935.0	2,555	192	169.0	878	93	160.5	1,724
Washington	736	2,059.4	2,796	388	283.7	731	195	370.4	1,896

Table D5 (continued)
Medicaid Enrollees, Expenditures, and Expenditures per Enrollee by Enrollment Group (non-DSH), 1993
(Expenditures in millions and enrollees in thousands, except where noted by [$])

	Elderly[12]			Blind and Disabled[13]		
	Enrollees	Expend.	Expend. per Enrollee ($)	Enrollees	Expend.	Expend. per Enrollee ($)
United States	3,936	$34,260.6	$8,704	5,478	$39,526.0	$7,216
New England	214	$2,790.8	$13,024	288	$2,862.8	$9,952
Connecticut	35	759.8	21,494	47	721.2	15,253
Maine	23	280.0	11,920	33	250.3	7,633
Massachusetts	97	1,249.2	12,877	144	1,308.3	9,097
New Hampshire	9	152.6	17,851	11	132.1	11,555
Rhode Island	39	265.7	6,777	39	354.2	8,983
Vermont	11	83.5	7,823	13	96.7	7,491
Middle Atlantic	622	$9,408.4	$15,129	904	$9,930.0	$10,990
New Jersey	89	1,137.8	12,807	137	1,510.8	11,020
New York	371	6,477.1	17,464	482	6,814.2	14,135
Pennsylvania	162	1,793.5	11,059	284	1,605.0	5,644
South Atlantic	722	$5,072.0	$7,028	919	$5,554.7	$6,042
Delaware	6	70.7	11,531	11	110.0	10,464
District of Columbia	10	177.2	17,538	25	277.2	10,950
Florida	220	1,531.0	6,972	274	1,349.0	4,923
Georgia	106	641.2	6,065	171	893.4	5,223
Maryland	49	509.6	10,439	89	704.3	7,888
North Carolina	135	838.4	6,195	107	801.5	7,485
South Carolina	75	374.4	4,972	82	469.6	5,723
Virginia	85	627.6	7,356	94	559.5	5,931
West Virginia	35	301.9	8,532	66	390.2	5,940
East South Central	342	$1,792.7	$5,243	601	$2,357.2	$3,920
Alabama	86	414.6	4,811	137	460.3	3,368
Kentucky	66	432.0	6,540	142	712.2	5,023
Mississippi	77	359.4	4,651	101	353.1	3,493
Tennessee	112	586.8	5,220	222	831.6	3,749
West South Central	502	$3,119.6	$6,219	517	$3,375.5	$6,528
Arkansas	55	337.2	6,116	84	421.3	4,998
Louisiana	98	689.3	7,047	133	1,085.9	8,193
Oklahoma	54	329.1	6,068	52	344.2	6,672
Texas	294	1,764.0	5,992	249	1,524.1	6,129
East North Central	501	$5,003.8	$9,996	873	$7,165.5	$8,209
Illinois	122	1,015.1	8,321	266	2,231.4	8,393
Indiana	57	681.9	12,021	73	914.4	12,501
Michigan	92	1,008.5	11,002	211	1,483.6	7,018
Ohio	163	1,485.7	9,138	217	1,715.6	7,888
Wisconsin	68	812.6	12,023	105	820.6	7,815
West North Central	252	$2,374.7	$9,425	279	$2,312.9	$8,283
Iowa	39	327.6	8,469	46	352.8	7,710
Kansas	30	202.0	6,814	37	282.7	7,742
Minnesota	57	789.7	13,927	60	755.2	12,617
Missouri	85	635.6	7,497	95	530.8	5,571
Nebraska	20	214.1	10,474	21	181.8	8,730
North Dakota	12	110.6	9,208	8	98.0	11,815
South Dakota	10	94.9	9,819	13	111.5	8,791
Mountain	106	$823.1	$7,771	161	$1,133.6	$7,039
Arizona	n/a	n/a	n/a	n/a	n/a	n/a
Colorado	36	303.5	8,462	50	345.4	6,935
Idaho	10	78.8	8,244	16	128.5	8,147
Montana	8	105.6	12,520	14	104.0	7,214
Nevada	11	84.7	7,716	13	127.4	9,510
New Mexico	27	125.8	4,588	44	219.2	4,959
Utah	10	83.8	8,467	18	168.8	9,360
Wyoming	4	40.8	10,868	5	40.3	7,424
Pacific	676	$3,875.6	$5,732	936	$4,833.8	$5,166
Alaska	5	44.1	9,264	6	60.2	9,916
California	571	2,814.7	4,929	767	3,561.1	4,641
Hawaii	13	106.6	8,500	17	112.1	6,682
Oregon	34	248.2	7,235	46	357.3	7,767
Washington	53	662.2	12,381	99	743.1	7,476

Source: Health Care Financing Administration Form 2082.
Note: See table notes for Section D.

Table D6a
Medicaid Spending for Non-Aged Acute Care (non-DSH), 1993:
All Enrollees

(Expenditures in millions and enrollees in thousands, except where noted by [$])

	Acute Expenditures[14]			Enrollees			Expenditures Per Enrollee ($)		
	Blind & Disabled	Adults	Children	Blind & Disabled	Adults	Children	Blind & Disabled	Adults	Children
United States	$19,449.2	$11,806.7	$13,391.8	5,478	8,922	20,000	$3,551	$1,323	$670
New England	$1,054.5	$518.5	$582.2	288	395	809	$3,666	$1,312	$720
Connecticut	191.4	124.7	158.1	47	83	189	4,047	1,509	837
Maine	100.0	57.0	52.9	33	49	90	3,050	1,154	588
Massachusetts	596.2	242.7	276.7	144	179	361	4,146	1,355	768
New Hampshire	38.3	29.0	33.2	11	20	46	3,352	1,449	727
Rhode Island	92.1	40.1	43.0	39	40	81	2,336	1,008	529
Vermont	36.4	24.9	18.2	13	24	42	2,821	1,025	432
Middle Atlantic	$4,471.1	$1,918.4	$2,375.3	904	1,156	2,925	$4,948	$1,660	$812
New Jersey	760.0	482.9	339.2	137	206	423	5,544	2,349	802
New York	3,046.5	1,143.3	1,589.6	482	599	1,652	6,319	1,909	962
Pennsylvania	664.6	292.2	446.5	284	351	850	2,337	832	525
South Atlantic	$3,110.1	$1,964.0	$2,625.0	919	1,477	3,541	$3,383	$1,329	$741
Delaware	42.7	24.7	30.6	11	17	43	4,064	1,411	708
District of Columbia	167.7	51.2	91.1	25	31	77	6,626	1,675	1,184
Florida	780.5	341.2	958.7	274	454	1,270	2,848	752	755
Georgia	527.1	478.5	358.7	171	240	545	3,082	1,997	658
Maryland	465.0	202.0	291.6	89	118	313	5,208	1,707	933
North Carolina	357.0	366.0	387.2	107	247	503	3,334	1,483	770
South Carolina	228.9	138.9	167.6	82	97	255	2,790	1,436	656
Virginia	307.1	197.0	222.2	94	134	347	3,255	1,466	641
West Virginia	234.0	164.6	117.4	66	140	187	3,562	1,179	627
East South Central	$1,492.5	$766.8	$929.4	601	575	1,420	$2,482	$1,333	$655
Alabama	246.9	83.8	153.1	137	125	309	1,807	672	496
Kentucky	463.0	245.3	231.5	142	150	308	3,266	1,639	750
Mississippi	217.0	151.1	139.1	101	101	291	2,146	1,503	478
Tennessee	565.6	286.6	405.8	222	200	512	2,550	1,430	793
West South Central	$1,572.0	$1,346.1	$1,707.6	517	899	2,334	$3,040	$1,497	$732
Arkansas	206.2	78.1	141.4	84	68	165	2,446	1,143	859
Louisiana	575.4	289.5	310.1	133	154	391	4,342	1,886	793
Oklahoma	102.5	126.7	189.7	52	96	236	1,987	1,314	805
Texas	687.9	851.8	1,066.4	249	581	1,542	2,766	1,466	692
East North Central	$3,392.6	$1,808.0	$2,196.8	873	1,426	3,244	$3,887	$1,268	$677
Illinois	1,099.1	498.8	718.9	266	398	955	4,134	1,253	752
Indiana	389.5	298.4	325.4	73	142	332	5,325	2,098	979
Michigan	854.0	428.3	382.6	211	390	739	4,040	1,099	518
Ohio	759.0	497.1	631.9	217	380	868	3,490	1,307	728
Wisconsin	291.1	85.4	138.0	105	116	349	2,772	738	396
West North Central	$825.0	$550.9	$686.7	279	501	1,122	$2,955	$1,099	$612
Iowa	136.6	107.7	126.8	46	75	155	2,984	1,437	820
Kansas	91.8	90.8	79.8	37	64	142	2,513	1,423	562
Minnesota	166.2	134.6	155.2	60	130	293	2,777	1,039	529
Missouri	279.8	130.3	164.2	95	172	355	2,936	760	463
Nebraska	73.5	41.9	99.9	21	32	101	3,528	1,305	991
North Dakota	30.6	25.1	27.5	8	14	35	3,690	1,741	784
South Dakota	46.6	20.3	33.4	13	15	42	3,670	1,367	798
Mountain	$551.1	$438.6	$445.2	161	288	632	$3,422	$1,523	$704
Arizona	n/a	n/a	n/a	n/a	n/a	n/a	n/a	n/a	n/a
Colorado	192.7	119.7	138.3	50	82	186	3,868	1,454	745
Idaho	47.2	35.8	37.8	16	26	63	2,994	1,378	599
Montana	53.1	30.6	34.3	14	34	42	3,683	904	817
Nevada	68.3	48.0	46.7	13	26	61	5,099	1,819	764
New Mexico	105.5	85.6	85.5	44	58	135	2,387	1,488	635
Utah	67.8	96.6	76.8	18	50	114	3,760	1,947	676
Wyoming	16.5	22.3	25.7	5	12	32	3,045	1,808	810
Pacific	$2,980.4	$2,495.5	$1,843.6	936	2,204	3,973	$3,185	$1,132	$464
Alaska	32.6	51.7	52.6	6	24	48	5,360	2,191	1,103
California	2,449.7	2,047.0	1,442.8	767	1,862	3,278	3,192	1,099	440
Hawaii	63.0	43.5	53.6	17	29	67	3,758	1,484	801
Oregon	104.6	80.5	85.7	46	93	192	2,273	864	446
Washington	330.5	272.9	208.9	99	195	388	3,324	1,397	538

Sources: Health Care Financing Administration Form 64 and Form 2082.
Note: See table notes for Section D.

Table D6b
Medicaid Spending for Non-Aged Acute Care (non-DSH), 1993:
Cash Assistance Enrollees

(Expenditures in millions and enrollees in thousands, except where noted by [$])

	Acute Expenditures[14]			Enrollees			Expenditures Per Enrollee ($)		
	Blind & Disabled	Adults	Children	Blind & Disabled	Adults	Children	Blind & Disabled	Adults	Children
United States	**$14,811.5**	**$6,770.4**	**$6,764.0**	**4,300**	**5,512**	**11,456**	**$3,445**	**$1,228**	**$590**
New England	**$715.4**	**$349.3**	**$320.1**	**203**	**280**	**524**	**$3,519**	**$1,246**	**$611**
Connecticut	121.8	72.1	87.2	29	51	115	4,255	1,412	756
Maine	65.2	36.8	25.9	23	33	44	2,857	1,109	588
Massachusetts	413.7	172.6	139.3	106	133	240	3,899	1,294	580
New Hampshire	25.0	17.0	19.0	7	12	28	3,607	1,375	681
Rhode Island	62.9	37.0	38.7	29	37	75	2,161	992	514
Vermont	26.9	13.9	10.0	10	13	21	2,765	1,052	476
Middle Atlantic	**$3,369.4**	**$1,258.7**	**$1,414.1**	**694**	**796**	**1,827**	**$4,854**	**$1,582**	**$774**
New Jersey	643.3	314.7	241.4	114	138	295	5,645	2,285	818
New York	2,201.6	730.3	898.2	380	426	1,042	5,795	1,715	862
Pennsylvania	524.5	213.7	274.5	200	232	490	2,618	920	561
South Atlantic	**$2,358.6**	**$1,121.1**	**$1,224.8**	**700**	**964**	**2,037**	**$3,368**	**$1,163**	**$601**
Delaware	36.2	16.7	16.2	8	12	25	4,354	1,418	648
District of Columbia	122.3	43.8	57.0	20	27	64	6,256	1,627	885
Florida	666.0	218.9	424.8	222	318	707	2,997	688	601
Georgia	463.9	273.3	188.9	148	148	317	3,126	1,847	596
Maryland	309.8	127.5	130.5	63	88	197	4,921	1,451	661
North Carolina	159.6	196.0	184.3	45	159	302	3,578	1,231	611
South Carolina	177.4	59.5	67.4	68	56	141	2,627	1,057	478
Virginia	248.8	95.1	84.5	76	80	168	3,253	1,185	502
West Virginia	174.6	90.3	71.1	50	76	115	3,468	1,193	619
East South Central	**$1,346.3**	**$432.1**	**$456.3**	**542**	**334**	**752**	**$2,485**	**$1,293**	**$607**
Alabama	240.0	45.7	53.0	131	65	143	1,827	708	371
Kentucky	427.3	148.1	124.5	130	94	173	3,293	1,575	718
Mississippi	189.1	82.7	83.2	90	65	178	2,093	1,267	468
Tennessee	489.9	155.6	195.6	190	110	258	2,575	1,412	757
West South Central	**$1,352.4**	**$639.8**	**$660.3**	**458**	**505**	**1,125**	**$2,951**	**$1,267**	**$587**
Arkansas	185.6	28.8	47.2	76	27	75	2,453	1,064	628
Louisiana	433.6	161.8	157.6	115	93	222	3,756	1,744	711
Oklahoma	78.8	47.0	77.6	43	57	143	1,847	827	541
Texas	654.4	402.1	378.0	225	328	685	2,914	1,226	552
East North Central	**$2,244.6**	**$1,206.9**	**$1,263.2**	**584**	**957**	**2,044**	**$3,844**	**$1,262**	**$618**
Illinois	732.8	318.8	438.8	169	243	595	4,335	1,313	737
Indiana	139.1	225.2	143.4	27	111	181	5,149	2,035	793
Michigan	636.6	317.3	266.8	164	289	535	3,885	1,097	499
Ohio	480.5	285.2	345.9	132	235	531	3,649	1,214	652
Wisconsin	255.6	60.3	68.3	92	79	203	2,767	767	337
West North Central	**$576.4**	**$339.8**	**$348.3**	**191**	**317**	**614**	**$3,018**	**$1,071**	**$567**
Iowa	112.6	63.6	56.5	36	45	80	3,110	1,411	703
Kansas	64.4	53.4	59.3	22	43	97	2,877	1,247	613
Minnesota	119.5	101.5	86.3	42	89	165	2,827	1,144	524
Missouri	159.0	78.3	94.9	59	108	205	2,717	727	463
Nebraska	56.1	22.9	28.5	15	19	37	3,668	1,205	770
North Dakota	22.8	8.9	8.9	6	5	11	3,951	1,729	808
South Dakota	42.1	11.2	13.9	11	9	19	3,971	1,272	717
Mountain	**$409.3**	**$241.5**	**$200.9**	**122**	**174**	**337**	**$3,361**	**$1,385**	**$596**
Arizona	n/a	n/a	n/a	n/a	n/a	n/a	n/a	n/a	n/a
Colorado	140.6	69.0	69.7	38	51	106	3,690	1,342	657
Idaho	16.5	12.3	12.2	5	9	20	3,258	1,336	619
Montana	41.1	17.9	17.7	11	18	19	3,649	989	919
Nevada	59.3	29.4	18.9	12	18	28	5,045	1,670	666
New Mexico	100.7	61.8	49.1	42	47	103	2,391	1,317	477
Utah	41.0	40.5	23.7	10	24	45	4,023	1,703	522
Wyoming	10.2	10.6	9.6	3	7	15	3,083	1,441	625
Pacific	**$2,439.2**	**$1,181.1**	**$876.2**	**805**	**1,184**	**2,196**	**$3,031**	**$998**	**$399**
Alaska	27.3	32.9	26.0	4	18	29	6,297	1,872	887
California	2,047.9	924.1	630.4	687	961	1,762	2,979	962	358
Hawaii	39.8	24.8	29.2	10	18	41	3,917	1,369	715
Oregon	57.7	40.1	42.4	21	62	115	2,756	651	369
Washington	266.5	159.3	148.1	82	125	249	3,251	1,269	595

Sources: Health Care Financing Administration Form 64 and Form 2082.
Note: See table notes for Section D.

Table D6c

Medicaid Spending for Non-Aged Acute Care (non-DSH), 1993:
Non-Cash Assistance Enrollees

(Expenditures in millions and enrollees in thousands, except where noted by [$])

	Acute Expenditures[14]			Enrollees			Expenditures Per Enrollee ($)		
	Blind & Disabled	Adults	Children	Blind & Disabled	Adults	Children	Blind & Disabled	Adults	Children
United States	**$4,637.7**	**$5,036.4**	**$6,627.8**	**1,178**	**3,411**	**8,543**	**$3,936**	**$1,477**	**$776**
New England	**$339.0**	**$169.1**	**$262.1**	**84**	**115**	**285**	**$4,019**	**$1,473**	**$921**
Connecticut	69.5	52.6	70.8	19	32	73	3,728	1,665	964
Maine	34.8	20.2	27.1	10	16	46	3,493	1,245	589
Massachusetts	182.6	70.2	137.4	38	46	120	4,841	1,534	1,143
New Hampshire	13.4	12.0	14.2	5	8	18	2,960	1,567	800
Rhode Island	29.2	3.1	4.3	10	3	6	2,829	1,251	707
Vermont	9.5	11.0	8.3	3	11	21	2,994	993	390
Middle Atlantic	**$1,101.7**	**$659.6**	**$961.2**	**209**	**360**	**1,098**	**$5,262**	**$1,833**	**$875**
New Jersey	116.8	168.2	97.7	23	68	127	5,045	2,479	767
New York	844.8	413.0	691.4	102	173	610	8,268	2,384	1,133
Pennsylvania	140.1	78.5	172.0	84	119	360	1,667	660	477
South Atlantic	**$751.5**	**$842.9**	**$1,400.2**	**219**	**513**	**1,504**	**$3,432**	**$1,643**	**$931**
Delaware	6.5	8.0	14.3	2	6	18	2,967	1,396	791
District of Columbia	45.4	7.4	34.1	6	4	13	7,881	2,035	2,714
Florida	114.5	122.3	533.9	52	136	563	2,208	901	948
Georgia	63.2	205.2	169.8	23	92	229	2,793	2,240	743
Maryland	155.2	74.5	161.1	26	30	115	5,896	2,447	1,400
North Carolina	197.5	170.0	202.8	62	88	201	3,160	1,942	1,009
South Carolina	51.5	79.4	100.2	15	40	114	3,544	1,965	876
Virginia	58.3	101.9	137.7	18	54	179	3,266	1,885	771
West Virginia	59.4	74.3	46.3	15	64	72	3,873	1,162	640
East South Central	**$146.2**	**$334.7**	**$473.1**	**60**	**241**	**668**	**$2,456**	**$1,388**	**$709**
Alabama	6.9	38.1	100.2	5	60	166	1,316	633	604
Kentucky	35.7	97.2	106.9	12	56	135	2,971	1,748	791
Mississippi	27.8	68.4	55.8	11	35	113	2,598	1,939	493
Tennessee	75.8	131.0	210.1	32	90	253	2,403	1,453	829
West South Central	**$219.6**	**$706.3**	**$1,047.4**	**59**	**394**	**1,208**	**$3,739**	**$1,791**	**$867**
Arkansas	20.6	49.3	94.3	9	41	90	2,385	1,195	1,052
Louisiana	141.9	127.7	152.5	17	61	169	8,292	2,102	900
Oklahoma	23.6	79.7	112.1	9	40	92	2,655	2,012	1,216
Texas	33.5	449.7	688.4	24	253	857	1,391	1,779	803
East North Central	**$1,148.0**	**$601.1**	**$933.6**	**289**	**470**	**1,200**	**$3,973**	**$1,280**	**$778**
Illinois	366.3	179.9	280.1	97	155	360	3,783	1,159	778
Indiana	250.4	73.2	182.0	46	32	151	5,428	2,319	1,202
Michigan	217.4	110.9	115.9	48	100	205	4,574	1,104	566
Ohio	278.5	211.9	285.9	86	145	338	3,246	1,458	847
Wisconsin	35.5	25.1	69.7	13	37	146	2,805	677	477
West North Central	**$248.6**	**$211.0**	**$338.4**	**88**	**184**	**508**	**$2,818**	**$1,147**	**$666**
Iowa	24.0	44.2	70.3	10	30	74	2,510	1,475	946
Kansas	27.4	37.4	20.5	14	21	45	1,938	1,783	451
Minnesota	46.8	33.1	68.9	18	41	129	2,658	810	536
Missouri	120.8	52.0	69.2	37	64	150	3,285	815	463
Nebraska	17.4	19.0	71.4	6	13	64	3,143	1,450	1,119
North Dakota	7.8	16.2	18.6	3	9	24	3,091	1,747	774
South Dakota	4.5	9.1	19.5	2	6	22	2,142	1,505	868
Mountain	**$141.9**	**$197.1**	**$244.4**	**39**	**114**	**295**	**$3,611**	**$1,735**	**$828**
Arizona	n/a	n/a	n/a	n/a	n/a	n/a	n/a	n/a	n/a
Colorado	52.1	50.7	68.6	12	31	80	4,447	1,641	862
Idaho	30.7	23.5	25.6	11	17	43	2,869	1,402	590
Montana	12.0	12.7	16.7	3	16	23	3,805	806	731
Nevada	9.0	18.7	27.9	2	9	33	5,479	2,118	848
New Mexico	4.8	23.8	36.5	2	11	32	2,314	2,245	1,146
Utah	26.8	56.1	53.1	8	26	68	3,419	2,171	778
Wyoming	6.4	11.7	16.1	2	5	16	2,987	2,354	984
Pacific	**$541.2**	**$1,314.4**	**$967.5**	**131**	**1,020**	**1,777**	**$4,137**	**$1,289**	**$544**
Alaska	5.3	18.8	26.6	2	6	18	3,035	3,126	1,449
California	401.8	1,122.9	812.4	80	901	1,516	5,025	1,246	536
Hawaii	23.2	18.7	24.4	7	11	26	3,515	1,671	936
Oregon	46.9	40.4	43.4	25	31	78	1,870	1,284	558
Washington	64.0	113.6	60.7	17	70	139	3,668	1,627	436

Sources: Health Care Financing Administration Form 64 and Form 2082.
Note: See table notes for Section D.

Table D7a
Medicaid Expenditures by Service:
All Expenditures, 1993

(Expenditures in millions)

	Total Expenditures	Expenditures				Percent of Total			
		Acute Care	Long-term Care	Medicare & HMOs	DSH	Acute Care	Long-term Care	Medicare & HMOs	DSH
United States	**$125,153.0**	**$57,300.8**	**$44,177.8**	**$6,730.5**	**$16,944.0**	**45.8%**	**35.3%**	**5.4%**	**13.5%**
New England	**$9,020.4**	**$3,066.5**	**$3,863.3**	**$526.1**	**$1,564.6**	**34.0%**	**42.8%**	**5.8%**	**17.3%**
Connecticut	2,277.9	607.3	1,165.6	87.6	417.3	26.7	51.2	3.8	18.3
Maine	851.1	317.7	342.7	26.6	164.1	37.3	40.3	3.1	19.3
Massachusetts	4,044.1	1,569.3	1,610.7	379.5	484.5	38.8	39.8	9.4	12.0
New Hampshire	762.9	135.8	227.7	16.5	382.9	17.8	29.8	2.2	50.2
Rhode Island	829.0	317.0	404.5	10.4	97.2	38.2	48.8	1.3	11.7
Vermont	255.5	119.4	112.1	5.4	18.6	46.7	43.9	2.1	7.3
Middle Atlantic	**$29,946.8**	**$11,475.4**	**$13,006.4**	**$1,006.9**	**$4,458.1**	**38.3%**	**43.4%**	**3.4%**	**14.9%**
New Jersey	4,706.0	1,895.9	1,642.5	79.5	1,088.2	40.3	34.9	1.7	23.1
New York	19,628.1	7,841.2	8,829.6	398.5	2,558.7	39.9	45.0	2.0	13.0
Pennsylvania	5,612.7	1,738.3	2,534.3	529.0	811.1	31.0	45.2	9.4	14.5
South Atlantic	**$18,218.7**	**$9,740.3**	**$5,668.0**	**$1,109.8**	**$1,700.6**	**53.5%**	**31.1%**	**6.1%**	**9.3%**
Delaware	253.0	134.9	109.3	3.6	5.2	53.3	43.2	1.4	2.1
District of Columbia	686.7	347.4	261.4	31.9	46.1	50.6	38.1	4.6	6.7
Florida	4,949.0	2,711.3	1,376.5	621.5	239.7	54.8	27.8	12.6	4.8
Georgia	2,798.7	1,657.1	748.4	83.7	309.4	59.2	26.7	3.0	11.1
Maryland	1,960.4	1,097.1	604.8	180.7	77.8	56.0	30.9	9.2	4.0
North Carolina	2,896.3	1,368.4	1,092.6	89.8	345.5	47.2	37.7	3.1	11.9
South Carolina	1,682.4	741.0	464.1	36.6	440.7	44.0	27.6	2.2	26.2
Virginia	1,791.8	942.8	682.4	35.8	130.8	52.6	38.1	2.0	7.3
West Virginia	1,200.4	740.5	328.5	26.1	105.3	61.7	27.4	2.2	8.8
East South Central	**$7,372.8**	**$3,885.8**	**$2,061.4**	**$286.9**	**$1,138.7**	**52.7%**	**28.0%**	**3.9%**	**15.4%**
Alabama	1,637.2	673.1	492.2	52.8	419.1	41.1	30.1	3.2	25.6
Kentucky	1,863.7	1,147.0	537.6	42.1	137.0	61.5	28.8	2.3	7.4
Mississippi	1,196.5	648.2	314.9	80.9	152.3	54.2	26.3	6.8	12.7
Tennessee	2,675.4	1,417.5	716.6	111.1	430.2	53.0	26.8	4.2	16.1
West South Central	**$12,969.8**	**$6,196.1**	**$3,704.8**	**$312.2**	**$2,756.7**	**47.8%**	**28.6%**	**2.4%**	**21.3%**
Arkansas	1,031.1	528.1	458.0	42.5	2.5	51.2	44.4	4.1	0.2
Louisiana	3,730.3	1,528.8	927.9	56.0	1,217.6	41.0	24.9	1.5	32.6
Oklahoma	1,089.7	535.5	491.9	38.9	23.5	49.1	45.1	3.6	2.2
Texas	7,118.6	3,603.7	1,827.0	174.8	1,513.0	50.6	25.7	2.5	21.3
East North Central	**$19,453.7**	**$8,940.8**	**$7,591.6**	**$1,646.1**	**$1,275.2**	**46.0%**	**39.0%**	**8.5%**	**6.6%**
Illinois	4,981.5	2,696.0	1,808.4	237.0	240.1	54.1	36.3	4.8	4.8
Indiana	2,815.5	1,234.0	1,081.9	465.9	33.8	43.8	38.4	16.5	1.2
Michigan	4,362.6	1,978.4	1,460.5	379.0	544.7	45.3	33.5	8.7	12.5
Ohio	5,179.1	2,248.6	2,175.8	305.8	449.0	43.4	42.0	5.9	8.7
Wisconsin	2,115.0	783.9	1,065.0	258.5	7.6	37.1	50.4	12.2	0.4
West North Central	**$7,395.6**	**$2,695.5**	**$3,300.1**	**$472.8**	**$927.1**	**36.4%**	**44.6%**	**6.4%**	**12.5%**
Iowa	987.2	476.7	423.9	82.6	4.0	48.3	42.9	8.4	0.4
Kansas	889.7	323.2	358.9	23.1	184.4	36.3	40.3	2.6	20.7
Minnesota	2,167.0	624.2	1,301.4	209.2	32.3	28.8	60.1	9.7	1.5
Missouri	2,251.6	764.7	658.3	125.4	703.1	34.0	29.2	5.6	31.2
Nebraska	564.2	276.9	261.0	22.9	3.3	49.1	46.3	4.1	0.6
North Dakota	269.7	107.5	159.6	2.6	0.0	39.8	59.2	1.0	0.0
South Dakota	266.3	122.3	137.0	7.0	0.0	45.9	51.4	2.6	0.0
Mountain	**$3,315.7**	**$1,783.4**	**$1,186.2**	**$120.5**	**$225.7**	**53.8%**	**35.8%**	**3.6%**	**6.8%**
Arizona	n/a	n/a	n/a	n/a	n/a	n/a	n/a	n/a	n/a
Colorado	1,091.7	543.6	384.7	32.8	130.5	49.8	35.2	3.0	12.0
Idaho	293.7	161.8	126.6	4.4	1.0	55.1	43.1	1.5	0.3
Montana	323.3	159.1	153.1	10.6	0.5	49.2	47.4	3.3	0.2
Nevada	423.4	202.7	121.1	19.4	80.3	47.9	28.6	4.6	19.0
New Mexico	571.2	364.6	188.0	9.8	8.8	63.8	32.9	1.7	1.5
Utah	477.6	277.3	157.2	38.6	4.5	58.1	32.9	8.1	0.9
Wyoming	134.8	74.4	55.5	4.8	0.1	55.2	41.2	3.6	0.1
Pacific	**$17,459.5**	**$9,517.0**	**$3,796.0**	**$1,249.1**	**$2,897.4**	**54.5%**	**21.7%**	**7.2%**	**16.6%**
Alaska	268.7	175.8	56.7	2.9	33.3	65.4	21.1	1.1	12.4
California	13,538.0	7,634.6	2,295.6	1,065.4	2,542.5	56.4	17.0	7.9	18.8
Hawaii	380.7	198.9	122.9	14.9	43.9	52.2	32.3	3.9	11.5
Oregon	955.6	425.5	430.7	78.8	20.6	44.5	45.1	8.2	2.2
Washington	2,316.5	1,082.2	890.1	87.2	257.0	46.7	38.4	3.8	11.1

Source: Health Care Financing Administration Form 64.
Note: See table notes for Section D.

Table D7b
Medicaid Expenditures by Service:
Acute Care Expenditures (non-DSH), 1993

(Expenditures in millions)

	Total	Basic Acute Care				Supplemental[17]		Percent of Direct Expend.[18]
		Inpatient	Physician Lab+X-Ray	Outpatient	Drugs	EPSDT	Other	
United States	$57,300.8	$25,507.8	$8,090.9	$9,321.4	$6,909.2	$606.8	$6,864.6	56.5%
New England	$3,066.5	$1,302.0	$317.4	$556.4	$358.4	$11.8	$520.5	44.3%
Connecticut	607.3	245.2	60.3	131.4	87.0	2.5	80.9	34.3
Maine	317.7	107.4	35.3	53.4	42.6	0.0	79.0	48.1
Massachusetts	1,569.3	727.8	178.8	260.5	160.1	7.5	234.6	49.3
New Hampshire	135.8	27.2	15.8	48.1	21.1	0.2	23.4	37.4
Rhode Island	317.0	162.8	9.1	40.7	28.4	1.5	74.5	43.9
Vermont	119.4	31.6	18.1	22.3	19.2	0.0	28.2	51.6
Middle Atlantic	$11,475.4	$5,516.2	$629.6	$2,489.1	$1,255.3	$125.8	$1,459.4	46.9%
New Jersey	1,895.9	974.3	113.9	417.5	251.5	3.8	135.0	53.6
New York	7,841.2	3,752.2	324.8	1,837.0	672.4	104.1	1,150.6	47.0
Pennsylvania	1,738.3	789.7	190.9	234.6	331.4	17.9	173.8	40.7
South Atlantic	$9,740.3	$4,076.6	$1,876.2	$1,569.7	$1,131.0	$95.7	$991.1	63.2%
Delaware	134.9	54.7	14.8	23.6	12.4	14.7	14.6	55.2
District of Columbia	347.4	214.4	26.6	67.0	20.3	0.3	18.7	57.1
Florida	2,711.3	1,109.1	498.6	399.9	342.0	11.6	350.0	66.3
Georgia	1,657.1	681.6	367.7	248.2	188.1	22.7	148.8	68.9
Maryland	1,097.1	625.9	189.9	142.7	92.7	8.0	37.9	64.5
North Carolina	1,368.4	557.2	287.7	248.4	158.0	12.0	105.1	55.6
South Carolina	741.0	294.3	121.4	122.0	88.0	6.6	108.6	61.5
Virginia	942.8	357.0	216.6	138.6	154.9	10.6	65.0	58.0
West Virginia	740.5	182.4	152.8	179.1	74.6	9.1	142.5	69.3
East South Central	$3,885.8	$1,387.2	$835.7	$708.4	$583.7	$46.1	$324.6	65.3%
Alabama	673.1	238.4	118.9	67.7	121.5	14.6	112.0	57.8
Kentucky	1,147.0	342.4	275.9	248.3	163.3	2.7	114.4	68.1
Mississippi	648.2	261.9	128.8	105.3	107.3	20.2	24.8	67.3
Tennessee	1,417.5	544.6	312.1	287.2	191.6	8.6	73.4	66.4
West South Central	$6,196.1	$2,712.5	$1,121.1	$696.0	$693.8	$79.8	$892.9	62.6%
Arkansas	528.1	208.5	115.8	88.3	62.6	8.5	44.6	53.6
Louisiana	1,528.8	675.3	285.3	178.0	192.5	35.4	162.4	62.2
Oklahoma	535.5	236.7	91.6	71.5	75.3	5.8	54.6	52.1
Texas	3,603.7	1,592.1	628.5	358.2	363.4	30.1	631.4	66.4
East North Central	$8,940.8	$4,276.4	$1,137.4	$1,462.6	$1,093.3	$60.2	$910.9	54.1%
Illinois	2,696.0	1,692.3	278.1	211.9	282.3	45.2	186.2	59.9
Indiana	1,234.0	480.2	201.2	253.4	168.0	2.7	128.5	53.3
Michigan	1,978.4	810.8	282.5	447.4	199.0	9.4	229.2	57.5
Ohio	2,248.6	1,047.4	307.7	414.0	306.0	0.0	173.5	50.8
Wisconsin	783.9	245.7	67.9	135.9	138.0	2.9	193.6	42.4
West North Central	$2,695.5	$1,103.7	$401.3	$389.3	$431.1	$55.1	$315.0	45.0%
Iowa	476.7	199.3	77.8	64.7	67.5	1.1	66.4	52.9
Kansas	323.2	137.3	58.4	40.7	50.4	2.1	34.3	47.4
Minnesota	624.2	238.0	120.2	69.3	83.4	6.0	107.3	32.4
Missouri	764.7	316.1	53.4	138.2	163.5	41.6	52.0	53.7
Nebraska	276.9	113.1	53.6	34.8	40.3	3.4	31.7	51.5
North Dakota	107.5	45.4	16.8	20.2	12.9	0.2	11.9	40.2
South Dakota	122.3	54.5	21.1	21.4	13.2	0.7	11.4	47.2
Mountain	$1,783.4	$766.6	$328.0	$291.6	$165.3	$18.5	$213.4	60.1%
Arizona	n/a	n/a	n/a	n/a	n/a	n/a	n/a	n/a
Colorado	543.6	266.6	84.6	97.9	49.5	4.8	40.1	58.6
Idaho	161.8	56.6	31.8	21.7	19.8	2.3	29.6	56.1
Montana	159.1	50.0	30.0	28.3	19.6	1.2	29.9	51.0
Nevada	202.7	95.1	48.3	19.5	12.6	3.4	23.8	62.6
New Mexico	364.6	141.2	72.3	56.1	29.0	3.0	63.0	66.0
Utah	277.3	123.7	45.1	57.5	27.3	3.2	20.7	63.8
Wyoming	74.4	33.4	15.8	10.7	7.5	0.6	6.4	57.2
Pacific	$9,517.0	$4,366.7	$1,444.1	$1,158.4	$1,197.4	$113.8	$1,236.7	71.5%
Alaska	175.8	52.2	44.4	34.7	12.4	2.6	29.5	75.6
California	7,634.6	3,775.0	1,085.6	810.1	986.8	98.7	878.3	76.9
Hawaii	198.9	86.3	39.1	27.2	22.7	2.8	20.8	61.8
Oregon	425.5	126.5	72.2	41.4	58.3	0.7	126.5	49.7
Washington	1,082.2	326.6	203.0	245.0	117.2	9.0	181.5	54.9

Source: Health Care Financing Administration Form 64.
Note: See table notes for Section D.

Table D7c
Medicaid Expenditures by Service:
Long-Term Care (non-DSH), 1993

(Expenditures in millions)

	Total	Long-term Care			Home and Community-Based Care			Percent of Direct Expend.[18]
		SNF/ICF -Other	ICF-MR	Mental Health	Waivers	Personal Care	Other[19]	
United States	$44,177.8	$26,076.9	$9,282.7	$2,077.4	$2,779.0	$2,459.6	$1,502.1	43.5%
New England	$3,863.3	$2,407.7	$671.1	$94.0	$453.2	$90.6	$146.6	55.7%
Connecticut	1,165.6	727.1	182.0	36.7	161.9	0.0	57.9	65.7
Maine	342.7	224.8	59.8	14.7	30.5	2.9	9.9	51.9
Massachusetts	1,610.7	1,039.4	307.6	24.5	84.0	86.0	69.2	50.7
New Hampshire	227.7	147.5	5.4	8.7	62.2	1.7	2.1	62.6
Rhode Island	404.5	203.4	105.2	8.8	83.4	0.0	3.8	56.1
Vermont	112.1	65.5	11.2	0.6	31.1	0.0	3.6	48.4
Middle Atlantic	$13,006.4	$6,608.1	$2,835.6	$844.5	$414.4	$1,672.7	$631.1	53.1%
New Jersey	1,642.5	987.8	286.2	66.1	157.9	50.9	93.6	46.4
New York	8,829.6	4,095.4	2,049.3	484.8	80.8	1,621.8	497.6	53.0
Pennsylvania	2,534.3	1,524.9	500.1	293.7	175.7	0.0	39.9	59.3
South Atlantic	$5,668.0	$3,517.3	$1,104.4	$255.5	$441.8	$100.7	$248.3	36.8%
Delaware	109.3	58.2	26.6	1.6	12.1	0.0	10.9	44.8
District of Columbia	261.4	138.6	64.0	42.4	0.0	5.0	11.4	42.9
Florida	1,376.5	1,011.9	192.2	14.4	82.8	2.5	72.7	33.7
Georgia	748.4	531.1	116.2	18.2	51.2	0.0	31.7	31.1
Maryland	604.8	401.1	60.8	11.3	77.8	19.4	34.4	35.5
North Carolina	1,092.6	585.9	316.6	33.7	66.6	35.7	54.0	44.4
South Carolina	464.1	208.8	165.3	39.2	43.5	0.6	6.7	38.5
Virginia	682.4	372.8	148.2	81.5	69.6	0.0	10.3	42.0
West Virginia	328.5	209.0	14.6	13.1	38.2	37.4	16.2	30.7
East South Central	$2,061.4	$1,399.4	$345.1	$112.1	$100.7	$0.0	$104.1	34.7%
Alabama	492.2	331.4	79.0	20.3	43.7	0.0	17.7	42.2
Kentucky	537.6	332.2	69.9	35.4	38.6	0.0	61.6	31.9
Mississippi	314.9	211.5	79.0	15.1	1.3	0.0	8.0	32.7
Tennessee	716.6	524.3	117.1	41.3	17.1	0.0	16.8	33.6
West South Central	$3,704.8	$2,065.7	$1,053.7	$135.7	$108.1	$240.8	$100.7	37.4%
Arkansas	458.0	251.9	89.6	45.9	15.5	49.3	5.9	46.4
Louisiana	927.9	526.1	324.0	41.3	14.6	0.0	21.8	37.8
Oklahoma	491.9	237.5	132.1	48.5	43.7	29.5	0.5	47.9
Texas	1,827.0	1,050.3	508.1	0.0	34.3	161.9	72.5	33.6
East North Central	$7,591.6	$4,885.2	$1,621.8	$362.7	$395.7	$181.8	$144.4	45.9%
Illinois	1,808.4	1,103.3	531.7	34.4	129.0	0.0	10.1	40.1
Indiana	1,081.9	712.7	283.5	43.7	4.9	0.0	37.1	46.7
Michigan	1,460.5	922.3	149.2	134.0	78.1	151.8	25.1	42.5
Ohio	2,175.8	1,497.4	449.6	115.5	88.2	0.0	25.1	49.2
Wisconsin	1,065.0	649.5	207.8	35.0	95.6	30.0	47.1	57.6
West North Central	$3,300.1	$1,907.6	$771.0	$112.9	$327.3	$114.4	$67.1	55.0%
Iowa	423.9	222.9	161.0	19.8	2.6	0.0	17.6	47.1
Kansas	358.9	176.8	106.6	28.7	37.2	3.6	6.0	52.6
Minnesota	1,301.4	740.2	288.7	31.8	134.6	83.4	22.7	67.6
Missouri	658.3	418.0	113.8	12.4	86.5	22.4	5.2	46.3
Nebraska	261.0	179.0	34.2	10.7	22.3	3.4	11.4	48.5
North Dakota	159.6	92.6	37.1	4.3	23.1	0.0	2.6	59.8
South Dakota	137.0	78.1	29.6	5.2	20.9	1.5	1.6	52.8
Mountain	$1,186.2	$651.6	$220.7	$87.4	$173.8	$23.8	$28.9	39.9%
Arizona	n/a	n/a	n/a	n/a	n/a	n/a	n/a	n/a
Colorado	384.7	220.1	50.7	22.0	81.1	0.0	10.8	41.4
Idaho	126.6	69.0	38.5	0.0	7.0	10.5	1.6	43.9
Montana	153.1	91.6	10.4	20.1	17.7	11.3	2.1	49.0
Nevada	121.1	73.7	26.8	8.7	5.1	1.3	5.6	37.4
New Mexico	188.0	99.6	42.8	20.4	20.2	0.0	4.9	34.0
Utah	157.2	72.1	45.2	6.9	29.5	0.7	2.7	36.2
Wyoming	55.5	25.6	6.2	9.2	13.1	0.0	1.4	42.8
Pacific	$3,796.0	$2,634.2	$659.3	$72.5	$364.1	$34.9	$31.0	28.5%
Alaska	56.7	42.3	10.4	1.0	0.0	2.6	0.5	24.4
California	2,295.6	1,878.5	356.3	0.2	41.9	0.0	18.7	23.1
Hawaii	122.9	101.8	6.2	0.0	13.4	0.0	1.6	38.2
Oregon	430.7	159.1	80.0	17.5	159.9	12.7	1.5	50.3
Washington	890.1	452.7	206.5	53.8	148.9	19.5	8.8	45.1

Source: Health Care Financing Administration Form 64.
Note: See table notes for Section D.

Table D7d
Medicaid Expenditures by Service:
Payments to HMOs and Medicare, 1993
(Expenditures in millions)

	Total	Payments to HMOs		Payments to Medicare	
		Expend.	Percent of Total Expend.	Expend.	Percent of Total Expend.
United States	$6,730.5	$3,939.5	3.1%	$2,791.0	2.2%
New England	$526.1	$324.5	3.6%	$201.7	2.2%
Connecticut	87.6	0.0	0.0	87.6	3.8
Maine	26.6	5.0	0.6	21.7	2.5
Massachusetts	379.5	309.7	7.7	69.9	1.7
New Hampshire	16.5	8.2	1.1	8.3	1.1
Rhode Island	10.4	1.6	0.2	8.7	1.1
Vermont	5.4	0.0	0.0	5.4	2.1
Middle Atlantic	$1,006.9	$720.3	2.4%	$286.6	1.0%
New Jersey	79.5	31.5	0.7	48.0	1.0
New York	398.5	256.7	1.3	141.9	0.7
Pennsylvania	529.0	432.2	7.7	96.8	1.7
South Atlantic	$1,109.8	$541.9	3.0%	$567.9	3.1%
Delaware	3.6	0.0	0.0	3.6	1.4
District of Columbia	31.9	25.0	3.6	6.9	1.0
Florida	621.5	369.3	7.5	252.3	5.1
Georgia	83.7	0.0	0.0	83.7	3.0
Maryland	180.7	141.7	7.2	39.0	2.0
North Carolina	89.8	5.9	0.2	83.9	2.9
South Carolina	36.6	0.0	0.0	36.5	2.2
Virginia	35.8	0.0	0.0	35.8	2.0
West Virginia	26.1	0.0	0.0	26.1	2.2
East South Central	$286.9	$31.4	0.4%	$255.6	3.5%
Alabama	52.8	0.5	0.0	52.3	3.2
Kentucky	42.1	0.0	0.0	42.1	2.3
Mississippi	80.9	0.0	0.0	80.9	6.8
Tennessee	111.1	30.8	1.2	80.2	3.0
West South Central	$312.2	$0.0	0.0%	$312.2	2.4%
Arkansas	42.5	0.0	0.0	42.5	4.1
Louisiana	56.0	0.0	0.0	56.0	1.5
Oklahoma	38.9	0.0	0.0	38.9	3.6
Texas	174.8	0.0	0.0	174.8	2.5
East North Central	$1,646.1	$1,226.4	6.3%	$419.7	2.2%
Illinois	236.9	119.0	2.4	118.0	2.4
Indiana	465.9	440.6	15.6	25.3	0.9
Michigan	379.0	307.4	7.0	71.7	1.6
Ohio	305.8	201.1	3.9	104.7	2.0
Wisconsin	258.5	158.4	7.5	100.1	4.7
West North Central	$472.8	$211.1	2.9%	$261.7	3.5%
Iowa	82.6	1.8	0.2	80.9	8.2
Kansas	23.1	0.1	0.0	23.1	2.6
Minnesota	209.2	183.1	8.4	26.1	1.2
Missouri	125.4	26.1	1.2	99.3	4.4
Nebraska	22.9	0.1	0.0	22.8	4.0
North Dakota	2.6	0.0	0.0	2.6	1.0
South Dakota	7.0	0.0	0.0	7.0	2.6
Mountain	$120.5	$59.3	1.8%	$61.2	1.8%
Arizona	n/a	n/a	n/a	n/a	n/a
Colorado	32.8	17.4	1.6	15.4	1.4
Idaho	4.4	0.1	0.0	4.3	1.5
Montana	10.6	0.2	0.1	10.4	3.2
Nevada	19.4	13.2	3.1	6.2	1.5
New Mexico	9.8	0.0	0.0	9.8	1.7
Utah	38.6	28.5	6.0	10.2	2.1
Wyoming	4.8	0.0	0.0	4.8	3.6
Pacific	$1,249.1	$824.6	4.7%	$424.5	2.4%
Alaska	2.9	0.0	0.0	2.9	1.1
California	1,065.4	712.1	5.3	353.3	2.6
Hawaii	14.9	5.9	1.5	9.1	2.4
Oregon	78.8	64.3	6.7	14.4	1.5
Washington	87.2	42.4	1.8	44.8	1.9

Source: Health Care Financing Administration Form 64.
Note: See table notes for Section D.

Table D7e
Medicaid Expenditures by Service:
Disproportionate Share Payments, 1992-93
(Expenditures in millions)

	1992 Total DSH		1993 Total DSH		1993 Inpatient DSH		1993 Mental Health DSH	
	DSH[20]	Percent of Total Expend.	DSH	Percent of Total Expend.	DSH	Percent of Inp. Expend.	DSH	Percent of MH Expend.
United States	**$17,525.6**	**15.3%**	**$16,944.0**	**13.5%**	**$14,400.4**	**36.1%**	**$2,543.6**	**55.0%**
New England	**$1,488.0**	**17.4%**	**$1,564.6**	**17.3%**	**$1,181.7**	**47.6%**	**$382.9**	**80.3%**
Connecticut	395.1	18.3	417.3	18.3	269.3	52.3	148.0	80.1
Maine	139.2	19.2	164.1	19.3	121.2	53.0	42.9	74.4
Massachusetts	457.3	11.8	484.5	12.0	324.1	30.8	160.4	86.8
New Hampshire	392.0	54.2	382.9	50.2	360.5	93.0	22.4	72.0
Rhode Island	81.3	10.5	97.2	11.7	97.1	37.4	0.1	0.9
Vermont	23.1	9.2	18.6	7.3	9.5	23.1	9.1	93.4
Middle Atlantic	**$5,180.9**	**16.4%**	**$4,458.1**	**14.9%**	**$3,325.2**	**37.6%**	**$1,132.9**	**57.3%**
New Jersey	1,094.1	24.3	1,088.2	23.1	769.7	44.1	318.6	82.8
New York	3,119.4	14.8	2,558.7	13.0	2,224.8	37.2	333.9	40.8
Pennsylvania	967.4	15.7	811.1	14.5	330.7	29.5	480.5	62.1
South Atlantic	**$1,642.2**	**10.5%**	**$1,700.6**	**9.3%**	**$1,191.5**	**22.6%**	**$509.1**	**66.6%**
Delaware	0.0	2.2	5.2	2.1	0.0	0.0	5.2	77.0
District of Columbia	32.9	5.6	46.1	6.7	32.1	13.0	14.0	24.8
Florida	191.4	4.7	239.7	4.8	175.7	13.7	64.0	81.6
Georgia	300.5	12.3	309.4	11.1	309.4	31.2	0.0	0.0
Maryland	113.0	5.8	77.8	4.0	22.9	3.5	55.0	83.0
North Carolina	332.4	13.7	345.5	11.9	13.2	2.3	332.3	90.8
South Carolina	439.8	29.3	440.7	26.2	412.5	58.4	28.2	41.8
Virginia	147.8	9.4	130.8	7.3	120.3	25.2	10.4	11.3
West Virginia	84.4	9.1	105.3	8.8	105.3	36.6	0.0	0.0
East South Central	**$1,265.7**	**18.8%**	**$1,138.7**	**15.4%**	**$1,135.4**	**45.0%**	**$3.3**	**2.9%**
Alabama	417.5	27.8	419.1	25.6	419.0	63.7	0.1	0.5
Kentucky	264.3	14.6	137.0	7.4	137.0	28.6	0.0	0.0
Mississippi	153.3	14.3	152.3	12.7	152.3	36.8	0.0	0.0
Tennessee	430.6	18.3	430.2	16.1	427.1	44.0	3.2	7.2
West South Central	**$2,755.5**	**24.2%**	**$2,756.7**	**21.3%**	**$2,724.9**	**50.1%**	**$31.8**	**19.0%**
Arkansas	2.5	0.3	2.5	0.2	2.5	1.2	0.0	0.0
Louisiana	1,217.6	36.6	1,217.6	32.6	1,190.7	63.8	27.0	39.5
Oklahoma	22.3	2.2	23.5	2.2	18.6	7.3	4.8	9.1
Texas	1,513.0	24.9	1,513.0	21.3	1,513.0	48.7	0.0	0.0
East North Central	**$1,530.2**	**9.0%**	**$1,275.2**	**6.6%**	**$1,208.6**	**22.0%**	**$66.6**	**15.5%**
Illinois	313.8	7.5	240.1	4.8	240.1	12.4	0.0	0.0
Indiana	211.6	9.5	33.8	1.2	24.9	4.9	8.9	16.9
Michigan	544.3	14.3	544.7	12.5	488.5	37.6	56.3	29.6
Ohio	451.8	9.5	449.0	8.7	449.0	30.0	0.0	0.0
Wisconsin	8.7	0.4	7.6	0.4	6.1	2.4	1.5	4.1
West North Central	**$970.6**	**13.9%**	**$927.1**	**12.5%**	**$599.2**	**35.2%**	**$327.9**	**74.4%**
Iowa	4.6	0.5	4.0	0.4	4.0	2.0	0.0	0.0
Kansas	188.9	20.7	184.4	20.7	4.4	3.1	180.0	86.3
Minnesota	42.0	2.2	32.3	1.5	24.6	9.4	7.7	19.5
Missouri	731.9	31.7	703.1	31.2	564.0	64.1	139.0	91.8
Nebraska	3.1	0.7	3.3	0.6	2.2	1.9	1.2	9.7
North Dakota	0.0	0.0	0.0	0.0	0.0	0.0	0.0	0.0
South Dakota	0.0	0.0	0.0	0.0	0.0	0.0	0.0	0.0
Mountain	**$212.4**	**13.4%**	**$225.7**	**6.8%**	**$223.4**	**22.6%**	**$2.3**	**2.5%**
Arizona	n/a	n/a	n/a	n/a	n/a	n/a	n/a	n/a
Colorado	120.8	30.6	130.5	12.0	129.6	32.7	0.9	4.0
Idaho	1.4	0.5	1.0	0.3	1.0	1.7	0.0	0.0
Montana	0.1	0.0	0.5	0.2	0.1	0.1	0.5	2.3
Nevada	73.6	20.3	80.3	19.0	80.3	45.8	0.0	0.0
New Mexico	11.8	2.3	8.8	1.5	8.8	5.9	0.0	0.0
Utah	4.5	1.1	4.5	0.9	3.6	2.8	0.9	11.0
Wyoming	0.1	0.1	0.1	0.1	0.1	0.3	0.0	0.0
Pacific	**$2,480.0**	**16.6%**	**$2,897.4**	**16.6%**	**$2,810.6**	**39.2%**	**$86.8**	**54.5%**
Alaska	0.0	7.9	33.3	12.4	0.0	0.0	33.3	97.2
California	2,191.5	18.8	2,542.5	18.8	2,542.5	40.2	0.0	0.0
Hawaii	40.4	11.8	43.9	11.5	43.9	33.7	0.0	0.0
Oregon	17.3	2.2	20.6	2.2	10.3	7.5	10.3	37.1
Washington	230.9	11.5	257.0	11.1	213.9	39.6	43.2	44.5

Source: Health Care Financing Administration Form 64.
Note: See table notes for Section D.

Table D8
Ratio of Medicaid Maximum Fees to New Medicare Fee Schedule Levels, 1993

	Primary Care	Hospital Visits	Surgery	Obstetrical Care	Laboratory Tests	Imaging Services	All Services
United States	**0.77**	**0.53**	**0.95**	**0.99**	**0.85**	**0.88**	**0.77**
New England	**0.79**	**0.50**	**0.87**	**0.81**	**0.71**	**0.71**	**0.70**
Connecticut	0.49	0.42	0.80	0.95	0.58	0.54	0.57
Maine	0.72	0.43	0.61	0.66	0.67	0.47	0.66
Massachusetts	0.93	0.58	1.01	0.72	0.71	0.83	0.87
New Hampshire	0.79	0.67	0.70	1.13	0.68	0.56	0.80
Rhode Island	0.46	0.30	0.59	0.50	0.52	0.42	0.46
Vermont	0.70	0.56	0.67	1.02	1.32	0.78	0.75
Middle Atlantic	**0.41**	**0.19**	**0.49**	**0.57**	**0.41**	**0.54**	**0.36**
New Jersey	0.39	0.28	0.45	0.39	0.50	0.42	0.39
New York	0.29	0.13	0.41	0.76	0.32	0.42	0.36
Pennsylvania	0.62	0.35	0.89	1.06	0.52	0.81	0.69
South Atlantic	**0.90**	**0.70**	**1.13**	**1.27**	**0.87**	**0.90**	**0.91**
Delaware	0.62	0.60	1.02	0.86	0.70	0.85	0.70
District of Columbia	0.57	0.36	0.67	0.96	0.42	0.70	0.62
Florida	0.76	0.60	0.96	1.02	0.61	0.83	0.80
Georgia	1.04	1.05	1.23	1.41	1.07	1.06	1.10
Maryland	0.80	0.30	0.68	1.13	0.71	0.51	0.77
North Carolina	0.96	0.96	1.03	1.19	0.83	0.96	0.99
South Carolina	0.70	0.28	1.00	1.08	0.63	0.62	0.73
Virginia	0.80	0.87	1.89	1.35	1.38	0.93	0.96
West Virginia	1.46	1.37	3.00	1.64	1.08	1.30	1.54
East South Central	**0.93**	**0.68**	**1.40**	**1.22**	**1.08**	**1.07**	**1.03**
Alabama	0.88	0.67	1.09	1.68	0.36	0.74	0.95
Kentucky	1.04	0.77	2.25	1.36	1.15	1.03	1.14
Mississippi	0.73	0.72	0.78	0.96	1.08	1.09	0.81
Tennessee	0.94	0.60	1.29	1.21	1.29	1.23	1.01
West South Central	**0.93**	**0.87**	**1.14**	**1.10**	**1.00**	**1.01**	**1.00**
Arkansas	1.26	1.06	1.65	1.01	1.16	1.32	1.24
Louisiana	0.89	0.78	1.36	1.37	1.04	1.13	0.99
Oklahoma	1.00	0.70	0.99	1.15	1.03	0.68	0.97
Texas	0.88	0.91	1.00	0.98	0.95	0.95	0.91
East North Central	**0.64**	**0.48**	**1.07**	**0.79**	**0.74**	**0.80**	**0.76**
Illinois	0.56	0.37	0.97	0.78	0.65	0.70	0.62
Indiana	0.88	0.96	1.82	1.06	1.21	0.99	0.98
Michigan	0.59	0.59	0.72	0.60	0.51	0.61	0.60
Ohio	0.58	0.32	1.07	0.73	0.70	0.86	0.64
Wisconsin	0.77	0.69	1.48	0.89	0.88	1.19	0.87
West North Central	**0.78**	**0.66**	**1.29**	**1.05**	**0.98**	**1.41**	**1.00**
Iowa	0.70	0.70	1.84	1.32	1.04	0.88	0.87
Kansas	0.66	0.35	1.20	1.22	1.32	1.19	0.81
Minnesota	0.84	1.05	1.56	1.09	0.83	1.27	0.96
Missouri	0.55	0.28	0.65	0.81	0.66	0.63	0.58
Nebraska	1.00	0.83	1.34	0.90	1.08	3.64	1.25
North Dakota	0.94	1.09	1.23	0.93	1.00	1.26	1.00
South Dakota	0.88	1.08	1.92	1.04	1.19	1.28	1.02
Mountain	**0.85**	**0.67**	**1.29**	**0.99**	**1.15**	**1.03**	**0.99**
Arizona	n/a	n/a	n/a	n/a	n/a	n/a	n/a
Colorado	0.74	0.47	0.88	0.86	1.04	0.72	0.76
Idaho	1.07	0.74	1.22	1.30	1.04	1.02	1.09
Montana	0.93	1.00	1.31	1.45	1.05	1.12	1.04
Nevada	0.93	0.86	1.80	1.21	1.19	1.32	1.05
New Mexico	0.79	0.65	1.64	0.97	1.54	1.36	0.93
Utah	0.78	0.74	1.19	0.85	0.78	0.64	0.80
Wyoming	1.05	1.05	2.04	1.36	1.26	1.26	1.17
Pacific	**0.63**	**0.52**	**0.89**	**0.76**	**0.78**	**0.72**	**0.71**
Alaska	1.74	1.05	2.30	1.25	0.90	1.68	1.64
California	0.51	0.51	0.86	0.58	0.78	0.67	0.56
Hawaii	0.83	0.87	1.57	0.67	0.81	0.89	0.86
Oregon	0.65	0.63	1.12	0.93	0.91	0.86	0.74
Washington	0.98	0.48	0.73	1.03	0.73	0.68	0.91

Source: Stephen A. Norton, 1994, "The Declining Gap between Medicaid and Medicare Physician Fees: Results of a 1993 Medicaid Fee Survey, Urban Institute Working Paper, 06375-01" (Washington, D.C.: Urban Institute).
Note: See table notes for Section D.

Notes to Tables, Section D

1. The eligible population is an estimate of all individuals (under age 65) who would qualify for Medicaid whether or not they actually applied for benefits. Eligibility for Medicaid was determined by the Urban Institute's Transfer Income Model (TRIM2). TRIM2 allows the application of family income and demographic information to individual state Medicaid eligibility rules to determine the number of eligible individuals. (See Appendix Three for more details.)

2. The eligibility rate is defined as the number of Medicaid-eligible individuals divided by the population.

3. The enrolled population is an estimate of the number of individuals under age 65 who were actually enrolled in the Medicaid program. The TRIM2 simulation model was used to correct for documented underreporting of Medicaid benefits on the CPS. (See Appendix Three for more details.)

4. The enrollment rate is defined as the number of Medicaid enrollees divided by the population.

5. The participation rate is defined as the number of Medicaid enrollees divided by the number of individuals determined to be eligible for benefits.

6. States that did not have more than 100 (unweighted) observations per age group were considered statistically unreliable and are not reported in this table.

7. Numbers of enrollees in Medicaid differ from those reported in table D1 for several reasons. First, the enrollment counts presented in table D1 do not include the elderly and are based on the Current Population Survey, which excludes institutionalized individuals. Furthermore, the numbers we present from the CPS are based on data for the years 1990, 1991, and 1992 (with emphasis on 1992) and are more representative of a 1990–92 three-year average. Finally, there may also be some differences introduced by the TRIM2 simulation of the counts presented in table D1. It is important to note that individuals may or may not be enrolled in Medicaid for the full year. As a result, enrollee counts tend to overstate the number of people enrolled in Medicaid at a point in time; expenditures per enrollee are affected because part- and full-time enrollees are given equal weight.

8. Growth in expenditures per enrollee does not include disproportionate share payments.

9. Children are defined as individuals under 21 years of age. It is probable that states vary in their age distinction for child enrollees, either including or excluding individuals between 18 and 21 years of age.

10. Total expenditures for children and adults include payments to HMOs. These payments are not itemized by enrollment group and were therefore distributed proportionally among cash assistance children and adults.

11. Adults in table D5 are defined as between 21 and 64 years of age. Some states may classify adults differently, including poverty-level pregnant women.

12. Medicaid payments for Medicare premiums and cost sharing were assumed to be made on behalf of elderly enrollees.

13. Expenditures and enrollment levels for blind persons and those with disabilities are not available by age. At the national level, approximately 13.5 percent of this population are children (under age 21), 76 percent are adults, and 10.5 percent are elderly.

14. Acute care services are defined here as inpatient hospital, physician/laboratory/X-ray, outpatient, and prescription drugs. The expenditures shown do not include "supplemental acute" care services such as EPSDT (early and periodic screening, diagnostic treatment), dental, or vision care.

15. Cash assistance enrollees refers to individuals who are eligible for Medicaid owing to their eligibility for AFDC or SSI.

16. Noncash assistance enrollees are defined as individuals who are eligible for Medicaid for reasons other than eligibility for AFDC or SSI. These groups include the medically needy and pregnant women and children covered under poverty-related rules.

17. Supplemental acute care includes EPSDT, family planning, dental services, and other practitioners' services.

18. Direct expenditures include payments for acute and long-term care services only. Payments to HMOs, Medicare, or disproportionate share institutions are not included.

19. Other home and community-based care includes home health services and home and community-based services for the functionally disabled elderly and mentally retarded/developmentally disabled (1915[c] waivers).

20. Disproportionate share expenditures were not available by type of institution for 1992.

All Tables:

Unless stated otherwise, the Medicaid expenditures shown in this section do not include disproportionate share payments (DSH) to inpatient hospitals and mental health institutions.

Medicaid enrollees are defined as individuals who are reported as enrolled in the Medicaid program, regardless of whether or not they actually received services.

For most of the tables in this section, data for the state of Arizona are not included.

Indices of Health Status

Section E's tables provide information on health status indicators within each state. Attention is concentrated on three subpopulations—pregnant women and infants, the total population, and selected populations, including persons with AIDS as well as those with disabilities that prevent or limit working.

PREGNANT WOMEN AND INFANTS

Newborn infants and pregnant women are the focus of the data in tables E1 through E3. Table El provides information on infant mortality rates per 1,000 births by race (white and black). Infant mortality is widely used as a measure of infant health status. The data show important variation between white and black infant mortality rates. On average there are twice as many black infant deaths as white infant deaths per 1,000 live births, a result that is fairly consistent across states.

Recent policy reforms have stressed the need to provide quality health care to pregnant women and infants. Data in these tables give some indication of the quality of care received. Table E2 lists the number of neonatal deaths, the number of births in which the mother received late or no prenatal care, and the number of low-weight births. Births in which the mother received prenatal care only after the seventh month of pregnancy, or not at all during the pregnancy, are classified as births receiving late or no prenatal care. Births under 2,500 grams are classified as low-weight births. The percentage of births in which the mother receives late or no prenatal care varies among the states. The rates in the District of Columbia, Arizona, New Mexico, and Texas, for example, are at least 50 percent higher than the national average of 6.3 percent.

Table E3 highlights racial differences in the number of births to unmarried women. Births to unmarried black women as a percentage of all births to black women range from 8 percent in North Dakota to 76.7 percent in Wisconsin, whereas the percentage for white women ranges from 11.6 percent in Alabama to about 30 percent in California and New Mexico. The variation between the races can be seen clearly when comparing national averages: of births to white women, 19.6 percent are to unmarried women; whereas among births to black women, 62.4 percent are to unmarried women.

TOTAL POPULATION

Table E4 shows birthrates and death rates per 1,000 population. Nationally, the birthrate is 16.3 per 1,000 population, and the death rate is 8.7 per 1,000 population. States with birthrates higher than the national average tend to have death rates below the national average. For example, California's birthrate of 19.6 per 1,000 population was almost 20 percent higher than the national average, while its death rate of 7.5 per 1,000 population was about 15 percent lower than the national average. The opposite of this is also true. The District of Columbia is an exception because both the birthrate and the death rate are significantly above the national average: 19.5 and 12.7 per 1,000 population, respectively. The information presented here along with the population characteristics found in Section G indicate relatively younger or older state populations.

Death rates by six selected causes are presented in table E5. These six leading causes of death account for over three-quarters of all deaths in the United States. In all of the states, heart disease is the leading cause of death and malignant neoplasms are second. However, there is variation across states in the rates of death due to these factors. For example, death rates from heart disease vary from 212.1 per 100,000 in the Mountain region to 355.8 per 100,000 in the Middle Atlantic region. Differences in death rates across states reflect, among other factors, differences in population characteristics such as age and income (tables G1 and G4–G7) and differences in state health care systems.

SELECTED POPULATIONS

Table E6 provides information on the number of AIDS cases in 1992, the rate of AIDS cases per 100,000 population, and cumulative state AIDS cases as a percentage of total U.S. AIDS cases since 1981. This information is important, since people with AIDS are high-cost users of our health care system as well as individuals who are likely to have difficulty obtaining or retaining health insurance. These data show that since 1981 six states—California (with the most cases), New York, Florida, Texas, New Jersey, and Illinois—have accounted for over 65 percent of the AIDS cases in this country. The data show that the AIDS virus affects all the states. However, there is wide variation in the number of cases per population across the states. For example, the number of AIDS cases per 100,000 ranges from 1 in North Dakota, South Dakota, and Wyoming to 123 in the District of Columbia.

Table E7 provides information on the distribution of the population aged 18 through 64 with self-reported disabilities that prevent or limit working. This is not a representative measure of the number of disabled people within a state, because the statistics are self-reported and only cover the adult population. Table E7 shows that the proportion of the adult population reporting disabilities that prevent or limit their ability to work ranges from 5.3 percent in Connecticut and Maryland to 11.5 percent in Kentucky, with most states falling within the range of 5 percent to 9 percent.

Table E1
Infant Mortality by Race, 1989

	All Races		Whites		Blacks	
	Infant Deaths under Age 1	Infant Deaths per 1,000 Births under Age 1[1]	Infant Deaths under Age 1	Infant Deaths per 1,000 Births under Age 1[1]	Infant Deaths under Age 1	Infant Deaths per 1,000 Births under Age 1[1]
United States	**39,655**	**9.8**	**25,794**	**8.2**	**12,527**	**17.7**
New England	**1,618**	**8.1**	**1,299**	**7.4**	**289**	**15.9**
Connecticut	433	8.8	298	7.2	130	18.6
Maine	129	7.4	124	7.3	0	0.0
Massachusetts	704	7.7	549	7.0	138	14.5
New Hampshire	142	8.0	141	8.1	1	5.4
Rhode Island	151	10.2	128	10.0	20	15.7
Vermont	59	6.9	59	7.0	0	0.0
Middle Atlantic	**5,943**	**10.1**	**3,593**	**8.1**	**2,248**	**18.9**
New Jersey	1,135	9.3	651	7.1	464	18.4
New York	3,094	10.6	1,831	8.6	1,205	18.2
Pennsylvania	1,714	10.2	1,111	8.0	579	21.2
South Atlantic	**7,531**	**11.0**	**3,906**	**8.4**	**3,545**	**17.6**
Delaware	127	11.8	76	9.6	50	19.3
District of Columbia	270	22.9	26	15.2	244	26.3
Florida	1,900	9.8	1,144	8.0	742	15.9
Georgia	1,358	12.3	624	9.1	725	18.1
Maryland	809	10.3	416	8.3	381	15.3
North Carolina	1,156	11.3	591	8.6	537	17.5
South Carolina	733	12.8	312	9.1	419	18.6
Virginia	969	10.0	519	7.5	436	18.1
West Virginia	209	9.4	198	9.4	11	11.9
East South Central	**2,539**	**10.9**	**1,423**	**8.7**	**1,100**	**16.8**
Alabama	755	12.1	375	9.3	377	17.3
Kentucky	494	9.2	399	8.4	92	17.2
Mississippi	500	11.6	190	8.6	304	14.8
Tennessee	790	10.8	459	8.4	327	18.3
West South Central	**4,420**	**9.5**	**2,916**	**8.1**	**1,412**	**15.8**
Arkansas	366	10.2	227	8.5	137	16.0
Louisiana	832	11.4	352	8.5	477	15.9
Oklahoma	405	8.5	294	8.3	70	12.7
Texas	2,817	9.2	2,043	8.0	728	16.1
East North Central	**7,012**	**10.7**	**4,568**	**8.7**	**2,369**	**19.8**
Illinois	2,235	11.7	1,282	9.2	931	20.6
Indiana	855	10.2	674	9.3	178	18.5
Michigan	1,646	11.1	950	8.3	673	21.8
Ohio	1,624	9.9	1,148	8.5	471	17.6
Wisconsin	652	9.1	514	8.3	116	16.1
West North Central	**2,288**	**8.5**	**1,780**	**7.6**	**381**	**16.5**
Iowa	323	8.3	291	7.9	23	18.3
Kansas	341	8.8	280	8.3	52	13.9
Minnesota	478	7.1	386	6.4	55	18.6
Missouri	771	9.9	541	8.6	223	16.7
Nebraska	192	7.9	156	7.1	26	16.8
North Dakota	77	8.0	62	7.5	1	8.9
South Dakota	106	9.6	64	7.1	1	7.7
Mountain	**2,109**	**8.9**	**1,754**	**8.5**	**153**	**15.7**
Arizona	620	9.2	495	8.8	55	17.8
Colorado	461	8.7	405	8.5	45	13.8
Idaho	154	9.7	144	9.5	1	10.8
Montana	132	11.3	98	9.9	0	0.0
Nevada	159	8.1	121	7.4	35	17.2
New Mexico	233	8.5	173	7.8	11	15.0
Utah	285	8.0	255	7.7	6	16.1
Wyoming	65	9.4	63	9.8	0	0.0
Pacific	**6,195**	**8.6**	**4,555**	**8.1**	**1,030**	**16.2**
Alaska	107	9.2	54	7.2	5	7.1
California	4,869	8.5	3,571	8.0	932	16.5
Hawaii	160	8.3	28	6.3	8	8.5
Oregon	368	8.9	329	8.8	22	18.3
Washington	691	9.2	573	8.9	63	15.8

Source: National Center for Health Statistics, 1989, <u>Vital Statistics of the United States: Volume II, Mortality</u> (Hyattsville, MD: NCHS).
Note: See table notes at end of Section E.

Table E2
Infant Health Indicators, 1989

	Neonatal Deaths (Ages 1-27 Days)		Births with Late or No Prenatal Care[3]		Low-Weight Births[5]	
	Number	per 1,000 Births[2]	Number	per 1,000 Births[4]	Number	per 1,000 Births
United States	25,168	6.2	254,911	6.3%	284,391	7.0%
New England	1,133	5.7	6,246	3.1%	11,933	6.0%
Connecticut	315	6.4	1,519	3.1	3,414	6.9
Maine	89	5.1	462	2.7	851	4.9
Massachusetts	484	5.3	2,969	3.2	5,388	5.9
New Hampshire	89	5.0	582	3.3	909	5.1
Rhode Island	115	7.8	433	2.9	909	6.2
Vermont	41	4.8	281	3.3	462	5.5
Middle Atlantic	4,024	6.8	41,188	7.0%	43,127	7.3%
New Jersey	751	6.2	9,205	7.6	8,902	7.3
New York	2,090	7.2	22,340	7.7	22,282	7.7
Pennsylvania	1,183	7.0	9,643	5.7	11,943	7.1
South Atlantic	4,997	7.3	44,623	6.5%	54,820	8.0%
Delaware	92	8.6	552	5.1	801	7.5
District of Columbia	188	15.9	1,613	13.7	1,867	15.9
Florida	1,253	6.5	15,552	8.1	14,808	7.7
Georgia	887	8.0	7,399	6.7	9,202	8.4
Maryland	509	6.5	3,026	3.9	6,260	8.0
North Carolina	775	7.6	5,793	5.7	8,270	8.1
South Carolina	467	8.1	5,065	8.8	5,268	9.2
Virginia	687	7.1	4,508	4.7	6,872	7.1
West Virginia	139	6.3	1,115	5.0	1,472	6.6
East South Central	1,595	6.9	11,868	5.1%	18,880	8.1%
Alabama	502	8.0	3,801	6.1	5,169	8.3
Kentucky	283	5.3	2,561	4.8	3,657	6.9
Mississippi	310	7.2	1,946	4.5	4,043	9.4
Tennessee	500	6.8	3,560	4.9	6,011	8.2
West South Central	2,709	5.8	43,688	9.4%	34,129	7.4%
Arkansas	216	6.0	2,534	7.1	2,973	8.3
Louisiana	529	7.3	4,550	6.3	6,626	9.1
Oklahoma	234	4.9	2,722	5.7	3,068	6.5
Texas	1,730	5.6	33,882	11.	21,462	7.0
East North Central	4,463	6.8	29,303	4.5%	47,061	7.1%
Illinois	1,428	7.5	9,901	5.2	14,645	7.7
Indiana	540	6.5	4,036	4.8	5,488	6.6
Michigan	1,071	7.2	6,123	4.1	11,275	7.6
Ohio	1,033	6.3	6,557	4.0	11,512	7.0
Wisconsin	391	5.4	2,686	3.7	4,141	5.8
West North Central	1,341	5.0	10,447	3.9%	15,658	5.8%
Iowa	214	5.5	1,047	2.7	2,116	5.4
Kansas	183	4.7	1,750	4.5	2,370	6.1
Minnesota	278	4.1	2,297	3.4	3,309	4.9
Missouri	462	5.9	3,726	4.8	5,386	6.9
Nebraska	108	4.5	763	3.2	1,402	5.8
North Dakota	45	4.7	316	3.3	481	5.0
South Dakota	51	4.6	548	4.9	594	5.4
Mountain	1,224	5.2	18,966	8.0%	15,699	6.6%
Arizona	371	5.5	7,961	11.9	4,262	6.3
Colorado	272	5.2	2,961	5.6	4,088	7.8
Idaho	100	6.3	970	6.1	879	5.5
Montana	65	5.6	565	4.8	647	5.5
Nevada	76	3.9	1,791	9.1	1,410	7.2
New Mexico	146	5.3	3,503	12.8	1,896	7.0
Utah	158	4.4	949	2.7	2,014	5.7
Wyoming	36	5.2	266	4.1	503	7.3
Pacific	3,682	5.1	48,582	6.8%	43,084	6.0%
Alaska	50	4.3	417	3.6	572	4.9
California	2,961	5.2	40,911	7.2	34,764	6.1
Hawaii	82	4.2	1,073	5.5	1,378	7.1
Oregon	208	5.0	2,262	5.5	2,151	5.2
Washington	381	5.1	3,919	5.2	4,219	5.6

Sources: Columns 1 and 2-- National Center for Health Statistics, 1989, <u>Vital Statistics of the United States: Volume II, Mortality</u> (Hyattsville, MD: NCHS); Columns 3-6-- ibid.: <u>Volume I, Natality</u>.

Note: See table notes at end of Section E.

Table E3
Births to Unmarried Women by Race, 1989

	All Races		White		Black	
	Number	As Percent of Births to All Women[6]	Number	As Percent of Births to White Women[6]	Number	As Percent of Births to Black Women[6]
United States	**1,094,169**	**27.1%**	**613,543**	**19.6%**	**442,395**	**62.4%**
New England	**46,775**	**23.4%**	**35,278**	**20.2%**	**10,120**	**55.8%**
Connecticut	13,005	26.3	8,461	20.5	4,260	60.8
Maine	3,806	21.8	3,717	21.8	25	20.2
Massachusetts	21,798	23.8	15,896	20.4	5,082	53.4
New Hampshire	2,797	15.7	2,750	15.8	34	18.5
Rhode Island	3,684	24.9	2,787	21.7	711	55.8
Vermont	1,685	19.8	1,667	19.9	8	20.0
Middle Atlantic	**169,453**	**28.8%**	**91,093**	**20.6%**	**76,186**	**64.2%**
New Jersey	29,364	24.1	13,933	15.2	15,125	60.1
New York	92,996	31.9	49,887	23.5	41,615	62.8
Pennsylvania	47,093	27.9	27,273	19.7	19,446	71.2
South Atlantic	**202,596**	**29.7%**	**75,338**	**16.2%**	**124,889**	**61.9%**
Delaware	3,125	29.1	1,297	16.3	1,813	70.0
District of Columbia	7,580	64.3	235	13.8	6,985	75.4
Florida	58,305	30.2	27,815	19.4	30,047	64.5
Georgia	34,926	31.7	9,713	14.2	25,084	62.6
Maryland	22,607	28.9	7,916	15.8	14,356	57.7
North Carolina	28,315	27.7	8,925	13.0	18,614	60.6
South Carolina	18,116	31.6	4,723	13.8	13,345	59.3
Virginia	24,410	25.2	10,061	14.4	14,094	58.5
West Virginia	5,212	23.5	4,653	22.0	551	59.4
East South Central	**68,927**	**29.7%**	**24,950**	**15.2%**	**43,664**	**66.5%**
Alabama	18,640	29.8	4,659	11.6	13,929	63.7
Kentucky	12,048	22.6	8,563	18.0	3,441	64.2
Mississippi	16,958	39.4	2,734	12.4	14,077	68.5
Tennessee	21,281	29.1	8,994	16.5	12,217	68.4
West South Central	**107,197**	**23.1%**	**53,410**	**14.9%**	**51,417**	**57.6%**
Arkansas	9,944	27.7	4,136	15.4	5,761	67.1
Louisiana	25,692	35.3	5,946	14.4	19,525	65.1
Oklahoma	11,258	23.8	6,390	18.0	3,262	59.1
Texas	60,303	19.6	36,938	14.5	22,869	50.6
East North Central	**177,942**	**27.0%**	**92,279**	**17.6%**	**83,816**	**70.1%**
Illinois	58,867	30.9	25,514	18.3	32,836	72.8
Indiana	19,898	23.8	13,379	18.4	6,410	66.6
Michigan	36,441	24.5	15,685	13.7	20,365	66.0
Ohio	45,921	28.0	27,039	20.0	18,671	69.6
Wisconsin	16,815	23.4	10,662	17.2	5,534	76.7
West North Central	**58,109**	**21.7%**	**39,082**	**16.7%**	**15,160**	**65.6%**
Iowa	7,575	19.4	6,613	17.9	811	64.4
Kansas	7,577	19.6	5,424	16.1	1,967	52.7
Minnesota	13,142	19.5	9,994	16.5	1,766	59.8
Missouri	21,123	27.1	11,336	17.9	9,620	72.0
Nebraska	4,662	19.3	3,412	15.6	969	62.7
North Dakota	1,615	16.9	1,079	13.0	9	8.0
South Dakota	2,415	21.8	1,224	13.6	18	13.8
Mountain	**56,429**	**23.8%**	**43,181**	**20.9%**	**4,637**	**47.6%**
Arizona	20,708	30.8	15,313	27.2	1,554	50.2
Colorado	10,787	20.5	8,987	18.9	1,465	45.0
Idaho	2,561	16.1	2,386	15.7	15	16.1
Montana	2,539	21.7	1,644	16.7	11	15.7
Nevada	4,607	23.5	3,191	19.6	1,164	57.2
New Mexico	9,447	34.5	6,586	29.8	294	40.2
Utah	4,504	12.7	3,935	11.8	103	27.7
Wyoming	1,276	18.5	1,139	17.7	31	31.3
Pacific	**206,741**	**28.8%**	**158,932**	**28.3%**	**32,506**	**51.2%**
Alaska	2,869	24.6	1,256	16.8	158	22.4
California	171,189	30.0	133,398	29.7	30,071	53.1
Hawaii	4,609	23.8	865	19.3	103	11.0
Oregon	10,436	25.3	9,226	24.6	631	52.4
Washington	17,638	23.4	14,187	22.1	1,543	38.6

Source: National Center for Health Statistics, 1989, <u>Vital Statistics of the United States: Volume I, Natality</u> (Hyattsville, MD: NCHS).
Note: See table notes at end of Section E.

Table E4
Total Births and Deaths, 1989
(Births and deaths in thousands)

	Births		Deaths	
	Total	per 1,000	Total	per 1,000
United States	**4,041**	**16.3**	**2,151**	**8.7**
New England	**200**	**15.3**	**116**	**8.9**
Connecticut	49	15.3	28	8.7
Maine	17	14.3	11	9.2
Massachusetts	92	15.5	54	9.1
New Hampshire	18	16.1	8	7.7
Rhode Island	15	14.8	10	9.6
Vermont	8	15.0	5	8.1
Middle Atlantic	**582**	**15.4**	**367**	**9.7**
New Jersey	122	15.7	71	9.2
New York	291	16.2	172	9.6
Pennsylvania	169	14.0	124	10.3
South Atlantic	**683**	**15.8**	**391**	**9.1**
Delaware	11	15.9	6	8.7
District of Columbia	12	19.5	8	12.7
Florida	193	15.2	133	10.5
Georgia	110	17.1	52	8.1
Maryland	78	16.7	38	8.2
North Carolina	102	15.5	57	8.7
South Carolina	57	16.3	30	8.4
Virginia	97	15.9	47	7.7
West Virginia	22	11.9	20	10.5
East South Central	**232**	**15.1**	**145**	**9.4**
Alabama	63	15.2	39	9.5
Kentucky	53	14.3	35	9.5
Mississippi	43	16.4	25	9.7
Tennessee	73	14.8	45	9.2
West South Central	**464**	**17.2**	**217**	**8.0**
Arkansas	36	14.9	25	10.2
Louisiana	73	16.6	38	8.6
Oklahoma	47	14.7	30	9.2
Texas	308	18.1	125	7.4
East North Central	**658**	**15.6**	**372**	**8.8**
Illinois	190	16.3	103	8.9
Indiana	83	14.9	49	8.8
Michigan	149	16.0	79	8.5
Ohio	164	15.0	98	9.0
Wisconsin	72	14.8	42	8.7
West North Central	**268**	**15.0**	**161**	**9.0**
Iowa	39	13.7	27	9.6
Kansas	39	15.4	22	8.9
Minnesota	68	15.5	34	7.9
Missouri	78	15.1	50	9.8
Nebraska	24	15.0	15	9.2
North Dakota	10	14.5	6	8.3
South Dakota	11	15.5	7	9.2
Mountain	**237**	**17.5**	**95**	**7.1**
Arizona	67	18.9	28	7.9
Colorado	53	15.9	21	6.4
Idaho	16	15.7	7	7.4
Montana	12	14.5	7	8.4
Nevada	20	17.6	9	7.8
New Mexico	27	17.9	11	6.9
Utah	36	20.8	9	5.4
Wyoming	7	14.5	3	6.9
Pacific	**718**	**18.7**	**286**	**7.5**
Alaska	12	22.1	2	4.0
California	570	19.6	217	7.5
Hawaii	19	17.4	7	5.8
Oregon	41	14.6	25	8.8
Washington	75	15.8	36	7.6

Sources: Columns 1 and 2-- National Center for Health Statistics, 1989, <u>Vital Statistics of the United States: Volume I, Natality</u> (Hyattsville, MD: NCHS); Columns 3 and 4-- ibid.: Volume II, Mortality.
Note: See table notes at end of Section E.

Table E5

Deaths per 100,000 Population by Cause, 1989

	Diseases of Heart	Malignant Neoplasms	Cerebrovascular Disease	Accidents and Adverse Effects	Chronic Obstructive Pulmonary Disease	Pneumonia
United States	295.6	199.9	58.6	38.3	34.0	30.2
New England	300.4	224.5	56.8	29.6	33.2	33.0
Connecticut	303.5	220.3	55.2	28.9	30.6	33.3
Maine	312.1	230.4	59.4	35.3	40.8	26.8
Massachusetts	301.6	230.5	58.0	27.4	32.1	36.8
New Hampshire	254.6	195.8	51.1	32.7	34.8	24.8
Rhode Island	342.4	245.4	60.7	28.8	33.5	27.2
Vermont	260.1	192.9	52.6	39.9	40.0	30.3
Middle Atlantic	355.8	226.1	55.6	31.8	33.2	34.8
New Jersey	314.3	232.5	53.1	27.4	31.8	29.1
New York	361.1	212.2	50.9	30.2	31.0	38.9
Pennsylvania	374.5	242.6	64.2	36.9	37.5	32.2
South Atlantic	303.2	212.2	62.1	42.6	34.1	26.2
Delaware	291.4	212.3	48.0	37.1	32.1	23.0
District of Columbia	326.7	282.0	73.8	36.6	27.2	40.1
Florida	365.4	257.1	66.4	42.1	43.2	25.3
Georgia	260.3	173.2	58.3	46.9	30.3	27.2
Maryland	257.9	202.3	48.7	30.1	28.8	25.4
North Carolina	288.8	197.5	70.2	48.3	29.4	28.6
South Carolina	272.1	184.9	70.1	52.7	29.1	20.7
Virginia	258.7	184.7	54.4	36.3	27.6	25.1
West Virginia	394.8	235.9	63.4	48.1	47.7	33.1
East South Central	328.0	209.6	70.3	50.7	35.5	30.5
Alabama	320.1	209.0	69.7	53.6	34.3	29.2
Kentucky	328.8	221.5	67.4	46.2	41.2	33.6
Mississippi	367.3	201.0	72.2	58.9	28.8	28.8
Tennessee	313.1	205.5	71.9	47.3	35.5	30.0
West South Central	266.9	178.2	56.2	41.5	28.7	25.1
Arkansas	346.7	229.7	84.6	53.7	38.1	34.8
Louisiana	291.1	194.2	56.4	43.7	27.8	20.7
Oklahoma	331.8	207.2	70.8	41.4	37.4	38.7
Texas	237.1	161.3	49.3	39.2	25.7	22.5
East North Central	312.5	204.9	60.0	34.9	33.8	29.7
Illinois	314.9	205.3	58.9	35.0	32.2	33.3
Indiana	306.0	203.1	67.9	36.7	36.6	26.7
Michigan	303.0	197.7	56.1	35.3	30.9	27.9
Ohio	342.2	212.9	57.6	33.4	37.6	27.7
Wisconsin	305.9	201.7	66.6	35.2	31.4	32.4
West North Central	310.4	207.0	68.0	39.1	37.8	34.1
Iowa	340.9	217.9	75.4	40.4	40.7	39.4
Kansas	307.8	199.4	64.5	38.8	39.1	34.5
Minnesota	249.9	184.2	65.4	35.4	30.5	29.2
Missouri	343.2	225.3	67.1	42.0	42.4	35.2
Nebraska	318.3	205.3	71.8	38.0	40.3	38.3
North Dakota	283.9	205.6	61.1	33.6	29.8	27.6
South Dakota	335.8	202.0	71.5	45.9	34.5	30.1
Mountain	212.1	158.0	42.9	41.7	39.7	25.9
Arizona	246.6	181.6	46.1	45.9	44.3	29.6
Colorado	184.0	141.8	39.9	33.3	39.9	26.0
Idaho	228.3	164.9	56.9	47.3	40.6	25.7
Montana	253.2	195.8	53.5	44.5	47.4	27.9
Nevada	245.6	187.2	40.5	43.0	48.3	24.4
New Mexico	197.3	147.2	36.8	56.7	53.3	24.7
Utah	159.8	108.8	37.4	32.5	48.3	24.4
Wyoming	203.8	158.7	35.8	44.4	42.5	22.5
Pacific	237.4	169.1	55.0	37.6	34.4	33.1
Alaska	90.3	83.5	18.4	70.6	16.3	8.2
California	239.5	165.7	54.2	37.1	33.6	35.0
Hawaii	179.3	141.5	44.2	27.2	18.1	24.6
Oregon	269.1	206.4	71.8	44.3	43.8	31.7
Washington	235.2	183.1	56.4	35.8	39.7	26.7

Source: National Center for Health Statistics, 1989, <u>Vital Statistics of the United States: Volume I, Mortality</u> (Hyattsville, MD: NCHS).
Note: See table notes at end of Section E.

Table E6
AIDS Cases and Rates

	AIDS Cases, 1992[7]	Annual Rates per 100,000 Population, 1992	Cumulative State AIDS Cases, 1981-92 as % of U.S. Cases[8]
United States	**45,904**	**18.0**	**100.0%**
New England	**1,737**	**13.1**	**3.9%**
Connecticut	648	19.8	1.2
Maine	44	3.6	0.1
Massachusetts	864	14.4	2.2
New Hampshire	48	4.3	0.1
Rhode Island	107	10.7	0.2
Vermont	26	4.6	0.0
Middle Atlantic	**11,759**	**30.8**	**30.0%**
New Jersey	2,030	26.0	6.3
New York	8,382	46.3	20.9
Pennsylvania	1,347	11.2	2.8
South Atlantic	**10,333**	**23.0**	**20.0%**
Delaware	138	20.0	0.2
District of Columbia	718	122.7	1.7
Florida	5,085	37.7	9.8
Georgia	1,374	20.3	2.9
Maryland	1,201	24.4	2.1
North Carolina	583	8.5	1.1
South Carolina	397	11.0	0.7
Virginia	781	12.2	1.4
West Virginia	56	3.1	0.1
East South Central	**1,324**	**8.5**	**2.2%**
Alabama	440	10.6	0.7
Kentucky	214	5.7	0.3
Mississippi	262	10.0	0.4
Tennessee	408	8.1	0.7
West South Central	**4,290**	**15.5**	**9.6%**
Arkansas	278	11.6	0.3
Louisiana	803	18.8	1.6
Oklahoma	271	8.5	0.5
Texas	2,938	16.6	7.2
East North Central	**4,024**	**9.5**	**7.2%**
Illinois	1,888	16.3	3.2
Indiana	398	7.0	0.7
Michigan	735	7.8	1.4
Ohio	773	7.0	1.5
Wisconsin	230	4.6	0.4
West North Central	**1,312**	**7.3**	**2.4%**
Iowa	112	4.0	0.2
Kansas	191	7.6	0.3
Minnesota	217	4.9	0.5
Missouri	714	13.8	1.3
Nebraska	61	3.8	0.1
North Dakota	9	1.4	0.0
South Dakota	8	1.1	0.0
Mountain	**1,342**	**9.3**	**2.8%**
Arizona	385	10.0	0.8
Colorado	407	11.7	1.0
Idaho	35	3.3	0.1
Montana	20	2.4	0.0
Nevada	248	18.6	0.4
New Mexico	107	6.8	0.2
Utah	135	7.5	0.2
Wyoming	5	1.1	0.0
Pacific	**9,783**	**24.1**	**21.9%**
Alaska	18	3.1	0.1
California	8,774	28.4	19.4
Hawaii	138	11.9	0.4
Oregon	288	9.7	0.6
Washington	565	11.0	1.4

Source: Centers for Disease Control, 1993, *HIV/AIDS Surveillance* 5(4).
Note: See table notes at end of Section E.

Table E7
Adults Ages 18-64 With Disabilities
That Prevent or Limit Work, 1990-92[9]
(Standard errors in parentheses)

	Number	Percent Disabled	Percent Not Disabled
United States	**153,323**	**7.4%**	**92.6%**
		(0.07)	**(0.07)**
New England	**8,206**	**6.8%**	**93.2%**
		(0.24)	**(0.24)**
Connecticut	2,011	5.3%	94.7%
		(0.61)	(0.61)
Maine	779	9.0%	91.0%
		(0.69)	(0.69)
Massachusetts	3,707	6.9%	93.1%
		(0.32)	(0.32)
New Hampshire	732	6.8%	93.2%
		(0.66)	(0.66)
Rhode Island	609	7.7%	92.3%
		(0.71)	(0.71)
Vermont	368	8.0%	92.0%
		(0.71)	(0.71)
Middle Atlantic	**23,156**	**6.9%**	**93.1%**
		(0.16)	**(0.16)**
New Jersey	4,866	4.7%	95.3%
		(0.26)	(0.26)
New York	11,004	7.0%	93.0%
		(0.24)	(0.24)
Pennsylvania	7,286	8.0%	92.0%
		(0.34)	(0.34)
South Atlantic	**26,924**	**7.5%**	**92.5%**
		(0.18)	**(0.18)**
Delaware	445	6.7%	93.3%
		(0.63)	(0.63)
District of Columbia	348	8.3%	91.7%
		(0.79)	(0.79)
Florida	7,913	7.4%	92.6%
		(0.31)	(0.31)
Georgia	3,954	8.3%	91.7%
		(0.65)	(0.65)
Maryland	3,020	5.2%	94.8%
		(0.56)	(0.56)
North Carolina	4,077	7.9%	92.1%
		(0.33)	(0.33)
South Carolina	2,180	9.1%	90.9%
		(0.62)	(0.62)
Virginia	3,898	6.5%	93.5%
		(0.52)	(0.52)
West Virginia	1,089	11.0%	89.0%
		(0.76)	(0.76)
East South Central	**9,329**	**10.1%**	**89.9%**
		(0.36)	**(0.36)**
Alabama	2,500	8.8%	91.2%
		(0.68)	(0.68)
Kentucky	2,237	11.5%	88.5%
		(0.77)	(0.77)
Mississippi	1,517	10.5%	89.5%
		(0.71)	(0.71)
Tennessee	3,076	10.0%	90.0%
		(0.68)	(0.68)
West South Central	**16,168**	**7.5%**	**92.5%**
		(0.25)	**(0.25)**
Arkansas	1,396	9.9%	90.1%
		(0.72)	(0.72)
Louisiana	2,484	8.9%	91.1%
		(0.72)	(0.72)
Oklahoma	1,876	8.4%	91.6%
		(0.67)	(0.67)
Texas	10,412	6.7%	93.3%
		(0.31)	(0.31)

Table E7 (continued)
Adults Ages 18-64 With Disabilities
That Prevent or Limit Work, 1990-92[9]

(Standard errors in parentheses)

	Number	Percent Disabled	Percent Not Disabled
East North Central	**25,998**	**7.2%**	**92.8%**
		(0.18)	**(0.18)**
Illinois	7,257	6.6%	93.4%
		(0.31)	(0.31)
Indiana	3,428	6.4%	93.6%
		(0.61)	(0.61)
Michigan	5,706	8.6%	91.4%
		(0.35)	(0.35)
Ohio	6,675	7.0%	93.0%
		(0.32)	(0.32)
Wisconsin	2,933	7.2%	92.8%
		(0.59)	(0.59)
West North Central	**10,790**	**6.7%**	**93.3%**
		(0.27)	**(0.27)**
Iowa	1,707	6.2%	93.8%
		(0.57)	(0.57)
Kansas	1,479	5.5%	94.5%
		(0.54)	(0.54)
Minnesota	2,725	7.0%	93.0%
		(0.62)	(0.62)
Missouri	3,188	7.3%	92.7%
		(0.64)	(0.64)
Nebraska	942	6.0%	94.0%
		(0.55)	(0.55)
North Dakota	357	5.7%	94.3%
		(0.55)	(0.55)
South Dakota	392	8.6%	91.4%
		(0.63)	(0.63)
Mountain	**8,110**	**7.3%**	**92.7%**
		(0.27)	**(0.27)**
Arizona	2,117	7.3%	92.7%
		(0.65)	(0.65)
Colorado	2,027	7.6%	92.4%
		(0.67)	(0.67)
Idaho	600	6.8%	93.2%
		(0.58)	(0.58)
Montana	471	8.3%	91.7%
		(0.66)	(0.66)
Nevada	786	6.6%	93.4%
		(0.59)	(0.59)
New Mexico	904	9.1%	90.9%
		(0.68)	(0.68)
Utah	932	5.5%	94.5%
		(0.57)	(0.57)
Wyoming	273	6.9%	93.1%
		(0.73)	(0.73)
Pacific	**24,642**	**7.3%**	**92.7%**
		(0.20)	**(0.20)**
Alaska	304	5.8%	94.2%
		(0.54)	(0.54)
California	18,827	7.1%	92.9%
		(0.23)	(0.23)
Hawaii	649	5.9%	94.1%
		(0.61)	(0.61)
Oregon	1,807	8.7%	91.3%
		(0.72)	(0.72)
Washington	3,056	8.4%	91.6%
		(0.65)	(0.65)

Source: Three-year merged March CPS: 1991, 1992, and 1993.
Note: See table notes at end of Section E.

Notes to Tables, Section E

1. "Infant Deaths per 1,000 Births under Age 1" in the indicated race group is the total number of infant deaths under one year of age in that race group per 1,000 live births in that race group. Infant deaths for all races do not equal the sum of white infant deaths and black infant deaths because other races are included in the all-races group.

2. The rate of neonatal deaths (age 1–27 days) is the number of total neonatal deaths (age 1–27 days) divided by total births per 1,000.

3. "Late or No Prenatal Care" refers to pregnant women who received no prenatal care before their seventh month or not at all during the pregnancy.

4. "Percentage with Late or No Prenatal Care" is a percentage of the total number of births. On average, 2.1 percent of mothers did not state the month in which they received prenatal care. The percentage reported is out of all births, including those with missing answers.

5. "Low-Weight Births" are defined as infants weighing under 2,500 grams at birth.

6. "Percentage of Births to Unmarried Women" in the indicated race group is the total number of births to unmarried women in that race group divided by the total number of births to women in that race group.

7. The number of AIDS cases does not include 277 persons whose state of residence is unknown.

8. AIDS cases per state are reported as a percentage of total U.S. cases spanning the 11-year period from 1981 to 1992. The figure is calculated by dividing the number of AIDS cases in this period for a particular state by the total cases nationwide for the same period.

9. Individuals included are those who reported that they have a disability that prevents work or limits their ability to work. Children with a disability are not included. These numbers do not necessarily reflect the population with handicaps where disability is based on a medical standard.

Health Care Costs, Access, and Utilization

Section F provides a set of broad-based indicators of health care costs, access, and utilization. The tables include information about hospital and physician costs, hospital utilization, and numbers of nursing homes, physicians, and health maintenance organizations.

HOSPITAL AND PHYSICIAN COSTS

Table F1 provides, first of all, information on short-term general hospital costs per patient day and per admission. These data reflect variations across states in cost of hospital care. The data generally show that costs per admission are highest in the Middle Atlantic and Pacific regions and lowest in the East South Central and West North Central regions.

The third column in table F1 presents the revised geographic adjustment factor to be used in the Medicare fee schedule for physician services in 1996. This is an index of physicians' practice input costs, including the cost of physician time, employee wages, office rents, and malpractice insurance. The index shown reflects input prices for the years 1990–93, depending on the category of input. The data show that costs faced by physicians are highest in the Middle Atlantic and Pacific regions and lowest in the East South Central.

The fourth column presents an index of private physicians' charges based on data reported on approximately 8,000 medical and surgical services to the Health Insurance Association of America. The data reflect variation across states in physicians' submitted charges. It is important to note that the indices do not represent variations in payments to physicians. To the extent that payments deviate from submitted charges because of, for example, discounts obtained by Blue Cross/Blue Shield plans or by managed care organizations, variations across states in payments to physicians could differ from the indices presented here. As with input costs, physician charges are highest in the Middle Atlantic and Pacific regions and lowest in the East South Central.

Columns five and six present data on expenditures per capita for hospital and physician services. These data were provided by the Health Care Financing Administration's Office of the Actuary and represent estimates of state expenditures based on a variety of health insurance industry and government surveys. Expenditures reflect both prices and the quantity of services provided. Expenditures for hospital services are highest in the New England and Middle Atlantic regions and lowest in the Mountain and Pacific regions. Expenditures for physician services are highest in the Pacific and New England regions and lowest in the East South Central region.

These data are based on HCFA estimates of expenditures on hospital and physician services in the state (jurisdiction) in which care was provided. Population data reflect numbers of individuals residing in the area. Thus, expenditures in one state include services provided to residents of other states. Likewise, expenditures in a state do not include services provided elsewhere to that state's residents. This problem, for example, explains the high level of expenditures per capita in the District of Columbia.

Hospitals and nursing homes

Table F2 provides data on hospital utilization. The table includes data on hospital beds as well as admissions and lengths of stay. The number of hospital beds per 1,000 population is highest in the East

South Central region and lowest in the Pacific region–4.5 compared to 2.5, respectively. The rate of hospital admissions is also highest in the East South Central states (about 153 per 1,000 population) and lowest in the Pacific region (about 103 per 1,000 population). Length of stays, measured by inpatient days per admission, are longest in the Middle Atlantic region (8.2 days) and shortest in the Mountain states (5.2 days), on average. Some of these geographic variations may arise from differences in the age and sex distribution and patient case mix across states.

Table F3 provides data on the availability of nursing home facilities in each state, including the number of nursing homes, the number of nursing home beds, the nursing home occupancy rate, and the number of beds per 1,000 elderly population. Nursing homes in the Middle Atlantic and South Atlantic regions tend to be larger than average, with 146 and 110 beds per home, respectively. Occupancy rates—the ratio of facilities' average daily census to their total number of licensed beds—range from 82 percent in Oklahoma, Indiana, and Texas to 99 percent in New York. There is a wide range in the number of licensed nursing home beds per 1,000 elderly population, from 24 in Nevada to 88 in Kansas.

Physicians and HMOs

Table F4 provides data on physician availability across states. Both the total number of physicians per 100,000 population as well as patient care physicians per 100,000 population are provided. The availability of physicians tends to be greatest in the New England and Middle Atlantic states and lowest in many of the southern and Mountain states.

Table F5 provides data on the number of HMOs as well as HMO membership per 1,000 population. The importance of HMOs varies considerably across the country. HMOs have become particularly important in California, Massachusetts, Minnesota, and Oregon, whereas penetration in most of the southern states is minimal. (HMO enrollment per 1,000 may be misleading in states where HMOs serve residents of multiple states. See note 14 after the tables.)

Table F1
Relative Hospital and Physician Costs

	Short-term General Hospital Cost[1]		Index of Physician Practice Costs[4]	Index of Physician Charges[5]	Expenditures per Capita for	
	Per Patient Day[2]	Per Admission[3]			Hospital Care[6]	Phys. Services[6]
United States	$914	$5,786	1.00	1.00	$1,134	$598
New England	$923	$6,168	1.04	1.00	$1,310	$641
Connecticut	1,005	7,096	1.11	1.03	1,242	679
Maine	815	5,077	0.96	0.90	1,018	443
Massachusetts	937	6,198	1.03	0.99	1,517	708
New Hampshire	859	5,450	1.00	0.95	1,022	581
Rhode Island	802	5,595	1.07	1.15	1,210	541
Vermont	793	4,999	0.96	0.88	886	429
Middle Atlantic	$815	$6,457	1.07	1.14	$1,342	$578
New Jersey	790	5,732	1.09	1.11	1,138	589
New York	819	7,390	1.12	1.18	1,404	588
Pennsylvania	828	5,771	0.99	1.10	1,390	559
South Atlantic	$905	$5,699	0.94	1.01	$1,137	$616
Delaware	952	5,956	1.02	1.10	1,177	718
District of Columbia	1,051	8,396	1.11	1.18	4,415	1,112
Florida	937	6,000	1.02	1.01	1,146	744
Georgia	911	5,235	0.97	1.03	1,148	589
Maryland	885	5,394	1.02	1.11	1,072	676
North Carolina	812	5,459	0.92	0.96	1,009	475
South Carolina	892	5,865	0.92	0.92	1,015	409
Virginia	947	5,539	0.94	0.97	1,019	551
West Virginia	794	4,927	0.92	0.92	1,111	500
East South Central	$777	$4,772	0.92	0.90	$1,111	$514
Alabama	791	4,978	0.93	0.93	1,105	561
Kentucky	756	4,679	0.92	0.88	1,052	489
Mississippi	642	3,894	0.90	0.83	936	356
Tennessee	857	5,163	0.92	0.91	1,260	579
West South Central	$878	$5,268	0.95	0.96	$1,068	$553
Arkansas	674	4,114	0.89	0.89	994	523
Louisiana	854	5,429	0.94	0.95	1,241	564
Oklahoma	772	4,835	0.91	0.91	950	463
Texas	948	5,506	0.96	0.97	1,042	562
East North Central	$929	$5,756	1.00	0.93	$1,134	$541
Illinois	988	6,289	1.01	1.01	1,195	496
Indiana	903	5,515	0.93	0.91	1,074	515
Michigan	932	5,931	1.08	0.86	1,138	549
Ohio	922	5,602	0.97	0.93	1,154	557
Wisconsin	845	4,981	0.97	0.95	1,005	621
West North Central	$876	$5,554	0.94	0.89	$1,130	$598
Iowa	756	5,513	0.91	0.85	1,049	463
Kansas	870	5,624	0.95	0.88	1,020	563
Minnesota	948	5,512	0.96	0.91	1,039	806
Missouri	911	5,897	0.95	0.91	1,291	546
Nebraska	839	5,262	0.89	0.76	1,123	489
North Dakota	791	5,153	0.90	0.95	1,255	697
South Dakota	861	5,276	0.88	0.83	1,136	487
Mountain	$1,077	$5,320	0.96	0.91	$968	$561
Arizona	1,148	5,442	1.00	0.96	964	619
Colorado	1,137	5,899	0.97	0.90	1,070	628
Idaho	971	4,329	0.91	0.82	733	382
Montana	932	4,885	0.91	0.82	944	388
Nevada	1,012	5,809	1.01	1.04	930	736
New Mexico	1,077	5,236	0.94	0.89	1,014	452
Utah	1,031	4,582	0.93	0.77	853	464
Wyoming	833	4,232	0.93	0.83	857	337
Pacific	$1,167	$6,184	1.04	1.03	$996	$724
Alaska	1,475	8,088	1.13	1.02	1,155	548
California	1,199	6,470	1.06	1.06	1,025	761
Hawaii	952	6,982	1.09	1.08	1,135	634
Oregon	1,051	4,857	0.95	0.85	877	595
Washington	1,065	5,303	0.98	0.93	913	665

Sources: Columns 1-2 — American Hospital Association's 1992 Annual Survey of Hospitals; Column 3— Federal Register 59
(121, June 24, 1994), Addendum D. Column 4 — Urban Institute Analysis of Health Insurance Association of America's Prevailing
Healthcare Charge System, 1993. Columns 5-6 — Health Care Financing Administration, Office of the Actuary, 1991.
Note: See table notes at end of Section F.

	Hospital Beds	Hospital Beds per 1,000 Population	Hospital Admissions[7]	Admissions per 1,000 Population	Inpatient Days[8]	Inpatient Days per Admission
United States	886,626	3.5	31,594,593	125.3	208,198,403	6.6
New England	42,807	3.3	1,619,364	124.1	11,230,227	6.9
Connecticut	9,546	2.9	360,232	110.9	2,649,132	7.4
Maine	4,272	3.4	151,497	120.5	1,017,811	6.7
Massachusetts	20,947	3.6	806,924	137.8	5,544,659	6.9
New Hampshire	3,204	2.8	117,340	103.2	752,802	6.4
Rhode Island	3,140	3.3	123,259	128.8	866,353	7.0
Vermont	1,698	2.9	60,112	101.8	399,470	6.6
Middle Atlantic	148,950	3.9	5,213,416	137.8	42,728,356	8.2
New Jersey	29,108	3.7	1,119,798	144.1	8,340,284	7.4
New York	71,267	4.0	2,344,050	131.1	21,605,402	9.2
Pennsylvania	48,575	4.0	1,749,568	143.4	12,782,670	7.3
South Atlantic	157,777	3.6	5,732,628	129.7	37,555,126	6.6
Delaware	2,074	2.9	83,541	116.7	545,711	6.5
District of Columbia	5,320	9.8	172,768	318.0	1,457,499	8.4
Florida	50,513	3.7	1,675,104	123.7	11,210,048	6.7
Georgia	24,170	3.8	891,501	138.5	5,418,506	6.1
Maryland	13,510	2.8	602,777	125.4	3,690,146	6.1
North Carolina	22,461	3.4	833,603	126.5	5,820,999	7.0
South Carolina	11,632	3.3	428,373	121.2	2,840,543	6.6
Virginia	19,923	3.2	753,879	120.5	4,690,965	6.2
West Virginia	8,174	4.6	291,082	162.7	1,880,709	6.5
East South Central	69,701	4.5	2,346,968	152.6	15,436,730	6.6
Alabama	18,197	4.4	617,519	149.9	4,064,070	6.6
Kentucky	16,047	4.4	556,426	152.9	3,605,562	6.5
Mississippi	12,213	4.6	395,739	147.5	2,575,353	6.5
Tennessee	23,244	4.7	777,284	157.3	5,191,745	6.7
West South Central	101,009	3.8	3,392,746	126.1	21,229,317	6.3
Arkansas	10,483	4.3	350,958	145.0	2,277,666	6.5
Louisiana	18,711	4.5	618,120	148.5	3,980,596	6.4
Oklahoma	12,387	3.9	402,043	126.5	2,529,985	6.3
Texas	59,428	3.5	2,021,625	118.0	12,441,070	6.2
East North Central	149,995	3.5	5,286,612	123.8	33,767,441	6.4
Illinois	43,107	3.6	1,521,099	128.0	9,991,283	6.6
Indiana	20,583	3.7	709,217	127.7	4,454,864	6.3
Michigan	29,853	3.2	1,068,479	115.3	6,909,466	6.5
Ohio	40,358	3.7	1,406,226	127.4	8,940,177	6.4
Wisconsin	16,094	3.2	581,591	117.1	3,471,651	6.0
West North Central	74,291	4.2	2,301,481	128.8	15,099,267	6.6
Iowa	12,288	4.3	365,111	128.4	2,470,512	6.8
Kansas	10,982	4.3	305,935	120.3	2,109,088	6.9
Minnesota	14,540	3.3	521,114	119.0	3,041,470	5.8
Missouri	22,371	4.3	709,666	137.7	4,842,745	6.8
Nebraska	6,860	4.2	186,619	114.6	1,212,718	6.5
North Dakota	3,386	5.4	101,427	162.0	670,992	6.6
South Dakota	3,864	5.5	111,609	158.9	751,742	6.7
Mountain	39,391	2.8	1,548,396	111.7	8,030,315	5.2
Arizona	10,035	2.8	429,828	118.9	2,178,886	5.1
Colorado	9,373	2.8	371,806	112.0	2,002,537	5.4
Idaho	2,701	2.5	102,858	96.9	468,694	4.6
Montana	3,088	3.7	107,809	130.8	583,044	5.4
Nevada	3,533	2.8	134,212	105.5	771,211	5.7
New Mexico	4,763	3.1	182,355	118.1	942,451	5.2
Utah	4,168	2.4	170,582	97.1	835,605	4.9
Wyoming	1,730	3.7	48,946	104.1	247,887	5.1
Pacific	102,705	2.5	4,152,982	102.9	23,121,624	5.6
Alaska	1,537	3.0	57,045	110.0	292,804	5.1
California	78,309	2.5	3,151,668	102.5	17,742,016	5.6
Hawaii	2,588	2.3	104,197	91.5	761,112	7.3
Oregon	7,761	2.6	309,228	103.7	1,535,272	5.0
Washington	12,510	2.5	530,844	106.3	2,790,420	5.3

Source: American Hospital Association's 1992 Annual Survey of Hospitals.
Note: See table notes at end of Section F.

Table F3
Nursing Home Facilities and Beds, 1992[9]

	Number of Nursing Home Facilities	Number of Nursing Home Beds	Average Number of Beds/Home	Average Occupancy Rate[10]	Number of Beds per 1,000 Pop. Aged 65 +
United States	16,783	1,718,192	102.4	91.0%	53.1
New England	1,287	114,015	88.6	96.3%	63.0
Connecticut	337	30,118	89.4	n/a	65.9
Maine	145	10,236	70.6	n/a	60.9
Massachusetts	571	52,828	92.5	96.5	63.3
New Hampshire	80	6,966	87.1	93.6	53.2
Rhode Island	103	10,222	99.6	96.6	66.8
Vermont	51	3,645	71.5	97.2	53.6
Middle Atlantic	1,650	240,401	145.7	99.0%	45.3
New Jersey	311	44,314	142.5	n/a	41.9
New York	632	106,124	167.9	99.0	44.7
Pennsylvania	707	89,963	127.2	n/a	47.8
South Atlantic	2,169	237,531	109.5	92.2%	39.3
Delaware	49	4,867	99.3	82.4	57.3
District of Columbia	18	3,129	173.8	n/a	40.6
Florida	597	71,162	119.2	91.2	28.6
Georgia	368	39,923	108.5	n/a	58.5
Maryland	226	27,587	122.1	93.6	51.2
North Carolina	369	35,174	95.3	n/a	41.6
South Carolina	167	16,125	96.6	94.4	38.7
Virginia	252	29,328	116.4	92.9	42.1
West Virginia	123	10,236	83.2	95.0	37.2
East South Central	969	98,400	101.5	95.8%	49.8
Alabama	222	23,025	103.7	95.3	42.8
Kentucky	262	23,145	88.3	97.7	48.5
Mississippi	172	16,051	93.3	96.7	49.2
Tennessee	313	36,179	115.6	94.5	56.5
West South Central	2,213	217,945	98.5	83.3%	71.0
Arkansas	232	23,790	102.5	86.9	66.5
Louisiana	343	37,496	109.3	86.4	78.0
Oklahoma	422	34,581	81.9	82.0	79.5
Texas	1,216	122,078	100.4	82.0	67.9
East North Central	3,321	351,613	105.9	87.7%	64.5
Illinois	853	100,557	117.9	n/a	68.7
Indiana	588	58,778	100.0	81.9	82.2
Michigan	453	50,961	112.5	90.5	44.3
Ohio	1,000	91,580	91.6	n/a	62.9
Wisconsin	427	49,737	116.5	91.6	74.5
West North Central	2,432	207,835	85.5	93.8%	82.9
Iowa	477	35,391	74.2	96.5	81.7
Kansas	436	30,622	70.2	89.9	87.5
Minnesota	451	45,073	99.9	94.9	80.2
Missouri	628	61,922	98.6	n/a	84.4
Nebraska	241	19,492	80.9	91.2	85.9
North Dakota	84	7,084	84.3	96.4	76.2
South Dakota	115	8,251	71.7	n/a	78.6
Mountain	769	71,050	92.4	86.8%	43.6
Arizona	135	16,719	123.8	90.0	32.6
Colorado	212	20,106	94.8	85.0	57.6
Idaho	75	5,804	77.4	85.7	45.7
Montana	95	6,495	68.4	n/a	58.5
Nevada	35	3,563	101.8	88.4	24.4
New Mexico	76	6,783	89.3	n/a	39.2
Utah	104	8,025	77.2	84.0	50.2
Wyoming	37	3,555	96.1	87.9	71.1
Pacific	1,973	179,402	90.9	88.8%	40.6
Alaska	22	1,033	47.0	n/a	41.3
California	1,433	130,955	91.4	n/a	40.3
Hawaii	43	3,415	79.4	96.5	25.7
Oregon	177	14,758	83.4	87.0	36.0
Washington	298	29,241	98.1	n/a	48.7

Source: R. DuNah, S. de Wit, C. Harrington, J. Swan, and B. Bedney, 1993, <u>State Data Book on Long Term</u>
<u>Programs & Market Characteristics</u> (San Francisco, CA: Institute for Health & Aging, University of CA).
Note: See table notes at end of Section F.

Table F4
Total and Patient Care Physicians, 1992[11]

	Total Physicians		Patient Care Physicians	
	Number	per 100,000	Number	per 100,000
United States	**623,378**	**247.2**	**513,620**	**203.7**
New England	**44,017**	**337.4**	**35,158**	**269.5**
Connecticut	11,335	349.0	9,189	282.9
Maine	2,678	212.9	2,115	168.2
Massachusetts	22,746	388.4	17,993	307.2
New Hampshire	2,625	230.9	2,132	187.6
Rhode Island	2,926	305.9	2,392	250.0
Vermont	1,707	289.2	1,337	226.5
Middle Atlantic	**119,730**	**316.4**	**98,840**	**261.2**
New Jersey	21,975	282.8	18,380	236.5
New York	64,927	363.2	53,245	297.9
Pennsylvania	32,828	269.1	27,215	223.1
South Atlantic	**109,854**	**248.5**	**88,836**	**200.9**
Delaware	1,549	216.4	1,292	180.5
District of Columbia	4,168	767.2	3,229	594.4
Florida	33,802	249.6	25,995	192.0
Georgia	12,849	199.7	11,106	172.6
Maryland	17,977	373.8	14,194	295.2
North Carolina	14,665	222.5	12,067	183.1
South Carolina	6,689	189.2	5,668	160.4
Virginia	14,638	234.0	12,296	196.6
West Virginia	3,517	196.6	2,989	167.1
East South Central	**29,665**	**192.9**	**25,541**	**166.1**
Alabama	7,435	180.5	6,383	155.0
Kentucky	7,175	197.2	6,195	170.3
Mississippi	3,846	143.4	3,333	124.3
Tennessee	11,209	226.9	9,630	194.9
West South Central	**52,445**	**195.0**	**44,766**	**166.4**
Arkansas	4,232	174.8	3,608	149.0
Louisiana	9,093	218.5	7,876	189.2
Oklahoma	5,274	166.0	4,486	141.2
Texas	33,846	197.5	28,796	168.0
East North Central	**93,835**	**219.7**	**78,946**	**184.9**
Illinois	28,467	239.5	23,937	201.4
Indiana	10,149	182.8	8,616	155.1
Michigan	19,810	213.9	16,630	179.5
Ohio	24,708	223.9	20,779	188.3
Wisconsin	10,701	215.5	8,984	180.9
West North Central	**38,349**	**214.6**	**32,138**	**179.8**
Iowa	4,890	171.9	3,947	138.8
Kansas	5,057	198.9	4,185	164.6
Minnesota	11,299	258.1	9,515	217.3
Missouri	11,460	222.4	9,685	188.0
Nebraska	3,199	196.5	2,721	167.1
North Dakota	1,260	201.2	1,096	175.0
South Dakota	1,184	168.6	989	140.8
Mountain	**29,838**	**215.2**	**24,355**	**175.7**
Arizona	8,687	240.3	6,847	189.4
Colorado	8,189	246.6	6,774	204.0
Idaho	1,556	146.7	1,289	121.5
Montana	1,546	187.5	1,283	155.6
Nevada	2,117	166.4	1,797	141.3
New Mexico	3,340	216.3	2,691	174.3
Utah	3,678	209.4	3,072	174.9
Wyoming	725	154.2	602	128.0
Pacific	**105,645**	**261.7**	**85,040**	**210.6**
Alaska	797	153.7	707	136.4
California	82,254	267.5	66,059	214.9
Hawaii	3,051	268.0	2,533	222.5
Oregon	7,094	237.8	5,737	192.3
Washington	12,449	249.4	10,004	200.4

Source: American Medical Association, Master File 1992.
Note: See table notes at end of Section F.

Table F5
HMOs and HMO Membership, 1992[12]

	HMOs[13]	HMO Membership	
		Number	Per 1,000[14]
United States	**556**	**38,767,556**	**153.7**
New England	**38**	**3,060,384**	**234.6**
Connecticut	13	665,693	205.0
Maine	3	48,663	38.7
Massachusetts	16	2,015,516	344.1
New Hampshire	2	121,877	107.2
Rhode Island	3	154,669	161.7
Vermont	1	53,966	91.4
Middle Atlantic	**68**	**5,861,395**	**154.9**
New Jersey	10	912,880	117.5
New York	39	3,209,788	179.6
Pennsylvania	19	1,738,727	142.5
South Atlantic	**92**	**4,807,240**	**108.7**
Delaware	3	81,431	113.8
District of Columbia	3	488,594	899.4
Florida	36	1,819,577	134.4
Georgia	8	378,685	58.8
Maryland	13	1,154,725	240.1
North Carolina	13	379,572	57.6
South Carolina	4	96,433	27.3
Virginia	12	408,223	65.3
West Virginia	0	0	0.0
East South Central	**23**	**682,025**	**44.3**
Alabama	9	217,314	52.8
Kentucky	5	248,955	68.4
Mississippi	0	0	0.0
Tennessee	9	215,756	43.7
West South Central	**46**	**2,004,928**	**74.5**
Arkansas	3	65,574	27.1
Louisiana	11	258,510	62.1
Oklahoma	7	221,990	69.9
Texas	25	1,458,854	85.1
East North Central	**120**	**6,310,339**	**147.8**
Illinois	26	1,716,593	144.4
Indiana	12	359,313	64.7
Michigan	20	1,578,218	170.4
Ohio	36	1,592,054	144.2
Wisconsin	26	1,064,161	214.3
West North Central	**50**	**2,230,281**	**124.8**
Iowa	4	107,178	37.7
Kansas	9	165,444	65.1
Minnesota	10	1,200,817	274.3
Missouri	18	615,386	119.4
Nebraska	6	114,874	70.6
North Dakota	2	6,072	9.7
South Dakota	1	20,510	29.2
Mountain	**47**	**2,194,639**	**158.3**
Arizona	10	714,802	197.7
Colorado	17	736,552	221.8
Idaho	2	20,351	19.2
Montana	1	10,731	13.0
Nevada	4	143,075	112.5
New Mexico	5	239,959	155.4
Utah	8	329,169	187.4
Wyoming	0	0	0.0
Pacific	**72**	**11,616,325**	**287.7**
Alaska	0	0	0.0
California	46	9,769,031	317.7
Hawaii	7	259,671	228.1
Oregon	9	777,812	260.7
Washington	10	809,811	162.2

Source: Interstudy Competitive Edge, <u>HMO Directory</u>, 1992.
Note: See table notes at end of Section F.

Notes to Tables, Section F

1. Only data from short-term general hospitals were used. Hospitals that reported long-term care units on the American Hospital Association's Annual Survey were omitted.

2. Short-term general hospital cost per patient day is total payroll and nonpayroll expenses divided by total adjusted patient days. The AHA defines adjusted patient days as the number of days of inpatient care, plus an estimated equivalent based on the volume of outpatient services. The outpatient estimate is derived by multiplying the number of outpatient visits by the ratio of outpatient revenue (per outpatient visit) to inpatient revenue (per inpatient day).

3. Short-term general hospital cost per admission is total payroll and nonpayroll expenses divided by total adjusted admissions. The AHA defines total adjusted admissions as the number of patients, excluding newborns accepted for inpatient service, plus an estimate of equivalent admissions attributed to outpatient admissions. The outpatient estimate is derived by multiplying outpatient admissions by the ratio of outpatient revenue to inpatient revenue.

4. The geographic adjustment factor (GAF) for the District of Columbia includes Washington, D.C., as well as Prince George's and Montgomery counties in Maryland; Fairfax and Arlington counties and the city of Alexandria in Virginia. These counties and the city of Alexandria are excluded from their respective states in the calculation of each state's GAF.

5. The private physician fee indices are derived from 1993 Health Insurance Association of America physician charge data for approximately 8,000 procedures. Services are weighted by national relative utilization rates (from HIAA) and relative resource use across services as specified by the Resource Based Relative Value Scale.

6. These data are based on HCFA estimates of expenditures on hospital and physician services in the state in which care was provided. Population data reflect numbers of individuals residing in the area. Thus, expenditures in one state include services provided to residents of other states. Likewise, expenditures in a state do not include services provided elsewhere to that state's residents. This problem, for example, explains the high level of expenditures per capita in the District of Columbia.

7. The number of hospital admissions is the total number of unadjusted admissions. These numbers do not include any outpatient visits and are not adjusted for patient case mix.

8. The number of inpatient days is the total number of unadjusted days. These numbers do not include any outpatient services.

9. The authors of the *State Data Book on Long Term Programs and Market Characteristics* compiled the data from a series of separate surveys of state officials. Due to incomplete data, some of the figures for certain states were estimated by the authors of that report. These states include Alaska, Arizona, California, Iowa, Montana, and Nevada.

10. The occupancy rate is the ratio of the facility's average daily census to its total number of licensed beds, expressed as a percentage. According to the data source, data on occupancy rates across states are difficult to obtain because many states have not collected occupancy data during the last three years. The United States and regional occupancy rates were calculated using only data from those states reporting occupancy rates.

11. "Total Physicians" is the sum of patient care and nonpatient care physicians. Patient care activities include office-based practice and hospital-based practice, which comprises physicians in residency training, clinical fellows, and full-time staff members of hospitals. Nonpatient care activities include administration, medical teaching, research, and other activities. They do not include federal physicians.

12. Data for table F5 were taken from the *1993 Area Resource File (ARF)* (Washington, D.C.: Office of Health Professions Analysis and Research, Bureau of Health Professions).

13. HMO location is based on the location of the organization's headquarters. HMOs in multistate areas may draw members from neighboring states. For example, the Health Plan of the Upper Ohio Valley and its members are included in counts for Ohio, although 51 percent of its members reside in West Virginia.

14. HMO membership per 1,000 population in areas where a plan services multiple states may be misstated, since this measure is based on the state population in which the plan's headquarters is located. For example, the high membership for the District of Columbia reflects residents of neighboring states who are members of plans with headquarters in the District.

State Demographic and Economic Profiles

The tables in this section provide background information on the demographic and economic characteristics of each state. The tables are broken down into five subsections encompassing general population characteristics, family income characteristics, worker characteristics, employer characteristics, and state finances. Information in this section may also be used in conjunction with the tables on the health insurance coverage of specific groups of individuals in Sections A and B.

POPULATION CHARACTERISTICS

Tables G1 through G3 show distributions for the nonelderly population by age (under 18, 18 to 34, 35 to 53, and 54 through 64), race and sex, and family type (married with no children, married with children, single with children, and single). This information is important because various health policy initiatives focus on these population subgroups.[1]

FAMILY INCOME CHARACTERISTICS

Tables G4 through G7 provide information on family income characteristics.[2] These data give states information about the distribution of family income in their state and allow comparisons with other states. Table G4 shows the upper limits for the 25th, median, and 75th income percentiles for 1992 in each state. These data are derived by sorting families into four income groups, each of which includes one-quarter of the population. Thus, the income distribution for families in the United States is: lowest quarter, up to $10,301; second quarter, $10,302 to $23,932; third quarter, $23,933 to $44,385; and upper quarter, all families with incomes above $44,385. Fifty percent of families earn less than the median ($23,933), and 50 percent of families earn more than the median.

These distributions indicate that the income ranges within quartiles of the population are uneven. That is, the range of income for the second quartile of the income distribution is much smaller than the range between the median and upper end of the third income quartile. This indicates that the income spread gets larger in higher-income quartiles. In addition, these data show that there are large differences in the levels of income across states. For example, family income at the upper end of the first income quartile is $5,950 in Mississippi, compared to $16,522 in Connecticut (table G4). In general, families in the southern regions have lower-than-average median incomes, and families in the other regions have higher-than-average median incomes. As with access to health insurance, important differences in family income also exist across states within regions. For example, families in Alaska have a $30,584 median income, compared to $24,177 for the Pacific region as a whole.

The remaining tables in the income subsection show people by their family's income as a percentage of poverty. Many of the health reform initiatives under consideration target subsidies or base special eligibility to families based on income as a percentage of poverty. Table G5 and the G6 and G7 table series provide information on family income relative to poverty (below 100 percent of poverty, 100–149 percent of poverty, 150–199 percent of poverty, 200–399 percent of poverty, and above 400 percent of poverty).

Table G5 shows all persons by their family's income relative to the poverty line. These data can be used in conjunction with data on insured status by income relative to poverty presented in Sections A and C. In addition, they stress that this measure of income well-being varies across states. For example, the percentage of persons below poverty ranges from 9.2 percent in Connecticut to 28 percent in Mississippi. Some of the states with the highest rates of uninsurance (table A1) also have the highest poverty rates: for example, New Mexico has an uninsured rate of 23.8 percent, and 24.9 percent of its population falls below poverty.

The G6 table series provides information on family income as a percentage of poverty separately for children and adults. A number of health reform proposals are likely to target expansions of health coverage to children. These tables can be used to estimate the proportion (and number) of children who would qualify for special subsidies or programs linked to family income. The tables show a wide variation in children's poverty rates across states. Nationally, 24.8 percent of children live in families with incomes below the poverty guideline; across states, this proportion ranges from 12.6 percent in New Hampshire to 43.2 percent in the District of Columbia. The proportion of children below poverty is between 20 and 30 percent in most states. Nationally, an additional 10.2 percent of children live in families with incomes between 100 and 149 percent of poverty, and 9.8 percent are in families between 150 and 199 percent of poverty.

The G7 table series provides information on all persons within each of the four family types by their family's income relative to poverty. Poverty rates are shown to vary greatly across family types. For example, table G7b shows that nationally, 5.5 percent of the persons in married-couple families without children have incomes below 100 percent of poverty, whereas table G7c shows that nationally, 49.6 percent of persons in single-person-with-children families have incomes below 100 percent of poverty. This information also varies greatly among the states. For example, table G7a shows that the percentage of persons in married-couple-with-children families who have incomes below 100 percent of poverty ranges from 2.8 percent in Delaware to 17.5 percent in New Mexico.

Worker characteristics

Table G8 provides information on labor force participation and unemployment rates for the working population. Labor force participation and unemployment rates indicate the employment environment that exists in each of the states. The information presented in this table is an average for 1990, 1991, and 1992 from our three-year merged CPS file, and therefore reflects the effects of the recession. The unemployment rate ranged from less than 4 percent in Hawaii, Nebraska, and Utah to over 9 percent in Maine, Rhode Island, and West Virginia.

Tables G9 through G11 provide data, respectively, on the working population by firm size (less than 25 workers, 25–99 workers, 100–499 workers, and 500 or more workers) and sector (private, government, and self-employed), and on the private-sector working population by industry (manufacturing, wholesale/retail, services, and other). The percentage of workers who work for small firms (100 workers or less) may be important in understanding the number of uninsured for a state, because workers in small firms tend to have lower rates of insurance. The same is true for self-employed workers and workers in the service and wholesale/retail trade industries. Thus, these data may be useful in integrating the health insurance status of workers described earlier in Section B.

Employer characteristics

Tables G12 through G14 provide information on the number of establishments, the number of workers by establishment size, and the annualized payroll per worker by establishment size.[3] These figures are based on tabulations from the Census Bureau's County Business Patterns data for 1991. Establishment size, characterized by the number of workers within each establishment, is broken into size categories: 1–4 workers, 5–9 workers, 10–19 workers, 20–99 workers, 100–499 workers, and 500 or more workers. The data in table G13 show that 26.5 percent of workers are employed by establishments with less than 20 employees, 29.2 percent of workers are in establishments with 20–99 workers, and 44.3 percent of workers are employed by establishments with more than 100 employees. As stated in Section A, firms with fewer than 25 workers are less likely to provide health insurance to their employees, whereas firms with over 100 workers are more likely to provide health insurance to their employees. These data show that, with few exceptions, there is not a wide variation in the distribution of workers by establishment size across the states. Some states in the West North Central, Mountain, and Pacific regions have higher-than-average concentrations of workers in small establishments. For example, the percentage of establishments with fewer than 20 workers is 45.1 percent in Montana, about 37 percent in each of the Dakotas, and 33.6 percent in New Mexico, compared to the national average of 26.5 percent.

Table G14 shows that the variation in average annual salary by establishment size is quite large. Nationally, persons working in large establishments (500 or more employees) have an average salary of $26,095. This is substantially higher than the salaries of workers in smaller establishments, which range from $18,573 (10–19 workers) to $17,644 (5–9 workers). Since large establishments are more likely to provide comprehensive health insurance for their workers, total compensation including health benefits is even higher. These data may be useful in evaluating employer mandates with subsidies targeted to firms with low average pay.[4]

STATE FINANCES

Tables G15 and G16 provide information on general revenue per capita and sources of general revenue, including the federal government and taxes. The data are for fiscal year 1990–91 and are reprinted from the Census Bureau. The data in G15 show that there is large variation in the amount of general revenue per capita among the states. For example, general revenue per capita ranges from $2,499 in Arkansas to $5,478 in Wyoming and $12,455 in Alaska.

In all of the states, 70 percent or more of general revenue comes from state and local sources. Many health care reform proposals at the state level depend on raising additional tax revenue. What form of tax to levy and how much revenue can be raised are important questions for implementation of reforms.

The percentage of funds raised from different types of taxes varies greatly across states (see table G16). Whereas the majority of state and local taxes are raised from a combination of property, sales/gross, and individual income taxes, there is considerable variation in the importance of these sources across states. Several states such as Washington and Wyoming have no individual income tax and raise a greater percentage of income from sales taxes.

Table G17 shows expenditure per capita data followed by the percentage of general expenditures spent on education, welfare, health and hospitals, police protection and corrections, highways, and other areas. (Outlays for Medicaid are included in general expenditures on welfare.) General expenditures per capita show the same variation found in the general revenue per capita data. The data do show variation among the states in specific expenditure groups. For example, education expenditures range from 23.4 percent in Alaska to 42.2 percent in Utah, and health and hospital expenditures range from 3.1 percent in Vermont to 16.5 percent in Alabama.

Notes, Section G

1. As discussed in the Introduction, the family unit definition in this edition has been changed from a nuclear family concept to the health insurance unit. Note 2, following the tables, explains this distinction.

2. These tables are based on the three-year merged CPS data. Because we group families using a health insurance unit concept, family incomes are lower and poverty rates are higher than if we used a nuclear family framework. Incomes used in these tables are primarily the incomes reported on the CPS. However, we incorporated some corrections to incomes estimated by the Urban Institute's TRIM2 model. The model corrects for underreporting of income from the cash welfare programs—AFDC and SSI—and makes corrections to reported interest and dividend incomes. See Linda Giannarelli, 1992, *An Analyst's Guide to TRIM2* (Washington, D.C.: Urban Institute Press).

3. The tables based on the County Business Patterns (CBP) data set show workers and employers by *establishment size*. Other tables in this volume, particularly tables based on the CPS, define employer size by *firm size*. Establishment and firm represent different employer units. An establishment is defined as a single physical location at which business is conducted or where services or industrial activities are performed. A firm is the aggregate of all establishments and/or subsidiaries owned by a parent company. If an employer operates in one location, establishment size and firm size are the same; otherwise, establishment size is smaller. Health reform policies which involve employers, such as an employer mandate, could be specified as enforceable at either the establishment level or the firm level. However, policies would most likely be enforced at business levels in between the firm and establishment levels, called *enterprises*. Enterprises are generally the individual subsidiary businesses held by a parent company (firm). Business enterprises are the entities that file payroll taxes and, therefore, would likely be the best business level for enforcement of employer requirements. When considering data shown by firm size from the CPS and establishment sizes from the CBP data, also note that the CPS firm size is based on a worker's report of the number of workers at his or her firm while the CBP establishment size is reported by the business establishment itself. Employer reports of number of workers are considered more reliable than worker reports.

4. Sheila Zedlewski, Greg Acs, Laura Wheaton, and Colin Winterbottom, 1992, "Exploring the Effects of Play or Pay Employer Mandates: Effects on Insurance Coverage and Costs," in U.S. Department of Labor, *Health Benefits and the Workforce* (Washington, D.C.: U.S. Department of Labor), 231–69.

Table G1
Nonelderly Population by Age, 1990-92[1]
(Persons in thousands, standard errors in parentheses)

	Total	Age			
		Under 18	18-34	35-53	54-64
United States	218,586	29.9% (0.15)	30.0% (0.15)	29.4% (0.15)	10.8% (0.10)
New England	11,286	27.3% (0.51)	31.1% (0.53)	31.2% (0.53)	10.4% (0.35)
Connecticut	2,820	28.7% (1.44)	29.1% (1.45)	31.6% (1.48)	10.6% (0.98)
Maine	1,102	29.3% (1.29)	28.8% (1.28)	32.7% (1.33)	9.2% (0.82)
Massachusetts	5,025	26.2% (0.67)	32.7% (0.72)	30.5% (0.70)	10.6% (0.47)
New Hampshire	1,016	28.0% (1.39)	29.7% (1.42)	32.5% (1.46)	9.8% (0.92)
Rhode Island	806	24.4% (1.38)	33.5% (1.52)	29.9% (1.48)	12.1% (1.05)
Vermont	518	28.9% (1.38)	30.2% (1.40)	30.8% (1.40)	10.1% (0.92)
Middle Atlantic	32,501	28.8% (0.35)	29.7% (0.35)	29.9% (0.35)	11.6% (0.24)
New Jersey	6,752	27.9% (0.66)	30.3% (0.68)	30.7% (0.68)	11.0% (0.46)
New York	15,479	28.9% (0.50)	30.4% (0.51)	29.6% (0.51)	11.1% (0.35)
Pennsylvania	10,270	29.1% (0.66)	28.3% (0.65)	29.9% (0.66)	12.7% (0.48)
South Atlantic	37,562	28.3% (0.37)	30.1% (0.38)	29.9% (0.38)	11.7% (0.26)
Delaware	623	28.6% (1.34)	32.0% (1.39)	28.8% (1.35)	10.6% (0.91)
District of Columbia	477	27.0% (1.51)	32.5% (1.59)	30.6% (1.56)	9.9% (1.01)
Florida	10,995	28.0% (0.63)	30.1% (0.64)	29.0% (0.64)	12.9% (0.47)
Georgia	5,612	29.5% (1.26)	29.9% (1.26)	30.3% (1.27)	10.3% (0.84)
Maryland	4,140	27.1% (1.32)	31.6% (1.38)	29.9% (1.36)	11.5% (0.95)
North Carolina	5,640	27.7% (0.65)	29.9% (0.66)	30.0% (0.66)	12.4% (0.48)
South Carolina	3,122	30.2% (1.14)	28.6% (1.13)	30.4% (1.15)	10.8% (0.77)
Virginia	5,428	28.2% (1.11)	30.0% (1.13)	31.2% (1.15)	10.6% (0.76)
West Virginia	1,523	28.5% (1.29)	28.5% (1.29)	29.4% (1.30)	13.6% (0.98)
East South Central	13,386	30.3% (0.64)	30.1% (0.64)	28.9% (0.63)	10.7% (0.43)
Alabama	3,600	30.6% (1.27)	30.7% (1.27)	27.4% (1.23)	11.3% (0.88)
Kentucky	3,132	28.6% (1.29)	30.9% (1.31)	30.0% (1.30)	10.5% (0.87)
Mississippi	2,351	35.5% (1.24)	29.5% (1.18)	25.7% (1.13)	9.4% (0.75)
Tennessee	4,304	28.5% (1.20)	29.3% (1.21)	31.1% (1.24)	11.0% (0.84)
West South Central	23,629	31.6% (0.50)	30.0% (0.50)	28.5% (0.49)	9.9% (0.32)
Arkansas	2,068	32.5% (1.29)	28.9% (1.25)	27.1% (1.23)	11.5% (0.88)
Louisiana	3,679	32.5% (1.36)	29.9% (1.33)	27.6% (1.29)	10.1% (0.87)
Oklahoma	2,719	31.0% (1.29)	28.7% (1.26)	29.1% (1.26)	11.1% (0.88)
Texas	15,163	31.3% (0.65)	30.5% (0.65)	28.8% (0.64)	9.4% (0.41)

Table G1 (continued)
Nonelderly Population by Age, 1990-92[1]
(Persons in thousands, standard errors in parentheses)

		Age			
	Total	Under 18	18-34	35-53	54-64
East North Central	**37,385**	**30.5%** (0.37)	**29.9%** (0.37)	**28.7%** (0.36)	**10.9%** (0.25)
Illinois	10,419	30.4% (0.67)	30.3% (0.67)	28.7% (0.66)	10.6% (0.45)
Indiana	4,858	29.4% (1.32)	31.2% (1.34)	27.4% (1.29)	12.0% (0.94)
Michigan	8,169	30.2% (0.67)	30.1% (0.67)	28.7% (0.66)	11.0% (0.46)
Ohio	9,628	30.7% (0.66)	29.0% (0.65)	29.4% (0.65)	11.0% (0.45)
Wisconsin	4,311	32.0% (1.22)	29.0% (1.19)	28.9% (1.18)	10.1% (0.79)
West North Central	**15,577**	**30.7%** (0.58)	**30.5%** (0.58)	**28.3%** (0.57)	**10.5%** (0.39)
Iowa	2,460	30.6% (1.25)	30.3% (1.25)	28.2% (1.22)	10.9% (0.85)
Kansas	2,205	32.9% (1.26)	28.8% (1.21)	28.1% (1.20)	10.1% (0.81)
Minnesota	3,844	29.1% (1.30)	31.8% (1.33)	28.7% (1.29)	10.4% (0.87)
Missouri	4,568	30.2% (1.32)	31.7% (1.33)	27.9% (1.29)	10.2% (0.87)
Nebraska	1,391	32.3% (1.24)	28.4% (1.20)	28.3% (1.20)	11.1% (0.83)
North Dakota	524	31.9% (1.26)	26.7% (1.20)	30.1% (1.24)	11.3% (0.86)
South Dakota	585	32.9% (1.20)	28.0% (1.15)	28.5% (1.15)	10.6% (0.79)
Mountain	**12,011**	**32.5%** (0.56)	**28.1%** (0.54)	**29.3%** (0.54)	**10.2%** (0.36)
Arizona	3,021	29.9% (1.33)	28.8% (1.31)	29.8% (1.33)	11.5% (0.92)
Colorado	2,882	29.7% (1.35)	30.0% (1.36)	30.5% (1.37)	9.8% (0.88)
Idaho	940	36.2% (1.24)	25.6% (1.12)	28.5% (1.16)	9.7% (0.76)
Montana	715	34.1% (1.29)	25.0% (1.17)	31.7% (1.26)	9.2% (0.79)
Nevada	1,114	29.5% (1.27)	27.9% (1.25)	31.5% (1.29)	11.1% (0.88)
New Mexico	1,341	32.6% (1.27)	26.3% (1.19)	29.9% (1.24)	11.2% (0.85)
Utah	1,584	41.2% (1.30)	28.2% (1.19)	22.9% (1.11)	7.7% (0.70)
Wyoming	414	33.9% (1.53)	25.2% (1.40)	30.8% (1.49)	10.1% (0.97)
Pacific	**35,249**	**30.1%** (0.41)	**30.2%** (0.41)	**29.8%** (0.41)	**9.9%** (0.27)
Alaska	451	32.6% (1.23)	27.9% (1.18)	31.7% (1.22)	7.9% (0.71)
California	27,030	30.3% (0.48)	31.0% (0.49)	28.9% (0.48)	9.7% (0.31)
Hawaii	903	28.1% (1.37)	27.5% (1.36)	31.6% (1.42)	12.8% (1.02)
Oregon	2,582	30.0% (1.36)	25.6% (1.29)	34.0% (1.41)	10.4% (0.91)
Washington	4,283	28.7% (1.25)	28.2% (1.25)	33.0% (1.30)	10.1% (0.83)

Source: Three-year merged March CPS: 1991, 1992, and 1993.
Note: See table notes at end of Section G.

Table G2
Nonelderly Population by Race and Sex, 1990-92[1]
(Persons in thousands, standard errors in parentheses)

	Total	Race		Sex	
		White	Nonwhite	Male	Female
United States	**218,586**	**82.9%**	**17.1%**	**49.7%**	**50.3%**
		(0.08)	**(0.08)**	**(0.11)**	**(0.11)**
New England	**11,286**	**92.0%**	**8.0%**	**49.9%**	**50.1%**
		(0.20)	**(0.21)**	**(0.37)**	**(0.37)**
Connecticut	2,820	86.7%	13.3%	49.2%	50.8%
		(0.70)	(0.73)	(1.03)	(1.03)
Maine	1,102	97.6%	2.4%	50.5%	49.5%
		(0.28)	(0.29)	(0.91)	(0.91)
Massachusetts	5,025	91.9%	8.1%	50.3%	49.7%
		(0.27)	(0.28)	(0.49)	(0.49)
New Hampshire	1,016	96.0%	4.0%	50.5%	49.5%
		(0.39)	(0.41)	(1.00)	(1.00)
Rhode Island	806	94.5%	5.5%	48.7%	51.3%
		(0.48)	(0.49)	(1.04)	(1.04)
Vermont	518	98.1%	1.9%	49.3%	50.7%
		(0.27)	(0.28)	(0.98)	(0.98)
Middle Atlantic	**32,501**	**82.5%**	**17.5%**	**49.4%**	**50.6%**
		(0.19)	**(0.19)**	**(0.25)**	**(0.25)**
New Jersey	6,752	80.4%	19.6%	50.1%	49.9%
		(0.38)	(0.39)	(0.47)	(0.47)
New York	15,479	78.8%	21.2%	48.9%	51.1%
		(0.29)	(0.31)	(0.36)	(0.36)
Pennsylvania	10,270	89.6%	10.4%	49.6%	50.4%
		(0.29)	(0.30)	(0.47)	(0.47)
South Atlantic	**37,562**	**74.0%**	**26.0%**	**49.2%**	**50.8%**
		(0.23)	**(0.24)**	**(0.26)**	**(0.26)**
Delaware	623	77.8%	22.2%	51.0%	49.0%
		(0.80)	(0.83)	(0.96)	(0.96)
District of Columbia	477	32.6%	67.4%	47.5%	52.5%
		(1.03)	(1.07)	(1.09)	(1.09)
Florida	10,995	80.2%	19.8%	48.8%	51.2%
		(0.36)	(0.37)	(0.45)	(0.45)
Georgia	5,612	65.5%	34.5%	48.5%	51.5%
		(0.85)	(0.88)	(0.89)	(0.89)
Maryland	4,140	69.7%	30.3%	50.5%	49.5%
		(0.88)	(0.91)	(0.96)	(0.96)
North Carolina	5,640	73.2%	26.8%	48.7%	51.3%
		(0.41)	(0.43)	(0.47)	(0.47)
South Carolina	3,122	65.4%	34.6%	49.5%	50.5%
		(0.77)	(0.80)	(0.80)	(0.80)
Virginia	5,428	76.6%	23.4%	49.7%	50.3%
		(0.68)	(0.70)	(0.80)	(0.80)
West Virginia	1,523	95.1%	4.9%	50.1%	49.9%
		(0.40)	(0.42)	(0.92)	(0.92)
East South Central	**13,386**	**77.2%**	**22.8%**	**49.2%**	**50.8%**
		(0.38)	**(0.39)**	**(0.45)**	**(0.45)**
Alabama	3,600	70.2%	29.8%	48.7%	51.3%
		(0.82)	(0.85)	(0.89)	(0.89)
Kentucky	3,132	94.2%	5.8%	49.4%	50.6%
		(0.43)	(0.45)	(0.92)	(0.92)
Mississippi	2,351	60.9%	39.1%	50.1%	49.9%
		(0.82)	(0.85)	(0.84)	(0.84)
Tennessee	4,304	79.6%	20.4%	49.1%	50.9%
		(0.69)	(0.72)	(0.86)	(0.86)
West South Central	**23,629**	**81.7%**	**18.3%**	**49.2%**	**50.8%**
		(0.27)	**(0.28)**	**(0.35)**	**(0.35)**
Arkansas	2,068	83.3%	16.7%	50.1%	49.9%
		(0.67)	(0.69)	(0.89)	(0.89)
Louisiana	3,679	68.5%	31.5%	47.6%	52.4%
		(0.87)	(0.90)	(0.93)	(0.93)
Oklahoma	2,719	82.8%	17.2%	49.2%	50.8%
		(0.68)	(0.70)	(0.90)	(0.90)
Texas	15,163	84.5%	15.5%	49.4%	50.6%
		(0.33)	(0.34)	(0.46)	(0.46)

Table G2 (continued)

Nonelderly Population by Race and Sex, 1990-92[1]

(Persons in thousands, standard errors in parentheses)

	Total	Race		Sex	
		White	Nonwhite	Male	Female
East North Central	**37,385**	**85.1%**	**14.9%**	**49.6%**	**50.4%**
		(0.18)	**(0.19)**	**(0.26)**	**(0.26)**
Illinois	10,419	79.1%	20.9%	49.4%	50.6%
		(0.38)	(0.40)	(0.47)	(0.47)
Indiana	4,858	90.2%	9.8%	48.8%	51.2%
		(0.56)	(0.58)	(0.93)	(0.93)
Michigan	8,169	83.3%	16.7%	50.0%	50.0%
		(0.35)	(0.37)	(0.47)	(0.47)
Ohio	9,628	87.4%	12.6%	49.9%	50.1%
		(0.31)	(0.32)	(0.46)	(0.46)
Wisconsin	4,311	92.0%	8.0%	49.8%	50.2%
		(0.46)	(0.48)	(0.84)	(0.84)
West North Central	**15,577**	**91.5%**	**8.5%**	**49.4%**	**50.6%**
		(0.23)	**(0.24)**	**(0.41)**	**(0.41)**
Iowa	2,460	96.2%	3.8%	50.4%	49.6%
		(0.33)	(0.35)	(0.88)	(0.88)
Kansas	2,205	90.5%	9.5%	50.7%	49.3%
		(0.51)	(0.53)	(0.86)	(0.86)
Minnesota	3,844	93.4%	6.6%	49.2%	50.8%
		(0.46)	(0.48)	(0.92)	(0.92)
Missouri	4,568	87.0%	13.0%	48.5%	51.5%
		(0.62)	(0.65)	(0.93)	(0.93)
Nebraska	1,391	94.6%	5.4%	48.2%	51.8%
		(0.39)	(0.40)	(0.86)	(0.86)
North Dakota	524	92.4%	7.6%	49.9%	50.1%
		(0.46)	(0.48)	(0.87)	(0.87)
South Dakota	585	89.8%	10.2%	51.7%	48.3%
		(0.50)	(0.52)	(0.83)	(0.83)
Mountain	**12,011**	**92.1%**	**7.9%**	**50.4%**	**49.6%**
		(0.21)	**(0.22)**	**(0.39)**	**(0.39)**
Arizona	3,021	94.3%	5.7%	50.0%	50.0%
		(0.43)	(0.45)	(0.94)	(0.94)
Colorado	2,882	89.8%	10.2%	51.2%	48.8%
		(0.58)	(0.60)	(0.96)	(0.96)
Idaho	940	96.4%	3.6%	49.8%	50.2%
		(0.31)	(0.32)	(0.83)	(0.83)
Montana	715	90.7%	9.3%	49.8%	50.2%
		(0.51)	(0.53)	(0.88)	(0.88)
Nevada	1,114	87.0%	13.0%	51.0%	49.0%
		(0.60)	(0.63)	(0.90)	(0.90)
New Mexico	1,341	86.9%	13.1%	50.2%	49.8%
		(0.59)	(0.61)	(0.87)	(0.87)
Utah	1,584	97.0%	3.0%	50.6%	49.4%
		(0.29)	(0.30)	(0.85)	(0.85)
Wyoming	414	98.0%	2.0%	49.2%	50.8%
		(0.29)	(0.30)	(1.04)	(1.04)
Pacific	**35,249**	**83.5%**	**16.5%**	**50.9%**	**49.1%**
		(0.22)	**(0.23)**	**(0.29)**	**(0.29)**
Alaska	451	74.8%	25.2%	51.0%	49.0%
		(0.74)	(0.77)	(0.85)	(0.85)
California	27,030	83.4%	16.6%	51.1%	48.9%
		(0.25)	(0.26)	(0.34)	(0.34)
Hawaii	903	28.4%	71.6%	50.8%	49.2%
		(0.89)	(0.92)	(0.98)	(0.98)
Oregon	2,582	94.2%	5.8%	50.1%	49.9%
		(0.45)	(0.46)	(0.96)	(0.96)
Washington	4,283	89.9%	10.1%	50.4%	49.6%
		(0.54)	(0.56)	(0.89)	(0.89)

Source: Three-year merged March CPS: 1991, 1992, and 1993.
Note: See table notes at end of Section G.

Table G3
Nonelderly Population by Family Type, 1990-92[1,2,3]
(Persons in thousands, standard errors in parentheses)

	Total	Married with Children	Married without Children	Single-Parent Family	Singles
United States	218,586	48.3% (0.17)	17.0% (0.12)	13.4% (0.11)	21.2% (0.14)
New England	11,286	47.7% (0.58)	17.0% (0.43)	11.9% (0.37)	23.3% (0.49)
Connecticut	2,820	49.4% (1.60)	16.6% (1.19)	12.3% (1.05)	21.8% (1.32)
Maine	1,102	50.7% (1.42)	17.5% (1.08)	13.3% (0.96)	18.5% (1.10)
Massachusetts	5,025	45.6% (0.76)	16.8% (0.57)	12.3% (0.50)	25.3% (0.66)
New Hampshire	1,016	51.8% (1.55)	17.6% (1.18)	9.1% (0.89)	21.5% (1.28)
Rhode Island	806	42.5% (1.59)	19.3% (1.27)	11.2% (1.02)	27.0% (1.43)
Vermont	518	53.3% (1.52)	15.5% (1.10)	10.1% (0.92)	21.1% (1.24)
Middle Atlantic	32,501	48.0% (0.38)	16.6% (0.28)	13.2% (0.26)	22.3% (0.32)
New Jersey	6,752	48.7% (0.73)	16.7% (0.55)	11.9% (0.48)	22.7% (0.62)
New York	15,479	46.6% (0.55)	15.6% (0.40)	14.7% (0.39)	23.2% (0.47)
Pennsylvania	10,270	49.6% (0.72)	18.0% (0.56)	11.8% (0.47)	20.6% (0.59)
South Atlantic	37,562	44.8% (0.41)	18.4% (0.32)	14.4% (0.29)	22.5% (0.34)
Delaware	623	45.1% (1.48)	15.6% (1.08)	15.2% (1.07)	24.1% (1.27)
District of Columbia	477	22.0% (1.41)	11.5% (1.08)	25.3% (1.48)	41.1% (1.67)
Florida	10,995	41.5% (0.69)	19.8% (0.56)	15.5% (0.51)	23.2% (0.59)
Georgia	5,612	46.5% (1.37)	16.7% (1.03)	14.9% (0.98)	21.9% (1.14)
Maryland	4,140	42.4% (1.46)	18.5% (1.15)	14.4% (1.04)	24.7% (1.28)
North Carolina	5,640	46.5% (0.72)	18.9% (0.56)	13.2% (0.49)	21.4% (0.59)
South Carolina	3,122	48.6% (1.25)	17.0% (0.94)	14.9% (0.89)	19.5% (0.99)
Virginia	5,428	47.5% (1.24)	18.3% (0.96)	12.1% (0.81)	22.1% (1.03)
West Virginia	1,523	52.3% (1.43)	18.0% (1.10)	11.8% (0.92)	17.8% (1.09)
East South Central	13,386	46.8% (0.70)	17.9% (0.53)	16.3% (0.52)	19.0% (0.55)
Alabama	3,600	46.0% (1.38)	19.4% (1.09)	15.1% (0.99)	19.5% (1.10)
Kentucky	3,132	49.6% (1.42)	19.0% (1.12)	13.9% (0.98)	17.5% (1.08)
Mississippi	2,351	49.6% (1.30)	12.7% (0.86)	19.9% (1.03)	17.9% (0.99)
Tennessee	4,304	44.1% (1.32)	18.6% (1.04)	17.1% (1.00)	20.2% (1.07)
West South Central	23,629	51.1% (0.54)	16.3% (0.40)	13.7% (0.37)	18.9% (0.43)
Arkansas	2,068	52.7% (1.38)	17.8% (1.06)	12.5% (0.91)	17.0% (1.04)
Louisiana	3,679	47.3% (1.45)	15.3% (1.04)	18.8% (1.13)	18.6% (1.13)
Oklahoma	2,719	53.0% (1.39)	18.5% (1.08)	11.3% (0.88)	17.1% (1.05)
Texas	15,163	51.4% (0.70)	15.9% (0.52)	13.1% (0.48)	19.6% (0.56)

Table G3 (continued)
Nonelderly Population by Family Type, 1990-92[1,2,3]
(Persons in thousands, standard errors in parentheses)

	Total	Married with Children	Married without Children	Single-Parent Family	Singles
East North Central	**37,385**	**48.7%**	**16.7%**	**14.2%**	**20.4%**
		(0.40)	**(0.30)**	**(0.28)**	**(0.32)**
Illinois	10,419	46.5%	16.5%	15.1%	21.9%
		(0.73)	(0.54)	(0.52)	(0.60)
Indiana	4,858	46.6%	18.2%	16.3%	18.9%
		(1.44)	(1.12)	(1.07)	(1.13)
Michigan	8,169	48.1%	16.2%	14.3%	21.4%
		(0.73)	(0.54)	(0.51)	(0.60)
Ohio	9,628	51.3%	17.2%	12.3%	19.2%
		(0.72)	(0.54)	(0.47)	(0.57)
Wisconsin	4,311	51.8%	15.6%	13.4%	19.2%
		(1.31)	(0.95)	(0.89)	(1.03)
West North Central	**15,577**	**52.0%**	**17.2%**	**11.7%**	**19.1%**
		(0.63)	**(0.48)**	**(0.41)**	**(0.50)**
Iowa	2,460	55.7%	16.1%	9.4%	18.8%
		(1.35)	(1.00)	(0.79)	(1.06)
Kansas	2,205	54.6%	15.4%	12.3%	17.7%
		(1.33)	(0.97)	(0.88)	(1.02)
Minnesota	3,844	48.2%	17.2%	12.2%	22.4%
		(1.43)	(1.08)	(0.93)	(1.19)
Missouri	4,568	49.2%	18.8%	13.3%	18.7%
		(1.43)	(1.12)	(0.97)	(1.12)
Nebraska	1,391	57.3%	17.6%	9.8%	15.2%
		(1.31)	(1.01)	(0.79)	(0.95)
North Dakota	524	59.4%	14.9%	8.2%	17.5%
		(1.33)	(0.96)	(0.74)	(1.03)
South Dakota	585	53.6%	15.8%	11.5%	19.1%
		(1.28)	(0.93)	(0.82)	(1.01)
Mountain	**12,011**	**52.2%**	**17.0%**	**11.9%**	**18.9%**
		(0.60)	**(0.45)**	**(0.39)**	**(0.47)**
Arizona	3,021	46.8%	19.7%	12.5%	21.0%
		(1.45)	(1.15)	(0.96)	(1.18)
Colorado	2,882	50.7%	17.4%	11.7%	20.2%
		(1.48)	(1.12)	(0.96)	(1.19)
Idaho	940	59.2%	16.4%	9.4%	15.0%
		(1.26)	(0.95)	(0.75)	(0.92)
Montana	715	54.9%	15.9%	11.9%	17.3%
		(1.35)	(0.99)	(0.88)	(1.03)
Nevada	1,114	44.3%	17.6%	14.0%	24.1%
		(1.38)	(1.06)	(0.97)	(1.19)
New Mexico	1,341	49.9%	15.8%	14.5%	19.7%
		(1.35)	(0.99)	(0.95)	(1.08)
Utah	1,584	65.8%	12.9%	8.7%	12.7%
		(1.25)	(0.88)	(0.74)	(0.88)
Wyoming	414	58.1%	16.5%	11.7%	13.8%
		(1.59)	(1.20)	(1.04)	(1.11)
Pacific	**35,249**	**48.1%**	**16.2%**	**12.5%**	**23.2%**
		(0.45)	**(0.33)**	**(0.30)**	**(0.38)**
Alaska	451	48.5%	14.6%	15.4%	21.5%
		(1.31)	(0.93)	(0.95)	(1.08)
California	27,030	47.9%	15.7%	12.7%	23.7%
		(0.53)	(0.38)	(0.35)	(0.45)
Hawaii	903	44.8%	18.2%	12.0%	25.0%
		(1.51)	(1.18)	(0.99)	(1.32)
Oregon	2,582	50.3%	18.4%	11.8%	19.6%
		(1.48)	(1.15)	(0.96)	(1.18)
Washington	4,283	49.1%	17.6%	11.2%	22.1%
		(1.38)	(1.05)	(0.87)	(1.15)

Source: Three-year merged March CPS: 1991, 1992, and 1993.
Note: See table notes at end of Section G.

Table G4
Nonelderly Family Income, 1990-92:
Upper Limit of Quartiles (1992 Dollars)[1,2,4]

(Families in thousands, standard errors in parentheses)

	Families	PERCENTILE		
		25th	Median	75th
United States	**102,141**	**$10,301**	**$23,932**	**$44,385**
		(70)	(103)	(154)
New England	**5,454**	**$13,425**	**$28,285**	**$50,026**
		(285)	**(345)**	**(612)**
Connecticut	1,316	16,522	32,245	56,236
		(886)	(1151)	(2270)
Maine	498	11,264	23,247	41,716
		(566)	(695)	(1324)
Massachusetts	2,503	12,900	28,184	50,250
		(393)	(444)	(803)
New Hampshire	479	14,380	29,003	50,000
		(873)	(833)	(1529)
Rhode Island	418	10,735	24,324	42,945
		(601)	(821)	(1292)
Vermont	239	12,500	25,000	44,577
		(579)	(1162)	(1093)
Middle Atlantic	**15,376**	**$10,816**	**$25,312**	**$47,161**
		(174)	**(266)**	**(404)**
New Jersey	3,229	13,132	28,983	54,531
		(364)	(509)	(770)
New York	7,417	10,000	24,648	46,032
		(247)	(354)	(571)
Pennsylvania	4,730	11,000	24,780	44,224
		(326)	(440)	(611)
South Atlantic	**18,212**	**$9,500**	**$22,113**	**$42,234**
		(140)	**(249)**	**(399)**
Delaware	305	12,810	25,874	46,000
		(519)	(877)	(1232)
District of Columbia	292	7,943	20,049	36,444
		(508)	(755)	(1428)
Florida	5,404	9,296	20,602	39,074
		(228)	(429)	(566)
Georgia	2,672	7,936	21,354	42,440
		(394)	(850)	(1821)
Maryland	2,096	12,500	26,807	50,420
		(782)	(975)	(2137)
North Carolina	2,703	9,670	21,612	41,513
		(247)	(418)	(714)
South Carolina	1,450	7,913	19,322	40,174
		(366)	(634)	(1165)
Virginia	2,605	11,403	25,870	46,488
		(558)	(791)	(1571)
West Virginia	684	7,282	18,052	35,090
		(454)	(727)	(1089)
East South Central	**6,123**	**$7,514**	**$19,000**	**$37,190**
		(214)	**(360)**	**(608)**
Alabama	1,664	6,886	18,542	37,057
		(434)	(729)	(1204)
Kentucky	1,418	8,643	20,932	41,204
		(411)	(911)	(1607)
Mississippi	1,018	5,950	15,143	32,000
		(378)	(664)	(1108)
Tennessee	2,023	7,952	20,000	37,084
		(433)	(705)	(1315)
West South Central	**10,630**	**$8,695**	**$21,210**	**$41,000**
		194	**358**	**579**
Arkansas	896	9,024	19,356	35,921
		(458)	(711)	(1230)
Louisiana	1,641	6,000	18,000	38,176
		(478)	(1076)	(1248)
Oklahoma	1,202	8,700	21,633	40,851
		(452)	(964)	(1502)
Texas	6,891	9,384	22,003	42,967
		(265)	(452)	(790)

Table G4 (continued)
Nonelderly Family Income, 1990-92:
Upper Limit of Quartiles (1992 Dollars)[1,2,4]
(Families in thousands, standard errors in parentheses)

| | | PERCENTILE | | |
	Families	25th	Median	75th
East North Central	**17,139**	**$11,000**	**$25,409**	**$45,085**
		(184)	**(275)**	**(397)**
Illinois	4,889	10,029	25,236	46,106
		(364)	(534)	(745)
Indiana	2,248	12,000	23,898	40,745
		(604)	(679)	(1113)
Michigan	3,790	9,702	25,290	46,804
		(242)	(582)	(758)
Ohio	4,299	11,500	25,753	45,258
		(300)	(486)	(658)
Wisconsin	1,913	13,000	27,196	45,630
		(614)	(777)	(1206)
West North Central	**6,930**	**$11,948**	**$24,689**	**$43,746**
		(264)	**(387)**	**(542)**
Iowa	1,075	12,890	24,457	41,705
		(534)	(789)	(1090)
Kansas	949	12,361	26,027	45,710
		(580)	(938)	(1118)
Minnesota	1,791	12,490	26,200	45,735
		(620)	(899)	(1455)
Missouri	2,072	10,683	22,911	43,050
		(598)	(862)	(1473)
Nebraska	570	12,956	26,901	44,100
		(539)	(960)	(942)
North Dakota	220	11,257	23,696	40,550
		(563)	(812)	(1211)
South Dakota	255	10,270	21,161	37,790
		(534)	(725)	(842)
Mountain	**5,313**	**$11,018**	**$24,432**	**$44,100**
		(264)	**(374)**	**(563)**
Arizona	1,413	11,018	23,996	43,501
		(666)	(829)	(1633)
Colorado	1,329	13,520	27,609	48,658
		(673)	(1050)	(1253)
Idaho	380	10,095	23,734	39,805
		(594)	(824)	(913)
Montana	304	9,891	22,333	39,695
		(461)	(827)	(970)
Nevada	545	11,331	23,798	42,952
		(549)	(912)	(1072)
New Mexico	610	7,679	19,365	38,349
		(398)	(860)	(1291)
Utah	566	12,209	26,929	45,500
		(702)	(1141)	(1117)
Wyoming	167	12,952	28,590	46,487
		(794)	(1001)	(1452)
Pacific	**16,964**	**$10,308**	**$24,177**	**$46,309**
		(174)	**(295)**	**(502)**
Alaska	211	12,846	30,584	56,120
		(571)	(1014)	(1921)
California	13,083	10,000	22,979	45,664
		(194)	(348)	(602)
Hawaii	450	13,955	27,711	50,000
		(684)	(848)	(1513)
Oregon	1,177	11,824	26,175	45,767
		(610)	(965)	(1533)
Washington	2,043	12,559	27,514	49,061
		(650)	(936)	(1449)

Source: Three-year merged March CPS: 1991, 1992, and 1993.
Note: See table notes at end of Section G.

Table G5

Nonelderly Family Income, 1990-92:
Persons in All Families[1,2,4]

(Persons in thousands, standard errors in parentheses)

	Number	Family Income as Percent of Poverty				
		< 100%	100-149%	150-199%	200-399%	400% +
United States	218,586	18.1%	8.8%	8.8%	32.3%	32.0%
		(0.18)	(0.13)	(0.13)	(0.22)	(0.22)
New England	11,286	12.8%	6.5%	7.0%	33.7%	40.1%
		(0.54)	(0.40)	(0.41)	(0.77)	(0.80)
Connecticut	2,820	9.2%	5.1%	6.0%	33.0%	46.7%
		(1.30)	(0.99)	(1.07)	(2.11)	(2.24)
Maine	1,102	16.2%	9.6%	10.4%	36.4%	27.4%
		(1.47)	(1.18)	(1.22)	(1.92)	(1.78)
Massachusetts	5,025	14.4%	6.2%	5.9%	31.9%	41.6%
		(0.75)	(0.52)	(0.51)	(1.00)	(1.06)
New Hampshire	1,016	10.6%	6.8%	7.8%	36.1%	38.7%
		(1.35)	(1.11)	(1.18)	(2.10)	(2.13)
Rhode Island	806	14.4%	6.8%	9.8%	35.8%	33.1%
		(1.59)	(1.14)	(1.35)	(2.18)	(2.14)
Vermont	518	12.1%	7.7%	9.7%	40.4%	30.1%
		(1.40)	(1.14)	(1.27)	(2.10)	(1.96)
Middle Atlantic	32,501	16.7%	7.4%	8.1%	32.1%	35.7%
		(0.40)	(0.28)	(0.29)	(0.50)	(0.52)
New Jersey	6,752	13.3%	5.3%	7.2%	29.1%	45.1%
		(0.70)	(0.46)	(0.54)	(0.94)	(1.03)
New York	15,479	19.2%	8.2%	8.1%	29.8%	34.7%
		(0.62)	(0.43)	(0.43)	(0.72)	(0.75)
Pennsylvania	10,270	15.2%	7.7%	8.7%	37.6%	30.9%
		(0.73)	(0.54)	(0.57)	(0.99)	(0.94)
South Atlantic	37,562	19.0%	8.8%	9.2%	31.6%	31.4%
		(0.45)	(0.33)	(0.33)	(0.54)	(0.54)
Delaware	623	11.7%	8.0%	10.2%	32.7%	37.5%
		(1.34)	(1.13)	(1.27)	(1.96)	(2.03)
District of Columbia	477	27.2%	9.4%	7.8%	25.4%	30.2%
		(2.13)	(1.40)	(1.28)	(2.08)	(2.20)
Florida	10,995	20.4%	9.7%	9.3%	32.8%	27.7%
		(0.79)	(0.58)	(0.57)	(0.93)	(0.88)
Georgia	5,612	21.1%	9.9%	8.8%	28.1%	32.1%
		(1.58)	(1.16)	(1.10)	(1.74)	(1.81)
Maryland	4,140	15.0%	5.7%	7.1%	29.3%	42.8%
		(1.49)	(0.97)	(1.08)	(1.90)	(2.07)
North Carolina	5,640	17.8%	8.5%	10.2%	34.1%	29.4%
		(0.78)	(0.57)	(0.61)	(0.96)	(0.93)
South Carolina	3,122	21.5%	10.2%	10.2%	31.9%	26.3%
		(1.44)	(1.06)	(1.06)	(1.64)	(1.55)
Virginia	5,428	15.5%	6.9%	8.9%	31.2%	37.4%
		(1.26)	(0.89)	(0.99)	(1.62)	(1.69)
West Virginia	1,523	24.0%	11.9%	10.1%	34.5%	19.4%
		(1.72)	(1.31)	(1.21)	(1.91)	(1.59)
East South Central	13,386	22.8%	11.2%	9.8%	33.3%	23.0%
		(0.82)	(0.62)	(0.58)	(0.93)	(0.83)
Alabama	3,600	21.9%	11.3%	10.1%	33.8%	22.9%
		(1.61)	(1.23)	(1.18)	(1.84)	(1.64)
Kentucky	3,132	21.7%	10.3%	8.4%	32.0%	27.5%
		(1.65)	(1.22)	(1.11)	(1.87)	(1.79)
Mississippi	2,351	28.0%	13.4%	10.0%	31.5%	17.0%
		(1.64)	(1.24)	(1.10)	(1.70)	(1.37)
Tennessee	4,304	21.4%	10.5%	10.3%	34.9%	22.9%
		(1.54)	(1.15)	(1.14)	(1.79)	(1.58)
West South Central	23,629	21.9%	10.4%	9.5%	30.4%	27.7%
		(0.63)	(0.47)	(0.45)	(0.70)	(0.68)
Arkansas	2,068	20.6%	11.8%	10.9%	36.2%	20.4%
		(1.58)	(1.26)	(1.21)	(1.87)	(1.57)
Louisiana	3,679	26.5%	9.7%	8.4%	30.8%	24.6%
		(1.80)	(1.21)	(1.13)	(1.88)	(1.76)
Oklahoma	2,719	19.1%	11.7%	11.2%	30.8%	27.1%
		(1.54)	(1.26)	(1.24)	(1.81)	(1.74)
Texas	15,163	21.5%	10.1%	9.3%	29.5%	29.6%
		(0.82)	(0.60)	(0.58)	(0.91)	(0.91)

Table G5 (continued)
Nonelderly Family Income, 1990-92:
Persons in All Families[1,2,4]
(Persons in thousands, standard errors in parentheses)

	Number	Family Income as Percent of Poverty				
		<100%	100-149%	150-199%	200-399%	400% +
East North Central	**37,385**	**16.9%**	**7.7%**	**8.4%**	**34.2%**	**32.9%**
		(0.42)	**(0.30)**	**(0.31)**	**(0.53)**	**(0.53)**
Illinois	10,419	18.7%	7.2%	7.8%	31.8%	34.5%
		(0.80)	(0.53)	(0.55)	(0.96)	(0.98)
Indiana	4,858	15.1%	9.2%	10.3%	38.0%	27.4%
		(1.46)	(1.18)	(1.24)	(1.98)	(1.82)
Michigan	8,169	19.4%	6.7%	7.7%	32.0%	34.2%
		(0.82)	(0.52)	(0.55)	(0.96)	(0.98)
Ohio	9,628	15.6%	8.0%	9.0%	35.6%	31.7%
		(0.73)	(0.55)	(0.58)	(0.97)	(0.94)
Wisconsin	4,311	12.6%	8.1%	7.9%	36.5%	34.9%
		(1.22)	(1.00)	(0.99)	(1.77)	(1.76)
West North Central	**15,577**	**14.8%**	**8.6%**	**10.6%**	**36.3%**	**29.6%**
		(0.63)	**(0.50)**	**(0.55)**	**(0.86)**	**(0.81)**
Iowa	2,460	13.1%	8.2%	12.2%	41.0%	25.4%
		(1.29)	(1.05)	(1.25)	(1.88)	(1.67)
Kansas	2,205	13.7%	8.2%	10.2%	37.2%	30.8%
		(1.30)	(1.03)	(1.14)	(1.82)	(1.74)
Minnesota	3,844	14.1%	7.9%	8.4%	35.1%	34.5%
		(1.40)	(1.09)	(1.12)	(1.92)	(1.91)
Missouri	4,568	17.2%	9.8%	11.6%	31.8%	29.6%
		(1.52)	(1.20)	(1.29)	(1.88)	(1.85)
Nebraska	1,391	12.3%	8.0%	10.9%	40.6%	28.2%
		(1.23)	(1.01)	(1.17)	(1.84)	(1.68)
North Dakota	524	15.7%	7.6%	11.8%	41.5%	23.5%
		(1.39)	(1.01)	(1.23)	(1.88)	(1.61)
South Dakota	585	17.4%	10.4%	11.0%	41.5%	19.7%
		(1.37)	(1.10)	(1.13)	(1.78)	(1.43)
Mountain	**12,011**	**16.6%**	**9.6%**	**10.3%**	**34.6%**	**29.0%**
		(0.63)	**(0.50)**	**(0.51)**	**(0.80)**	**(0.76)**
Arizona	3,021	17.7%	9.4%	9.7%	32.6%	30.7%
		(1.56)	(1.19)	(1.21)	(1.91)	(1.88)
Colorado	2,882	13.9%	8.4%	8.2%	34.3%	35.3%
		(1.45)	(1.16)	(1.14)	(1.98)	(2.00)
Idaho	940	16.8%	10.5%	12.1%	40.7%	19.9%
		(1.36)	(1.11)	(1.18)	(1.78)	(1.45)
Montana	715	18.7%	10.8%	11.9%	36.1%	22.5%
		(1.49)	(1.19)	(1.24)	(1.84)	(1.60)
Nevada	1,114	15.7%	8.3%	10.1%	33.6%	32.3%
		(1.43)	(1.08)	(1.18)	(1.85)	(1.83)
New Mexico	1,341	24.9%	10.9%	10.8%	29.1%	24.3%
		(1.65)	(1.19)	(1.18)	(1.73)	(1.63)
Utah	1,584	12.9%	10.8%	13.3%	38.7%	24.4%
		(1.24)	(1.15)	(1.26)	(1.81)	(1.60)
Wyoming	414	12.5%	9.2%	9.5%	40.5%	28.4%
		(1.50)	(1.31)	(1.33)	(2.23)	(2.05)
Pacific	**35,249**	**18.8%**	**9.8%**	**8.1%**	**29.0%**	**34.3%**
		(0.50)	**(0.38)**	**(0.35)**	**(0.58)**	**(0.60)**
Alaska	451	17.7%	9.4%	9.4%	31.1%	32.4%
		(1.41)	(1.08)	(1.08)	(1.71)	(1.73)
California	27,030	20.3%	10.4%	8.2%	27.2%	33.9%
		(0.60)	(0.45)	(0.41)	(0.66)	(0.70)
Hawaii	903	15.6%	7.5%	9.4%	34.1%	33.3%
		(1.56)	(1.13)	(1.25)	(2.03)	(2.02)
Oregon	2,582	13.7%	9.7%	10.2%	32.4%	33.9%
		(1.44)	(1.24)	(1.27)	(1.96)	(1.98)
Washington	4,283	13.5%	6.2%	5.7%	37.0%	37.5%
		(1.33)	(0.94)	(0.91)	(1.88)	(1.89)

Source: Three-year merged March CPS: 1991, 1992, and 1993.
Note: See table notes at end of Section G.

Table G6a
Nonelderly Family Income, 1990-92:
Children under Age 18[1,2,4]

(Persons in thousands, standard errors in parentheses)

	Number	Family Income as Percent of Poverty				
		< 100%	100-149%	150-199%	200-399%	400% +
United States	65,262	24.8%	10.2%	9.8%	33.2%	21.9%
		(0.37)	(0.26)	(0.25)	(0.40)	(0.35)
New England	3,080	18.8%	7.6%	8.1%	36.8%	28.8%
		(1.21)	(0.82)	(0.85)	(1.50)	(1.41)
Connecticut	809	15.5%	6.2%	6.7%	35.6%	36.0%
		(3.04)	(2.02)	(2.10)	(4.02)	(4.03)
Maine	323	22.3%	11.3%	12.1%	36.9%	17.4%
		(3.07)	(2.34)	(2.41)	(3.56)	(2.79)
Massachusetts	1,318	21.6%	7.2%	6.8%	35.2%	29.2%
		(1.73)	(1.08)	(1.06)	(2.01)	(1.91)
New Hampshire	284	12.6%	9.2%	9.0%	40.7%	28.5%
		(2.75)	(2.39)	(2.36)	(4.07)	(3.74)
Rhode Island	197	20.2%	6.4%	12.6%	39.6%	21.2%
		(3.69)	(2.25)	(3.05)	(4.50)	(3.76)
Vermont	150	14.9%	9.2%	10.1%	45.5%	20.3%
		(2.84)	(2.31)	(2.40)	(3.97)	(3.21)
Middle Atlantic	9,345	22.5%	8.7%	9.5%	34.1%	25.2%
		(0.84)	(0.57)	(0.59)	(0.95)	(0.87)
New Jersey	1,886	17.7%	6.1%	7.3%	32.4%	36.4%
		(1.50)	(0.94)	(1.02)	(1.83)	(1.89)
New York	4,475	27.0%	9.6%	10.0%	31.0%	22.5%
		(1.29)	(0.86)	(0.87)	(1.35)	(1.22)
Pennsylvania	2,984	19.0%	9.0%	10.1%	39.9%	22.0%
		(1.48)	(1.08)	(1.14)	(1.85)	(1.57)
South Atlantic	10,637	26.8%	10.2%	9.7%	31.6%	21.7%
		(0.96)	(0.66)	(0.64)	(1.01)	(0.90)
Delaware	178	16.1%	11.3%	12.9%	33.2%	26.5%
		(2.88)	(2.48)	(2.62)	(3.69)	(3.46)
District of Columbia	129	43.2%	13.2%	7.4%	21.0%	15.1%
		(4.56)	(3.12)	(2.42)	(3.75)	(3.30)
Florida	3,082	30.7%	11.1%	8.5%	32.6%	17.2%
		(1.72)	(1.17)	(1.04)	(1.75)	(1.40)
Georgia	1,658	28.9%	10.9%	10.4%	27.3%	22.5%
		(3.24)	(2.22)	(2.18)	(3.18)	(2.98)
Maryland	1,120	22.7%	7.6%	7.8%	29.5%	32.4%
		(3.36)	(2.12)	(2.16)	(3.66)	(3.76)
North Carolina	1,563	25.2%	9.7%	11.2%	33.9%	20.0%
		(1.68)	(1.14)	(1.22)	(1.83)	(1.54)
South Carolina	942	29.3%	11.0%	11.0%	31.5%	17.2%
		(2.91)	(2.00)	(2.00)	(2.97)	(2.41)
Virginia	1,531	18.9%	8.3%	10.1%	33.4%	29.3%
		(2.57)	(1.81)	(1.98)	(3.10)	(2.99)
West Virginia	434	30.5%	13.4%	10.6%	33.3%	12.3%
		(3.47)	(2.57)	(2.32)	(3.55)	(2.48)
East South Central	4,057	30.7%	13.1%	10.4%	31.0%	14.9%
		(1.65)	(1.21)	(1.09)	(1.65)	(1.27)
Alabama	1,100	28.8%	12.9%	10.2%	32.2%	15.9%
		(3.19)	(2.36)	(2.13)	(3.29)	(2.58)
Kentucky	896	29.7%	11.4%	8.2%	31.8%	19.0%
		(3.42)	(2.38)	(2.05)	(3.49)	(2.94)
Mississippi	834	35.9%	14.7%	10.1%	28.9%	10.4%
		(2.94)	(2.17)	(1.85)	(2.78)	(1.88)
Tennessee	1,228	29.5%	13.5%	12.3%	30.8%	14.0%
		(3.21)	(2.40)	(2.31)	(3.25)	(2.44)
West South Central	7,461	29.8%	11.9%	9.7%	29.9%	18.8%
		(1.24)	(0.88)	(0.80)	(1.25)	(1.06)
Arkansas	671	28.1%	14.4%	9.8%	33.5%	14.3%
		(3.07)	(2.40)	(2.03)	(3.22)	(2.39)
Louisiana	1,195	37.6%	10.9%	6.1%	30.4%	14.9%
		(3.47)	(2.23)	(1.72)	(3.29)	(2.55)
Oklahoma	843	24.4%	14.2%	13.5%	30.9%	16.9%
		(3.03)	(2.46)	(2.40)	(3.25)	(2.64)
Texas	4,751	29.0%	11.3%	9.9%	29.0%	20.8%
		(1.61)	(1.13)	(1.06)	(1.61)	(1.44)

Table G6a (continued)
Nonelderly Family Income, 1990-92:
Children under Age 18[1,2,4]
(Persons in thousands, standard errors in parentheses)

	Number	Family Income as Percent of Poverty				
		<100%	100-149%	150-199%	200-399%	400% +
East North Central	**11,387**	**23.1%**	**8.8%**	**9.9%**	**36.2%**	**22.0%**
		(0.86)	**(0.58)**	**(0.61)**	**(0.98)**	**(0.84)**
Illinois	3,162	26.3%	8.1%	9.2%	34.4%	22.0%
		(1.65)	(1.02)	(1.08)	(1.78)	(1.55)
Indiana	1,430	20.6%	12.0%	13.1%	35.9%	18.3%
		(3.04)	(2.44)	(2.54)	(3.60)	(2.91)
Michigan	2,464	26.6%	7.1%	8.7%	34.1%	23.6%
		(1.66)	(0.96)	(1.05)	(1.78)	(1.59)
Ohio	2,953	21.2%	9.1%	10.7%	38.5%	20.4%
		(1.49)	(1.05)	(1.13)	(1.78)	(1.47)
Wisconsin	1,378	16.5%	9.2%	8.9%	39.5%	26.0%
		(2.41)	(1.88)	(1.85)	(3.18)	(2.86)
West North Central	**4,787**	**20.0%**	**10.3%**	**12.3%**	**37.6%**	**19.8%**
		(1.28)	**(0.98)**	**(1.05)**	**(1.56)**	**(1.28)**
Iowa	754	15.8%	9.6%	15.3%	42.6%	16.7%
		(2.53)	(2.04)	(2.50)	(3.42)	(2.58)
Kansas	726	17.8%	9.7%	12.0%	38.8%	21.8%
		(2.51)	(1.94)	(2.14)	(3.20)	(2.71)
Minnesota	1,119	20.1%	10.0%	9.9%	37.5%	22.5%
		(2.99)	(2.24)	(2.22)	(3.61)	(3.12)
Missouri	1,380	24.1%	11.8%	12.6%	31.9%	19.6%
		(3.15)	(2.37)	(2.44)	(3.43)	(2.92)
Nebraska	449	17.4%	8.3%	12.3%	42.1%	19.9%
		(2.50)	(1.82)	(2.17)	(3.25)	(2.63)
North Dakota	167	19.0%	8.4%	13.6%	42.5%	16.5%
		(2.65)	(1.87)	(2.31)	(3.33)	(2.50)
South Dakota	193	22.3%	12.1%	12.5%	40.6%	12.5%
		(2.61)	(2.05)	(2.08)	(3.08)	(2.08)
Mountain	**3,901**	**21.6%**	**11.1%**	**12.5%**	**36.4%**	**18.4%**
		(1.22)	**(0.93)**	**(0.98)**	**(1.42)**	**(1.15)**
Arizona	904	24.6%	10.9%	12.9%	33.2%	18.3%
		(3.22)	(2.33)	(2.50)	(3.52)	(2.89)
Colorado	855	19.4%	9.6%	10.0%	36.7%	24.3%
		(3.04)	(2.26)	(2.30)	(3.70)	(3.29)
Idaho	340	21.1%	11.9%	14.3%	41.6%	11.1%
		(2.46)	(1.95)	(2.11)	(2.97)	(1.89)
Montana	244	24.0%	13.1%	13.7%	37.1%	12.2%
		(2.80)	(2.21)	(2.25)	(3.16)	(2.14)
Nevada	328	19.8%	11.0%	11.0%	36.0%	22.2%
		(2.88)	(2.26)	(2.26)	(3.47)	(3.00)
New Mexico	437	32.5%	11.1%	11.8%	29.3%	15.3%
		(3.13)	(2.10)	(2.15)	(3.04)	(2.40)
Utah	653	14.7%	12.1%	15.6%	40.3%	17.2%
		(2.05)	(1.88)	(2.10)	(2.84)	(2.19)
Wyoming	140	15.1%	11.5%	10.9%	45.3%	17.2%
		(2.79)	(2.49)	(2.44)	(3.89)	(2.94)
Pacific	**10,606**	**26.0%**	**11.3%**	**8.5%**	**30.1%**	**24.1%**
		(1.02)	**(0.73)**	**(0.65)**	**(1.06)**	**(0.99)**
Alaska	147	23.4%	11.3%	10.6%	34.1%	20.7%
		(2.75)	(2.05)	(1.99)	(3.08)	(2.63)
California	8,203	28.2%	12.0%	8.5%	27.7%	23.7%
		(1.21)	(0.87)	(0.75)	(1.20)	(1.14)
Hawaii	254	26.7%	7.8%	10.1%	32.6%	22.8%
		(3.58)	(2.17)	(2.44)	(3.79)	(3.39)
Oregon	776	17.7%	12.5%	12.2%	36.4%	21.2%
		(2.91)	(2.52)	(2.50)	(3.67)	(3.12)
Washington	1,227	17.1%	6.6%	6.2%	40.6%	29.5%
		(2.74)	(1.81)	(1.75)	(3.58)	(3.32)

Source: Three-year merged March CPS: 1991, 1992, and 1993.
Note: See table notes at end of Section G.

Table G6b
Nonelderly Family Income, 1990-92:
Adults Ages 18-64[1,2,4]

(Persons in thousands, standard errors in parentheses)

	Number	Family Income as Percent of Poverty				
		< 100%	100-149%	150-199%	200-399%	400% +
United States	**153,323**	**15.2%**	**8.2%**	**8.4%**	**31.9%**	**36.4%**
		(0.20)	**(0.15)**	**(0.15)**	**(0.26)**	**(0.27)**
New England	**8,206**	**10.6%**	**6.0%**	**6.6%**	**32.5%**	**44.3%**
		(0.58)	**(0.45)**	**(0.47)**	**(0.89)**	**(0.95)**
Connecticut	2,011	6.7%	4.7%	5.7%	31.9%	50.9%
		(1.33)	(1.13)	(1.24)	(2.48)	(2.66)
Maine	779	13.6%	8.9%	9.7%	36.2%	31.6%
		(1.63)	(1.35)	(1.41)	(2.28)	(2.21)
Massachusetts	3,707	11.8%	5.9%	5.5%	30.8%	46.0%
		(0.81)	(0.59)	(0.57)	(1.16)	(1.25)
New Hampshire	732	9.8%	5.9%	7.4%	34.3%	42.6%
		(1.54)	(1.22)	(1.35)	(2.45)	(2.55)
Rhode Island	609	12.5%	6.9%	8.9%	34.6%	37.0%
		(1.73)	(1.33)	(1.49)	(2.49)	(2.52)
Vermont	368	11.0%	7.1%	9.6%	38.3%	34.0%
		(1.59)	(1.30)	(1.50)	(2.47)	(2.41)
Middle Atlantic	**23,156**	**14.4%**	**6.9%**	**7.6%**	**31.3%**	**39.9%**
		(0.45)	**(0.32)**	**(0.34)**	**(0.59)**	**(0.62)**
New Jersey	4,866	11.6%	4.9%	7.2%	27.8%	48.5%
		(0.78)	(0.53)	(0.63)	(1.09)	(1.22)
New York	11,004	16.0%	7.6%	7.4%	29.3%	39.7%
		(0.68)	(0.49)	(0.49)	(0.85)	(0.91)
Pennsylvania	7,286	13.6%	7.2%	8.1%	36.6%	34.5%
		(0.83)	(0.63)	(0.66)	(1.17)	(1.15)
South Atlantic	**26,924**	**15.9%**	**8.3%**	**9.0%**	**31.6%**	**35.3%**
		(0.50)	**(0.38)**	**(0.39)**	**(0.64)**	**(0.65)**
Delaware	445	9.9%	6.7%	9.2%	32.4%	41.9%
		(1.48)	(1.23)	(1.43)	(2.32)	(2.44)
District of Columbia	348	21.3%	8.1%	7.9%	27.0%	35.7%
		(2.29)	(1.52)	(1.51)	(2.49)	(2.68)
Florida	7,913	16.4%	9.2%	9.6%	32.9%	31.9%
		(0.86)	(0.67)	(0.69)	(1.09)	(1.08)
Georgia	3,954	17.8%	9.5%	8.1%	28.5%	36.1%
		(1.77)	(1.36)	(1.27)	(2.09)	(2.22)
Maryland	3,020	12.1%	5.1%	6.9%	29.3%	46.7%
		(1.59)	(1.07)	(1.24)	(2.22)	(2.44)
North Carolina	4,077	14.9%	8.1%	9.8%	34.1%	33.0%
		(0.85)	(0.65)	(0.71)	(1.13)	(1.12)
South Carolina	2,180	18.1%	9.8%	9.8%	32.0%	30.2%
		(1.62)	(1.25)	(1.25)	(1.96)	(1.93)
Virginia	3,898	14.2%	6.4%	8.4%	30.4%	40.6%
		(1.43)	(1.01)	(1.14)	(1.89)	(2.02)
West Virginia	1,089	21.5%	11.3%	9.9%	35.1%	22.3%
		(1.96)	(1.51)	(1.42)	(2.27)	(1.98)
East South Central	**9,329**	**19.3%**	**10.3%**	**9.5%**	**34.3%**	**26.5%**
		(0.93)	**(0.72)**	**(0.69)**	**(1.12)**	**(1.04)**
Alabama	2,500	18.9%	10.6%	10.1%	34.5%	26.0%
		(1.83)	(1.44)	(1.41)	(2.22)	(2.05)
Kentucky	2,237	18.5%	9.9%	8.5%	32.1%	30.9%
		(1.84)	(1.42)	(1.32)	(2.22)	(2.19)
Mississippi	1,517	23.7%	12.7%	10.0%	32.9%	20.7%
		(1.93)	(1.51)	(1.37)	(2.14)	(1.84)
Tennessee	3,076	18.2%	9.3%	9.5%	36.5%	26.5%
		(1.71)	(1.29)	(1.30)	(2.14)	(1.96)
West South Central	**16,168**	**18.3%**	**9.7%**	**9.4%**	**30.7%**	**31.8%**
		(0.72)	**(0.55)**	**(0.54)**	**(0.85)**	**(0.86)**
Arkansas	1,396	17.0%	10.6%	11.5%	37.5%	23.4%
		(1.78)	(1.46)	(1.51)	(2.29)	(2.00)
Louisiana	2,484	21.2%	9.2%	9.4%	31.0%	29.2%
		(2.03)	(1.43)	(1.45)	(2.30)	(2.26)
Oklahoma	1,876	16.7%	10.6%	10.2%	30.8%	31.6%
		(1.76)	(1.45)	(1.43)	(2.18)	(2.20)
Texas	10,412	18.1%	9.6%	9.0%	29.7%	33.6%
		(0.92)	(0.71)	(0.69)	(1.10)	(1.13)

Table G6b (continued)
Nonelderly Family Income, 1990-92:
Adults Ages 18-64[1,2,4]
(Persons in thousands, standard errors in parentheses)

	Number	Family Income as Percent of Poverty				
		<100%	100-149%	150-199%	200-399%	400% +
East North Central	**25,998**	**14.2%**	**7.2%**	**7.7%**	**33.3%**	**37.6%**
		(0.47)	**(0.35)**	**(0.36)**	**(0.64)**	**(0.65)**
Illinois	7,257	15.4%	6.8%	7.1%	30.7%	40.0%
		(0.89)	(0.62)	(0.64)	(1.14)	(1.21)
Indiana	3,428	12.8%	8.0%	9.1%	38.8%	31.3%
		(1.62)	(1.32)	(1.40)	(2.37)	(2.25)
Michigan	5,706	16.4%	6.6%	7.2%	31.0%	38.8%
		(0.91)	(0.61)	(0.64)	(1.14)	(1.20)
Ohio	6,675	13.1%	7.5%	8.2%	34.4%	36.7%
		(0.82)	(0.64)	(0.67)	(1.15)	(1.17)
Wisconsin	2,933	10.8%	7.5%	7.4%	35.1%	39.1%
		(1.39)	(1.18)	(1.17)	(2.13)	(2.18)
West North Central	**10,790**	**12.5%**	**7.9%**	**9.9%**	**35.7%**	**34.0%**
		(0.71)	**(0.58)**	**(0.64)**	**(1.02)**	**(1.01)**
Iowa	1,707	11.9%	7.6%	10.8%	40.3%	29.3%
		(1.49)	(1.22)	(1.43)	(2.26)	(2.09)
Kansas	1,479	11.7%	7.5%	9.3%	36.4%	35.2%
		(1.48)	(1.21)	(1.33)	(2.22)	(2.20)
Minnesota	2,725	11.7%	7.0%	7.8%	34.1%	39.4%
		(1.53)	(1.22)	(1.28)	(2.27)	(2.34)
Missouri	3,188	14.1%	8.9%	11.2%	31.8%	34.0%
		(1.69)	(1.38)	(1.52)	(2.25)	(2.29)
Nebraska	942	9.9%	7.8%	10.3%	39.9%	32.1%
		(1.36)	(1.22)	(1.38)	(2.23)	(2.12)
North Dakota	357	14.2%	7.2%	10.9%	40.9%	26.8%
		(1.61)	(1.19)	(1.44)	(2.27)	(2.04)
South Dakota	392	15.0%	9.6%	10.2%	41.9%	23.2%
		(1.57)	(1.29)	(1.33)	(2.17)	(1.86)
Mountain	**8,110**	**14.2%**	**8.8%**	**9.2%**	**33.7%**	**34.1%**
		(0.72)	**(0.58)**	**(0.59)**	**(0.97)**	**(0.97)**
Arizona	2,117	14.7%	8.8%	8.3%	32.3%	35.9%
		(1.73)	(1.38)	(1.34)	(2.28)	(2.34)
Colorado	2,027	11.6%	7.9%	7.4%	33.2%	39.9%
		(1.60)	(1.34)	(1.30)	(2.35)	(2.44)
Idaho	600	14.4%	9.7%	10.9%	40.1%	24.9%
		(1.59)	(1.35)	(1.41)	(2.22)	(1.96)
Montana	471	15.9%	9.7%	10.9%	35.6%	27.9%
		(1.72)	(1.39)	(1.47)	(2.25)	(2.11)
Nevada	786	14.0%	7.2%	9.7%	32.6%	36.5%
		(1.62)	(1.20)	(1.38)	(2.19)	(2.25)
New Mexico	904	21.2%	10.9%	10.3%	28.9%	28.7%
		(1.90)	(1.44)	(1.41)	(2.10)	(2.10)
Utah	932	11.5%	9.8%	11.7%	37.5%	29.4%
		(1.55)	(1.44)	(1.55)	(2.35)	(2.21)
Wyoming	273	11.1%	7.9%	8.7%	38.0%	34.2%
		(1.76)	(1.51)	(1.58)	(2.71)	(2.65)
Pacific	**24,642**	**15.7%**	**9.1%**	**7.9%**	**28.6%**	**38.7%**
		(0.55)	**(0.44)**	**(0.41)**	**(0.69)**	**(0.74)**
Alaska	304	14.9%	8.4%	8.9%	29.7%	38.1%
		(1.61)	(1.25)	(1.28)	(2.06)	(2.19)
California	18,827	16.8%	9.8%	8.1%	27.0%	38.3%
		(0.66)	(0.53)	(0.48)	(0.79)	(0.86)
Hawaii	649	11.3%	7.4%	9.1%	34.7%	37.4%
		(1.60)	(1.33)	(1.46)	(2.41)	(2.45)
Oregon	1,807	12.0%	8.5%	9.4%	30.7%	39.4%
		(1.63)	(1.40)	(1.46)	(2.30)	(2.44)
Washington	3,056	12.0%	6.1%	5.6%	35.6%	40.8%
		(1.50)	(1.10)	(1.06)	(2.21)	(2.27)

Source: Three-year merged March CPS: 1991, 1992, and 1993.
Note: See table notes at end of Section G.

Table G7a

Nonelderly Family Income, 1990-92:
Persons in Married Couple with Children Families[1,2,4]

(Persons in thousands, standard errors in parentheses)

	Number	Family Income as Percent of Poverty				
		<100%	100-149%	150-199%	200-399%	400% +
United States	105,670	9.3%	8.4%	9.2%	38.9%	34.2%
		(0.19)	(0.19)	(0.19)	(0.33)	(0.32)
New England	5,387	5.1%	4.8%	6.5%	40.2%	43.4%
		(0.52)	(0.50)	(0.58)	(1.15)	(1.16)
Connecticut	1,392	2.8%	3.4%	3.7%	39.3%	50.7%
		(1.06)	(1.16)	(1.21)	(3.13)	(3.20)
Maine	559	9.3%	8.7%	10.3%	42.4%	29.2%
		(1.63)	(1.58)	(1.71)	(2.77)	(2.55)
Massachusetts	2,291	5.8%	4.3%	5.6%	37.9%	46.5%
		(0.74)	(0.64)	(0.73)	(1.55)	(1.59)
New Hampshire	526	2.9%	6.2%	8.3%	43.7%	38.9%
		(1.02)	(1.46)	(1.68)	(3.02)	(2.97)
Rhode Island	342	6.2%	3.8%	12.1%	43.1%	34.8%
		(1.68)	(1.34)	(2.27)	(3.45)	(3.32)
Vermont	276	5.4%	6.6%	9.0%	49.5%	29.4%
		(1.33)	(1.46)	(1.68)	(2.93)	(2.67)
Middle Atlantic	15,585	7.2%	6.4%	8.4%	38.9%	39.2%
		(0.40)	(0.38)	(0.43)	(0.76)	(0.76)
New Jersey	3,287	4.0%	4.0%	6.0%	33.2%	52.8%
		(0.58)	(0.58)	(0.71)	(1.40)	(1.48)
New York	7,207	9.2%	7.4%	9.4%	36.3%	37.7%
		(0.66)	(0.60)	(0.67)	(1.10)	(1.11)
Pennsylvania	5,091	6.3%	6.4%	8.6%	46.2%	32.5%
		(0.70)	(0.71)	(0.81)	(1.44)	(1.36)
South Atlantic	16,829	8.7%	8.5%	9.3%	38.1%	35.4%
		(0.49)	(0.48)	(0.50)	(0.84)	(0.83)
Delaware	281	2.8%	5.1%	9.0%	39.4%	43.7%
		(1.04)	(1.37)	(1.78)	(3.05)	(3.09)
District of Columbia	105	15.4%	12.5%	4.0%	31.6%	36.5%
		(3.68)	(3.37)	(2.00)	(4.74)	(4.91)
Florida	4,563	10.9%	9.8%	9.2%	40.0%	30.1%
		(0.95)	(0.91)	(0.89)	(1.50)	(1.40)
Georgia	2,611	9.4%	10.0%	9.8%	32.9%	37.9%
		(1.66)	(1.71)	(1.69)	(2.67)	(2.76)
Maryland	1,755	4.0%	4.3%	7.3%	33.1%	51.2%
		(1.26)	(1.30)	(1.67)	(3.02)	(3.21)
North Carolina	2,623	7.9%	7.7%	9.8%	41.4%	33.2%
		(0.80)	(0.79)	(0.89)	(1.47)	(1.40)
South Carolina	1,517	8.5%	9.4%	12.0%	41.4%	28.6%
		(1.41)	(1.47)	(1.64)	(2.48)	(2.28)
Virginia	2,576	6.8%	6.3%	7.8%	37.5%	41.6%
		(1.27)	(1.23)	(1.36)	(2.45)	(2.49)
West Virginia	797	15.2%	13.1%	10.9%	40.1%	20.8%
		(2.00)	(1.88)	(1.73)	(2.73)	(2.26)
East South Central	6,269	9.8%	10.9%	11.0%	42.6%	25.8%
		(0.86)	(0.89)	(0.90)	(1.42)	(1.26)
Alabama	1,655	7.6%	11.3%	10.7%	43.8%	26.6%
		(1.52)	(1.82)	(1.78)	(2.85)	(2.54)
Kentucky	1,553	12.9%	8.6%	7.8%	40.1%	30.6%
		(1.91)	(1.59)	(1.53)	(2.79)	(2.63)
Mississippi	1,165	13.2%	14.1%	10.1%	43.1%	19.6%
		(1.75)	(1.81)	(1.56)	(2.57)	(2.06)
Tennessee	1,896	7.2%	10.4%	14.3%	43.2%	24.9%
		(1.47)	(1.73)	(1.98)	(2.81)	(2.45)
West South Central	12,070	13.3%	10.5%	9.5%	36.7%	30.0%
		(0.73)	(0.66)	(0.63)	(1.03)	(0.98)
Arkansas	1,090	11.1%	13.3%	12.3%	41.5%	21.8%
		(1.68)	(1.82)	(1.76)	(2.64)	(2.22)
Louisiana	1,740	10.2%	9.5%	6.2%	43.6%	30.5%
		(1.80)	(1.74)	(1.43)	(2.94)	(2.73)
Oklahoma	1,441	12.1%	11.5%	12.7%	36.1%	27.7%
		(1.75)	(1.72)	(1.79)	(2.59)	(2.41)
Texas	7,800	14.5%	10.1%	9.2%	34.6%	31.5%
		(0.98)	(0.84)	(0.80)	(1.32)	(1.29)

Table G7a (continued)
Nonelderly Family Income, 1990-92:
Persons in Married Couple with Children Families[1,2,4]

(Persons in thousands, standard errors in parentheses)

	Number	Family Income as Percent of Poverty				
		<100%	100-149%	150-199%	200-399%	400% +
East North Central	**18,208**	**7.5%**	**7.0%**	**8.6%**	**41.9%**	**34.9%**
		(0.43)	**(0.41)**	**(0.45)**	**(0.80)**	**(0.77)**
Illinois	4,842	7.4%	7.0%	7.7%	40.6%	37.3%
		(0.79)	(0.77)	(0.80)	(1.48)	(1.46)
Indiana	2,262	5.9%	9.8%	11.0%	43.9%	29.5%
		(1.41)	(1.77)	(1.87)	(2.97)	(2.72)
Michigan	3,933	9.5%	5.7%	8.0%	40.3%	36.5%
		(0.87)	(0.69)	(0.80)	(1.46)	(1.43)
Ohio	4,939	7.6%	7.1%	9.8%	43.5%	32.1%
		(0.75)	(0.73)	(0.84)	(1.40)	(1.32)
Wisconsin	2,232	6.0%	6.4%	7.0%	41.9%	38.8%
		(1.21)	(1.25)	(1.30)	(2.52)	(2.49)
West North Central	**8,095**	**7.8%**	**8.3%**	**10.8%**	**42.9%**	**30.2%**
		(0.66)	**(0.68)**	**(0.77)**	**(1.22)**	**(1.13)**
Iowa	1,370	6.5%	7.9%	13.8%	47.3%	24.6%
		(1.26)	(1.38)	(1.77)	(2.56)	(2.21)
Kansas	1,204	6.3%	7.5%	11.2%	43.2%	31.8%
		(1.24)	(1.34)	(1.61)	(2.53)	(2.38)
Minnesota	1,855	7.2%	8.0%	8.5%	40.7%	35.6%
		(1.50)	(1.57)	(1.62)	(2.85)	(2.77)
Missouri	2,245	9.8%	10.1%	10.2%	38.8%	31.1%
		(1.71)	(1.74)	(1.75)	(2.81)	(2.67)
Nebraska	798	6.7%	6.5%	11.7%	46.4%	28.8%
		(1.24)	(1.22)	(1.59)	(2.46)	(2.24)
North Dakota	311	10.0%	6.4%	12.0%	47.9%	23.8%
		(1.48)	(1.21)	(1.61)	(2.47)	(2.10)
South Dakota	313	9.6%	9.4%	11.0%	50.8%	19.2%
		(1.45)	(1.44)	(1.54)	(2.46)	(1.94)
Mountain	**6,268**	**10.3%**	**9.8%**	**11.9%**	**40.2%**	**27.8%**
		(0.71)	**(0.69)**	**(0.75)**	**(1.14)**	**(1.05)**
Arizona	1,413	11.5%	10.4%	11.7%	37.1%	29.3%
		(1.90)	(1.82)	(1.92)	(2.88)	(2.72)
Colorado	1,461	7.7%	8.7%	9.4%	38.7%	35.4%
		(1.57)	(1.66)	(1.71)	(2.86)	(2.81)
Idaho	556	12.1%	9.7%	14.4%	47.6%	16.2%
		(1.54)	(1.40)	(1.66)	(2.35)	(1.73)
Montana	393	12.8%	10.5%	13.4%	42.9%	20.4%
		(1.72)	(1.58)	(1.75)	(2.55)	(2.08)
Nevada	493	8.5%	7.5%	10.1%	39.9%	34.0%
		(1.64)	(1.55)	(1.77)	(2.88)	(2.79)
New Mexico	670	17.5%	10.4%	12.4%	34.9%	24.9%
		(2.05)	(1.64)	(1.78)	(2.57)	(2.33)
Utah	1,042	7.7%	11.3%	14.7%	42.5%	23.8%
		(1.22)	(1.45)	(1.62)	(2.26)	(1.95)
Wyoming	240	6.4%	8.5%	9.5%	50.9%	24.8%
		(1.46)	(1.66)	(1.75)	(2.98)	(2.57)
Pacific	**16,959**	**12.4%**	**9.9%**	**8.4%**	**34.1%**	**35.3%**
		(0.60)	**(0.55)**	**(0.51)**	**(0.87)**	**(0.88)**
Alaska	219	10.0%	7.3%	10.1%	37.8%	34.8%
		(1.59)	(1.38)	(1.60)	(2.58)	(2.53)
California	12,937	13.9%	11.1%	8.6%	31.8%	34.5%
		(0.74)	(0.67)	(0.60)	(1.00)	(1.02)
Hawaii	405	9.8%	5.5%	10.4%	37.3%	37.1%
		(1.90)	(1.46)	(1.96)	(3.10)	(3.10)
Oregon	1,298	6.7%	10.2%	10.2%	41.1%	31.8%
		(1.48)	(1.79)	(1.78)	(2.90)	(2.75)
Washington	2,101	7.2%	3.8%	4.9%	42.5%	41.5%
		(1.44)	(1.07)	(1.20)	(2.75)	(2.74)

Source: Three-year merged March CPS: 1991, 1992, and 1993.
Note: See table notes at end of Section G.

Table G7b
Nonelderly Family Income, 1990-92:
Persons in Married Couple without Children Families[1,2,4]

(Persons in thousands, standard errors in parentheses)

	Number	Family Income as Percent of Poverty				
		<100%	100-149%	150-199%	200-399%	400% +
United States	**37,122**	5.5%	4.5%	5.4%	26.7%	57.8%
		(0.26)	(0.24)	(0.26)	(0.50)	(0.56)
New England	**1,920**	**2.5%**	**2.7%**	**4.1%**	**23.0%**	**67.8%**
		(0.62)	**(0.64)**	**(0.78)**	**(1.65)**	**(1.84)**
Connecticut	468	1.4%	1.2%	3.7%	18.6%	75.1%
		(1.31)	(1.21)	(2.09)	(4.29)	(4.78)
Maine	192	3.5%	5.6%	5.8%	32.3%	52.8%
		(1.75)	(2.19)	(2.24)	(4.47)	(4.77)
Massachusetts	846	2.9%	3.0%	2.9%	22.0%	69.3%
		(0.88)	(0.89)	(0.87)	(2.17)	(2.42)
New Hampshire	179	2.7%	2.1%	5.7%	22.6%	66.9%
		(1.70)	(1.48)	(2.42)	(4.36)	(4.91)
Rhode Island	155	1.7%	3.1%	5.7%	28.4%	61.2%
		(1.32)	(1.79)	(2.39)	(4.66)	(5.04)
Vermont	80	3.8%	2.6%	7.6%	26.2%	59.7%
		(2.09)	(1.74)	(2.89)	(4.79)	(5.34)
Middle Atlantic	**5,386**	**4.8%**	**3.5%**	**4.4%**	**25.3%**	**62.0%**
		(0.57)	**(0.48)**	**(0.54)**	**(1.15)**	**(1.28)**
New Jersey	1,126	4.4%	2.3%	5.0%	18.4%	70.0%
		(1.03)	(0.76)	(1.11)	(1.96)	(2.32)
New York	2,415	5.4%	3.6%	4.1%	23.2%	63.8%
		(0.89)	(0.74)	(0.79)	(1.67)	(1.91)
Pennsylvania	1,845	4.4%	4.0%	4.4%	32.2%	54.9%
		(0.99)	(0.95)	(0.99)	(2.25)	(2.40)
South Atlantic	**6,897**	**5.6%**	**4.4%**	**6.3%**	**27.7%**	**56.1%**
		(0.62)	**(0.55)**	**(0.66)**	**(1.21)**	**(1.34)**
Delaware	97	1.1%	2.5%	2.9%	24.5%	68.9%
		(1.10)	(1.66)	(1.78)	(4.56)	(4.90)
District of Columbia	55	6.9%	2.5%	4.9%	24.0%	61.8%
		(3.57)	(2.18)	(3.03)	(6.02)	(6.85)
Florida	2,177	6.4%	5.0%	7.4%	29.8%	51.4%
		(1.08)	(0.97)	(1.16)	(2.03)	(2.21)
Georgia	937	5.0%	4.7%	5.9%	26.6%	57.9%
		(2.06)	(2.01)	(2.24)	(4.20)	(4.69)
Maryland	765	2.3%	1.5%	4.2%	20.9%	71.1%
		(1.45)	(1.18)	(1.96)	(3.95)	(4.40)
North Carolina	1,066	6.7%	4.4%	6.8%	29.9%	52.1%
		(1.17)	(0.96)	(1.18)	(2.14)	(2.33)
South Carolina	530	5.9%	6.3%	6.3%	26.9%	54.6%
		(2.00)	(2.08)	(2.07)	(3.78)	(4.24)
Virginia	995	4.9%	2.7%	5.2%	24.5%	62.6%
		(1.76)	(1.33)	(1.81)	(3.50)	(3.94)
West Virginia	275	8.8%	9.6%	8.2%	40.3%	33.1%
		(2.68)	(2.80)	(2.61)	(4.65)	(4.46)
East South Central	**2,392**	**7.6%**	**8.3%**	**6.8%**	**34.0%**	**43.4%**
		(1.23)	**(1.28)**	**(1.17)**	**(2.20)**	**(2.31)**
Alabama	697	7.9%	9.5%	7.8%	33.9%	40.9%
		(2.39)	(2.59)	(2.38)	(4.19)	(4.35)
Kentucky	595	7.8%	7.6%	7.0%	32.4%	45.2%
		(2.47)	(2.43)	(2.35)	(4.30)	(4.58)
Mississippi	297	9.1%	11.3%	9.5%	30.3%	39.7%
		(2.96)	(3.25)	(3.02)	(4.72)	(5.02)
Tennessee	803	6.5%	6.6%	4.6%	36.7%	45.6%
		(2.14)	(2.16)	(1.82)	(4.19)	(4.34)
West South Central	**3,847**	**7.9%**	**6.7%**	**6.9%**	**28.1%**	**50.3%**
		(1.03)	**(0.95)**	**(0.96)**	**(1.70)**	**(1.90)**
Arkansas	368	8.6%	6.7%	8.2%	39.3%	37.2%
		(2.59)	(2.31)	(2.53)	(4.51)	(4.46)
Louisiana	562	8.9%	6.2%	9.4%	29.4%	46.1%
		(2.98)	(2.51)	(3.04)	(4.76)	(5.20)
Oklahoma	504	7.1%	5.9%	6.2%	30.1%	50.7%
		(2.34)	(2.15)	(2.20)	(4.18)	(4.55)
Texas	2,413	7.8%	7.0%	6.3%	25.7%	53.2%
		(1.33)	(1.27)	(1.21)	(2.18)	(2.49)

Nonelderly Family Income, 1990-92:
Persons in Married Couple without Children Families[1,2,4]

(Persons in thousands, standard errors in parentheses)

	Number	Family Income as Percent of Poverty				
		<100%	100-149%	150-199%	200-399%	400% +
East North Central	**6,251**	**4.0%**	**4.0%**	**4.5%**	**26.0%**	**61.5%**
		(0.54)	**(0.54)**	**(0.57)**	**(1.21)**	**(1.34)**
Illinois	1,723	3.9%	3.5%	3.8%	23.9%	65.0%
		(0.98)	(0.93)	(0.97)	(2.16)	(2.42)
Indiana	883	1.7%	5.6%	5.3%	35.9%	51.4%
		(1.24)	(2.20)	(2.15)	(4.59)	(4.78)
Michigan	1,321	3.7%	3.7%	4.8%	23.2%	64.6%
		(0.97)	(0.97)	(1.09)	(2.16)	(2.45)
Ohio	1,653	5.6%	3.8%	4.3%	24.5%	61.8%
		(1.13)	(0.93)	(0.99)	(2.10)	(2.37)
Wisconsin	671	3.4%	4.5%	4.9%	27.9%	59.3%
		(1.69)	(1.94)	(2.01)	(4.18)	(4.58)
West North Central	**2,674**	**3.9%**	**4.4%**	**6.3%**	**28.5%**	**56.9%**
		(0.83)	**(0.88)**	**(1.05)**	**(1.94)**	**(2.13)**
Iowa	397	4.4%	5.5%	7.5%	29.2%	53.3%
		(1.96)	(2.17)	(2.52)	(4.34)	(4.76)
Kansas	340	4.8%	3.4%	3.7%	27.4%	60.7%
		(2.04)	(1.74)	(1.82)	(4.29)	(4.69)
Minnesota	662	2.1%	1.6%	3.8%	24.2%	68.3%
		(1.39)	(1.23)	(1.85)	(4.15)	(4.51)
Missouri	860	4.1%	6.1%	8.7%	27.8%	53.4%
		(1.85)	(2.22)	(2.62)	(4.17)	(4.64)
Nebraska	245	4.2%	4.5%	5.6%	37.9%	47.9%
		(1.78)	(1.85)	(2.04)	(4.33)	(4.46)
North Dakota	78	7.7%	4.5%	8.3%	35.1%	44.3%
		(2.63)	(2.05)	(2.73)	(4.71)	(4.90)
South Dakota	92	5.8%	8.4%	7.5%	35.4%	42.9%
		(2.12)	(2.51)	(2.40)	(4.34)	(4.50)
Mountain	**2,045**	**5.7%**	**4.7%**	**5.6%**	**28.8%**	**55.3%**
		(0.95)	**(0.86)**	**(0.94)**	**(1.85)**	**(2.03)**
Arizona	596	7.4%	5.0%	4.0%	26.3%	57.2%
		(2.41)	(2.00)	(1.81)	(4.05)	(4.55)
Colorado	501	2.8%	4.6%	5.3%	27.5%	59.8%
		(1.66)	(2.09)	(2.24)	(4.48)	(4.92)
Idaho	154	5.4%	4.3%	7.1%	37.4%	45.9%
		(2.02)	(1.81)	(2.30)	(4.33)	(4.46)
Montana	114	7.5%	4.2%	5.4%	31.3%	51.6%
		(2.53)	(1.92)	(2.17)	(4.45)	(4.79)
Nevada	196	6.5%	2.7%	7.0%	24.2%	59.5%
		(2.31)	(1.53)	(2.39)	(4.00)	(4.59)
New Mexico	213	7.4%	6.5%	6.8%	27.4%	51.9%
		(2.51)	(2.36)	(2.41)	(4.27)	(4.78)
Utah	204	4.7%	4.4%	8.1%	36.3%	46.6%
		(2.20)	(2.11)	(2.82)	(4.98)	(5.17)
Wyoming	68	4.1%	4.7%	4.0%	31.2%	56.0%
		(2.22)	(2.37)	(2.20)	(5.19)	(5.56)
Pacific	**5,710**	**6.8%**	**3.8%**	**4.9%**	**23.2%**	**61.2%**
		(0.80)	**(0.61)**	**(0.69)**	**(1.34)**	**(1.54)**
Alaska	66	6.4%	4.9%	5.6%	20.9%	62.2%
		(2.36)	(2.09)	(2.23)	(3.93)	(4.69)
California	4,253	7.7%	4.2%	5.4%	21.5%	61.2%
		(0.99)	(0.75)	(0.85)	(1.54)	(1.82)
Hawaii	164	3.6%	2.9%	5.6%	28.1%	59.8%
		(1.87)	(1.70)	(2.32)	(4.52)	(4.93)
Oregon	474	3.8%	2.6%	4.6%	24.2%	64.7%
		(1.88)	(1.55)	(2.05)	(4.18)	(4.66)
Washington	752	4.4%	2.8%	2.2%	31.5%	59.0%
		(1.91)	(1.55)	(1.37)	(4.32)	(4.57)

Source: Three-year merged March CPS: 1991, 1992, and 1993.
Note: See table notes at end of Section G.

Table G7c
Nonelderly Family Income, 1990-92:
Persons in Single-Parent Families[1,2,4]
(Persons in thousands, standard errors in parentheses)

	Number	Family Income as Percent of Poverty				
		<100%	100-149%	150-199%	200-399%	400% +
United States	**29,398**	**49.6%**	**12.8%**		**20.4%**	**7.1%**
		(0.64)	**(0.42)**	**(0.38)**	**(0.51)**	(0.33)
New England	**1,344**	**45.3%**	**11.8%**	**10.1%**	**23.9%**	**8.9%**
		(2.34)	**(1.52)**	**(1.42)**	**(2.01)**	**(1.34)**
Connecticut	346	38.6%	8.9%	13.7%	22.0%	16.7%
		(6.25)	(3.66)	(4.42)	(5.32)	(4.79)
Maine	146	47.2%	14.6%	15.2%	20.3%	2.6%
		(5.47)	(3.87)	(3.93)	(4.41)	(1.75)
Massachusetts	616	48.3%	12.4%	7.4%	24.6%	7.4%
		(3.07)	(2.03)	(1.61)	(2.65)	(1.60)
New Hampshire	93	46.2%	13.0%	8.9%	25.0%	6.9%
		(7.23)	(4.87)	(4.13)	(6.28)	(3.67)
Rhode Island	90	46.8%	11.6%	7.3%	32.7%	1.6%
		(6.76)	(4.35)	(3.53)	(6.36)	(1.68)
Vermont	53	44.0%	13.6%	10.6%	21.3%	10.5%
		(6.67)	(4.61)	(4.13)	(5.51)	(4.13)
Middle Atlantic	**4,287**	**48.4%**	**13.1%**	**9.6%**	**20.9%**	**7.9%**
		(1.48)	**(1.00)**	**(0.87)**	**(1.21)**	**(0.80)**
New Jersey	803	45.1%	11.0%	11.1%	24.2%	8.7%
		(2.99)	(1.88)	(1.89)	(2.57)	(1.69)
New York	2,269	50.8%	13.6%	8.2%	20.0%	7.3%
		(2.05)	(1.40)	(1.13)	(1.64)	(1.07)
Pennsylvania	1,215	46.1%	13.7%	11.2%	20.4%	8.6%
		(2.96)	(2.04)	(1.87)	(2.39)	(1.66)
South Atlantic	**5,393**	**50.8%**	**13.0%**	**10.3%**	**20.2%**	**5.7%**
		(1.53)	**(1.03)**	**(0.93)**	**(1.23)**	**(0.71)**
Delaware	95	35.2%	20.3%	17.5%	21.1%	5.9%
		(5.13)	(4.32)	(4.08)	(4.38)	(2.52)
District of Columbia	121	48.8%	13.8%	11.0%	18.9%	7.5%
		(4.75)	(3.28)	(2.98)	(3.72)	(2.50)
Florida	1,702	51.0%	12.9%	8.5%	22.8%	4.8%
		(2.51)	(1.68)	(1.40)	(2.10)	(1.07)
Georgia	835	57.1%	12.3%	8.7%	17.4%	4.4%
		(4.98)	(3.31)	(2.83)	(3.82)	(2.07)
Maryland	596	50.6%	13.0%	7.0%	20.8%	8.6%
		(5.50)	(3.70)	(2.81)	(4.47)	(3.09)
North Carolina	743	49.0%	13.1%	13.7%	19.2%	5.0%
		(2.80)	(1.89)	(1.92)	(2.21)	(1.23)
South Carolina	465	56.9%	13.1%	8.3%	15.2%	6.5%
		(4.50)	(3.07)	(2.51)	(3.26)	(2.24)
Virginia	657	40.1%	12.5%	16.9%	23.1%	7.5%
		(4.92)	(3.31)	(3.76)	(4.22)	(2.64)
West Virginia	180	59.6%	13.0%	9.3%	14.3%	3.8%
		(5.76)	(3.95)	(3.40)	(4.10)	(2.25)
East South Central	**2,182**	**57.3%**	**14.8%**	**8.5%**	**14.7%**	**4.7%**
		(2.41)	**(1.73)**	**(1.36)**	**(1.73)**	**(1.03)**
Alabama	545	57.0%	14.6%	7.9%	16.8%	3.8%
		(4.96)	(3.53)	(2.70)	(3.74)	(1.92)
Kentucky	435	55.7%	15.8%	9.4%	13.9%	5.3%
		(5.34)	(3.92)	(3.14)	(3.72)	(2.41)
Mississippi	468	61.3%	14.4%	9.4%	11.7%	3.2%
		(3.99)	(2.88)	(2.39)	(2.63)	(1.44)
Tennessee	735	56.0%	14.7%	7.8%	15.6%	5.8%
		(4.52)	(3.23)	(2.44)	(3.31)	(2.13)
West South Central	**3,240**	**55.3%**	**13.4%**	**10.1%**	**15.9%**	**5.3%**
		(2.05)	**(1.41)**	**(1.24)**	**(1.51)**	**(0.93)**
Arkansas	259	56.9%	13.5%	3.9%	22.3%	3.4%
		(5.45)	(3.76)	(2.13)	(4.58)	(1.98)
Louisiana	692	67.7%	10.4%	8.8%	10.5%	2.6%
		(4.40)	(2.87)	(2.66)	(2.89)	(1.49)
Oklahoma	309	45.0%	20.9%	10.7%	19.5%	3.8%
		(5.79)	(4.74)	(3.60)	(4.61)	(2.23)
Texas	1,980	52.4%	13.2%	11.3%	16.4%	6.8%
		(2.75)	(1.86)	(1.74)	(2.04)	(1.38)

Table G7c (continued)
Nonelderly Family Income, 1990-92:
Persons in Single-Parent Families[1,2,4]
(Persons in thousands, standard errors in parentheses)

	Number	Family Income as Percent of Poverty				
		<100%	100-149%	150-199%	200-399%	400% +
East North Central	**5,301**	**48.4%**	**11.7%**		**23.1%**	**6.7%**
		(1.49)	**(0.96)**	**(0.90)**	**(1.26)**	**(0.75)**
Illinois	1,571	53.4%	9.4%	10.5%	19.6%	7.0%
		(2.65)	(1.54)	(1.63)	(2.11)	(1.36)
Indiana	793	43.0%	14.0%	13.9%	24.6%	4.5%
		(5.00)	(3.50)	(3.49)	(4.35)	(2.09)
Michigan	1,169	52.9%	9.6%	8.5%	21.0%	8.0%
		(2.72)	(1.60)	(1.52)	(2.22)	(1.48)
Ohio	1,188	48.6%	13.7%	7.5%	24.1%	6.0%
		(2.88)	(1.98)	(1.52)	(2.46)	(1.37)
Wisconsin	580	32.5%	14.9%	12.3%	32.5%	7.8%
		(4.70)	(3.58)	(3.30)	(4.70)	(2.69)
West North Central	**1,825**	**45.8%**	**13.1%**	**14.0%**	**21.6%**	**5.6%**
		(2.59)	**(1.75)**	**(1.80)**	**(2.14)**	**(1.19)**
Iowa	231	45.2%	12.2%	12.4%	26.6%	3.6%
		(6.23)	(4.10)	(4.12)	(5.53)	(2.33)
Kansas	272	42.8%	12.2%	11.1%	27.5%	6.5%
		(5.31)	(3.52)	(3.37)	(4.79)	(2.64)
Minnesota	468	45.0%	11.6%	11.3%	25.5%	6.7%
		(5.74)	(3.70)	(3.65)	(5.03)	(2.88)
Missouri	608	48.4%	14.2%	18.3%	14.0%	5.1%
		(5.54)	(3.87)	(4.29)	(3.85)	(2.44)
Nebraska	137	44.3%	13.5%	11.7%	23.0%	7.6%
		(5.93)	(4.08)	(3.84)	(5.02)	(3.16)
North Dakota	43	46.9%	14.9%	14.0%	19.9%	4.4%
		(6.64)	(4.74)	(4.61)	(5.31)	(2.73)
South Dakota	67	44.2%	17.4%	16.1%	19.6%	2.7%
		(5.27)	(4.03)	(3.90)	(4.21)	(1.71)
Mountain	**1,424**	**43.8%**	**12.1%**	**11.6%**	**25.0%**	**7.5%**
		(2.43)	**(1.59)**	**(1.57)**	**(2.12)**	**(1.29)**
Arizona	376	42.5%	11.0%	13.7%	26.6%	6.1%
		(5.72)	(3.62)	(3.98)	(5.11)	(2.77)
Colorado	338	45.7%	8.5%	8.0%	25.5%	12.3%
		(6.08)	(3.40)	(3.31)	(5.32)	(4.01)
Idaho	88	42.4%	17.7%	12.2%	22.1%	5.6%
		(5.85)	(4.51)	(3.87)	(4.91)	(2.73)
Montana	85	42.6%	18.3%	14.2%	23.7%	1.1%
		(5.49)	(4.29)	(3.87)	(4.72)	(1.18)
Nevada	156	34.4%	15.2%	12.9%	28.3%	9.3%
		(4.97)	(3.75)	(3.50)	(4.71)	(3.03)
New Mexico	194	54.5%	13.9%	9.2%	18.9%	3.4%
		(4.99)	(3.47)	(2.89)	(3.92)	(1.83)
Utah	137	41.9%	9.0%	14.0%	28.4%	6.6%
		(6.22)	(3.61)	(4.38)	(5.69)	(3.14)
Wyoming	48	37.4%	15.6%	14.5%	20.1%	12.3%
		(6.43)	(4.82)	(4.69)	(5.33)	(4.37)
Pacific	**4,402**	**47.5%**	**12.9%**	**8.6%**	**20.2%**	**10.8%**
		(1.80)	**(1.21)**	**(1.01)**	**(1.45)**	**(1.12)**
Alaska	69	38.8%	17.7%	10.2%	25.5%	7.8%
		(4.60)	(3.60)	(2.86)	(4.11)	(2.53)
California	3,439	49.6%	12.4%	8.1%	19.0%	11.0%
		(2.08)	(1.37)	(1.13)	(1.63)	(1.30)
Hawaii	108	48.1%	13.4%	5.6%	25.4%	7.5%
		(6.20)	(4.22)	(2.85)	(5.40)	(3.26)
Oregon	305	44.1%	13.8%	15.1%	16.8%	10.1%
		(6.04)	(4.19)	(4.36)	(4.55)	(3.67)
Washington	481	35.5%	14.9%	9.2%	29.2%	11.3%
		(5.57)	(4.14)	(3.35)	(5.28)	(3.68)

Source: Three-year merged March CPS: 1991, 1992, and 1993.
Note: See table notes at end of Section G.

Table G7d
Nonelderly Family Income, 1990-92:
Single Persons[1,2,4]

(Persons in thousands, standard errors in parentheses)

	Number	Family Income as Percent of Poverty				
		<100%	100-149%	150-199%	200-399%	400% +
United States	**46,395**	28.1%	10.6%	10.0%	29.1%	22.2%
		(0.45)	(0.31)	(0.30)	(0.46)	(0.42)
New England	**2,635**	19.6%	9.9%	8.6%	33.1%	28.9%
		(1.33)	(1.00)	(0.94)	(1.58)	(1.52)
Connecticut	614	13.2%	10.0%	8.6%	35.6%	32.6%
		(3.26)	(2.89)	(2.70)	(4.61)	(4.52)
Maine	204	24.7%	12.0%	11.6%	35.5%	16.3%
		(4.00)	(3.01)	(2.97)	(4.44)	(3.43)
Massachusetts	1,272	21.1%	9.0%	7.6%	31.4%	30.9%
		(1.74)	(1.22)	(1.13)	(1.99)	(1.98)
New Hampshire	218	20.5%	9.8%	7.9%	33.5%	28.4%
		(3.82)	(2.81)	(2.55)	(4.46)	(4.26)
Rhode Island	217	23.0%	12.1%	10.3%	31.0%	23.6%
		(3.68)	(2.86)	(2.66)	(4.05)	(3.71)
Vermont	109	19.8%	11.3%	12.7%	36.9%	19.3%
		(3.71)	(2.95)	(3.10)	(4.50)	(3.68)
Middle Atlantic	**7,243**	27.3%	9.3%	9.3%	29.2%	24.9%
		(1.02)	(0.66)	(0.66)	(1.04)	(0.99)
New Jersey	1,536	23.3%	7.3%	9.3%	30.7%	29.3%
		(1.84)	(1.13)	(1.26)	(2.00)	(1.98)
New York	3,589	28.6%	9.3%	8.3%	27.3%	26.5%
		(1.47)	(0.95)	(0.90)	(1.45)	(1.44)
Pennsylvania	2,119	28.1%	10.6%	11.1%	31.3%	18.9%
		(2.02)	(1.38)	(1.41)	(2.08)	(1.76)
South Atlantic	**8,443**	30.1%	10.6%	10.5%	29.0%	19.9%
		(1.12)	(0.75)	(0.75)	(1.11)	(0.97)
Delaware	150	20.1%	9.1%	12.7%	32.7%	25.4%
		(3.42)	(2.45)	(2.84)	(4.00)	(3.71)
District of Columbia	196	25.9%	7.1%	8.6%	26.5%	31.9%
		(3.27)	(1.91)	(2.09)	(3.29)	(3.48)
Florida	2,553	28.9%	11.6%	11.7%	29.0%	18.8%
		(1.86)	(1.31)	(1.31)	(1.86)	(1.60)
Georgia	1,230	33.6%	12.1%	9.0%	26.3%	19.0%
		(3.92)	(2.70)	(2.37)	(3.65)	(3.25)
Maryland	1,024	22.5%	7.1%	9.0%	34.1%	27.2%
		(3.51)	(2.16)	(2.41)	(3.98)	(3.74)
North Carolina	1,208	29.9%	11.3%	11.7%	30.9%	16.1%
		(2.01)	(1.39)	(1.41)	(2.03)	(1.61)
South Carolina	610	40.3%	13.1%	10.3%	25.3%	11.0%
		(3.89)	(2.68)	(2.41)	(3.45)	(2.49)
Virginia	1,200	29.5%	8.6%	10.0%	27.8%	24.1%
		(3.38)	(2.08)	(2.23)	(3.32)	(3.17)
West Virginia	272	41.9%	10.1%	10.1%	25.9%	12.0%
		(4.70)	(2.88)	(2.87)	(4.17)	(3.09)
East South Central	**2,543**	39.4%	11.6%	10.8%	25.8%	12.5%
		(2.20)	(1.44)	(1.40)	(1.97)	(1.49)
Alabama	703	42.4%	10.5%	12.9%	23.1%	11.1%
		(4.36)	(2.70)	(2.95)	(3.72)	(2.77)
Kentucky	549	34.8%	14.0%	10.9%	23.3%	17.0%
		(4.56)	(3.33)	(2.98)	(4.05)	(3.60)
Mississippi	421	45.6%	11.7%	11.0%	22.3%	9.4%
		(4.30)	(2.78)	(2.70)	(3.59)	(2.52)
Tennessee	870	36.8%	10.8%	8.9%	31.2%	12.2%
		(4.03)	(2.60)	(2.38)	(3.87)	(2.74)
West South Central	**4,473**	33.1%	11.2%	11.2%	26.1%	18.4%
		(1.65)	(1.11)	(1.11)	(1.54)	(1.36)
Arkansas	351	36.1%	11.5%	14.8%	26.7%	10.9%
		(4.54)	(3.02)	(3.35)	(4.18)	(2.94)
Louisiana	685	40.6%	12.6%	12.5%	20.0%	14.3%
		(4.64)	(3.14)	(3.13)	(3.78)	(3.31)
Oklahoma	466	36.8%	12.7%	12.7%	22.8%	15.0%
		(4.57)	(3.15)	(3.15)	(3.98)	(3.38)
Texas	2,971	30.4%	10.7%	10.3%	27.9%	20.7%
		(2.07)	(1.39)	(1.36)	(2.01)	(1.82)

Table G7d (continued)
Noneelderly Family Income, 1990-92:
Single Persons[1,2,4]

(Persons in thousands, standard errors in parentheses)

	Number	Family Income as Percent of Poverty				
		<100%	100-149%	150-199%	200-399%	400% +
East North Central	**7,625**	**28.0%**	**9.4%**	**9.9%**	**30.1%**	**22.6%**
		(1.12)	**(0.73)**	**(0.74)**	**(1.14)**	**(1.04)**
Illinois	2,283	30.1%	8.9%	9.1%	27.5%	24.5%
		(2.02)	(1.25)	(1.27)	(1.96)	(1.89)
Indiana	920	26.5%	7.1%	10.4%	36.8%	19.2%
		(4.14)	(2.40)	(2.86)	(4.52)	(3.69)
Michigan	1,746	31.4%	9.5%	8.5%	27.1%	23.5%
		(2.07)	(1.30)	(1.24)	(1.98)	(1.89)
Ohio	1,848	24.8%	10.7%	11.9%	32.1%	20.5%
		(2.00)	(1.43)	(1.49)	(2.16)	(1.87)
Wisconsin	828	24.3%	10.6%	9.7%	31.9%	23.6%
		(3.60)	(2.58)	(2.48)	(3.92)	(3.57)
West North Central	**2,982**	**24.6%**	**10.6%**	**11.9%**	**34.5%**	**18.4%**
		(1.75)	**(1.25)**	**(1.31)**	**(1.93)**	**(1.58)**
Iowa	463	24.3%	9.8%	11.6%	39.5%	14.8%
		(3.79)	(2.62)	(2.83)	(4.32)	(3.14)
Kansas	390	24.0%	11.7%	11.8%	34.0%	18.4%
		(3.83)	(2.89)	(2.90)	(4.25)	(3.48)
Minnesota	860	21.4%	10.6%	10.1%	36.5%	21.3%
		(3.49)	(2.62)	(2.57)	(4.10)	(3.48)
Missouri	855	27.5%	9.6%	13.3%	30.3%	19.3%
		(4.17)	(2.75)	(3.17)	(4.29)	(3.68)
Nebraska	212	22.1%	14.0%	13.9%	33.6%	16.5%
		(3.98)	(3.32)	(3.31)	(4.53)	(3.56)
North Dakota	92	27.5%	10.8%	12.8%	35.3%	13.6%
		(4.06)	(2.82)	(3.04)	(4.35)	(3.12)
South Dakota	112	32.8%	10.8%	10.6%	33.5%	12.3%
		(3.87)	(2.56)	(2.54)	(3.89)	(2.71)
Mountain	**2,273**	**26.6%**	**11.8%**	**9.2%**	**30.4%**	**22.0%**
		(1.71)	**(1.25)**	**(1.12)**	**(1.78)**	**(1.60)**
Arizona	635	26.4%	10.5%	8.0%	31.8%	23.3%
		(3.92)	(2.73)	(2.42)	(4.15)	(3.76)
Colorado	582	20.7%	10.6%	7.7%	34.0%	27.1%
		(3.77)	(2.86)	(2.47)	(4.41)	(4.13)
Idaho	141	32.1%	16.1%	8.4%	28.4%	15.1%
		(4.36)	(3.43)	(2.59)	(4.22)	(3.35)
Montana	124	31.1%	12.8%	11.4%	27.6%	17.1%
		(4.25)	(3.07)	(2.92)	(4.10)	(3.46)
Nevada	268	25.0%	9.7%	10.7%	31.8%	22.8%
		(3.45)	(2.37)	(2.47)	(3.72)	(3.35)
New Mexico	265	36.1%	13.7%	11.0%	23.2%	16.0%
		(4.12)	(2.95)	(2.69)	(3.62)	(3.15)
Utah	201	27.9%	15.4%	11.1%	28.2%	17.3%
		(4.68)	(3.77)	(3.27)	(4.69)	(3.95)
Wyoming	57	26.8%	12.0%	11.7%	25.1%	24.5%
		(5.43)	(3.98)	(3.94)	(5.31)	(5.27)
Pacific	**8,178**	**25.1%**	**12.0%**	**9.5%**	**27.4%**	**26.1%**
		(1.14)	**(0.86)**	**(0.77)**	**(1.18)**	**(1.16)**
Alaska	97	27.5%	11.1%	9.8%	27.1%	24.4%
		(3.57)	(2.51)	(2.38)	(3.55)	(3.43)
California	6,401	25.6%	12.3%	9.3%	26.2%	26.6%
		(1.33)	(1.00)	(0.88)	(1.34)	(1.35)
Hawaii	226	19.4%	11.7%	12.2%	37.0%	19.7%
		(3.39)	(2.75)	(2.81)	(4.14)	(3.41)
Oregon	506	22.8%	12.8%	12.7%	27.2%	24.6%
		(3.96)	(3.15)	(3.14)	(4.20)	(4.07)
Washington	949	23.4%	9.8%	8.7%	33.2%	25.0%
		(3.51)	(2.46)	(2.33)	(3.90)	(3.58)

Source: Three-year merged March CPS: 1991, 1992, and 1993.
Note: See table notes at end of Section G.

Table G8
Labor Force Status, 1991-93: Adults Ages 18-64[1,5]

(Persons in thousands, standard errors in parentheses)

	Adults Ages 18-64	Labor Force Participation Rate	Employment Rate	Adults Ages 18-64 In Labor Force	Unemployment Rate In Labor Force
United States	153,323	77.6% (0.12)	72.0% (0.13)	118,917	7.2% (0.08)
New England	8,206	80.9% (0.38)	74.3% (0.43)	6,638	8.1% (0.29)
Connecticut	2,011	82.2% (1.04)	76.9% (1.15)	1,653	6.5% (0.72)
Maine	779	79.3% (0.98)	71.9% (1.09)	618	9.3% (0.77)
Massachusetts	3,707	80.2% (0.51)	73.4% (0.57)	2,971	8.5% (0.39)
New Hampshire	732	82.7% (1.00)	75.4% (1.14)	605	8.8% (0.80)
Rhode Island	609	80.3% (1.06)	72.6% (1.19)	489	9.5% (0.85)
Vermont	368	81.6% (1.01)	75.3% (1.12)	301	7.7% (0.75)
Middle Atlantic	23,156	75.1% (0.28)	69.3% (0.30)	17,394	7.7% (0.20)
New Jersey	4,866	78.6% (0.51)	72.3% (0.56)	3,823	8.0% (0.37)
New York	11,004	72.9% (0.42)	67.3% (0.45)	8,027	7.7% (0.29)
Pennsylvania	7,286	76.1% (0.53)	70.5% (0.57)	5,545	7.4% (0.36)
South Atlantic	26,924	78.3% (0.29)	73.3% (0.31)	21,094	6.5% (0.19)
Delaware	445	80.0% (1.01)	74.6% (1.10)	356	6.7% (0.69)
District of Columbia	348	76.5% (1.21)	70.2% (1.31)	267	8.3% (0.88)
Florida	7,913	77.5% (0.50)	72.3% (0.53)	6,132	6.8% (0.33)
Georgia	3,954	77.9% (0.98)	72.7% (1.05)	3,079	6.7% (0.65)
Maryland	3,020	81.8% (0.96)	76.9% (1.05)	2,471	6.0% (0.64)
North Carolina	4,077	78.6% (0.50)	74.3% (0.53)	3,204	5.5% (0.31)
South Carolina	2,180	76.8% (0.91)	70.9% (0.98)	1,674	7.6% (0.63)
Virginia	3,898	81.9% (0.81)	77.4% (0.88)	3,192	5.5% (0.52)
West Virginia	1,089	66.0% (1.15)	59.3% (1.20)	719	10.3% (0.89)
East South Central	9,329	74.2% (0.53)	68.8% (0.56)	6,918	7.2% (0.35)
Alabama	2,500	73.8% (1.05)	68.2% (1.11)	1,846	7.6% (0.72)
Kentucky	2,237	74.3% (1.06)	69.1% (1.12)	1,661	7.0% (0.70)
Mississippi	1,517	74.2% (1.02)	68.6% (1.08)	1,126	7.6% (0.70)
Tennessee	3,076	74.3% (0.99)	69.3% (1.05)	2,286	6.8% (0.64)
West South Central	16,168	76.4% (0.40)	71.3% (0.43)	12,359	6.7% (0.26)
Arkansas	1,396	76.9% (1.02)	71.3% (1.10)	1,074	7.3% (0.70)
Louisiana	2,484	71.2% (1.15)	66.7% (1.20)	1,768	6.4% (0.72)
Oklahoma	1,876	74.9% (1.05)	70.2% (1.10)	1,406	6.3% (0.66)
Texas	10,412	77.9% (0.51)	72.6% (0.55)	8,110	6.8% (0.34)

Table G8 (continued)
Labor Force Status, 1991-93: Adults Ages 18-64[1,5]
(Persons in thousands, standard errors in parentheses)

	Adults Ages 18-64	Labor Force Participation Rate	Employment Rate	Adults Ages 18-64 In Labor Force	Unemployment Rate In Labor Force
East North Central	**25,998**	**78.2%** **(0.29)**	**72.4%** **(0.31)**	**20,328**	**7.4%** **(0.20)**
Illinois	7,257	78.8% (0.52)	72.3% (0.56)	5,716	8.2% (0.38)
Indiana	3,428	77.7% (1.03)	73.4% (1.10)	2,664	5.6% (0.63)
Michigan	5,706	75.3% (0.54)	68.7% (0.58)	4,298	8.8% (0.40)
Ohio	6,675	77.9% (0.52)	72.3% (0.56)	5,199	7.1% (0.35)
Wisconsin	2,933	83.6% (0.85)	79.1% (0.93)	2,451	5.3% (0.55)
West North Central	**10,790**	**82.4%** **(0.42)**	**78.0%** **(0.45)**	**8,895**	**5.4%** **(0.27)**
Iowa	1,707	83.8% (0.87)	80.0% (0.94)	1,429	4.5% (0.52)
Kansas	1,479	82.1% (0.90)	78.1% (0.97)	1,214	4.9% (0.55)
Minnesota	2,725	84.7% (0.88)	80.4% (0.97)	2,308	5.0% (0.57)
Missouri	3,188	79.6% (1.00)	73.6% (1.09)	2,538	7.6% (0.71)
Nebraska	942	83.9% (0.85)	81.6% (0.90)	791	2.8% (0.41)
North Dakota	357	82.4% (0.90)	78.3% (0.97)	294	5.1% (0.56)
South Dakota	392	81.6% (0.87)	78.1% (0.93)	320	4.3% (0.49)
Mountain	**8,110**	**78.4%** **(0.43)**	**73.7%** **(0.46)**	**6,356**	**5.9%** **(0.27)**
Arizona	2,117	77.5% (1.04)	73.3% (1.10)	1,642	5.5% (0.63)
Colorado	2,027	79.8% (1.02)	75.5% (1.10)	1,617	5.3% (0.62)
Idaho	600	78.0% (0.96)	72.6% (1.04)	468	7.0% (0.65)
Montana	471	79.9% (0.96)	73.6% (1.06)	377	7.8% (0.71)
Nevada	786	79.3% (0.97)	73.9% (1.05)	623	6.9% (0.66)
New Mexico	904	73.1% (1.05)	67.2% (1.11)	661	8.1% (0.74)
Utah	932	80.3% (0.98)	77.3% (1.04)	748	3.8% (0.51)
Wyoming	273	80.5% (1.13)	75.9% (1.22)	220	5.8% (0.72)
Pacific	**24,642**	**76.8%** **(0.33)**	**70.2%** **(0.36)**	**18,936**	**8.6%** **(0.24)**
Alaska	304	79.2% (0.94)	72.3% (1.03)	241	8.7% (0.71)
California	18,827	76.0% (0.39)	69.2% (0.42)	14,299	8.9% (0.29)
Hawaii	649	81.0% (1.02)	78.4% (1.07)	525	3.2% (0.50)
Oregon	1,807	79.8% (1.03)	73.5% (1.13)	1,442	7.9% (0.75)
Washington	3,056	79.5% (0.95)	72.7% (1.05)	2,429	8.6% (0.72)

Source: Three-year merged March CPS: 1991, 1992, and 1993.
Note: See table notes at end of Section G.

Table G9
Employment by Firm Size, 1990-92:
Workers Ages 18-64[1,6]
(Persons in thousands, standard errors in parentheses)

| | Number | Number of Workers | | | |
		<25	25-99	100-499	500+
United States	**124,269**	**29.3%**	**13.3%**	**14.5%**	**42.9%**
		(0.14)	**(0.11)**	**(0.11)**	**(0.16)**
New England	**6,866**	**28.7%**	**13.6%**	**16.2%**	**41.4%**
		(0.48)	**(0.36)**	**(0.39)**	**(0.52)**
Connecticut	1,704	27.4%	12.7%	15.6%	44.4%
		(1.32)	(0.98)	(1.07)	(1.47)
Maine	652	35.0%	13.4%	16.9%	34.8%
		(1.27)	(0.90)	(1.00)	(1.26)
Massachusetts	3,063	26.5%	13.4%	16.0%	44.1%
		(0.62)	(0.48)	(0.52)	(0.70)
New Hampshire	627	31.1%	14.7%	17.8%	36.5%
		(1.32)	(1.01)	(1.09)	(1.37)
Rhode Island	502	29.8%	15.9%	17.3%	37.0%
		(1.35)	(1.08)	(1.11)	(1.42)
Vermont	317	39.1%	14.8%	16.2%	30.0%
		(1.36)	(0.99)	(1.03)	(1.28)
Middle Atlantic	**18,166**	**27.2%**	**14.2%**	**16.9%**	**41.7%**
		(0.33)	**(0.26)**	**(0.28)**	**(0.36)**
New Jersey	3,953	26.4%	14.7%	16.6%	42.3%
		(0.61)	(0.49)	(0.52)	(0.68)
New York	8,401	27.7%	14.1%	16.5%	41.7%
		(0.49)	(0.38)	(0.40)	(0.54)
Pennsylvania	5,811	27.0%	14.1%	17.6%	41.2%
		(0.62)	(0.48)	(0.53)	(0.68)
South Atlantic	**21,968**	**28.9%**	**12.0%**	**12.9%**	**46.2%**
		(0.35)	**(0.25)**	**(0.26)**	**(0.39)**
Delaware	382	25.5%	11.9%	12.6%	50.0%
		(1.19)	(0.89)	(0.91)	(1.37)
District of Columbia	274	23.4%	12.6%	15.7%	48.3%
		(1.37)	(1.07)	(1.18)	(1.61)
Florida	6,363	32.8%	12.7%	12.3%	42.2%
		(0.62)	(0.44)	(0.44)	(0.65)
Georgia	3,198	28.8%	11.9%	12.6%	46.7%
		(1.19)	(0.85)	(0.87)	(1.31)
Maryland	2,551	26.5%	11.5%	11.9%	50.2%
		(1.20)	(0.87)	(0.88)	(1.36)
North Carolina	3,376	27.6%	11.5%	13.3%	47.6%
		(0.60)	(0.43)	(0.46)	(0.67)
South Carolina	1,753	26.2%	11.2%	14.6%	48.0%
		(1.05)	(0.76)	(0.85)	(1.20)
Virginia	3,319	27.1%	12.0%	13.2%	47.7%
		(1.01)	(0.74)	(0.77)	(1.14)
West Virginia	754	28.6%	12.9%	13.6%	45.0%
		(1.32)	(0.98)	(1.00)	(1.46)
East South Central	**7,221**	**29.1%**	**12.2%**	**14.1%**	**44.6%**
		(0.62)	**(0.45)**	**(0.48)**	**(0.68)**
Alabama	1,919	31.1%	10.9%	12.4%	45.6%
		(1.26)	(0.85)	(0.90)	(1.36)
Kentucky	1,729	30.1%	13.1%	14.3%	42.5%
		(1.27)	(0.93)	(0.97)	(1.36)
Mississippi	1,166	30.2%	13.1%	16.9%	39.8%
		(1.22)	(0.89)	(0.99)	(1.30)
Tennessee	2,407	26.2%	12.2%	13.8%	47.7%
		(1.13)	(0.84)	(0.89)	(1.28)
West South Central	**12,938**	**31.8%**	**12.5%**	**12.0%**	**43.7%**
		(0.49)	**(0.35)**	**(0.34)**	**(0.52)**
Arkansas	1,122	32.8%	13.1%	13.9%	40.2%
		(1.27)	(0.91)	(0.94)	(1.33)
Louisiana	1,858	31.9%	12.5%	11.6%	44.0%
		(1.37)	(0.97)	(0.94)	(1.46)
Oklahoma	1,508	33.5%	13.7%	14.3%	38.5%
		(1.27)	(0.93)	(0.94)	(1.31)
Texas	8,451	31.3%	12.1%	11.5%	45.1%
		(0.63)	(0.44)	(0.43)	(0.68)

Table G9 (continued)
Employment by Firm Size, 1990-92:
Workers Ages 18-64[1,6]

(Persons in thousands, standard errors in parentheses)

	Number	Number of Workers			
		<25	25-99	100-499	500+
East North Central	**21,282**	**26.2%**	**13.5%**	**16.5%**	**43.8%**
		(0.34)	**(0.26)**	**(0.28)**	**(0.38)**
Illinois	5,894	25.9%	13.5%	17.1%	43.5%
		(0.61)	(0.48)	(0.53)	(0.69)
Indiana	2,849	26.3%	13.6%	17.1%	43.1%
		(1.20)	(0.93)	(1.02)	(1.35)
Michigan	4,528	27.0%	12.5%	14.4%	46.1%
		(0.63)	(0.47)	(0.50)	(0.71)
Ohio	5,418	25.1%	13.5%	16.3%	45.2%
		(0.60)	(0.47)	(0.51)	(0.69)
Wisconsin	2,594	27.6%	15.5%	18.5%	38.4%
		(1.08)	(0.88)	(0.94)	(1.18)
West North Central	**9,406**	**31.6%**	**13.9%**	**15.0%**	**39.5%**
		(0.54)	**(0.41)**	**(0.42)**	**(0.57)**
Iowa	1,504	34.1%	13.7%	15.1%	37.1%
		(1.19)	(0.86)	(0.90)	(1.21)
Kansas	1,290	32.1%	12.8%	14.6%	40.5%
		(1.18)	(0.84)	(0.89)	(1.24)
Minnesota	2,447	30.8%	14.9%	14.3%	40.0%
		(1.19)	(0.92)	(0.90)	(1.26)
Missouri	2,679	27.6%	13.8%	16.2%	42.4%
		(1.21)	(0.93)	(1.00)	(1.33)
Nebraska	830	34.5%	13.2%	14.5%	37.8%
		(1.18)	(0.84)	(0.87)	(1.20)
North Dakota	311	42.3%	13.7%	13.7%	30.4%
		(1.25)	(0.87)	(0.87)	(1.16)
South Dakota	343	38.2%	14.4%	14.5%	32.9%
		(1.17)	(0.84)	(0.85)	(1.13)
Mountain	**6,777**	**30.7%**	**12.2%**	**12.7%**	**44.4%**
		(0.53)	**(0.38)**	**(0.38)**	**(0.57)**
Arizona	1,724	30.4%	10.5%	14.2%	44.9%
		(1.27)	(0.85)	(0.96)	(1.37)
Colorado	1,738	27.7%	13.1%	12.7%	46.6%
		(1.23)	(0.93)	(0.92)	(1.37)
Idaho	510	36.5%	12.6%	13.1%	37.9%
		(1.21)	(0.83)	(0.85)	(1.22)
Montana	405	43.1%	13.9%	10.8%	32.2%
		(1.29)	(0.90)	(0.81)	(1.21)
Nevada	652	26.5%	12.3%	11.9%	49.3%
		(1.16)	(0.86)	(0.85)	(1.31)
New Mexico	706	34.3%	13.1%	11.1%	41.5%
		(1.27)	(0.90)	(0.84)	(1.32)
Utah	804	26.0%	12.3%	11.7%	50.0%
		(1.17)	(0.88)	(0.86)	(1.33)
Wyoming	238	39.2%	10.9%	15.6%	34.3%
		(1.50)	(0.95)	(1.11)	(1.45)
Pacific	**19,644**	**31.9%**	**14.3%**	**13.7%**	**40.1%**
		(0.41)	**(0.31)**	**(0.30)**	**(0.43)**
Alaska	259	36.2%	11.8%	12.3%	39.6%
		(1.20)	(0.81)	(0.82)	(1.22)
California	14,774	31.9%	14.6%	13.7%	39.9%
		(0.48)	(0.36)	(0.35)	(0.50)
Hawaii	545	27.4%	14.6%	14.0%	44.0%
		(1.26)	(1.00)	(0.98)	(1.40)
Oregon	1,517	34.5%	12.7%	14.5%	38.2%
		(1.33)	(0.93)	(0.98)	(1.36)
Washington	2,548	31.1%	13.9%	13.4%	41.5%
		(1.20)	(0.90)	(0.88)	(1.27)

Source: Three-year merged March CPS: 1991, 1992, and 1993.
Note: See table notes at end of Section G.

Table G10
Employment by Sector, 1990-92:
Workers Ages 18-64[1,6]

(Persons in thousands, standard errors in parentheses)

	Number	Private	Government	Self-Employed[7]
United States	**124,269**	**76.9%**	**15.4%**	**7.5%**
		(0.13)	**(0.11)**	**(0.08)**
New England	**6,866**	**79.6%**	**13.1%**	**7.2%**
		(0.43)	**(0.36)**	**(0.28)**
Connecticut	1,704	81.1%	12.4%	6.4%
		(1.16)	(0.98)	(0.72)
Maine	652	72.9%	15.1%	11.9%
		(1.18)	(0.95)	(0.86)
Massachusetts	3,063	80.1%	13.7%	6.1%
		(0.56)	(0.48)	(0.34)
New Hampshire	627	80.6%	10.5%	8.7%
		(1.13)	(0.87)	(0.80)
Rhode Island	502	81.6%	12.0%	6.3%
		(1.14)	(0.96)	(0.72)
Vermont	317	74.3%	15.0%	10.6%
		(1.22)	(1.00)	(0.86)
Middle Atlantic	**18,166**	**78.6%**	**15.1%**	**6.2%**
		(0.30)	**(0.26)**	**(0.18)**
New Jersey	3,953	79.8%	14.9%	5.1%
		(0.56)	(0.49)	(0.31)
New York	8,401	75.8%	17.3%	6.7%
		(0.47)	(0.41)	(0.27)
Pennsylvania	5,811	81.8%	11.9%	6.0%
		(0.54)	(0.45)	(0.33)
South Atlantic	**21,968**	**76.6%**	**16.5%**	**6.7%**
		(0.33)	**(0.29)**	**(0.19)**
Delaware	382	83.1%	11.8%	5.0%
		(1.02)	(0.88)	(0.60)
District of Columbia	274	65.6%	28.4%	6.0%
		(1.54)	(1.46)	(0.77)
Florida	6,363	77.5%	15.1%	7.1%
		(0.55)	(0.47)	(0.34)
Georgia	3,198	78.9%	14.4%	6.4%
		(1.07)	(0.92)	(0.65)
Maryland	2,551	70.4%	22.2%	7.2%
		(1.24)	(1.13)	(0.70)
North Carolina	3,376	78.0%	14.6%	7.3%
		(0.56)	(0.47)	(0.35)
South Carolina	1,753	78.5%	15.4%	5.8%
		(0.98)	(0.87)	(0.56)
Virginia	3,319	75.5%	18.2%	6.3%
		(0.98)	(0.88)	(0.55)
West Virginia	754	75.9%	18.5%	5.2%
		(1.25)	(1.14)	(0.65)
East South Central	**7,221**	**76.6%**	**15.4%**	**7.7%**
		(0.58)	**(0.49)**	**(0.37)**
Alabama	1,919	76.1%	14.9%	8.8%
		(1.16)	(0.97)	(0.77)
Kentucky	1,729	75.6%	16.1%	7.8%
		(1.19)	(1.01)	(0.74)
Mississippi	1,166	75.2%	17.0%	7.3%
		(1.14)	(1.00)	(0.69)
Tennessee	2,407	78.2%	14.4%	7.0%
		(1.06)	(0.90)	(0.66)
West South Central	**12,938**	**75.5%**	**16.3%**	**7.9%**
		(0.45)	**(0.39)**	**(0.28)**
Arkansas	1,122	73.7%	15.9%	9.9%
		(1.19)	(0.99)	(0.81)
Louisiana	1,858	74.5%	17.8%	7.4%
		(1.28)	(1.12)	(0.77)
Oklahoma	1,508	72.2%	16.8%	10.5%
		(1.21)	(1.01)	(0.82)
Texas	8,451	76.5%	15.9%	7.2%
		(0.58)	(0.50)	(0.35)

Table G10 (continued)
Employment by Sector, 1990-92:
Workers Ages 18-64[1,6]
(Persons in thousands, standard errors in parentheses)

	Number	Private	Government	Self-Employed[7]
East North Central	**21,282**	**79.6%**	**14.0%**	**6.2%**
		(0.31)	**(0.26)**	**(0.18)**
Illinois	5,894	79.9%	13.5%	6.5%
		(0.56)	(0.48)	(0.34)
Indiana	2,849	79.3%	13.1%	7.4%
		(1.10)	(0.92)	(0.71)
Michigan	4,528	80.1%	14.0%	5.8%
		(0.56)	(0.49)	(0.33)
Ohio	5,418	80.1%	14.3%	5.4%
		(0.55)	(0.48)	(0.31)
Wisconsin	2,594	77.3%	15.3%	7.2%
		(1.02)	(0.87)	(0.63)
West North Central	**9,406**	**74.4%**	**15.0%**	**10.0%**
		(0.51)	**(0.42)**	**(0.35)**
Iowa	1,504	72.6%	15.1%	11.7%
		(1.12)	(0.90)	(0.81)
Kansas	1,290	73.1%	15.3%	10.7%
		(1.12)	(0.91)	(0.78)
Minnesota	2,447	75.8%	14.2%	9.7%
		(1.11)	(0.90)	(0.76)
Missouri	2,679	78.3%	14.1%	7.2%
		(1.11)	(0.94)	(0.70)
Nebraska	830	70.7%	16.7%	12.2%
		(1.13)	(0.92)	(0.81)
North Dakota	311	64.4%	19.4%	14.9%
		(1.21)	(1.00)	(0.90)
South Dakota	343	65.8%	18.8%	13.9%
		(1.14)	(0.94)	(0.83)
Mountain	**6,777**	**73.4%**	**17.5%**	**8.7%**
		(0.51)	**(0.44)**	**(0.32)**
Arizona	1,724	76.8%	14.3%	8.5%
		(1.17)	(0.97)	(0.77)
Colorado	1,738	75.3%	16.6%	8.0%
		(1.19)	(1.02)	(0.75)
Idaho	510	70.8%	17.8%	10.8%
		(1.14)	(0.96)	(0.78)
Montana	405	61.9%	23.3%	14.0%
		(1.26)	(1.10)	(0.90)
Nevada	652	79.5%	13.4%	6.9%
		(1.06)	(0.89)	(0.67)
New Mexico	706	65.3%	23.6%	10.7%
		(1.28)	(1.14)	(0.83)
Utah	804	74.1%	19.1%	6.4%
		(1.17)	(1.05)	(0.65)
Wyoming	238	66.2%	23.5%	9.6%
		(1.45)	(1.30)	(0.90)
Pacific	**19,644**	**75.3%**	**15.6%**	**8.9%**
		(0.38)	**(0.32)**	**(0.25)**
Alaska	259	63.1%	26.3%	10.6%
		(1.21)	(1.10)	(0.77)
California	14,774	76.4%	14.5%	8.9%
		(0.44)	(0.36)	(0.29)
Hawaii	545	71.8%	21.3%	6.9%
		(1.27)	(1.16)	(0.71)
Oregon	1,517	73.6%	16.5%	9.5%
		(1.23)	(1.04)	(0.82)
Washington	2,548	71.6%	19.5%	8.7%
		(1.17)	(1.02)	(0.73)

Source: Three-year merged March CPS: 1991, 1992, and 1993.
Note: See table notes at end of Section G.

Table G11
Employment by Industry, 1990-92:
Private-Sector Workers Ages 18-64[1,6]

(Persons in thousands, standard errors in parentheses)

	Number	Manufacturing	Wholesale/ Retail	Services	Other[8]
United States	**95,569**	**21.8%**	**25.3%**	**29.2%**	**23.7%**
		(0.15)	**(0.16)**	**(0.16)**	**(0.15)**
New England	**5,463**	**23.8%**	**23.1%**	**32.1%**	**21.0%**
		(0.51)	**(0.50)**	**(0.56)**	**(0.49)**
Connecticut	1,382	25.9%	22.6%	29.2%	22.4%
		(1.44)	(1.37)	(1.49)	(1.37)
Maine	475	24.1%	24.9%	30.4%	20.6%
		(1.33)	(1.34)	(1.43)	(1.26)
Massachusetts	2,455	21.3%	23.1%	35.0%	20.6%
		(0.64)	(0.66)	(0.75)	(0.64)
New Hampshire	506	26.7%	24.2%	30.3%	18.8%
		(1.40)	(1.36)	(1.46)	(1.24)
Rhode Island	410	28.8%	21.8%	28.8%	20.6%
		(1.48)	(1.34)	(1.48)	(1.32)
Vermont	236	22.1%	22.7%	33.0%	22.1%
		(1.35)	(1.36)	(1.53)	(1.35)
Middle Atlantic	**14,270**	**20.5%**	**23.7%**	**32.8%**	**22.9%**
		(0.34)	**(0.35)**	**(0.39)**	**(0.35)**
New Jersey	3,153	20.4%	24.0%	30.3%	25.4%
		(0.62)	(0.66)	(0.71)	(0.67)
New York	6,365	19.1%	22.9%	35.2%	22.8%
		(0.49)	(0.53)	(0.60)	(0.52)
Pennsylvania	4,752	22.5%	24.8%	31.2%	21.5%
		(0.64)	(0.66)	(0.71)	(0.63)
South Atlantic	**16,837**	**20.7%**	**25.4%**	**28.3%**	**25.5%**
		(0.36)	**(0.38)**	**(0.40)**	**(0.39)**
Delaware	318	22.1%	21.9%	27.9%	28.1%
		(1.25)	(1.24)	(1.35)	(1.35)
District of Columbia	179	7.3%	20.0%	56.1%	16.6%
		(1.03)	(1.60)	(1.98)	(1.49)
Florida	4,933	13.3%	28.0%	30.3%	28.4%
		(0.51)	(0.68)	(0.69)	(0.68)
Georgia	2,524	23.0%	26.0%	26.0%	25.0%
		(1.25)	(1.30)	(1.30)	(1.28)
Maryland	1,797	12.5%	24.8%	35.6%	27.1%
		(1.07)	(1.40)	(1.55)	(1.44)
North Carolina	2,633	33.5%	23.0%	23.4%	20.1%
		(0.72)	(0.64)	(0.64)	(0.61)
South Carolina	1,377	32.0%	24.5%	22.0%	21.4%
		(1.26)	(1.16)	(1.12)	(1.11)
Virginia	2,504	20.8%	23.6%	29.1%	26.5%
		(1.07)	(1.12)	(1.19)	(1.16)
West Virginia	572	17.8%	27.7%	25.8%	28.7%
		(1.29)	(1.50)	(1.47)	(1.52)
East South Central	**5,529**	**27.3%**	**25.1%**	**25.1%**	**22.5%**
		(0.70)	**(0.68)**	**(0.68)**	**(0.65)**
Alabama	1,461	27.8%	25.6%	24.9%	21.7%
		(1.40)	(1.37)	(1.35)	(1.29)
Kentucky	1,307	22.5%	27.2%	26.2%	24.1%
		(1.32)	(1.41)	(1.40)	(1.36)
Mississippi	878	27.3%	24.6%	22.6%	25.5%
		(1.36)	(1.32)	(1.28)	(1.33)
Tennessee	1,883	30.4%	23.4%	25.6%	20.5%
		(1.34)	(1.23)	(1.27)	(1.17)
West South Central	**9,764**	**18.2%**	**26.9%**	**28.3%**	**26.7%**
		(0.47)	**(0.54)**	**(0.55)**	**(0.54)**
Arkansas	827	28.0%	25.7%	22.5%	23.8%
		(1.41)	(1.38)	(1.32)	(1.34)
Louisiana	1,385	14.0%	25.6%	28.6%	31.9%
		(1.18)	(1.48)	(1.54)	(1.59)
Oklahoma	1,088	20.2%	27.6%	28.5%	23.7%
		(1.27)	(1.42)	(1.43)	(1.35)
Texas	6,465	17.5%	27.2%:	28.9%	26.5%
		(0.59)	(0.69)	(0.71)	(0.69)

Table G11 (continued)
Employment by Industry, 1990-92:
Private-Sector Workers Ages 18-64[1,6]

(Persons in thousands, standard errors in parentheses)

	Number	Manufacturing	Wholesale/ Retail	Services	Other[8]
East North Central	**16,940**	**27.8%**	**24.8%**	**27.1%**	**20.3%**
		(0.38)	**(0.37)**	**(0.38)**	**(0.34)**
Illinois	4,707	23.1%	25.2%	28.9%	22.8%
		(0.66)	(0.68)	(0.71)	(0.66)
Indiana	2,259	32.0%	25.0%	22.8%	20.3%
		(1.43)	(1.32)	(1.28)	(1.23)
Michigan	3,628	29.4%	25.9%	26.4%	18.3%
		(0.72)	(0.69)	(0.70)	(0.61)
Ohio	4,341	28.1%	24.5%	28.2%	19.2%
		(0.69)	(0.66)	(0.69)	(0.61)
Wisconsin	2,005	30.7%	22.2%	26.9%	20.2%
		(1.27)	(1.15)	(1.22)	(1.11)
West North Central	**7,001**	**20.1%**	**26.9%**	**29.9%**	**23.1%**
		(0.54)	**(0.60)**	**(0.62)**	**(0.57)**
Iowa	1,092	22.2%	29.8%	25.7%	22.3%
		(1.22)	(1.34)	(1.29)	(1.22)
Kansas	942	20.9%	26.3%	27.9%	25.0%
		(1.20)	(1.30)	(1.32)	(1.28)
Minnesota	1,854	20.3%	27.8%	30.4%	21.6%
		(1.19)	(1.33)	(1.36)	(1.22)
Missouri	2,099	20.2%	24.3%	32.5%	23.0%
		(1.22)	(1.31)	(1.43)	(1.28)
Nebraska	587	19.0%	27.5%	28.7%	24.8%
		(1.16)	(1.31)	(1.33)	(1.27)
North Dakota	201	9.8%	32.8%	31.1%	26.3%
		(0.94)	(1.48)	(1.46)	(1.39)
South Dakota	226	15.3%	27.8%	31.2%	25.6%
		(1.07)	(1.33)	(1.37)	(1.30)
Mountain	**4,977**	**14.5%**	**26.3%**	**32.6%**	**26.5%**
		(0.47)	**(0.59)**	**(0.63)**	**(0.59)**
Arizona	1,324	14.8%	26.5%	33.5%	25.2%
		(1.12)	(1.39)	(1.49)	(1.37)
Colorado	1,308	16.4%	23.8%	32.7%	27.1%
		(1.18)	(1.35)	(1.49)	(1.41)
Idaho	361	21.1%	27.5%	26.6%	24.8%
		(1.22)	(1.34)	(1.32)	(1.29)
Montana	251	10.9%	32.7%	28.6%	27.9%
		(1.03)	(1.55)	(1.49)	(1.48)
Nevada	519	6.2%	23.1%	44.2%	26.5%
		(0.71)	(1.24)	(1.46)	(1.30)
New Mexico	461	10.9%	29.8%	31.6%	27.7%
		(1.04)	(1.52)	(1.55)	(1.49)
Utah	596	19.3%	27.7%	28.5%	24.5%
		(1.22)	(1.39)	(1.40)	(1.33)
Wyoming	158	7.9%	28.3%	24.3%	39.5%
		(1.01)	(1.70)	(1.62)	(1.84)
Pacific	**14,788**	**20.2%**	**25.8%**	**29.0%**	**25.1%**
		(0.40)	**(0.44)**	**(0.46)**	**(0.44)**
Alaska	163	7.9%	28.4%	29.6%	34.2%
		(0.85)	(1.42)	(1.44)	(1.49)
California	11,292	20.9%	25.2%	28.8%	25.2%
		(0.48)	(0.51)	(0.53)	(0.51)
Hawaii	392	6.9%	26.6%	35.3%	31.2%
		(0.84)	(1.47)	(1.59)	(1.54)
Oregon	1,117	21.4%	27.8%	28.0%	22.8%
		(1.33)	(1.46)	(1.46)	(1.36)
Washington	1,823	19.0%	27.7%	29.4%	24.0%
		(1.20)	(1.37)	(1.39)	(1.30)

Source: **Three-year merged March CPS: 1991, 1992, and 1993.**
Note: See table notes at end of Section G.

Table G12
Private Establishments by Size, 1991[9]

	Total	Number of Workers at Establishment					
		1-4	5-9	10-19	20-99	100-499	500+
United States	**6,200,650**	**54.5%**	**20.0%**	**12.4%**	**10.9%**	**1.9%**	**0.2%**
New England	**357,428**	**55.7%**	**19.7%**	**12.2%**	**10.1%**	**2.0%**	**0.3%**
Connecticut	90,498	55.7	19.6	12.3	10.1	2.0	0.3
Maine	34,270	58.6	19.8	11.7	8.4	1.3	0.2
Massachusetts	153,939	53.9	19.9	12.6	11.0	2.3	0.3
New Hampshire	32,254	56.9	20.1	11.8	9.3	1.7	0.2
Rhode Island	26,895	57.4	18.9	11.8	9.9	1.8	0.3
Vermont	19,572	60.4	19.1	11.2	8.1	1.1	0.1
Middle Atlantic	**950,734**	**57.2%**	**18.8%**	**11.6%**	**10.2%**	**1.9%**	**0.3%**
New Jersey	210,113	57.8	18.4	11.5	10.1	2.0	0.3
New York	461,152	59.4	18.0	11.0	9.6	1.8	0.3
Pennsylvania	279,469	53.0	20.5	12.8	11.2	2.2	0.3
South Atlantic	**1,108,978**	**54.4%**	**20.4%**	**12.4%**	**10.6%**	**1.9%**	**0.2%**
Delaware	19,154	54.8	20.0	12.6	10.4	1.9	0.4
District of Columbia	19,257	49.9	19.5	14.0	13.4	2.8	0.4
Florida	364,572	57.2	19.9	11.5	9.6	1.6	0.2
Georgia	158,637	53.0	20.5	12.6	11.4	2.2	0.3
Maryland	114,999	51.7	20.8	13.8	11.7	1.9	0.2
North Carolina	164,799	54.0	20.5	12.2	10.9	2.1	0.3
South Carolina	80,288	53.3	21.3	12.5	10.7	2.0	0.3
Virginia	149,369	52.6	20.9	13.3	11.0	1.9	0.3
West Virginia	37,903	54.6	21.0	12.6	10.0	1.6	0.2
East South Central	**333,990**	**53.3%**	**20.7%**	**12.6%**	**11.1%**	**2.1%**	**0.3%**
Alabama	87,317	52.7	21.2	12.7	11.2	2.0	0.3
Kentucky	79,598	52.7	20.8	12.9	11.3	2.1	0.2
Mississippi	53,109	56.1	20.4	11.7	9.6	2.0	0.2
Tennessee	113,966	52.9	20.3	12.7	11.5	2.3	0.3
West South Central	**618,893**	**54.4%**	**20.3%**	**12.3%**	**10.9%**	**1.9%**	**0.2%**
Arkansas	53,961	56.0	20.3	12.0	9.5	1.9	0.3
Louisiana	88,993	52.2	21.2	12.9	11.4	2.0	0.2
Oklahoma	75,827	56.2	20.1	11.7	10.2	1.5	0.2
Texas	400,112	54.4	20.1	12.3	11.0	1.9	0.2
East North Central	**989,801**	**51.6%**	**20.9%**	**13.3%**	**11.8%**	**2.2%**	**0.3%**
Illinois	275,351	52.9	19.8	12.9	11.8	2.3	0.3
Indiana	129,506	50.4	21.5	13.5	12.0	2.3	0.3
Michigan	211,569	51.7	21.2	13.5	11.4	1.9	0.2
Ohio	249,546	50.6	21.4	13.4	12.0	2.3	0.3
Wisconsin	123,829	51.8	20.8	13.2	11.6	2.2	0.3
West North Central	**469,811**	**54.3%**	**20.4%**	**12.6%**	**10.7%**	**1.8%**	**0.2%**
Iowa	74,320	54.1	21.2	12.6	10.2	1.7	0.2
Kansas	65,941	54.7	20.4	12.5	10.6	1.7	0.2
Minnesota	114,342	52.4	20.1	13.4	11.7	2.2	0.3
Missouri	131,078	54.7	20.0	12.2	10.9	2.0	0.3
Nebraska	44,405	54.7	21.1	12.3	10.1	1.5	0.2
North Dakota	18,979	57.9	20.1	11.8	8.9	1.3	0.1
South Dakota	20,746	57.9	19.8	11.9	9.0	1.3	0.1
Mountain	**360,471**	**55.5%**	**20.3%**	**12.2%**	**10.3%**	**1.6%**	**0.2%**
Arizona	87,681	54.0	20.5	12.4	11.1	1.8	0.2
Colorado	99,630	57.3	19.5	11.3	10.1	1.6	0.2
Idaho	27,383	56.1	20.6	12.8	9.1	1.2	0.1
Montana	25,651	60.4	19.7	10.8	8.1	0.8	0.1
Nevada	30,905	52.5	20.5	13.3	11.5	1.8	0.4
New Mexico	36,336	55.7	20.6	12.1	10.0	1.4	0.1
Utah	37,905	51.5	21.3	13.7	11.3	2.0	0.2
Wyoming	14,980	58.8	20.5	11.5	8.1	1.1	0.0
Pacific	**1,010,544**	**54.6%**	**19.5%**	**12.5%**	**11.4%**	**1.8%**	**0.2%**
Alaska	15,131	57.5	20.6	12.0	8.4	1.4	0.1
California	747,688	54.6	19.2	12.5	11.7	1.8	0.2
Hawaii	29,736	50.7	21.5	13.5	12.2	1.9	0.2
Oregon	82,466	55.0	20.4	12.6	10.4	1.5	0.2
Washington	135,523	55.1	20.0	12.7	10.5	1.5	0.2

Source: U.S. Bureau of the Census, <u>County Business Patterns</u>, 1991, (Washington, D.C.: Bureau of the Census).
Note: See table notes at end of Section G.

Table G13
Employment by Establishment Size:
Private-Sector Jobs, 1991[9]
(Persons in thousands)

	Total	Number of Workers at Establishment					
		1-4	5-9	10-19	20-99	100-499	500+
United States	92,286	6.4%	8.9%	11.2%	29.2%	24.2%	20.1%
New England	5,446	6.4%	8.5%	10.8%	26.6%	24.8%	22.9%
Connecticut	1,433	6.2	8.2	10.4	25.6	24.4	25.2
Maine	402	8.4	11.1	13.4	27.9	20.9	18.3
Massachusetts	2,615	5.7	7.7	10.0	26.0	26.2	24.5
New Hampshire	417	7.6	10.2	12.3	28.4	24.1	17.5
Rhode Island	374	7.1	8.9	11.5	28.4	24.5	19.6
Vermont	206	9.9	11.9	14.1	30.3	20.1	13.6
Middle Atlantic	14,439	6.5%	8.2%	10.3%	26.8%	24.5%	23.7%
New Jersey	3,087	6.7	8.3	10.5	27.8	26.1	20.7
New York	6,804	6.9	8.0	10.0	25.9	23.1	26.1
Pennsylvania	4,547	6.0	8.3	10.6	27.6	25.5	22.1
South Atlantic	16,058	6.6%	9.3%	11.5%	29.4%	24.5%	18.8%
Delaware	308	5.6	8.3	10.6	25.8	22.2	27.6
District of Columbia	402	4.3	6.2	9.0	26.3	25.6	28.6
Florida	4,571	7.8	10.4	12.3	30.7	22.9	16.0
Georgia	2,469	6.0	8.7	10.8	29.4	26.5	18.5
Maryland	1,731	6.0	9.2	12.2	30.6	23.8	18.2
North Carolina	2,607	6.2	8.5	10.3	27.9	25.8	21.1
South Carolina	1,243	6.2	9.0	10.8	27.5	25.4	21.1
Virginia	2,243	6.2	9.2	11.8	29.2	24.4	19.1
West Virginia	484	7.8	10.9	13.2	30.5	22.8	14.8
East South Central	5,143	6.3%	8.8%	11.0%	28.7%	26.3%	18.8%
Alabama	1,351	6.2	9.0	11.0	28.8	24.9	20.1
Kentucky	1,195	6.4	9.1	11.5	29.8	26.0	17.1
Mississippi	730	7.5	9.7	11.5	27.6	27.8	16.0
Tennessee	1,867	5.9	8.2	10.4	28.5	26.9	20.2
West South Central	9,015	6.7%	9.1%	11.3%	29.6%	24.3%	18.9%
Arkansas	760	7.2	9.5	11.4	26.7	26.2	19.1
Louisiana	1,305	6.6	9.5	11.9	31.2	24.6	16.2
Oklahoma	968	7.9	10.3	12.4	31.8	22.8	14.8
Texas	5,983	6.5	8.8	11.0	29.2	24.3	20.2
East North Central	16,217	5.6%	8.4%	10.9%	29.0%	25.1%	21.0%
Illinois	4,636	5.5	7.8	10.3	28.4	25.9	22.1
Indiana	2,130	5.6	8.7	11.0	29.4	25.3	20.0
Michigan	3,301	5.9	9.0	11.6	29.2	22.6	21.7
Ohio	4,192	5.5	8.4	10.7	28.9	25.2	21.2
Wisconsin	1,959	5.8	8.7	11.3	29.4	27.0	17.9
West North Central	6,779	6.7%	9.3%	11.7%	29.5%	23.6%	19.2%
Iowa	1,019	7.1	10.2	12.3	29.9	22.4	18.0
Kansas	895	7.3	9.9	12.3	31.0	22.6	16.9
Minnesota	1,842	5.6	8.3	11.2	28.9	25.2	20.8
Missouri	1,990	6.4	8.7	10.8	28.6	24.4	21.1
Nebraska	604	7.3	10.2	12.1	29.3	21.0	20.2
North Dakota	201	9.6	12.5	14.7	33.3	21.9	8.0
South Dakota	228	9.0	11.9	14.5	31.7	20.7	12.1
Mountain	4,737	7.3%	10.2%	12.4%	30.6%	21.9%	17.9%
Arizona	1,234	6.6	9.5	11.9	31.0	23.4	17.6
Colorado	1,286	7.6	10.0	11.7	31.0	22.4	17.4
Idaho	309	8.5	12.0	15.1	30.9	18.5	14.9
Montana	214	12.3	15.5	17.3	36.6	18.3	3.1
Nevada	541	5.0	7.8	10.3	25.7	19.6	31.6
New Mexico	428	8.3	11.5	13.8	33.2	20.9	12.2
Utah	593	5.7	9.0	11.7	28.3	23.9	21.4
Wyoming	133	11.4	15.1	17.4	34.5	21.6	1.9
Pacific	14,452	6.5%	9.0%	11.8%	31.7%	22.8%	18.2%
Alaska	164	8.7	12.4	14.8	29.9	24.2	9.9
California	11,020	6.3	8.6	11.4	31.6	23.1	18.9
Hawaii	443	6.3	9.5	12.3	32.7	23.0	16.2
Oregon	1,033	7.6	10.8	13.5	32.7	22.6	12.9
Washington	1,792	7.0	10.0	12.9	31.4	20.7	18.0

Source: U.S. Bureau of the Census, <u>County Business Patterns</u>, 1991, (Washington, D.C.: Bureau of the Census).
Note: See table notes at end of Section G.

Table G14
Annualized Payroll Per Private-Sector Worker by Establishment Size, 1991[9,10]

	All Sizes	Number of Workers at Establishment					
		1-4	5-9	10-19	20-99	100-499	500+
United States	**$20,536**	**$17,832**	**$17,644**	**$18,573**	**$18,304**	**$21,289**	**$26,095**
New England	**$24,725**	**$19,457**	**$19,549**	**$20,449**	**$22,324**	**$25,694**	**$31,856**
Connecticut	27,906	22,181	22,034	23,008	24,998	28,545	35,592
Maine	19,343	14,639	15,074	16,551	17,112	19,137	29,779
Massachusetts	25,374	20,393	20,252	20,892	23,077	26,361	31,338
New Hampshire	21,299	17,304	17,500	18,485	19,624	22,045	28,912
Rhode Island	20,703	17,794	18,233	18,650	19,442	22,116	24,137
Vermont	19,060	14,267	15,414	16,660	17,750	20,570	28,945
Middle Atlantic	**$22,865**	**$19,769**	**$20,322**	**$21,609**	**$23,179**	**$26,340**	**$21,187**
New Jersey	26,682	21,501	21,732	22,622	24,804	28,121	33,118
New York	21,750	21,276	22,042	23,411	24,844	28,096	12,453
Pennsylvania	21,941	15,850	16,895	18,387	19,720	22,725	29,065
South Atlantic	**$20,563**	**$17,271**	**$17,170**	**$17,969**	**$18,461**	**$20,866**	**$27,877**
Delaware	24,748	16,969	17,007	18,787	19,849	22,744	37,124
District of Columbia	29,806	29,746	27,523	27,016	29,062	31,894	30,003
Florida	19,406	18,176	17,722	18,047	17,862	18,960	25,748
Georgia	21,051	18,110	17,460	18,680	18,895	21,535	27,817
Maryland	22,796	19,585	18,570	19,035	20,739	23,368	31,248
North Carolina	19,306	14,692	15,650	16,523	16,830	19,552	26,465
South Carolina	18,379	14,328	14,885	16,029	15,713	18,793	25,261
Virginia	21,281	16,721	16,965	17,925	19,058	22,018	29,394
West Virginia	19,702	12,533	14,057	15,586	17,252	22,438	32,139
East South Central	**$18,562**	**$13,951**	**$14,904**	**$15,808**	**$16,683**	**$19,141**	**$25,484**
Alabama	18,684	14,027	14,938	15,983	16,648	18,845	25,999
Kentucky	18,395	13,721	14,643	15,158	16,314	19,858	25,754
Mississippi	16,534	12,565	13,691	14,603	15,335	17,462	21,963
Tennessee	19,374	14,746	15,628	16,652	17,468	19,572	26,055
West South Central	**$20,740**	**$17,055**	**$16,671**	**$17,286**	**$18,203**	**$22,007**	**$28,416**
Arkansas	16,876	13,484	14,073	15,060	15,493	18,030	20,993
Louisiana	19,378	15,815	15,385	16,544	17,205	20,909	27,113
Oklahoma	19,219	15,102	15,394	15,661	16,569	21,649	29,004
Texas	21,774	18,220	17,568	18,047	19,038	22,849	29,464
East North Central	**$22,326**	**$16,726**	**$16,721**	**$17,835**	**$19,493**	**$23,126**	**$31,357**
Illinois	24,000	19,224	18,782	19,726	21,544	25,175	30,797
Indiana	20,416	14,653	14,970	16,051	17,446	20,864	30,600
Michigan	23,527	17,095	16,886	18,320	19,997	24,041	35,043
Ohio	21,603	15,836	16,269	17,195	18,754	22,348	30,449
Wisconsin	19,966	14,533	14,897	16,087	17,736	21,031	28,695
West North Central	**$19,617**	**$14,313**	**$14,937**	**$16,215**	**$17,338**	**$20,637**	**$28,031**
Iowa	17,792	13,032	13,827	15,026	15,745	19,139	25,525
Kansas	19,239	14,185	15,111	16,499	17,137	20,588	27,893
Minnesota	21,647	15,973	15,819	17,185	18,865	22,317	30,948
Missouri	20,487	14,840	15,541	16,795	18,007	21,112	28,740
Nebraska	17,215	13,223	14,167	15,073	15,843	18,531	22,098
North Dakota	15,805	12,229	13,561	14,381	15,099	16,559	27,097
South Dakota	14,985	11,928	12,847	14,129	14,057	16,115	20,896
Mountain	**$19,788**	**$16,431**	**$16,083**	**$16,695**	**$17,666**	**$20,847**	**$27,534**
Arizona	20,145	18,038	17,027	17,235	17,460	19,702	29,901
Colorado	21,745	17,325	17,389	18,089	19,329	22,488	31,980
Idaho	17,707	13,342	14,032	14,875	16,009	19,258	27,594
Montana	15,983	12,616	13,126	14,144	15,234	20,010	23,321
Nevada	19,920	20,131	18,235	18,896	18,934	19,737	21,551
New Mexico	17,990	14,114	14,436	15,171	15,855	20,417	28,822
Utah	18,727	15,962	14,513	15,174	17,180	20,514	23,242
Wyoming	18,505	13,801	14,655	15,089	16,067	27,316	33,840
Pacific	**$15,842**	**$21,031**	**$19,518**	**$20,129**	**$12,729**	**$13,158**	**$18,167**
Alaska	26,901	20,700	21,271	22,623	24,436	28,620	49,156
California	13,992	22,368	20,326	20,880	10,573	10,276	14,416
Hawaii	21,156	20,547	19,108	19,088	19,691	22,610	25,058
Oregon	19,871	15,843	15,888	16,703	18,544	21,995	28,549
Washington	22,573	17,037	17,386	18,085	19,779	23,179	34,984

Source: U.S. Bureau of the Census, <u>County Business Patterns</u>, 1991, (Washington, D.C.: Bureau of the Census).
Note: See table notes at end of Section G.

Table G15
General Revenue and Revenue Sources, Fiscal Year 1990-91[11,12]

	State/Local General Revenue per Capita	Source of General Revenue (%)		
		Federal Government	State Sources	Local Sources
United States	**$3,578**	**17.1%**	**45.2%**	**37.7%**
New England	**$3,896**	**18.5%**	**50.2%**	**31.3%**
Connecticut	4,088	17.1	49.2	33.8
Maine	3,405	19.5	51.0	29.5
Massachusetts	4,094	18.9	53.0	28.1
New Hampshire	3,104	14.3	35.1	50.6
Rhode Island	3,642	22.6	49.4	28.0
Vermont	3,864	21.9	49.9	28.1
Middle Atlantic	**$4,370**	**16.6%**	**41.1%**	**42.3%**
New Jersey	4,240	13.9	47.6	38.5
New York	5,273	17.3	37.5	45.2
Pennsylvania	3,129	17.2	44.2	38.6
South Atlantic	**$3,178**	**15.5%**	**45.3%**	**39.1%**
Delaware	4,065	14.9	67.0	18.1
District of Columbia	n/a	n/a	n/a	n/a
Florida	3,245	12.6	40.1	47.3
Georgia	3,203	17.9	39.6	42.4
Maryland	3,577	15.1	47.9	37.0
North Carolina	2,910	17.9	48.8	33.2
South Carolina	3,000	21.0	49.4	29.6
Virginia	3,297	13.4	48.8	37.8
West Virginia	3,039	20.9	56.0	23.1
East South Central	**$2,880**	**22.6%**	**47.4%**	**30.0%**
Alabama	2,876	21.7	49.4	29.0
Kentucky	3,095	20.7	56.3	23.0
Mississippi	2,826	27.2	42.4	30.3
Tennessee	2,755	22.4	41.1	36.4
West South Central	**$3,037**	**17.6%**	**43.6%**	**38.8%**
Arkansas	2,499	21.8	52.4	25.9
Louisiana	3,391	21.6	45.4	33.0
Oklahoma	3,014	17.4	53.3	29.3
Texas	3,031	16.1	40.3	43.6
East North Central	**$3,351**	**16.6%**	**46.1%**	**37.3%**
Illinois	3,318	15.2	44.1	40.7
Indiana	3,075	16.3	49.5	34.2
Michigan	3,614	16.8	45.7	37.6
Ohio	3,176	18.3	45.0	36.8
Wisconsin	3,637	16.0	50.5	33.5
West North Central	**$3,385**	**16.9%**	**46.9%**	**36.1%**
Iowa	3,441	16.7	48.7	34.6
Kansas	3,262	14.7	43.9	41.3
Minnesota	4,189	15.8	48.7	35.5
Missouri	2,723	18.3	45.7	36.0
Nebraska	3,414	15.7	45.1	39.2
North Dakota	3,746	22.6	52.3	25.1
South Dakota	3,066	25.5	42.0	32.5
Mountain	**$3,407**	**17.2%**	**46.8%**	**36.0%**
Arizona	3,297	14.6	46.7	38.7
Colorado	3,508	15.0	38.9	46.1
Idaho	2,954	19.2	51.9	28.9
Montana	3,288	25.5	46.0	28.5
Nevada	3,366	13.7	46.8	39.5
New Mexico	3,628	18.7	59.6	21.6
Utah	3,051	20.2	49.0	30.8
Wyoming	5,478	23.5	45.7	30.9
Pacific	**$3,296**	**16.5%**	**48.0%**	**35.5%**
Alaska	12,455	11.3	69.8	18.8
California	2,966	16.6	45.3	38.2
Hawaii	4,704	15.1	67.6	17.3
Oregon	3,726	20.0	41.3	38.7
Washington	3,800	16.4	52.0	31.6

Source: U.S. Bureau of the Census, 1991, Government Finances: 1990-91, GF/91-5
(Washington, D.C.: Bureau of the Census).
Note: See table notes at end of Section G.

Table G16
Tax Revenue and Tax Revenue Sources, Fiscal Year 1990-91[11]

	State/Local Taxes Per Capita	Source of Tax Revenues (%)			
		Property Taxes	Sales/Gross Taxes	Individual Income Taxes[13]	Corporate Income and Other Taxes[14]
United States	**$2,083**	**32.0%**	**35.3%**	**20.8%**	**11.9%**
New England	**$2,388**	**40.0%**	**26.8%**	**22.5%**	**10.8%**
Connecticut	2,668	42.7	38.8	5.4	13.1
Maine	2,034	39.2	29.7	23.1	8.0
Massachusetts	2,469	33.6	20.2	36.1	10.1
New Hampshire	1,916	70.0	14.7	1.7	13.6
Rhode Island	2,130	41.3	31.6	20.1	7.0
Vermont	2,121	43.6	26.1	21.4	8.9
Middle Atlantic	**$2,756**	**34.8%**	**27.9%**	**24.8%**	**12.3%**
New Jersey	2,781	45.2	29.6	15.7	9.5
New York	3,337	33.0	26.9	28.8	11.3
Pennsylvania	1,888	29.8	29.3	23.2	17.7
South Atlantic	**$1,822**	**30.1%**	**38.8%**	**20.2%**	**10.9%**
Delaware	2,081	15.0	12.2	34.3	38.5
District of Columbia	n/a	n/a	n/a	n/a	n/a
Florida	1,831	37.5	51.0	0.0	11.5
Georgia	1,797	28.2	40.0	24.8	7.0
Maryland	2,284	27.0	25.4	39.0	8.6
North Carolina	1,673	22.9	35.2	31.4	10.5
South Carolina	1,560	27.1	38.3	25.0	9.6
Virginia	1,962	32.6	30.5	26.3	10.6
West Virginia	1,628	16.7	42.9	19.6	20.8
East South Central	**$1,455**	**19.0%**	**48.6%**	**17.2%**	**15.3%**
Alabama	1,363	12.5	49.6	22.0	15.9
Kentucky	1,730	16.0	35.0	31.9	17.1
Mississippi	1,304	26.4	48.2	14.2	11.2
Tennessee	1,410	23.3	60.2	1.4	15.1
West South Central	**$1,693**	**31.1%**	**49.3%**	**6.2%**	**13.4%**
Arkansas	1,334	18.1	46.7	25.1	10.1
Louisiana	1,653	16.7	51.5	11.4	20.4
Oklahoma	1,671	15.0	43.1	23.0	18.9
Texas	1,757	38.7	50.1	0.0	11.2
East North Central	**$2,013**	**35.7%**	**30.9%**	**23.8%**	**9.6%**
Illinois	2,133	36.8	35.8	18.4	9.0
Indiana	1,739	32.8	35.0	25.6	6.6
Michigan	2,104	42.4	23.1	21.2	13.3
Ohio	1,851	29.2	31.8	30.2	8.8
Wisconsin	2,226	35.8	28.4	27.2	8.6
West North Central	**$1,917**	**31.3%**	**34.6%**	**23.3%**	**10.8%**
Iowa	1,947	35.2	28.6	24.7	11.5
Kansas	1,930	35.8	34.1	18.3	11.8
Minnesota	2,348	30.6	30.0	28.6	10.8
Missouri	1,596	23.6	42.4	24.9	9.1
Nebraska	1,955	38.1	34.7	19.4	7.8
North Dakota	1,734	29.1	40.0	10.4	20.5
South Dakota	1,487	38.9	46.9	0.0	14.2
Mountain	**$1,851**	**29.8%**	**41.6%**	**17.4%**	**11.2%**
Arizona	2,006	33.0	42.8	16.6	7.6
Colorado	1,959	35.2	35.5	22.2	7.1
Idaho	1,602	26.6	35.7	26.8	10.9
Montana	1,466	35.7	15.5	23.9	24.9
Nevada	1,944	23.5	63.2	0.0	13.3
New Mexico	1,721	12.9	55.8	13.9	17.4
Utah	1,601	26.0	40.7	25.2	8.1
Wyoming	2,253	40.5	26.8	0.0	32.7
Pacific	**$2,302**	**28.5%**	**36.3%**	**21.5%**	**13.7%**
Alaska	4,411	27.5	7.6	0.0	64.9
California	2,283	28.0	34.8	24.3	12.9
Hawaii	2,862	15.0	51.4	26.8	6.8
Oregon	2,017	43.5	9.0	33.7	13.8
Washington	2,239	28.0	62.1	0.0	9.9

Source: U.S. Bureau of the Census, 1991, <u>Government Finances: 1990-91</u>, GF/91-5
(Washington, D.C.: Bureau of the Census).
Note: See table notes at end of Section G.

	State/Local General Expend. Per Capita[15]	Class of Expenditure (%)					
		Education	Welfare[16]	Health/ Hospitals	Police/ Corrections	Highways	Other
United States	**3,590**	**34.2%**	**14.0%**	**9.0%**	**8.2%**	**7.2%**	**27.4%**
New England	**$4,025**	**29.5%**	**18.4%**	**7.4%**	**7.9%**	**6.7%**	**30.0%**
Connecticut	4,446	29.7	14.5	7.6	8.2	8.8	31.2
Maine	3,631	35.3	19.7	4.9	5.6	9.1	25.4
Massachusetts	4,105	25.8	21.9	8.8	8.4	4.5	30.6
New Hampshire	3,061	37.0	13.2	4.6	7.6	8.4	29.2
Rhode Island	3,863	31.2	16.4	6.6	8.4	6.3	31.1
Vermont	3,865	41.1	15.3	3.1	4.4	10.5	25.6
Middle Atlantic	**$4,449**	**30.8%**	**16.8%**	**8.1%**	**8.0%**	**6.1%**	**30.2%**
New Jersey	4,098	33.2	13.5	5.2	7.9	6.5	33.7
New York	5,458	28.2	18.2	10.1	8.7	5.4	29.4
Pennsylvania	3,194	35.2	15.9	5.6	6.4	7.4	29.5
South Atlantic	**$3,273**	**35.5%**	**11.4%**	**10.3%**	**8.8%**	**7.6%**	**26.4%**
Delaware	4,093	36.4	9.2	5.4	6.6	10.8	31.6
District of Columbia	n/a	n/a	n/a	n/a	n/a	n/a	n/a
Florida	3,415	32.6	10.5	9.5	10.2	6.6	30.6
Georgia	3,213	33.8	12.7	15.8	8.5	7.2	22.0
Maryland	3,717	35.6	11.9	4.9	9.9	7.9	29.8
North Carolina	3,036	38.9	12.0	12.1	7.7	7.6	21.7
South Carolina	3,138	37.9	13.8	15.0	7.2	5.5	20.6
Virginia	3,322	38.1	9.8	8.6	8.2	9.8	25.5
West Virginia	2,862	38.3	13.7	7.0	3.6	10.4	27.0
East South Central	**$2,840**	**35.0%**	**13.4%**	**12.8%**	**6.6%**	**8.6%**	**23.6%**
Alabama	2,941	36.3	11.6	16.5	6.2	7.5	21.9
Kentucky	2,949	34.4	17.9	7.1	6.1	8.8	25.7
Mississippi	2,691	37.1	12.7	15.2	5.1	9.5	20.4
Tennessee	2,757	33.3	11.9	12.6	8.1	9.0	25.1
West South Central	**$2,924**	**37.8%**	**12.0%**	**9.8%**	**7.7%**	**8.4%**	**24.2%**
Arkansas	2,439	40.1	16.5	8.5	5.8	9.4	19.7
Louisiana	3,349	31.3	13.0	12.5	7.1	8.2	27.9
Oklahoma	2,888	36.7	13.3	10.5	7.3	10.1	22.1
Texas	2,896	39.6	11.0	9.0	8.2	8.1	24.1
East North Central	**$3,339**	**36.8%**	**15.2%**	**8.3%**	**7.7%**	**7.3%**	**24.7%**
Illinois	3,294	33.4	13.1	6.5	8.4	8.6	30.0
Indiana	2,994	41.3	14.0	10.1	6.0	6.8	21.8
Michigan	3,599	38.5	15.3	10.3	7.9	5.8	22.2
Ohio	3,194	35.7	17.5	8.6	7.7	7.2	23.3
Wisconsin	3,671	38.8	15.9	6.4	7.5	7.9	23.5
West North Central	**$3,364**	**37.1%**	**13.5%**	**9.1%**	**5.9%**	**10.2%**	**24.2%**
Iowa	3,417	38.7	13.3	10.8	5.0	11.6	20.6
Kansas	3,200	38.6	10.6	8.8	7.2	11.7	23.1
Minnesota	4,250	33.2	15.9	9.5	4.9	8.8	27.7
Missouri	2,664	38.8	13.3	9.1	7.6	9.1	22.1
Nebraska	3,467	41.2	11.9	8.5	5.7	10.5	22.2
North Dakota	3,541	37.8	12.5	4.1	3.5	11.0	31.1
South Dakota	2,949	36.1	10.7	5.7	5.2	14.9	27.4
Mountain	**$3,450**	**37.7%**	**9.8%**	**6.9%**	**8.4%**	**9.5%**	**27.7%**
Arizona	3,537	38.0	9.9	4.9	9.7	9.4	28.1
Colorado	3,418	37.5	10.6	6.9	8.5	9.5	27.0
Idaho	2,849	38.7	10.4	8.8	6.5	10.9	24.7
Montana	3,499	37.3	12.4	5.8	5.2	12.0	27.3
Nevada	3,743	31.9	6.2	7.4	11.6	8.2	34.7
New Mexico	3,461	38.1	10.6	9.2	7.9	8.8	25.4
Utah	3,015	42.2	10.2	7.2	6.8	7.0	26.6
Wyoming	5,064	36.0	6.5	10.5	5.6	14.9	26.5
Pacific	**$4,024**	**32.3%**	**13.6%**	**8.6%**	**9.5%**	**5.4%**	**30.7%**
Alaska	9,776	23.4	6.5	3.6	5.2	10.3	51.0
California	3,978	31.9	14.4	9.1	10.3	4.6	29.7
Hawaii	4,589	24.3	9.1	7.2	5.8	6.6	47.0
Oregon	3,630	36.7	11.1	7.2	8.2	7.7	29.1
Washington	3,815	37.2	12.7	8.0	6.9	7.3	27.9

Source: U.S. Bureau of the Census, 1991, <u>Government Finances: 1990-91</u>, GF/91-5
(Washington, D.C.: Bureau of the Census).
Note: See table notes at end of Section G.

Notes to Tables, Section G

1. Population excludes persons over age 65, those living in institutions, and those in families with active military service members. Percentages may not sum to 100 owing to rounding.

2. We define families as health insurance units. A health insurance unit includes the members of a nuclear family who can be covered under one health policy. The standard we use follows a typical insurance industry standard: a policy-holder may cover his or her spouse, all children under age 18, and children between ages 18 and 21 who are full-time students. Thus, whereas a single 25-year-old child living with his or her parents may be included in the parents' nuclear family, he or she would be treated as a separate, single health unit.

3. The distribution listed is the number of individuals in families of a given type. A family of the type "Single" will have fewer persons than a family of the type "Married with Children."

4. Incomes used in these tables are primarily the incomes reported on the CPS. However, we incorporated some corrections to incomes estimated by the Urban Institute's TRIM2 model. The model corrects for underreporting of income from the cash welfare programs—AFDC and SSI—and makes corrections to reported interest and dividend incomes. See Linda Giannarelli, 1992, *An Analyst's Guide to TRIM2* (Washington, D.C.: Urban Institute Press) for details.

In tables showing family income as a percentage of poverty, poverty is defined using the federal poverty guidelines from the U.S. Department of Health and Human Services.

5. The worker and unemployed populations are defined as individuals who reported working or being unemployed, respectively, in the week before the interview. Workers are furthermore defined as individuals who reported a positive number of usual hours of work per week in the previous year. The labor force participation rate is defined as the number of individuals in the labor force divided by the population ages 18 to 64. The labor force is defined as workers plus the unemployed. The employment rate is defined as the number of employed workers divided by the population ages 18 to 64. The unemployment rate is defined as the number of individuals who reported themselves as unemployed divided by the number of individuals in the labor force.

6. Workers are defined as persons 18 to 64 years old reporting a positive number of usual hours worked. Firm size, sector, and industry are based on the job held for the longest period during the year preceding the March CPS interview.

7. The self-employed sector includes self-employed unincorporated workers; the self-employed incorporated are classified as private-sector workers.

8. "Other" includes these industries: agriculture, forestry, fisheries, mining, construction, transportation, communication, other public utilities, finance, insurance, and real estate. Public-sector workers are not included in table G11.

9. Establishment size is based on the number of workers at a single location of a business establishment. Firm size, used in tables based on the merged CPS file, is based on worker reports of the number of workers at all locations that their

employer operates. If an employer operates in one location, establishment and firm size are the same; otherwise, establishment size will be smaller. See note 3 following the text in Section G.

10. The Census Bureau's County Business Patterns provides first-quarter payroll and employment for the week including March 12. We define annualized payroll per worker as first-quarter pay divided by reported number of employees and multiplied by 4.

11. State finance data from the U.S. Department of Commerce are reproduced in the publication *States in Profile, The State Policy Reference Book, 1994, First Edition* (Washington, D.C.: U.S. Department of Commerce). Data for the District of Columbia are not included.

12. General revenues exclude employee retirement fund revenue and revenue of certain utility-type operations. The categories of revenues in table G15 differ from the categories used in the 1993 edition of this volume. In the prior edition, revenues were categorized as federal government, other sources, and state/local taxes. This edition shows revenue sources by government level: federal, state, and local. This change corresponds to a change in our source for these data. Instead of combining state and local sources into one category, the Census Bureau reports state and local sources separately, along with the federal sources, and eliminates the "Other" category.

13. South Dakota and Texas have no state income tax but do have local option income taxes.

14. "Corporate Income and Other Taxes" includes corporate income taxes, severance tax, parimutual tax, lottery tax, alcohol tax, tobacco tax, and motor fuel tax.

15. General expenditures exclude expenditures on utilities, liquor stores, and employee retirement funds.

16. Outlays for Medicaid are included in general expenditures on welfare.

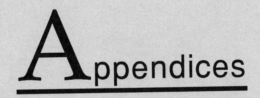

Appendices

APPENDIX ONE: TRENDS IN HEALTH INSURANCE COVERAGE

APPENDIX TWO: THE THREE-YEAR MERGED MARCH CURRENT POPULATION SURVEY

APPENDIX THREE: ISSUES IN USING THE CPS TO MEASURE HEALTH INSURANCE COVERAGE

Trends in Health Insurance Coverage

In this appendix, we discuss state-level trends in health insurance coverage. We compare health insurance coverage as indicated in the three-year CPS merge for the years 1988–1990 to the file for 1990–1992. The three-year CPS file for 1988–1990 is the file used in the first *State-Level Data Book on Health Care Access and Financing*; the latter data set is used for the tables in this edition. In the introduction to this volume, we discuss a number of changes made to our analysis of CPS data since the first edition was prepared. Briefly, these are: first, the change in our definition of family from a nuclear family concept to health insurance units; second, a change to our definition of children's coverage; and third, our merge previously took all observations from the middle year whereas we now take all observations from the last year. (See the Introduction for a more detailed discussion.) The comparisons between the two files in this appendix control for the first two differences; that is, we apply our new definitions to the old data here. The method used to merge the files is not changed. Therefore, the average health coverage for the period 1988–1990 is dominated by the middle year—1989—and the average health coverage for the period 1990–1992 is dominated by the last year—1992. Therefore, the changes in coverage shown may be thought of as changes over a period somewhat over two years.

Table 1.1 and the 1.2 table series are presented to facilitate comparison of coverage for the period covered by the first data book to tables in this edition. These tables apply our new definitions to the old data. Table 1.1 shows coverage for all nonelderly using our new definition of children's coverage (analogous to table A1); the 1.2 table series shows the same by age group (analogous to the A2 table series). Table 1.3 and the 1.4 table series show the changes in health insurance coverage between the two periods. These tables subtract the most recent data (in table A1 and the A2 table series) from the older data (in table 1.1 and the 1.2 table series). Statistical significance (at the 95 percent level) is indicated.[1] We provide analysis of table 1.3 and the 1.4 table series below.

TRENDS FOR TOTAL NONELDERLY POPULATION

Table 1.3 shows the change in health insurance coverage for the nonelderly population. We show the four major types of health coverage: employer coverage (own-employer coverage and coverage as a dependent are grouped together here), Medicaid, other coverage (private nongroup coverage, Medicare, CHAMPUS, and military and VA health), and the uninsured. Average coverage for the period 1990–1992 is shown relative to coverage for 1988–1990. *Therefore, a negative number indicates the prevalence of the group has declined between the periods; conversely, a positive number indicates an increase for the group over time.*

For the nation, employer coverage fell 2.8 percent between the two periods. Employer coverage decreased in all but five states. In the few states with an apparent increase in employer coverage, the changes are not statistically significant. Declines in employer coverage were particularly strong in the South Atlantic region, where coverage fell in each state (though not statistically significant in Delaware) and averaged -4.8 percent for the region as a whole. Among the 29 states with a statistically significant change in employer health coverage, the declines range from -7 percent in South Carolina and -5.8 percent in the District of Columbia to -2 percent in Michigan.

Medicaid coverage increased by 1.9 percent nationally. Medicaid coverage increased in most states. Increases in Medicaid were statistically significant in 15 states, where growth ranged from 4.1 percent in the District of Columbia and 3.6 percent in Florida to 1.1 percent in Michigan. In other states, the statistical evidence is not sufficient (at the 95 percent confidence level) to assert a real change in Medicaid coverage.[2] Only three states have significant changes in other coverage; other coverage increased in Connecticut and Washington by 1.6 and 1.2 percent, respectively, and declined in Iowa by -1.9 percent.

Nationally, the uninsured rate increased by 0.7 percent. The South Atlantic region, which had the greatest decline in employer coverage, had a correspondingly high increase in its uninsured rate: 1.8 percent. The uninsured rate increased in 35 states and fell in 16; however, increases are statistically significant in 22 states, and declines significant in only 7 states. Among states where changes in the uninsured rate were statistically significant, the changes ranged from increases of 3.1 percent in the District of Columbia and South Carolina to a decline of -3.6 percent in New Mexico. In the remaining 22 states, the statistical evidence is not sufficient (at the 95 percent confidence interval) to assert a change in the true uninsured rate. The data show that there can be considerable variation in the uninsured trend across states within a single region; in New England, two states had significant declines in the uninsured rate (-1.2 percent in Connecticut and -1.8 percent in New Hampshire), and two states experienced significant increases in the uninsured rate (1.6 percent in Maine and 1.8 percent in Massachusetts).

Because the primary source of health insurance coverage throughout the United States is employer-sponsored coverage, one would expect that states with significant declines in employer coverage would have the highest increases in uninsured rates. To a large extent this is true; there is a strong negative correlation between the change in employer coverage and the uninsured rate. In fact, the two states with the steepest declines in employer coverage, South Carolina and the District of Columbia (-7.0 and -5.8 percent, respectively), also had the highest increase in state uninsured rates (3.1 percent each)[3]. However, changes in Medicaid coverage offset declines in employer coverage more in some states than in others. For example, Maryland, New Jersey, and North Carolina experienced similar declines in employer coverage between the periods analyzed (-3.7 percent, -3.6 percent, and -3.7 percent, respectively). However, more rapid growth of Medicaid in North Carolina (2.6 percent) than in Maryland and New Jersey (1.1 percent and 1.7 percent, respectively) moderated the growth in the population without health coverage: the uninsured rate grew 1.1 percent in North Carolina versus 2.0 percent in Maryland and 2.3 percent in New Jersey. While growth in Medicaid offsets declines in employer coverage in aggregate, it is not necessarily true that the growth in Medicaid is helping the same families which are losing employer coverage. While CPS data does not follow families across time, analysis of earlier data suggests that the types of families gaining Medicaid in recent years are different from the types of families losing employer coverage.[4]

TRENDS FOR CHILDREN AND ADULTS

Table 1.4a shows changes in health insurance coverage for children under age 18, and table 1.4b shows changes for adults ages 18–64. The loss of employer coverage and growth in Medicaid observed for the whole nonelderly population generally hold for children and adults as well. In most cases, however, the magnitude of the shifts for children were somewhat greater than the changes for adults. Overall, employer coverage of children declined -3.0 percent relative to a -2.7 percent decline for adults. Often the gap between the loss of employer coverage among children and adults is greater than at the national level: for example, in Rhode Island children's employer coverage dropped -8.8 percent relative to -3.1 percent for adults, and in Florida children's employer coverage dropped -7.9 percent versus a drop of -4.3 percent for adults. Coverage of children through employer coverage dropped in 38 states and increased in 13. However, the change is statistically significant (at the 95 percent level) in only 25 states, and in each case indicates a decline in coverage. Among adults, employer coverage declined in 46 states and grew in only 5, but changes were statistically significant in 24 states, and in each such case was a decline. Among the 19 states where employer coverage declines were statistically significant for both children and adults, the loss of coverage was greater among children in all but 4 states (New Jersey, South Carolina, Virginia, and Illinois).

The contrast in coverage trends for children and adults is most clear with regard to Medicaid coverage. Nationally, the prevalence of children with Medicaid as a primary source of coverage increased by 4.0 percentage points relative to a gain of 1.0 percentage point for adults. Children's Medicaid gains were statistically significant in 17 states, ranging from 7.2 percent in Missouri and 7.1 percent in Rhode Island to the lowest statistically significant gain of 1.9 percent in Illinois. Medicaid gains among adults were statistically significant in only 13 states, ranging from 2.8 percent in the District of Columbia to 1.0 percent in California and Illinois.

Changes in the prevalence of uninsurance were considerably different for children and adults. Nationally, the uninsured rate *declined* for children by -1.0 percent, but *grew* for adults by 1.4 percent. Uninsured rates fell for children in 26 states and for adults in only 12, but declines were statistically significant in 16 states for children and only 3 states for adults. Changes in children's uninsured rates ranged from declines in excess of -6 percent in Arizona, New Mexico, and Colorado to increases of 3.7 percent in the District of Columbia and 4.5 percent in Nevada. Among adults, changes in uninsurance ranged from declines of greater than 2 percent in Colorado and New Mexico to increases of 3.3 percent in Florida and 4.6 percent in South Carolina.

Improvements in the uninsured rates for children are usually associated with growth in the Medicaid program. However, Medicaid growth alone is not enough to ensure an overall expansion of coverage for children. While many states with improved coverage of children experienced Medicaid growth greater than the national average, some of these states also tended to have little change in employer coverage among children. And several states with significant *increases* in uninsurance among children had strong gains in Medicaid which were not sufficient to offset greater losses in employer coverage (the District of Columbia, Maine, Massachusetts, and Nevada).

Notes, Appendix One

1. An asterisk indicates that there is sufficient statistical evidence (at the 95 percent level) to assert that there was a real change (increase or decrease) in the prevalence of the group over time. If no asterisk appears, there is too much uncertainty to assert that the change shown for the CPS sample population represents a change in the true prevalence of the coverage group for the whole state population.

2. Data in table D4 show growth in Medicaid enrollment over a similar time period. Those data are not subject to the same limitations on statistical significance associated with these survey-based data.

3. Note that changes in coverage were extreme in the District in each coverage category: the District had the third largest decline in employer coverage, the greatest growth in Medicaid, and the second largest drop in other coverage and was tied for the greatest increase in the uninsured rate.

4. See, for example, Colin Winterbottom, 1993, "Trends in Health Insurance Coverage" (Washington, D.C.: Urban Institute).

Table 1.1
Health Insurance Coverage of the Nonelderly, 1988-90[1]

(Persons in thousands)

	Number	Employer (own)	Employer (other)[2]	Medicaid[3]	Other Public[4]	Other Private[5]	Uninsured[6]
United States	213,580	33.2% (0.10)	33.3% (0.10)	9.0% (0.06)	2.0% (0.03)	7.5% (0.06)	15.1% (0.08)
New England	11,157	37.9% (0.36)	36.4% (0.36)	6.8% (0.19)	1.4% (0.09)	7.1% (0.19)	10.4% (0.23)
Connecticut	2,761	41.6% (1.03)	37.4% (1.01)	4.5% (0.43)	0.9% (0.20)	5.9% (0.49)	9.7% (0.62)
Maine	1,055	33.2% (0.87)	35.9% (0.89)	9.6% (0.55)	2.0% (0.26)	8.4% (0.52)	10.9% (0.58)
Massachusetts	5,062	37.5% (0.48)	36.1% (0.47)	8.3% (0.27)	1.6% (0.12)	7.0% (0.25)	9.5% (0.29)
New Hampshire	972	35.9% (0.97)	35.9% (0.97)	3.0% (0.34)	1.4% (0.24)	8.4% (0.56)	15.5% (0.73)
Rhode Island	823	38.3% (1.00)	36.3% (0.99)	6.9% (0.52)	1.2% (0.22)	6.8% (0.52)	10.7% (0.63)
Vermont	485	36.4% (0.97)	35.4% (0.96)	6.6% (0.50)	1.4% (0.23)	9.2% (0.58)	11.1% (0.63)
Middle Atlantic	32,415	35.9% (0.24)	34.9% (0.24)	9.5% (0.15)	1.3% (0.06)	6.9% (0.13)	11.6% (0.16)
New Jersey	6,631	39.7% (0.47)	35.0% (0.46)	6.5% (0.23)	0.8% (0.09)	7.5% (0.25)	10.4% (0.29)
New York	15,507	33.9% (0.36)	33.0% (0.36)	11.8% (0.25)	1.4% (0.09)	6.6% (0.19)	13.3% (0.26)
Pennsylvania	10,277	36.4% (0.45)	37.8% (0.45)	7.8% (0.25)	1.4% (0.11)	6.8% (0.23)	9.8% (0.28)
South Atlantic	36,005	35.1% (0.26)	31.1% (0.25)	7.7% (0.14)	2.5% (0.08)	7.0% (0.14)	16.7% (0.20)
Delaware	574	37.9% (0.96)	32.9% (0.93)	5.5% (0.45)	2.2% (0.29)	6.5% (0.49)	15.0% (0.71)
District of Columbia	493	36.7% (1.02)	18.2% (0.82)	15.5% (0.77)	1.9% (0.29)	8.0% (0.57)	19.8% (0.85)
Florida	10,334	32.2% (0.43)	28.0% (0.41)	7.0% (0.23)	3.1% (0.16)	8.6% (0.26)	21.2% (0.38)
Georgia	5,475	34.4% (0.85)	31.1% (0.82)	8.9% (0.51)	2.0% (0.25)	6.4% (0.43)	17.3% (0.67)
Maryland	3,977	39.3% (0.95)	35.1% (0.93)	7.9% (0.53)	1.7% (0.25)	5.3% (0.44)	10.7% (0.60)
North Carolina	5,469	37.9% (0.46)	30.3% (0.43)	7.5% (0.25)	2.5% (0.15)	7.5% (0.25)	14.3% (0.33)
South Carolina	2,932	36.3% (0.80)	32.1% (0.77)	7.5% (0.44)	3.1% (0.29)	5.8% (0.39)	15.2% (0.59)
Virginia	5,166	36.0% (0.78)	33.9% (0.77)	5.8% (0.38)	2.7% (0.27)	6.1% (0.39)	15.5% (0.59)
West Virginia	1,586	29.4% (0.83)	35.3% (0.87)	13.2% (0.61)	2.1% (0.26)	5.8% (0.42)	14.1% (0.63)
East South Central	13,214	30.5% (0.42)	32.2% (0.42)	10.9% (0.28)	2.9% (0.15)	6.8% (0.23)	16.7% (0.34)
Alabama	3,570	30.3% (0.82)	32.8% (0.84)	7.9% (0.48)	3.5% (0.33)	6.2% (0.43)	19.3% (0.71)
Kentucky	3,123	31.2% (0.86)	33.4% (0.87)	12.2% (0.60)	2.6% (0.29)	6.8% (0.47)	13.8% (0.64)
Mississippi	2,285	25.3% (0.74)	29.2% (0.77)	15.2% (0.61)	3.5% (0.31)	7.3% (0.44)	19.5% (0.67)
Tennessee	4,236	33.0% (0.82)	32.6% (0.82)	10.2% (0.53)	2.3% (0.26)	6.9% (0.44)	15.1% (0.62)
West South Central	23,455	28.1% (0.32)	30.4% (0.32)	8.4% (0.20)	2.9% (0.12)	7.5% (0.19)	22.7% (0.30)
Arkansas	2,103	27.1% (0.79)	32.1% (0.83)	9.5% (0.52)	3.7% (0.33)	7.8% (0.48)	19.9% (0.71)
Louisiana	3,701	25.0% (0.81)	30.3% (0.86)	12.8% (0.63)	3.2% (0.33)	7.2% (0.48)	21.5% (0.77)
Oklahoma	2,679	28.4% (0.82)	30.8% (0.84)	8.3% (0.50)	3.2% (0.32)	8.7% (0.51)	20.6% (0.73)
Texas	14,973	28.9% (0.42)	30.2% (0.42)	7.1% (0.24)	2.7% (0.15)	7.3% (0.24)	23.8% (0.39)

Table 1.1 (Continued)
Health Insurance Coverage of the Nonelderly, 1988-90[1]
(Persons in thousands)

	Number	Employer (own)	Employer (other)[2]	Medicaid[3]	Other Public[4]	Other Private[5]	Uninsured[6]
East North Central	**36,786**	**34.5%**	**37.3%**	**9.2%**	**1.5%**	**6.9%**	**10.6%**
		(0.25)	**(0.25)**	**(0.15)**	**(0.06)**	**(0.13)**	**(0.16)**
Illinois	10,171	34.9%	34.5%	10.4%	1.5%	7.5%	11.2%
		(0.46)	(0.45)	(0.29)	(0.12)	(0.25)	(0.30)
Indiana	4,773	34.2%	36.4%	5.5%	2.0%	8.0%	13.8%
		(0.89)	(0.91)	(0.43)	(0.27)	(0.51)	(0.65)
Michigan	8,201	33.6%	37.7%	11.4%	1.4%	6.3%	9.6%
		(0.45)	(0.46)	(0.30)	(0.11)	(0.23)	(0.28)
Ohio	9,537	34.4%	39.2%	8.9%	1.6%	6.0%	9.8%
		(0.44)	(0.45)	(0.27)	(0.12)	(0.22)	(0.28)
Wisconsin	4,104	35.8%	40.4%	6.3%	1.0%	7.7%	8.8%
		(0.83)	(0.85)	(0.42)	(0.17)	(0.46)	(0.49)
West North Central	**15,279**	**32.3%**	**36.1%**	**6.9%**	**1.6%**	**11.8%**	**11.3%**
		(0.38)	**(0.4)**	**(0.21)**	**(0.1)**	**(0.27)**	**(0.26)**
Iowa	2,386	31.1%	37.5%	6.1%	1.3%	15.4%	8.7%
		(0.82)	(0.86)	(0.43)	(0.20)	(0.64)	(0.50)
Kansas	2,078	32.5%	38.7%	7.0%	1.2%	10.5%	10.2%
		(0.83)	(0.87)	(0.45)	(0.19)	(0.55)	(0.54)
Minnesota	3,849	33.7%	34.1%	8.3%	1.6%	11.6%	10.6%
		(0.87)	(0.87)	(0.51)	(0.23)	(0.59)	(0.57)
Missouri	4,475	33.8%	36.3%	6.6%	1.9%	7.9%	13.4%
		(0.88)	(0.90)	(0.47)	(0.26)	(0.50)	(0.64)
Nebraska	1,361	30.8%	36.3%	5.7%	1.6%	14.3%	11.3%
		(0.80)	(0.83)	(0.40)	(0.22)	(0.61)	(0.55)
North Dakota	546	24.8%	34.9%	5.9%	2.1%	22.8%	9.5%
		(0.74)	(0.82)	(0.40)	(0.24)	(0.72)	(0.50)
South Dakota	585	26.5%	33.2%	5.7%	2.7%	17.2%	14.7%
		(0.73)	(0.77)	(0.38)	(0.27)	(0.62)	(0.58)
Mountain	**11,712**	**30.2%**	**34.7%**	**6.2%**	**2.5%**	**8.4%**	**18.0%**
		(0.36)	**(0.37)**	**(0.19)**	**(0.12)**	**(0.22)**	**(0.3)**
Arizona	3,016	31.6%	31.6%	7.0%	2.9%	7.8%	19.2%
		(0.87)	(0.87)	(0.48)	(0.31)	(0.50)	(0.74)
Colorado	2,836	32.2%	34.8%	5.9%	2.5%	7.5%	17.2%
		(0.90)	(0.92)	(0.46)	(0.30)	(0.51)	(0.73)
Idaho	896	27.5%	36.2%	4.4%	1.9%	12.4%	17.6%
		(0.76)	(0.82)	(0.35)	(0.24)	(0.56)	(0.65)
Montana	711	27.2%	31.7%	8.0%	2.4%	13.6%	17.0%
		(0.78)	(0.82)	(0.48)	(0.27)	(0.60)	(0.66)
Nevada	1,010	37.7%	30.8%	3.8%	2.4%	6.5%	18.7%
		(0.92)	(0.87)	(0.36)	(0.29)	(0.47)	(0.74)
New Mexico	1,302	24.1%	30.1%	7.7%	3.4%	7.3%	27.4%
		(0.75)	(0.81)	(0.47)	(0.32)	(0.46)	(0.79)
Utah	1,525	27.5%	46.6%	6.0%	1.3%	8.4%	10.2%
		(0.77)	(0.86)	(0.41)	(0.20)	(0.48)	(0.52)
Wyoming	414	28.9%	38.3%	5.8%	2.3%	10.6%	14.1%
		(0.94)	(1.01)	(0.49)	(0.31)	(0.64)	(0.72)
Pacific	**33,556**	**31.6%**	**29.1%**	**11.9%**	**1.9%**	**7.4%**	**18.0%**
		(0.29)	**(0.29)**	**(0.21)**	**(0.09)**	**(0.17)**	**(0.24)**
Alaska	435	29.4%	30.4%	8.3%	3.7%	6.0%	22.3%
		(0.80)	(0.80)	(0.48)	(0.33)	(0.42)	(0.73)
California	25,588	30.5%	27.7%	13.2%	1.7%	7.4%	19.5%
		(0.35)	(0.34)	(0.25)	(0.10)	(0.20)	(0.30)
Hawaii	850	41.1%	31.8%	8.6%	2.3%	6.2%	10.1%
		(0.99)	(0.93)	(0.56)	(0.30)	(0.48)	(0.60)
Oregon	2,464	34.4%	35.5%	6.8%	1.6%	6.8%	14.9%
		(0.93)	(0.94)	(0.49)	(0.24)	(0.49)	(0.70)
Washington	4,219	35.0%	33.5%	8.3%	2.9%	8.1%	12.1%
		(0.86)	(0.85)	(0.50)	(0.30)	(0.49)	(0.59)

Source: **Three-year merged March CPS, 1989, 1990, and 1991.**
Note: **See table notes at end of Appendix One.**

Table 1.2a
Health Insurance Coverage of the Nonelderly by Age, 1988-90:
Children Under Age 18[1]
(Persons in thousands)

	Number	Employer[9]	Medicaid[3]	Other Coverage[7]	Uninsured[9]
United States	63,262	64.7%	17.1%	5.8%	12.4%
		(0.19)	(0.15)	(0.09)	(0.19)
New England	2,994	74.5%	13.4%	4.6%	7.5%
		(0.63)	(0.49)	(0.30)	(0.38)
Connecticut	740	79.7%	9.3%	3.0%	7.9%
		(1.62)	(1.17)	(0.69)	(1.09)
Maine	308	70.5%	16.8%	6.2%	6.5%
		(1.57)	(1.28)	(0.83)	(0.84)
Massachusetts	1,331	72.9%	16.9%	4.4%	5.8%
		(0.85)	(0.72)	(0.39)	(0.45)
New Hampshire	271	71.1%	4.6%	6.7%	17.7%
		(1.74)	(0.80)	(0.96)	(1.47)
Rhode Island	216	78.2%	13.3%	3.3%	5.1%
		(1.66)	(1.37)	(0.72)	(0.88)
Vermont	130	71.2%	12.0%	9.1%	7.8%
		(1.77)	(1.26)	(1.12)	(1.05)
Middle Atlantic	9,153	69.5%	18.9%	4.4%	7.2%
		(0.44)	(0.38)	(0.20)	(0.25)
New Jersey	1,776	73.9%	13.9%	5.0%	7.2%
		(0.81)	(0.64)	(0.40)	(0.48)
New York	4,430	65.2%	23.5%	4.1%	7.3%
		(0.68)	(0.61)	(0.28)	(0.37)
Pennsylvania	2,947	73.4%	15.0%	4.5%	7.2%
		(0.77)	(0.62)	(0.36)	(0.45)
South Atlantic	10,038	64.3%	15.2%	5.4%	15.1%
		(0.49)	(0.37)	(0.23)	(0.36)
Delaware	157	70.0%	12.6%	3.8%	13.6%
		(1.73)	(1.26)	(0.72)	(1.30)
District of Columbia	124	47.8%	35.3%	3.9%	13.1%
		(2.11)	(2.02)	(0.82)	(1.42)
Florida	2,815	58.2%	14.6%	6.8%	20.4%
		(0.87)	(0.62)	(0.44)	(0.71)
Georgia	1,610	62.5%	17.6%	5.5%	14.4%
		(1.59)	(1.25)	(0.75)	(1.15)
Maryland	1,042	73.7%	17.2%	1.6%	7.5%
		(1.68)	(1.44)	(0.48)	(1.01)
North Carolina	1,470	66.7%	14.7%	5.9%	12.7%
		(0.86)	(0.65)	(0.43)	(0.61)
South Carolina	845	66.0%	14.0%	5.1%	14.9%
		(1.46)	(1.07)	(0.68)	(1.10)
Virginia	1,497	68.4%	10.4%	5.7%	15.4%
		(1.41)	(0.93)	(0.71)	(1.10)
West Virginia	476	64.2%	21.1%	4.5%	10.2%
		(1.59)	(1.35)	(0.68)	(1.00)
East South Central	4,001	59.8%	20.0%	5.4%	14.8%
		(0.81)	(0.66)	(0.37)	(0.59)
Alabama	1,100	61.7%	14.1%	6.3%	17.8%
		(1.57)	(1.12)	(0.79)	(1.24)
Kentucky	890	63.6%	20.5%	4.3%	11.6%
		(1.66)	(1.40)	(0.70)	(1.11)
Mississippi	772	50.7%	28.8%	6.2%	14.3%
		(1.46)	(1.33)	(0.71)	(1.03)
Tennessee	1,239	60.9%	19.5%	4.8%	14.8%
		(1.57)	(1.27)	(0.69)	(1.14)
West South Central	7,493	56.0%	15.9%	6.6%	21.5%
		(0.62)	(0.46)	(0.31)	(0.51)
Arkansas	693	57.6%	17.2%	6.1%	19.1%
		(1.52)	(1.17)	(0.74)	(1.21)
Louisiana	1,173	50.2%	23.6%	6.5%	19.7%
		(1.66)	(1.41)	(0.82)	(1.32)
Oklahoma	796	56.5%	17.0%	7.9%	18.7%
		(1.65)	(1.25)	(0.90)	(1.30)
Texas	4,831	57.1%	13.7%	6.5%	22.7%
		(0.80)	(0.55)	(0.40)	(0.68)

Table 1.2a (Continued)
Health Insurance Coverage of the Nonelderly by Age, 1988-90: Children Under Age 18[1]
(Persons in thousands)

	Number	Employer[9]	Medicaid[3]	Other Coverage[7]	Uninsured[6]
East North Central	**10,951**	**70.6%**	**17.5%**	**5.0%**	**6.9%**
		(0.43)	**(0.36)**	**(0.21)**	**(0.24)**
Illinois	2,997	66.2%	21.5%	5.1%	7.2%
		(0.83)	(0.72)	(0.39)	(0.46)
Indiana	1,382	67.8%	10.8%	7.9%	13.6%
		(1.63)	(1.08)	(0.94)	(1.20)
Michigan	2,446	70.3%	20.2%	4.0%	5.4%
		(0.79)	(0.69)	(0.34)	(0.39)
Ohio	2,920	73.7%	17.0%	4.0%	5.4%
		(0.74)	(0.63)	(0.33)	(0.38)
Wisconsin	1,205	77.9%	11.1%	5.9%	5.1%
		(1.32)	(1.00)	(0.75)	(0.70)
West North Central	**4,731**	**69.3%**	**12.5%**	**9.3%**	**8.9%**
		(0.68)	**(0.49)**	**(0.43)**	**(0.42)**
Iowa	731	72.8%	10.8%	11.3%	5.1%
		(1.43)	(1.00)	(1.02)	(0.71)
Kansas	634	73.8%	13.0%	6.4%	6.8%
		(1.42)	(1.09)	(0.79)	(0.81)
Minnesota	1,192	67.0%	15.4%	10.0%	7.6%
		(1.55)	(1.19)	(0.99)	(0.88)
Missouri	1,375	69.3%	12.1%	6.1%	12.5%
		(1.56)	(1.10)	(0.81)	(1.11)
Nebraska	433	69.1%	10.4%	12.0%	8.5%
		(1.42)	(0.94)	(1.00)	(0.86)
North Dakota	180	61.7%	10.4%	20.9%	7.0%
		(1.45)	(0.91)	(1.22)	(0.76)
South Dakota	186	61.8%	9.7%	13.7%	14.7%
		(1.42)	(0.86)	(1.00)	(1.03)
Mountain	**3,841**	**65.0%**	**11.4%**	**7.2%**	**16.4%**
		(0.65)	**(0.43)**	**(0.35)**	**(0.51)**
Arizona	939	60.5%	14.3%	5.5%	19.7%
		(1.64)	(1.18)	(0.76)	(1.33)
Colorado	898	66.3%	10.9%	5.6%	17.1%
		(1.62)	(1.07)	(0.79)	(1.29)
Idaho	314	66.0%	7.3%	12.3%	14.4%
		(1.37)	(0.75)	(0.95)	(1.01)
Montana	231	58.0%	13.9%	13.9%	14.1%
		(1.52)	(1.07)	(1.07)	(1.08)
Nevada	285	69.3%	8.1%	7.3%	15.3%
		(1.64)	(0.97)	(0.92)	(1.28)
New Mexico	424	53.5%	13.5%	6.5%	26.5%
		(1.54)	(1.05)	(0.76)	(1.36)
Utah	617	77.2%	9.0%	6.8%	7.0%
		(1.14)	(0.78)	(0.69)	(0.69)
Wyoming	133	69.3%	10.1%	10.4%	10.2%
		(1.69)	(1.10)	(1.12)	(1.11)
Pacific	**10,061**	**57.7%**	**22.1%**	**5.9%**	**14.3%**
		(0.57)	**(0.48)**	**(0.27)**	**(0.41)**
Alaska	140	60.2%	17.1%	6.6%	16.1%
		(1.51)	(1.16)	(0.77)	(1.14)
California	7,718	54.4%	24.1%	5.8%	15.7%
		(0.68)	(0.58)	(0.32)	(0.50)
Hawaii	224	68.0%	18.1%	4.8%	9.1%
		(1.82)	(1.51)	(0.84)	(1.12)
Oregon	750	69.2%	12.5%	5.1%	13.2%
		(1.64)	(1.17)	(0.78)	(1.20)
Washington	1,229	69.1%	16.7%	7.0%	7.1%
		(1.54)	(1.24)	(0.85)	(0.86)

Source: Three-year merged March CPS, 1989, 1990, and 1991.
Note: See table notes at end of Appendix One.

Table 1.2b
Health Insurance Coverage of the Nonelderly by Age, 1988-90:
Adults 18-64[1]

(Persons in thousands)

	Number	Employer (own)	Employer (other)[2]	Medicaid[3]	Other Coverage[7]	Uninsured[6]
United States	150,318	47.1%	20.1%	5.5%	11.1%	16.2%
		(0.13)	(0.10)	(0.06)	(0.08)	(0.10)
New England	8,163	51.8%	22.4%	4.4%	10.0%	11.4%
		(0.44)	(0.36)	(0.18)	(0.26)	(0.28)
Connecticut	2,022	56.7%	22.0%	2.7%	8.3%	10.3%
		(1.21)	(1.01)	(0.39)	(0.67)	(0.74)
Maine	747	46.9%	21.6%	6.6%	12.2%	12.7%
		(1.10)	(0.91)	(0.55)	(0.72)	(0.73)
Massachusetts	3,731	50.8%	23.0%	5.2%	10.2%	10.9%
		(0.57)	(0.48)	(0.25)	(0.35)	(0.36)
New Hampshire	701	49.7%	22.3%	2.3%	11.0%	14.6%
		(1.20)	(1.00)	(0.36)	(0.75)	(0.84)
Rhode Island	607	51.7%	21.6%	4.6%	9.5%	12.7%
		(1.20)	(0.98)	(0.50)	(0.70)	(0.80)
Vermont	355	49.6%	22.4%	4.7%	11.1%	12.3%
		(1.18)	(0.98)	(0.50)	(0.74)	(0.77)
Middle Atlantic	23,262	50.0%	21.4%	5.8%	9.6%	13.3%
		(0.30)	(0.25)	(0.14)	(0.18)	(0.20)
New Jersey	4,855	54.2%	20.8%	3.7%	9.6%	11.6%
		(0.56)	(0.45)	(0.21)	(0.33)	(0.36)
New York	11,077	47.4%	20.2%	7.2%	9.6%	15.7%
		(0.45)	(0.36)	(0.23)	(0.27)	(0.33)
Pennsylvania	7,330	51.0%	23.5%	5.0%	9.7%	10.8%
		(0.55)	(0.47)	(0.24)	(0.33)	(0.34)
South Atlantic	25,967	48.6%	18.3%	4.7%	11.1%	17.3%
		(0.32)	(0.24)	(0.13)	(0.20)	(0.24)
Delaware	417	52.1%	19.0%	2.8%	10.6%	15.5%
		(1.16)	(0.91)	(0.38)	(0.71)	(0.84)
District of Columbia	369	49.1%	8.2%	8.8%	11.9%	22.1%
		(1.23)	(0.67)	(0.69)	(0.79)	(1.02)
Florida	7,518	44.1%	16.8%	4.1%	13.5%	21.5%
		(0.54)	(0.40)	(0.21)	(0.37)	(0.44)
Georgia	3,865	48.7%	18.1%	5.2%	9.5%	18.5%
		(1.06)	(0.82)	(0.47)	(0.62)	(0.82)
Maryland	2,936	53.3%	21.4%	4.6%	8.9%	11.8%
		(1.13)	(0.93)	(0.47)	(0.65)	(0.73)
North Carolina	3,998	51.8%	16.9%	4.8%	11.5%	14.9%
		(0.55)	(0.41)	(0.24)	(0.35)	(0.39)
South Carolina	2,087	51.0%	18.4%	4.8%	10.5%	15.3%
		(0.98)	(0.76)	(0.42)	(0.60)	(0.71)
Virginia	3,669	50.7%	19.8%	3.9%	10.1%	15.6%
		(0.97)	(0.77)	(0.37)	(0.58)	(0.70)
West Virginia	1,110	42.0%	23.0%	9.8%	9.4%	15.8%
		(1.07)	(0.91)	(0.64)	(0.63)	(0.79)
East South Central	9,213	43.7%	20.3%	7.0%	11.6%	17.5%
		(0.54)	(0.44)	(0.28)	(0.35)	(0.41)
Alabama	2,469	43.6%	20.0%	5.2%	11.3%	19.9%
		(1.07)	(0.86)	(0.48)	(0.68)	(0.86)
Kentucky	2,233	43.6%	21.3%	8.9%	11.5%	14.7%
		(1.08)	(0.89)	(0.62)	(0.70)	(0.77)
Mississippi	1,513	38.2%	18.2%	8.3%	13.2%	22.1%
		(1.02)	(0.81)	(0.58)	(0.71)	(0.87)
Tennessee	2,997	46.6%	20.9%	6.4%	11.0%	15.2%
		(1.03)	(0.84)	(0.50)	(0.65)	(0.74)
West South Central	15,962	41.3%	18.4%	4.8%	12.1%	23.3%
		(0.42)	(0.33)	(0.18)	(0.28)	(0.36)
Arkansas	1,410	40.5%	19.5%	5.6%	14.1%	20.3%
		(1.06)	(0.86)	(0.50)	(0.75)	(0.87)
Louisiana	2,528	36.6%	21.0%	7.9%	12.2%	22.3%
		(1.09)	(0.92)	(0.61)	(0.74)	(0.94)
Oklahoma	1,882	40.5%	19.9%	4.6%	13.5%	21.4%
		(1.06)	(0.86)	(0.46)	(0.74)	(0.89)
Texas	10,142	42.7%	17.3%	4.0%	11.6%	24.4%
		(0.55)	(0.42)	(0.22)	(0.36)	(0.48)

Table 1.2b (Continued)
Health Insurance Coverage of the Nonelderly by Age, 1988-90:
Adults 18-64[1]
(Persons in thousands)

	Number	Employer (own)	Employer (other)[2]	Medicaid[3]	Other Coverage[7]	Uninsured[6]
East North Central	25,836	49.1% (0.31)	23.3% (0.26)	5.6% (0.14)	9.9% (0.19)	12.1% (0.20)
Illinois	7,174	49.5% (0.57)	21.3% (0.47)	5.8% (0.27)	10.6% (0.35)	12.8% (0.38)
Indiana	3,391	48.1% (1.12)	23.7% (0.95)	3.3% (0.40)	11.0% (0.70)	13.9% (0.77)
Michigan	5,755	47.9% (0.56)	23.8% (0.48)	7.6% (0.30)	9.2% (0.33)	11.4% (0.36)
Ohio	6,617	49.5% (0.56)	24.0% (0.48)	5.4% (0.25)	9.3% (0.32)	11.8% (0.36)
Wisconsin	2,898	50.7% (1.03)	24.9% (0.89)	4.3% (0.41)	9.9% (0.61)	10.3% (0.62)
West North Central	10,548	46.8% (0.49)	21.2% (0.40)	4.3% (0.20)	15.3% (0.36)	12.3% (0.33)
Iowa	1,655	44.7% (1.06)	21.9% (0.88)	4.0% (0.42)	19.1% (0.84)	10.2% (0.65)
Kansas	1,444	46.8% (1.07)	23.2% (0.90)	4.3% (0.43)	14.0% (0.74)	11.6% (0.69)
Minnesota	2,657	48.8% (1.10)	19.4% (0.87)	5.2% (0.49)	14.6% (0.78)	12.0% (0.72)
Missouri	3,100	48.8% (1.12)	21.7% (0.93)	4.2% (0.45)	11.5% (0.72)	13.9% (0.78)
Nebraska	927	45.1% (1.05)	21.1% (0.86)	3.5% (0.38)	17.7% (0.80)	12.7% (0.70)
North Dakota	366	37.0% (1.01)	21.8% (0.87)	3.7% (0.39)	26.8% (0.93)	10.8% (0.65)
South Dakota	399	38.7% (0.97)	19.9% (0.80)	3.8% (0.38)	22.7% (0.84)	14.7% (0.71)
Mountain	7,871	44.9% (0.47)	19.9% (0.38)	3.7% (0.18)	12.7% (0.32)	18.7% (0.37)
Arizona	2,078	45.8% (1.12)	18.7% (0.88)	3.7% (0.42)	13.0% (0.76)	18.9% (0.88)
Colorado	1,938	47.1% (1.17)	20.2% (0.94)	3.6% (0.44)	12.0% (0.76)	17.2% (0.88)
Idaho	582	42.3% (1.05)	20.2% (0.85)	2.9% (0.35)	15.4% (0.76)	19.3% (0.84)
Montana	480	40.2% (1.05)	19.1% (0.84)	5.1% (0.47)	17.1% (0.81)	18.4% (0.83)
Nevada	725	52.4% (1.11)	15.8% (0.81)	2.2% (0.32)	9.6% (0.66)	20.1% (0.89)
New Mexico	878	35.8% (1.03)	18.8% (0.84)	5.0% (0.47)	12.7% (0.71)	27.8% (0.96)
Utah	909	46.1% (1.12)	25.7% (0.98)	3.9% (0.44)	11.8% (0.72)	12.4% (0.74)
Wyoming	281	42.5% (1.25)	23.8% (1.07)	3.7% (0.48)	14.1% (0.88)	15.9% (0.92)
Pacific	23,495	45.1% (0.38)	17.0% (0.28)	7.6% (0.20)	10.8% (0.23)	19.6% (0.30)
Alaska	295	43.2% (1.05)	16.3% (0.79)	4.1% (0.42)	11.2% (0.67)	25.2% (0.92)
California	17,870	43.6% (0.45)	16.2% (0.33)	8.5% (0.25)	10.6% (0.28)	21.1% (0.37)
Hawaii	626	55.6% (1.16)	19.0% (0.92)	5.2% (0.52)	9.7% (0.69)	10.5% (0.72)
Oregon	1,714	49.4% (1.17)	20.7% (0.95)	4.4% (0.48)	9.8% (0.70)	15.7% (0.85)
Washington	2,990	49.4% (1.07)	18.9% (0.84)	4.9% (0.46)	12.7% (0.71)	14.2% (0.75)

Source: Three-year merged March CPS, 1989, 1990, and 1991.
Note: See table notes at end of Appendix One.

Table 1.3

Change in Nonelderly Health Insurance Coverage, 1990-92 Relative to 1988-90[8]

(An asterisk(*) indicates the change is statistically significant at the 95 percent level)

	Employer[9]	Medicaid[3]	Other Coverage[7]	Uninsured[6]
United States	-2.8% *	1.9% *	0.1%	0.7% *
New England	-3.3% *	2.1% *	0.7% *	0.5% *
Connecticut	-2.6% *	2.3% *	1.6% *	-1.2% *
Maine	-4.1% *	1.8%	0.7%	1.6% *
Massachusetts	-4.1% *	2.0% *	0.3%	1.8% *
New Hampshire	-0.5%	1.8%	0.5%	-1.8% *
Rhode Island	-4.6% *	3.1% *	1.1%	0.3%
Vermont	-1.4%	2.7% *	-0.9%	-0.4%
Middle Atlantic	-3.0% *	1.6% *	0.1%	1.3% *
New Jersey	-3.6% *	1.7% *	-0.3%	2.3% *
New York	-3.2% *	1.4% *	0.5%	1.3% *
Pennsylvania	-2.5% *	1.9% *	-0.1%	0.7% *
South Atlantic	-4.8% *	2.5% *	0.5% *	1.8% *
Delaware	-0.1%	0.9%	-0.3%	-0.5%
District of Columbia	-5.8% *	4.1% *	-1.5%	3.1% *
Florida	-5.3% *	3.6% *	-0.2%	1.9% *
Georgia	-5.2% *	2.6% *	1.2%	1.4% *
Maryland	-3.7% *	1.1%	0.7%	2.0% *
North Carolina	-3.7% *	2.6% *	0.0%	1.1% *
South Carolina	-7.0% *	3.2% *	0.7%	3.1% *
Virginia	-4.5% *	1.3%	1.0%	2.2% *
West Virginia	-4.6% *	2.9% *	1.0%	0.7%
East South Central	-2.3% *	1.9% *	-0.3%	0.7% *
Alabama	-1.2%	1.5%	-0.7%	0.3%
Kentucky	-1.5%	1.0%	0.2%	0.3%
Mississippi	-1.9%	0.6%	-0.4%	1.7% *
Tennessee	-3.9% *	3.5% *	-0.2%	0.6%
West South Central	-2.7% *	2.9% *	-0.2%	0.0%
Arkansas	-3.5% *	2.3% *	1.2%	0.0%
Louisiana	-2.9% *	2.4% *	0.2%	0.3%
Oklahoma	-3.0% *	1.6%	0.4%	0.9%
Texas	-2.5% *	3.4% *	-0.6%	-0.2%
East North Central	-2.3% *	1.4% *	0.1%	0.8% *
Illinois	-3.2% *	1.4% *	0.1%	1.6% *
Indiana	-0.5%	1.7%	-0.4%	-0.9%
Michigan	-2.0% *	1.1% *	-0.1%	1.0% *
Ohio	-2.7% *	1.2% *	0.4%	1.1% *
Wisconsin	-2.3% *	1.9% *	0.3%	0.0%
West North Central	-2.5% *	1.3% *	0.0%	1.2% *
Iowa	-1.0%	1.1%	-1.9% *	1.8% *
Kansas	-3.2% *	0.0%	1.3%	1.8% *
Minnesota	-1.3%	-0.1%	-0.2%	1.6% *
Missouri	-5.2% *	3.1% *	1.0%	1.0%
Nebraska	0.4%	1.7%	-0.6%	-1.5% *
North Dakota	-0.3%	1.1%	-1.1%	0.3%
South Dakota	-2.0%	1.4%	-1.5%	2.1% *
Mountain	-0.5%	1.8% *	-0.1%	-1.2% *
Arizona	-0.9%	2.4% *	0.1%	-1.6% *
Colorado	1.2%	1.1%	1.2%	-3.4% *
Idaho	-1.0%	2.4% *	-1.6%	0.2%
Montana	0.3%	2.1% *	-1.7%	-0.7%
Nevada	-4.0% *	1.8% *	-0.3%	2.6% *
New Mexico	-0.3%	3.7% *	0.1%	-3.6% *
Utah	-1.1%	0.2%	-1.0%	2.0% *
Wyoming	-0.3%	2.1% *	-0.9%	-0.9%
Pacific	-1.5% *	1.8% *	0.0%	-0.3%
Alaska	0.0%	2.1% *	-1.3%	-0.8%
California	-1.6% *	2.0% *	-0.1%	-0.3%
Hawaii	2.2%	0.1%	-0.5%	-1.8% *
Oregon	-1.1%	1.7% *	0.0%	-0.6%
Washington	-1.9% *	0.7%	1.2% *	0.0%

Source: Three-year merged March CPS files from 1989-1991 and 1991-1993.
Note: See table notes at end of Appendix One.

Table 1.4a

Change in Nonelderly Health Insurance Coverage by Age, 1990-92 Relative to 1988-90: Children Under 18[8]

(An asterisk(*) indicates the change is statistically significant at the 95 percent level)

	Employer[9]	Medicaid[3]	Other Coverage[7]	Uninsured[6]
United States	-3.0% *	4.0% *	0.0%	-1.0% *
New England	-4.6% *	4.2% *	0.5%	0.0%
Connecticut	-4.3% *	4.3% *	2.5% *	-2.4% *
Maine	-7.9% *	3.3% *	1.9%	2.6% *
Massachusetts	-5.6% *	4.2% *	-0.6%	2.0% *
New Hampshire	2.0%	3.2% *	-0.1%	-5.1% *
Rhode Island	-8.8% *	7.1% *	1.4%	0.2%
Vermont	2.0%	5.2% *	-4.5% *	-2.6% *
Middle Atlantic	-3.1% *	3.0% *	-0.1%	0.1%
New Jersey	-3.1% *	2.3% *	-0.4%	1.2% *
New York	-3.4% *	2.9% *	0.1%	0.4%
Pennsylvania	-2.8% *	3.9% *	-0.1%	-1.0% *
South Atlantic	-6.0% *	5.7% *	0.7% *	-0.4%
Delaware	0.4%	0.9%	1.4%	-2.6% *
District of Columbia	-7.1% *	5.9% *	-2.5% *	3.7% *
Florida	-7.9% *	9.2% *	0.4%	-1.7% *
Georgia	-5.7% *	4.7% *	0.4%	0.6%
Maryland	-6.8% *	2.4%	2.6% *	1.8%
North Carolina	-5.2% *	6.1% *	0.1%	-0.9%
South Carolina	-5.5% *	4.5% *	1.3%	-0.4%
Virginia	-3.7% *	3.1% *	1.0%	-0.3%
West Virginia	-5.9% *	6.7% *	-0.6%	-0.2%
East South Central	-2.4% *	3.4% *	0.0%	-1.0%
Alabama	-2.4%	3.1% *	-1.2%	0.6%
Kentucky	-1.7%	2.0%	0.5%	-0.7%
Mississippi	-0.6%	-0.7%	0.5%	0.8%
Tennessee	-3.5%	6.9% *	0.5%	-3.9% *
West South Central	-2.7% *	6.1% *	-0.5%	-2.9% *
Arkansas	-5.2% *	3.9% *	1.0%	0.4%
Louisiana	0.5%	4.5% *	-1.1%	-3.9% *
Oklahoma	0.2%	2.2%	-1.3%	-1.1%
Texas	-3.7% *	7.5% *	-0.4%	-3.4% *
East North Central	-2.7% *	2.8% *	0.0%	-0.1%
Illinois	-2.9% *	1.9% *	0.5%	0.5%
Indiana	1.2%	3.6% *	-1.0%	-3.7% *
Michigan	-3.0% *	2.0% *	-0.2%	1.2% *
Ohio	-3.9% *	3.6% *	0.5%	-0.2%
Wisconsin	-3.6% *	4.0% *	-1.2%	0.8%
West North Central	-4.4% *	3.3% *	0.4%	0.8%
Iowa	-2.9%	2.4%	-1.2%	1.7% *
Kansas	-3.7% *	-0.6%	1.4%	2.9% *
Minnesota	-2.8%	1.4%	0.9%	0.5%
Missouri	-8.7% *	7.2% *	1.3%	0.2%
Nebraska	-2.3%	4.5% *	-1.2%	-1.0%
North Dakota	1.4%	1.4%	-2.2%	-0.6%
South Dakota	-4.6% *	3.7% *	0.2%	0.7%
Mountain	0.2%	3.6% *	-0.5%	-3.3% *
Arizona	1.1%	5.5% *	0.7%	-7.4% *
Colorado	2.9%	2.6%	0.9%	-6.4% *
Idaho	-2.9%	4.1% *	-1.5%	0.3%
Montana	1.3%	4.3% *	-3.8% *	-1.7%
Nevada	-5.1% *	2.8% *	-2.2% *	4.5% *
New Mexico	-0.7%	8.1% *	-0.8%	-6.6% *
Utah	-1.1%	-0.3%	-0.8%	2.2% *
Wyoming	0.8%	3.1% *	-4.5% *	0.5%
Pacific	-0.5%	3.5% *	-0.6% *	-2.3% *
Alaska	-2.2%	2.6%	-0.6%	0.2%
California	-0.5%	4.1% *	-0.8% *	-2.8% *
Hawaii	3.3%	-0.4%	0.0%	-2.9% *
Oregon	1.1%	3.5% *	-1.2%	-3.5% *
Washington	-1.7%	-0.2%	0.8%	1.1%

Source: Three-year merged March CPS files from 1989-1991 and 1991-1993.

Note: See table notes at end of Appendix One.

Table 1.4b
Change in Nonelderly Health Insurance Coverage by Age, 1990-92 Relative to 1988-90:
Adults 18 - 64[8]

(An asterisk(*) indicates the change is statistically significant at the 95 percent level)

	Employer[9]	Medicaid[3]	Other Coverage[7]	Uninsured[6]
United States	-2.7% *	1.0% *	0.2%	1.4% *
New England	-2.8% *	1.3% *	0.8%	0.7% *
Connecticut	-2.0%	1.3%	1.3%	-0.7%
Maine	-2.5%	1.2%	0.2%	1.1%
Massachusetts	-3.5% *	1.2% *	0.7%	1.7% *
New Hampshire	-1.5%	1.3%	0.8%	-0.6%
Rhode Island	-3.1% *	2.1% *	0.9%	0.2%
Vermont	-2.8%	1.5%	0.6%	0.7%
Middle Atlantic	-3.0% *	0.9% *	0.3%	1.8% *
New Jersey	-3.8% *	1.3% *	-0.2%	2.7% *
New York	-3.1% *	0.6%	0.7%	1.7% *
Pennsylvania	-2.4% *	1.1% *	-0.1%	1.4% *
South Atlantic	-4.3% *	1.2% *	0.4%	2.7% *
Delaware	-0.3%	0.7%	-0.8%	0.4%
District of Columbia	-5.1% *	2.8% *	-0.9%	3.2% *
Florida	-4.3% *	1.3% *	-0.3%	3.3% *
Georgia	-5.0% *	1.8%	1.5%	1.7% *
Maryland	-2.6%	0.4%	0.0%	2.1% *
North Carolina	-3.1% *	1.2% *	0.1%	1.9% *
South Carolina	-7.7% *	2.5% *	0.5%	4.6% *
Virginia	-4.9% *	0.6%	1.0%	3.2% *
West Virginia	-4.2% *	1.6%	1.6%	1.0%
East South Central	-2.2% *	1.2% *	-0.4%	1.4% *
Alabama	-0.6%	0.9%	-0.4%	0.2%
Kentucky	-1.4%	0.6%	0.1%	0.7%
Mississippi	-2.5%	0.8%	-0.7%	2.4% *
Tennessee	-4.1% *	2.3% *	-0.6%	2.4% *
West South Central	-2.7% *	1.5% *	-0.1%	1.4% *
Arkansas	-2.7%	1.6%	1.2%	-0.2%
Louisiana	-4.5% *	1.2%	0.9%	2.4% *
Oklahoma	-4.3% *	1.2%	1.3%	1.9% *
Texas	-2.1% *	1.7% *	-0.8%	1.2% *
East North Central	-2.1% *	0.7% *	0.2%	1.3% *
Illinois	-3.2% *	1.0% *	0.1%	2.1% *
Indiana	-1.1%	0.9%	-0.1%	0.3%
Michigan	-1.5% *	0.6%	0.0%	0.9% *
Ohio	-2.2% *	0.2%	0.3%	1.7% *
Wisconsin	-1.7% *	0.7%	1.2%	-0.1%
West North Central	-1.6% *	0.4%	-0.2%	1.4% *
Iowa	-0.2%	0.5%	-2.2%	1.9% *
Kansas	-3.1% *	0.1%	1.6%	1.4% *
Minnesota	-0.8%	-0.5%	-0.8%	2.0% *
Missouri	-3.6% *	1.4%	0.9%	1.4%
Nebraska	1.7%	0.3%	-0.2%	-1.8% *
North Dakota	-1.0%	1.0%	-0.6%	0.6%
South Dakota	-0.8%	0.2%	-2.1%	2.8% *
Mountain	-0.9% *	1.0% *	0.0%	-0.2%
Arizona	-1.8%	1.3%	-0.3%	0.8%
Colorado	0.4%	0.7%	1.1%	-2.2% *
Idaho	0.1%	1.3%	-1.6%	0.2%
Montana	-0.2%	0.8%	-0.5%	-0.1%
Nevada	-3.6%	1.2%	0.5%	1.9% *
New Mexico	-0.1%	1.6%	0.6%	-2.1% *
Utah	-1.2%	0.4%	-1.1%	1.9% *
Wyoming	-0.9%	1.3%	1.0%	-1.4%
Pacific	-1.9% *	1.0% *	0.3%	0.6% *
Alaska	1.0%	1.7% *	-1.6%	-1.2%
California	-2.0% *	1.0% *	0.3%	0.8% *
Hawaii	1.9%	0.0%	-0.5%	-1.4%
Oregon	-2.0%	1.0%	0.4%	0.7%
Washington	-2.0% *	1.1%	1.3%	-0.4%

Source: Three-year merged March CPS files from 1989-1991 and 1991-1993.
Note: See table notes at end of Appendix One.

Notes to Tables, Appendix One

1. These tables apply modified definitions of children's coverage to the data presented in the previous edition of the *State-Level Data Book*. We present these tables because we changed the way we interpret data from the Current Population Survey to count the coverage of children since the first edition was prepared. While this change is small (it increases employer coverage and reduces the uninsured rate by about 0.5 percent), it makes it difficult to compare coverage in tables from the previous version to data in this update. (The nature of the change is discussed in the Introduction.)

Population in the merged CPS file excludes persons aged 65 and over, those living in institutions, and those in families with active military service members. Persons with more than one type of health coverage are included only in the first category shown. Percentages may not sum to 100 owing to rounding.

2. "Employer (other)" includes persons covered as dependents on the employer group insurance of another family member.

3. Medicaid coverage reflects corrections to the reports of Medicaid on the Current Population Survey made by the Urban Institute's TRIM2 model (see Appendix Three).

4. "Other Public" includes persons covered under Medicare, CHAMPUS, VA, and military health programs.

5. "Other Private" includes persons covered through privately purchased coverage that is not obtained through an employer or union (often referred to as "nongroup" coverage).

6. "Uninsured" includes persons without insurance coverage for the entire reference year. The CPS does not currently collect information on persons who are without coverage for less than 12 months (see Appendix Three).

7. These categories are hierarchical, so each person is shown only in the first appropriate category. For example, a person in a health unit where the head works full-time and the spouse part-time would be classified only in the one full-time worker group.

8. These tables show the changes in coverage. They are coverage rates for the more recent period (tables A1, A2a, and A2b) less the rates for the previous period (tables 1.1, 1.2a, and 1.2b). Therefore, a negative number indicates the prevalence of the group has declined between the periods; conversely, a positive number indicates an increase for the group over time.

9. We have combined "own" employer coverage and "other" employer coverage for these tables.

The Three-Year Merged March Current Population Survey

The estimates in Sections A, B, C, and G of this report are from a sample constructed from three years of the March Current Population Survey: 1991, 1992, and 1993.[1] The purpose of merging three years of data was to produce more reliable estimates, particularly estimates calculated using relatively small subsamples of the data. Three-year merged CPS samples have also been used to calculate state-level poverty rates.[2]

The March CPS sample does not include persons living in institutions. For this volume, we have also eliminated people aged 65 and over and individuals who were in the military at the time of the survey and their families. We eliminated the elderly because the vast majority of that group have coverage through Medicare, and most proposed health reforms deal primarily with the nonelderly. To obtain estimates for the civilian population, we also eliminated families with an active military member.

THREE-YEAR MERGED SAMPLE

Because the Current Population Survey is an interview of a sample population rather than the whole population, estimates based on the sample are subject to sampling error. Great care is taken to select a sample that is "representative" of the whole population in a state, but these estimates—such as the uninsured rate—obtained from the CPS sample can only be characterized as the best estimate of the uninsured rate for the whole population. The standard error is a measure of the uncertainty associated with using a sample to measure a population mean; in other words, it is a measure of "how far off" the estimate based on the sample is likely to be. A smaller standard error indicates greater confidence that the sample estimate is close to the true value for the whole population. Standard errors vary with several factors, including what is being estimated (health insurance counts versus poverty rates) and the size of the sample population drawn. With a larger sample, we can have more confidence that our estimates are closer to the true value for the whole population, and the standard error is thus smaller. This is the reason we merged individual CPS files to obtain a larger sample.

The estimates derived from the merged sample are averages over the three years. Estimates from this sample are more meaningful if the true number (such as the percentage uninsured) remains relatively unchanged over the period of the files merged. Merging more years would reduce the standard errors further (see discussion following), but would require assuming little change over a longer period. For this reason, we merged three years to balance this concern against gaining larger sample sizes.

Due to the CPS sampling frame, using three years of the March CPS only doubles the CPS sample size. In the CPS design, each sample household is surveyed in two consecutive years. In a given March survey, half of the households were interviewed the previous year, and half of the households will be interviewed again in the next year. To ensure that all observations in the merged sample were independent, we included each household only once. For this edition, we chose to include each household that was interviewed in more than one of the files in the most recent year the household was interviewed. Thus, we included all households in the last file (the 1993 CPS). Those households in the 1993 file that were interviewed in the 1992 file were dropped from the 1992 file, leaving half of the 1992 file. Each of the households remaining in the 1992 file were interviewed for the 1991 CPS, so we dropped them from that file, leaving half of the 1991 file. The final merged file thus draws half of its observations from the 1993 survey, one-quarter from the 1992 survey, and one-quarter from the 1991 file.

The population numbers cited in this report's tables reflect the weighted population for the appropriate subsample being used. There are an associated number of unweighted observations for every sample and subsample used. For example, the population in New Jersey under age 65 is 6,752,000. In the three-year merged CPS sample there are 11,341 unweighted observations under age 65 for New Jersey. There are too many tables to report the unweighted subsample size for each estimate. However, to give the reader an idea of the number of unweighted observations underlying population estimates, we reproduce here as appendix table 2.1 the health insurance coverage for the population under age 65 (see also table A1 in section A), showing the unweighted counts in each cell. The first column shows the total number of unweighted observations from the three-year merged CPS under age 65 for each state. The total unweighted count varies from 2,097 for Vermont to 26,672 for California. This total is then broken down into six categories of health insurance coverage.

Even after doubling the sample size, some state subsamples of interest may have small numbers of unweighted observations. For this reason, we have included standard errors, which reflect the reliability of a given estimate. They are reported in parentheses under each estimate for tables from the three-year merged CPS. In addition, we do not report estimates where the denominator used to calculate a percentage is based on fewer than 100 unweighted observations. These estimates are replaced with a triple dash (---) in the tables.

CALCULATING STANDARD ERRORS

In calculating the standard errors of estimates from the CPS data, we needed to make adjustments for the sample design of the CPS. The Census Bureau provides adjustment factors and formulas that can be used to calculate correct standard errors. There are two types of adjustment factors, one for the characteristic being estimated, such as marital status or insurance coverage, and one for each state. The factors used in this monograph were obtained from the March CPS

Technical Documentation from 1991, 1992, and 1993, and directly from the Census Bureau.

The formula used to calculate the standard error of a percentage is as follows,[3]

$$SE(p) = \sqrt{\frac{f^2 b}{x} p \, (100 - p)} \, , \qquad \text{(A.1)}$$

where $SE(p)$ is the standard error of the percentage, b is the adjustment factor for the characteristic estimated, f^2 is the state adjustment factor, p is the estimated percentage, and x is the population base of the percentage. The base of the percentage, x, is two times larger for the three-year merged CPS sample than for a one-year sample. This translates into approximately a 30 percent reduction in standard errors.

USING STANDARD ERRORS

The standard error is a measure of the reliability of a given estimate. The numbers from the CPS are estimates, because only a sample of the entire population is surveyed each year. We do not know exactly how many people are, for example, working part-time, but we have an estimate based on a sample of the population. The CPS represents one possible sample of the entire population and gives one estimate of the percentage working part-time. These are the estimates presented in this volume. It is also possible to draw other samples from the entire population, using the same general design as the CPS. We could then calculate other estimates of the percentage working part-time, which could be different from the first estimate. Standard errors allow us to construct a confidence interval around an estimate and to state that the average estimated percentage from all samples falls within that interval with a specified probability, called the level of confidence.

For example, if the estimate of the percentage of part-time workers is p, and the standard error is s, then we can create an interval around p that contains the true percentage of part-time workers with a 95 percent probability. The interval around p for the 95 percent confidence level would be:

$$p - (1.96 * s) \le p \le p + (1.96 * s). \qquad \text{(A.2)}$$

For example, if we estimate 10 percent of the population works part-time with a standard error of 2, then the 95 percent confidence interval ranges from 6.1 to 13.9. With 95 percent confidence, we can report that the percentage of the population working part-time falls within this range.

Standard errors can also be used to distinguish whether two estimates are different from each other at a certain level of significance. Again, because these reported numbers are estimates, two estimates that appear to be different (for example, 20 percent and 23 percent) may not be "significantly different" when we take into account that these numbers are calculated from one sample. If the difference between two estimates is greater than the standard error of the difference multiplied by 1.96, then the two estimates are different at the 95 percent confidence level.

To calculate this, the formula for the standard error of the difference of two estimates is as follows:

$$SE\ (X_1 - X_2) = \sqrt{SE\ (X_1)^2 + SE\ (X_2)^2} \qquad \text{(A.3)}$$

where SE stands for standard error, X_1 is one estimate, and X_2 is the other.

For example, the percentage uninsured in Maine is 12.5 with a standard error of 0.60, and the percentage uninsured in New Hampshire is 13.6 with a standard error of 0.69. We can verify these two numbers are different at the 95 percent confidence level. We can check this by calculating the standard error of the difference between the two estimates. Using the preceding formula, the standard error of the difference is calculated as 0.91. The difference between the two estimates is 1.1 percent. The two estimates are considered significantly different at the 95 percent confidence level if

$$\frac{X_1 - X_2}{SE\ (X_1 - X_2)} \geq 1.96. \qquad \text{(A.4)}$$

In our example, 1.1 divided by .91 is not greater than 1.96. Therefore, these two estimates are not significantly different at the 95 percent level. This test is referred to as the *t*-test.

In general, it is important to remember that small differences in estimates, even if statistically significant, should be used with caution. This applies to any comparison of a certain characteristic across states or rank-ordering of states when the differences are small.

Also note that the standard errors and these related tests only provide an estimate of one potential source of error—random variations in the sample drawn for the CPS interview. There are other potential sources of error, such as drawing samples from limited areas within small states, unclear question structures, respondent errors, and in the case of corrections made to the reports of Medicaid, errors in modeling program rules. Instances of these problems on the CPS interview are detailed in Appendix Three. However, the effect of some of these kinds of errors is consistent across regions; if respondents tend to interpret questions about employer coverage incorrectly, they are as likely to do so in one state as another, so the estimates still provide a basis for comparison.

SELECTED CONFIDENCE INTERVALS

To provide additional information for some key statistics in this volume and to emphasize the importance of standard errors, we have included several graphic representations of confidence intervals. For example, figure 2.1 shows the point estimates for the uninsured rates from table A1 as well as a horizontal black bar representing the 95 percent confidence interval based on the standard error for each estimate (the point estimate is the "tall" section at the middle of each bar). Looking at the confidence interval for the uninsured rate in Maine, for example, we see the 12.5 percent point estimate from table A1 at the center of the horizontal bar. We also see that the standard error for Maine (0.85) implies a 95 percent confidence interval ranging from about 11 percent to about 14 percent. Note that the confidence intervals tend to be narrower in larger states and also narrower for regions than for individual states. This occurs because the sample size from larger states is generally larger, so our confidence in these estimates is greater. For example, the confidence interval for the District of Columbia is clearly larger than that for Florida. As shown in appendix table 2.1, there are only 2,124 unweighted observations in the District of Columbia, whereas Florida has 12,141.

We can also compare confidence intervals across states and regions to *roughly* estimate whether estimates in several states are significantly different. For example, because the confidence intervals for Maine and Connecticut do not overlap, we can assert with *at least* 95 percent confidence that the true uninsured rate in Connecticut is less than the rate in Maine. Where confidence intervals overlap, we *cannot* assert with 95 percent confidence that the true uninsured rates are different. It is more precise to apply the *t*-test described earlier when comparing rates across states, but this method is a rough and generally reliable way to check for statistical significance of geographic variations.

We have added a shaded vertical bar representing the confidence interval for the estimate of the national uninsured rate to simplify comparison of regional and state estimates to the national rate. If a region's or state's confidence interval does not intersect the national confidence interval, we can assert with 95 percent confidence that the true uninsured rate in that state is different from the national average. But, in cases where the confidence interval for the state or region intersects with the confidence interval for the national average, there is too much uncertainty to say (with 95 percent confidence) that the true uninsured rate is different from the national average. For example, we can assert with at least 95 percent confidence that the uninsured rate of each of the New England states is lower than the national uninsured rate. But even though the point estimate for uninsurance in West Virginia is below the national average, we cannot assert that this difference is statistically significant (at the 95 percent confidence level), because the confidence interval for West Virginia intersects the confidence interval for the national rate.

Figures 2.1 and 2.2 present the point estimates and confidence intervals for two important estimates related to Medicaid eligibility and enrollment. The data corresponding to each of these figures are presented in table D1. The enrollment rate (figure 2.2) is the number of enrollees divided by the total population, whereas the participation rate (figure 2.3) is the number of enrollees divided by the number of people eligible for Medicaid under program rules.[4] The confidence intervals for the Medicaid enrollment rate are relatively narrow, usually within five percentage points. Statistically significant differences relative to the national rate can be asserted in 24 of the 51 states and 4 of the 9 regions. (Note that enrollment rates reported in table D3 are from administrative data, and thus are not subject to sampling error.) Confidence intervals for the participation rate are wider, however. This occurs because the standard error for a percentage is defined relative to the sample size used to estimate the denominator. For the enrollment rate, the denominator is the total state population; by contrast the denominator for the participation rate is the number of people eligible for Medicaid—a much smaller number. Therefore, *the uncertainty related to the Medicaid participation rate is greater than that for other statistics included in this book.* In particular, note that the degree of uncertainty is considerable in states like New Hampshire and Indiana, which have relatively few persons eligible for Medicaid, versus the regional averages or states like California or Ohio. Even with wide confidence intervals, however, we can assert (with at least 95 percent confidence) that the participation rates in 22 of the 51 states are different from the national average participation rate.

As mentioned earlier, standard errors estimate the degree of uncertainty resulting from one type of error—random sampling. Because the Medicaid enrollment and participation rates are based on microsimulation of Medicaid program rules, these estimates may also be subject to "modeling" errors (see Appendix Three). We include these graphics primarily to emphasize the importance of interpreting point estimates provided in this volume with reference to the standard error indicated.

Notes, Appendix Two

1. The March CPS collects information from the previous year, so the period covered by this sample is 1990, 1991, and 1992.

2. For other studies using three years of CPS data, see Jon Haveman, Sheldon Danziger, and Robert Plotnick, 1991, "State Poverty Rates for Whites, Blacks, and Hispanics in the Late 1980s," *Focus* 13 (Spring):1–7; and U.S. Department of Commerce, Bureau of the Census, 1991, "Poverty in the United States: 1991," *Current Population Reports*, ser. P-60 (Washington, D.C.: U.S. Government Printing Office). For more information on the CPS design and reliability of estimates, see Bureau of the Census, "The Current Population Survey: Design and Methodology," Technical Paper 40 (Washington, D.C.: Author).

3. This formula and the parameters for various characteristics and for states can be found in the March Current Population Survey "Technical Documentation" in the "Source and Accuracy Statement" appendix.

4. Medicaid eligibility is modeled for each household on the three-year CPS file using the Urban Institute's TRIM2 microsimulation model. This process is discussed in Appendix Three. Eligibility rules applied to each household correspond to the reference year of each CPS file. For example, eligibility for households on the 1990 file is based on state-specific eligibility rules in effect during 1989.

Table 2.1
Unweighted Nonelderly Counts by Type of Health Insurance Coverage

	Number	Employer (own)	Employer (other)[2]	Medicaid[3]	Other Public[4]	Other Private[5]	Uninsured[6]
United States	271,454	83,622	88,066	30,584	5,552	20,487	43,143
New England	21,260	7,336	7,499	2,122	354	1,604	2,345
Connecticut	2,448	915	954	177	23	176	203
Maine	2,655	831	901	303	67	228	325
Massachusetts	9,762	3,399	3,329	1,108	145	698	1,083
New Hampshire	2,162	726	824	103	52	172	285
Rhode Island	2,136	780	708	232	25	161	230
Vermont	2,097	685	783	199	42	169	219
Middle Atlantic	42,032	13,785	14,250	5,128	558	2,784	5,527
New Jersey	11,341	4,062	3,926	991	124	774	1,464
New York	19,644	5,912	6,183	3,032	283	1,294	2,940
Pennsylvania	11,047	3,811	4,141	1,105	151	716	1,123
South Atlantic	42,646	13,805	12,356	4,528	1,164	3,046	7,747
Delaware	2,317	824	843	145	43	150	312
District of Columbia	2,124	713	339	407	32	146	487
Florida	12,141	3,544	3,100	1,266	353	1,048	2,830
Georgia	2,929	906	878	349	74	192	530
Maryland	2,604	963	881	236	46	136	342
North Carolina	10,145	3,614	3,012	999	267	740	1,513
South Carolina	3,545	1,129	1,098	370	127	211	610
Virginia	3,814	1,280	1,212	264	124	251	683
West Virginia	3,027	832	993	492	98	172	440
East South Central	13,165	3,729	4,146	1,746	429	834	2,281
Alabama	3,227	952	1,057	309	110	187	612
Kentucky	3,011	903	1,005	396	93	194	420
Mississippi	3,657	867	1,055	592	128	261	754
Tennessee	3,270	1,007	1,029	449	98	192	495
East North Central	24,210	6,262	6,766	2,906	661	1,705	5,910
Illinois	3,366	907	987	385	126	304	657
Indiana	2,711	631	816	407	61	225	571
Michigan	3,211	816	994	318	118	270	695
Ohio	14,922	3,908	3,969	1,796	356	906	3,987
Wisconsin	40,542	13,537	14,823	4,358	668	2,680	4,476
West South Central	11,265	3,714	3,799	1,334	172	817	1,429
Arkansas	2,982	1,003	1,127	188	82	211	371
Louisiana	10,996	3,612	4,074	1,362	153	663	1,132
Oklahoma	11,549	3,909	4,325	1,172	204	714	1,225
Texas	3,750	1,299	1,498	302	57	275	319
West North Central	23,024	6,755	8,071	1,812	447	3,168	2,771
Iowa	3,424	1,047	1,276	247	50	454	350
Kansas	3,405	1,033	1,297	245	45	389	396
Minnesota	2,893	950	974	251	36	335	347
Missouri	2,976	952	953	301	63	274	433
Nebraska	3,425	1,006	1,303	261	82	445	328
North Dakota	3,295	804	1,142	251	64	712	322
South Dakota	3,606	963	1,126	256	107	559	595
Mountain	26,019	7,319	9,157	2,221	651	2,117	4,554
Arizona	2,967	871	902	346	69	215	564
Colorado	3,097	1,029	1,092	224	109	226	417
Idaho	3,645	961	1,315	260	83	374	652
Montana	3,438	900	1,151	333	74	421	559
Nevada	3,091	1,079	926	168	71	186	661
New Mexico	3,870	893	1,190	460	130	236	961
Utah	3,478	926	1,599	229	54	246	424
Wyoming	2,433	660	982	201	61	213	316
Pacific	38,556	11,094	10,998	5,763	620	2,549	7,532
Alaska	3,787	1,145	1,187	362	116	211	766
California	26,672	7,040	7,066	4,677	350	1,731	5,808
Hawaii	2,348	950	819	211	52	129	187
Oregon	2,843	934	1,011	243	32	201	422
Washington	2,906	1,025	915	270	70	277	349

Source: Three-year merged March CPS, 1991, 1992, and 1993.
Note: See table notes at end of Section A.

Figure 2.1
Nonelderly Uninsured Rate, 1990-1992:
Point Estimate and Confidence Interval By Region and State

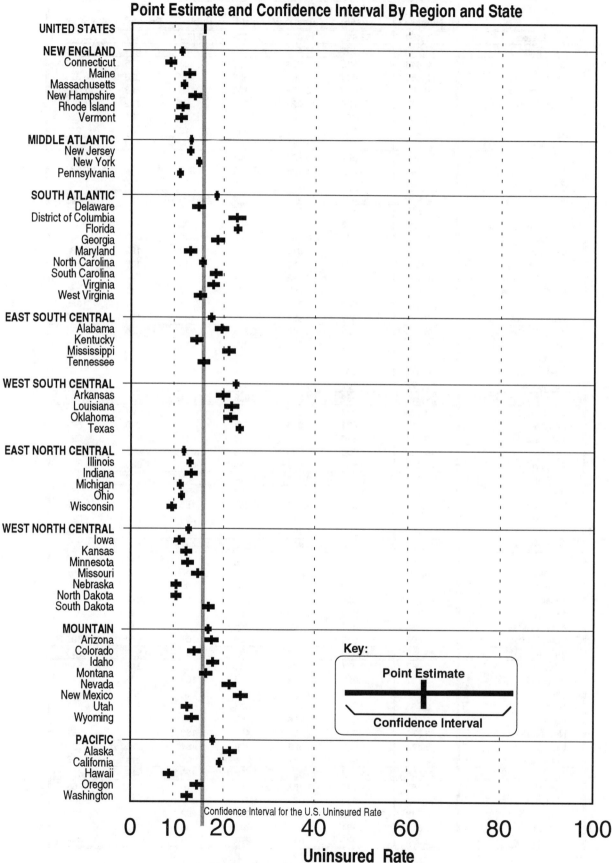

Source: Three-year merged March CPS, 1991,1992, and 1993.
Notes: 1.Confidence interval is 95 percent.
    2.Population excludes the elderly, the institutionalized and the families of active military members.
    3.Uninsured are those without coverage for a 12 month period. See table A1.

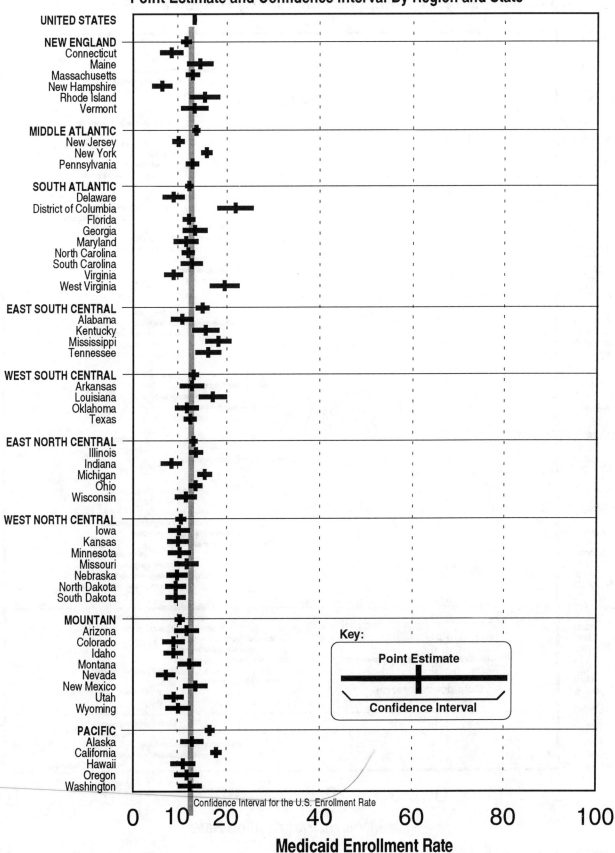

Figure 2.2
Nonelderly Medicaid Enrollment Rate, 1990-1992:
Point Estimate and Confidence Interval By Region and State

Medicaid Enrollment Rate

Source: Three-year merged March CPS, 1991,1992, and 1993.
Notes: 1.Confidence interval is 95 percent.
2.Population excludes the elderly, the institutionalized and the families of active military members.
3.The enrollment rate is the proportion of the nonelderly population enrolled in Medicaid. See Table D1.

Figure 2.3
Nonelderly Medicaid Participation Rate, 1990-1992:
Point Estimate and Confidence Interval By Region and State

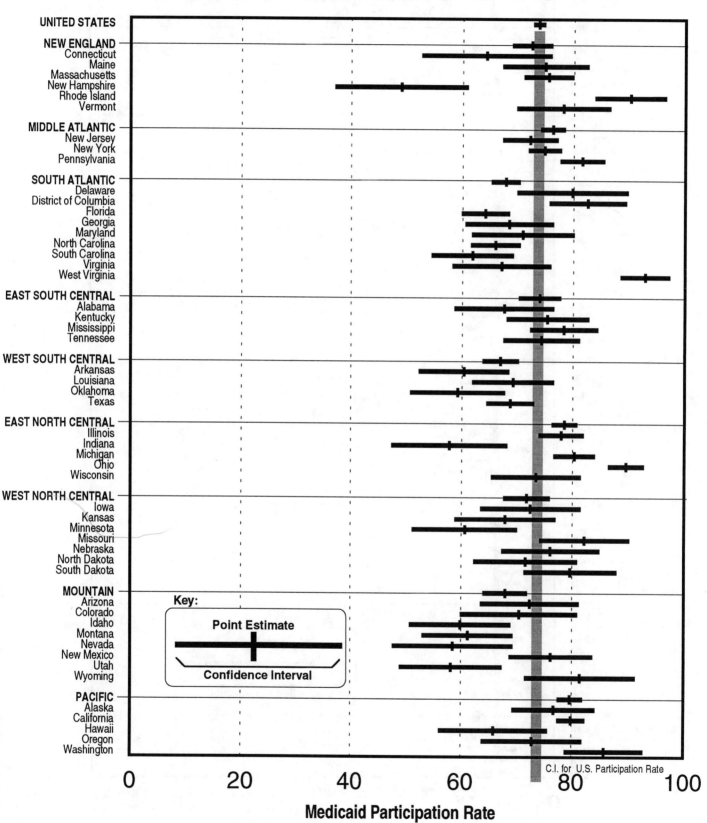

Medicaid Participation Rate

C.I. for U.S. Participation Rate

Key:
Point Estimate
Confidence Interval

Source: Three-year merged March CPS, 1991,1992, and 1993.
Notes: 1.Confidence interval is 95 percent.
2.Population excludes the elderly, the institutionalized and the families of active military members.
3.The participation rate is the proportion of the nonelderly eligible for Medicaid who actually enroll. See Table D1.

Issues in Using the CPS to Measure Health Insurance Coverage

The March Current Population Survey is an important source of information on the health insurance coverage of Americans. Administered annually by the U.S. Bureau of the Census, the survey covers a representative sample of about 57,000 households including about 160,000 people. In addition to questions about household composition and income, the survey has contained questions related to health insurance coverage since 1980. Much of the current discussion related to health insurance coverage and the reorganization of the U.S. health care system is framed with reference to data from the CPS. This appendix discusses the CPS health insurance questions and general issues related to these important data.

The interpretation of survey-based data requires careful consideration of the survey itself and the comparison of results to other sources of data. Such scrutiny of health insurance data from the CPS has raised a few concerns about the data, including concerns about whether all possible forms of coverage are represented, the apparent underreporting of Medicaid coverage, the handling of inconsistent answers to different questions, and the possibility that information provided by survey respondents reflects their health insurance coverage at the time of the interview rather than during the previous year. There are also concerns that samples in small states are drawn from limited areas (often urban centers) which may not be representative of the whole state population. Before discussing most of these concerns individually, we review the questions as they appear in the CPS.

Appendix table 3.1 shows the questions as they appear on the CPS questionnaire. The first set of questions (74 through 75F) inquires about coverage of household members under the major forms of public and private health coverage during the previous calendar year. Question 74 asks which members, if any, were covered under the major forms of public coverage—Medicare, Medicaid, CHAMPUS, Veteran's Administration (VA), and military health care. Questions 75A through 75F ask about private sources of health coverage, including whether coverage is employment-related. Dependent coverage is captured through question 75F, which asks which other family members are covered under the private plan or plans. The second set of questions (80 through 81A) asks about the coverage status of children under 15. These questions try to capture children's coverage overlooked during the interview—in particular, children's coverage as dependents on policies of persons outside the household (question 81A)—and to confirm coverage of children under public programs.

It is important to note that at no point in the CPS are respondents asked if any members of the household were uninsured for either part or all of the previous year. Estimates of the uninsured from the CPS reflect the number of persons for whom none of the specified types of coverage are reported for the year. Therefore, if survey respondents are answering the questions as intended, a person reported as uninsured on the CPS is without insurance for the entire year. For example, if a person has coverage under an employer-sponsored plan for six months of the previous year and is uninsured for the remainder of the year, the person's accurate response to the CPS questions would indicate coverage under employment-related insurance for some part of the year, but the period without insurance would not be captured. When respondents answer the questions accurately, the survey captures any type of coverage held for even part of the year, but captures as uninsured only those who were without insurance for the entire year.

COVERAGE UNDER OTHER GOVERNMENT PROGRAMS

Note also that the CPS questions do not offer respondents the opportunity to report coverage under government programs other than those specified. Coverage under state-funded programs for the ill and

---

APPENDIX TABLE 3.1

CPS Health Insurance Questions

---

74. There are several government programs which provide medical care or help pay medical bills.

    During *[previous year]* was anyone in this household covered by:

    74A. Medicare *(for the disabled and elderly)*?

       74B. [If yes. . .] Who was that? *(Anyone else?)*

    74C. Medicaid *(for the needy)*?

       74D. [If yes. . .] Who was that? *(Anyone else?)*

    74E. CHAMPUS, VA, or military health care?

       74F. [If yes. . .] Who was that? *(Anyone else?)*

75A. Other than government sponsored policies, health insurance can be obtained privately or through a current or former employer or union. Was anyone in this household covered by health insurance of this type at any time during *[previous year]*?

    [If yes. . .]

    75B. Who was that? *(Anyone else?)*

    [For each person with such coverage . . .]

    75C. Was . . .'s health insurance coverage from a plan in . . .'s own name?

    75D. Was this health insurance plan offered through . . .'s current or former employer or union?

    75E. Did . . .'s employer or union pay for all, part, or none of the cost of this plan?

    75F. What other persons were covered by this health insurance policy? *(Mark all that apply)*

    ❑ Spouse
    ❑ Child(ren) in the household
    ❑ Child(ren) not in the household
    ❑ Other
    ❑ No one

(continued)

Appendix Table 3.1 *(continued)*

Supplemental Questions if Children Under 15

80. During *[previous year]*, how many of the children under age 15 in this household were covered by Medicare or Medicaid?

❏ All
❏ Some, but not all *(indicate number)*
❏ None

81. During *[previous year]*, how many children under age 15 in this household were covered by a health insurance plan *(excluding Medicaid or Medicare)*?

❏ All
❏ Some, but not all *(indicate number)*
❏ None

[If all or some . . .]

81A. How many of these children were covered by the health insurance plan of someone not residing in this household?

❏ All
❏ Some, but not all *(indicate number)*
❏ None

medically indigent, for example, is not represented by the questions on the CPS. In response to growing concerns about the uninsured, a number of states have introduced state-funded programs to extend coverage to those in need. Hawaii, for example, has an independent program that extends coverage to families which might otherwise be uninsured. California and Vermont are providing coverage to pregnant women whose incomes are just over the Medicaid limits. In addition to programs covering poor and near-poor families who do not qualify for Medicaid, a number of states have developed and funded programs targeted to persons with specific medical conditions, such as those with mental retardation or persons infected with HIV. The CPS questions also do not allow a category for reporting coverage through the Indian Health Service. Although the Indian Health Service does not extend formal coverage, it guarantees access to care for Native Americans who qualify.

The CPS questions, however, do not directly capture coverage under special state-funded programs or the Indian Health Service.

A person with coverage under such a program may mistakenly report coverage as Medicaid, or if he or she is aware of the distinction and reports no form of private coverage, may fall into the residual uninsured category.

Still other states—21 states as of 1991—have facilitated state-sponsored "pools" to help persons who are considered "uninsurable" owing to high medical risks;[1] it is unclear how a person with such coverage would report it on the CPS. Although coverage under such programs should be captured as private, nongroup coverage, survey respondents may mistakenly believe that the opening to question 75, which asks about coverage that is *not* "government sponsored" and is "obtained privately," precludes this type of coverage.

Few good estimates are available for the number of people who obtain coverage through these state-funded programs. In 1983, the Health Care Financing Administration estimated that at least 875,000 persons were covered through state-only programs for the indigent in 29 states at a cost of $1.7 billion.[2] Programs of this sort have been considered and adopted in an increasing number of states in recent years and are expected to grow further. The U.S. General Accounting Office estimates that only 77,000 persons gained access to private insurance through state-sponsored high-risk pools in 1989.[3] A systematic collection of data from states on the extent of such programs, if any, was beyond the scope of this project. If your use of these data focuses on a few states, we suggest that it may be worthwhile to check if these states have such programs, and request estimates of the number of persons covered during 1988–92. These data should also be interpreted with care in states with significant Native American populations, such as Arizona, Arkansas, the Dakotas, Montana, New Mexico, and Oklahoma because these populations may qualify for health care services through the Indian Health Service.

Medicaid reporting

The underreporting of Medicaid coverage on the CPS also raises concerns. Participation in Medicaid and other income-related programs, such as Aid to Families with Dependent Children and Supplemental Security Income, is said to be underreported because the number of persons on the survey file reporting participation in these programs is significantly lower than the number of program participants shown in the programs' administrative data systems. For example, the number of nonelderly, noninstitutionalized persons reporting Medicaid coverage on the March 1991 CPS is about 21 percent lower than the "unduplicated" counts of nonelderly, noninstitutionalized persons reported in data from the HCFA.[4] Thus, relying completely on self-reported Medicaid coverage from the CPS understates the significance of Medicaid in providing coverage and overstates the number of uninsured. The enhanced version of the CPS used in this analysis, however, corrects for the underreporting of Medicaid coverage by imputing Medicaid coverage. The Urban Institute's Transfer Income Model (TRIM2), a microsimulation model, passes each person's record on the CPS through the various state rules for Medicaid eligibility to identify which persons are *eligible* for coverage. Statistical procedures are used to choose enough additional persons from the pool of eligibles who did not report coverage on the CPS to match the known enrollment figures.[5] The TRIM2 model aligns program enrollees to known enrollment figures in each state by age and disability group. Giannarelli provides further discussion of the methodology of these corrections.[6]

These edits to Medicaid reporting can also correct some of the errors described in the previous section. Suppose, for example, a person who receives care through the Indian Health Service is coded during the CPS interview as having Medicaid. If the TRIM2 models that the person could not possibly qualify for Medicaid given his family composition and other characteristics, the person's report of Medicaid would be changed. However, if the interviewee reported no other type of health coverage, he would be classified as uninsured.

INCONSISTENT RESPONSES

There are also cases in which the reported coverage of children from the multipartite questions 74–75 conflicts with the information provided in the more direct questions 80 and 81. For example, survey respondents may report that their children are covered under their employer-sponsored plan in response to question 75F, but then report on question 81 that their children are without insurance. Likewise, the reverse may occur: a child may be categorized as uninsured based on the first set of questions, but categorized as insured under the second set. The 1991 CPS includes about 7 million weighted children with such conflicting information.[7] These discrepancies may be difficult to reconcile. Some analysts have employed a series of assumptions about children covered by plans outside the household to assign coverage status in these cases.[8] Others have counted children as covered if coverage is indicated under either set of questions.[9]

In the previous edition of this volume, we defined children as covered through employer or nongroup coverage if indicated under the first set of questions *or* the second set indicated a child had coverage from outside the household. *We have modified the definition for this edition.* In this edition, we have expanded this definition to count additional children as covered if the second set of questions indicates coverage from within the household *and* there is an adult in the health insurance unit with health coverage. This change affects about 800,000 children, and increases private coverage and reduces the uninsured rate by about 0.5 percent for the whole nonelderly population and by about 1.2 percent for children. Coverage of adults is not affected by this change. In its published estimates of the uninsured rate, the Census Bureau does not check if an adult in the unit has coverage. As a result, the Census Bureau's count of uninsured children is lower by about 800,000. The definition used by the Employee Benefits Research Institute (EBRI) is more restrictive than ours; as a result, their count of uninsured children is higher. However, the TRIM2 corrections for the underreporting of Medicaid are more significant to the difference in the CPS-based uninsured counts from TRIM2, Census, and EBRI. Once we make these corrections, our uninsured counts are lower than both the Census and the EBRI counts. For example, for 1992 Census reported 37.0 million nonelderly without insurance, EBRI estimated 38.5 million, and TRIM2 estimated 34.9 million without coverage.

TIMING OF COVERAGE

Finally, there is concern that persons responding to the CPS may be reporting their coverage status at the time of the interview, rather than their status during the previous calendar year, as requested. These concerns are based on comparisons of estimates of health insurance coverage based on the CPS to other surveys of health insurance coverage. For example, Swartz found that if the number of uninsured from the CPS is compared to counts of persons uninsured for the entire year from other surveys (e.g., the Health Interview Survey and the National Medical Care Utilization and Expenditure Survey), the CPS number is considerably larger.[10] If, however, comparisons of the CPS estimates are made to "point-in-time" estimates of the uninsured from other surveys—estimates of the number who are without insurance at a particular time (a given month, for example)—the numbers are much closer. Similarly, Swartz found that CPS estimates of persons with Medicaid and private coverage were more similar to point-in-time estimates than annual estimates from other surveys. The Census Bureau arrives at similar conclusions in comparing results from the Survey of Income and Program Participation (SIPP) to CPS data.[11] We believe the evidence suggests that there is at best a mix of responses among respondents to the CPS: some are reporting their current coverage while others are reporting coverage during the previous year, as requested. The results in this volume assume the latter.

Notes, Appendix Three

1. U.S. General Accounting Office, 1992, *Access to Health Care: States Respond to Growing Crisis*, GAO/HRD-92-70 (Washington, D.C.: Author), June.

2. Health Care Financing Administration, 1985, *Health Care Financing Program Statistics: Analysis of State Medicaid Program Characteristics, 1984* (Baltimore, Md.: U.S. Department of Health and Human Services).

3. U.S. General Accounting Office, *Access to Health Care*.

4. Institutionalized persons are not represented on the CPS. On the 1991 CPS, 19.6 million noninstitutionalized nonelderly persons reported Medicaid coverage. Comparable data from the Health Care Financing Administration indicate that 24.7 million were enrolled in Medicaid for that period.

5. For example, after correction, TRIM2 identified 24.3 million Medicaid enrollees on the March 1991 CPS, a figure significantly closer to the 24.7 million known to have been enrolled than the 19.6 million reporting coverage on the uncorrected CPS. Medicaid adjustments are made separately for each CPS file based on eligibility rules and administrative data on enrollment applicable for the prior year *before* the three CPS files are merged.

6. Linda Giannarelli, 1992, *An Analyst's Guide to TRIM2* (Washington, D.C.: Urban Institute Press).

7. Employee Benefits Research Institute, 1992, *Sources of Health Insurance and Characteristics of the Uninsured, Analysis of the March 1991 Current Population Survey* (Washington, D.C.: Author), February.

8. Ibid.

9. Richard Kronick, 1991, "Health Insurance, 1979–1989: The Frayed Connection between Employment and Insurance," *Inquiry* 28: 318–32.

10. Katherine Swartz, 1986, "Interpreting the Estimates from Four National Surveys of the Number of People without Health Insurance," *Journal of Economic and Social Measurement* 14:233–42.

11. U.S. Department of Commerce, Bureau of the Census, 1990, "Health Insurance Coverage: 1986–88," *Current Population Reports*, ser. P-70, no. 17 (Washington, D.C.: U.S. Government Printing Office).